MW01490030

TEACHING THE SEVERELY MENTALLY RETARDED

Adaptive Skills Training

Allen A. Mori, Ph.D.

Department of Special Education
University of Nevada
Las Vegas, Nevada

and

Lowell F. Masters, Ed.D.

Southern Nevada Mental
Retardation Services
Las Vegas, Nevada

AN ASPEN PUBLICATION®
Aspen Systems Corporation
Germantown, Maryland
London, England
1980

Library of Congress Cataloging in Publication Data

Mori, Allen A.
Teaching the severely mentally retarded.

Includes bibliographies and index.
1. Mentally handicapped children—Care and
treatment. 2. Mentally handicapped children—
Education. I. Masters, Lowell F., joint author. II. Title
RJ506.M4M66   371.92'84   79-27489
ISBN: 0-89443-173-0

Library of Congress Catalog Card Number: 79-27489
ISBN: 0-89443-173-0

Printed in the United States of America
1 2 3 4 5

Table of Contents

Preface vii

Acknowledgments ix

Chapter 1—Nature and Needs of the Severely Retarded 1

   The Need for the Right People 1
   Definition of Mental Retardation 10
   Characteristics of the Severely Mentally Retarded 12
   Educating the Severely Retarded 17
   Summary 19

Chapter 2—Defining and Assessing Adaptive Behavior 23

   Defining Adaptive Behavior 23
   Assessing Adaptive Behavior 25
   Psycho-Educational Assessment 27
   Task Analytical Assessment 37
   Summary 41

Chapter 3—Planning Educational Activities for Adaptive Skills
            Training 45

   Assessment—The Establishment of Entering Behavior ... 46
   Selecting and Specifying Target Behaviors 46
   Writing Instructional Objectives 50
   Skill Sequencing 51

Task Analysis: General Format 52
Task Analysis: Structure 54
Reinforcing Behaviors to Promote Change 61
Decreasing Inappropriate Behavior 66
Focusing Learner Attention 72
Evaluating Student Progress 76
Summary 78

Chapter 4—Motor Skills Training **81**

Righting and Equilibrium Reactions 81
Postural Reflexes 87
Development of Gross Motor Skills 90
Developing Fine Motor Skills 98
Summary 102

Chapter 5—Communication Skills Training **105**

The Development of Language 105
Basic Skills in Speech Acquisition 108
A Skill Sequence for Language 109
Instructional Programs 110
Summary 129

Chapter 6—Self-Help Skills Training **133**

Basic Skill Areas for Self-Help Training 133
Toilet Training the Severely Retarded Learner 136
Teaching Independent Eating Skills 142
Teaching Independent Dressing Skills 152
Dressing 155
Summary 161

Chapter 7—Social Skills Training **163**

Basic Skill Areas for Social Skills Training 163
Teaching Grooming and Hygiene 166
Other Social Skill Development 173
Physical Appearance and Personal Care of Belongings ... 175
Summary 181

Chapter 8—Personality Skills Training **183**

Overview of Personality Factors in the Mentally Retarded 184
Developing the Self-Concept and Relating to Others 188
Teaching Play Behaviors 190
Summary 213

Chapter 9—Mobility Skills Training **215**

Early Programs of Travel Instruction for the Mentally
  Retarded 215
The Laus Orientation and Mobility Program for Sighted
  Mentally Retarded Individuals 218
Summary 226

Chapter 10—Occupational Skills Training **229**

Basic Skill Areas for Occupational Education 230
The Activity Center 249
Summary 266

Chapter 11—The Sheltered Workshop for Severely Retarded
  Learners **269**

History of Sheltered Workshops 269
Workshops for the Mentally Retarded 270
Program Planning and Occupational Training in the
  Sheltered Workshop 271
Job Skills in the Sheltered Workshop 276
Sheltered Workshop Layout 277
Sheltered Workshop Staff 279
The Industrial Sheltered Workshop 282
The Sheltered Workshop in the Public School 287
Summary 291

Chapter 12—Adapted Physical Education and Recreation Skills
  Training **293**

Components of Adapted Physical Education 293
The Need 294

Setting Up the Program—A Team Approach 294
Team Members 295
Assessment 296
Instructional Levels 296
Organizing Instruction 309
Instructional Techniques 310
Recreation Training 313
Summary 330

Chapter 13—Aquatic Therapy and Emergency Procedures **333**

Conceptualizing Instruction 334
Administrative Considerations in Aquatic Programming .. 335
Emergency Procedures 338
Sudden Illnesses 346
Aquatic Instruction 349
Activities for Instruction 355
Summary 359

Appendix A **361**

Index **395**

Preface

Certainly mental retardation is not a new phenomenon, since anthropological and historical evidence suggests it has existed as long as people have existed. Only recently has public attention focused on mentally retarded persons. The 1960s might well be called the era of awareness, as President John F. Kennedy appointed the President's Panel on Mental Retardation; President Lyndon Johnson skillfully ensured the passage of federal legislation, including the establishment of the Bureau of Education for the Handicapped; and Dr. Burton Blatt exposed us all to the horrors of institutions in *Christmas in Purgatory*. The 1970s can be called the era of litigation, which eventually prompted "civil rights for the handicapped." The 1971 Pennsylvania case, *Pennsylvania Association for Retarded Children, Nancy Beth Bowman et al., v. the Commonwealth of Pennsylvania, David H. Kurtzman, et al.,* and the 1972 Alabama case, *Wyatt v. Stickney* (later *Wyatt v. Aderholt,* 1974) gave the retarded a right to education and a right to treatment. Litigation led to the passage of P.L. 94-142, the Education for All Handicapped Children Act of 1975 that guaranteed a free, appropriate public education for all handicapped children.

How will the 1980s affect the severely retarded? We believe that this decade will eventually become known as the era of expanding instructional and mechanical technology. Yet, initially, this era will be hampered by a lack of appropriate materials, methodological suggestions, and guides for instructing the severely retarded. This textbook will fill the existing gap between the dire need for services and the lack of a guide to deliver those services. Instead of being the definitive work in this emergent field, this text is a sourcebook and guide for the practitioner working with an important part of the mentally retarded population.

The first three chapters provide an overview of employment prospects in the area of severe retardation, as well as a description of the population's characteristics, service delivery system models, and service needs of the severely retarded learner. Chapters 2 and 3 are designed to acquaint the reader with assessment models, the principles of reinforcement, writing instructional objectives, doing task analyses, and the evaluation of learner progress. Chapters 4 through 10 provide intensive coverage of the adaptive skills, with a chapter on mobility skills or independent travel training. Almost all the chapters describe the teaching process beginning with determining a present functional level and continuing with task analyses and skill sequences of important target behaviors. The final three chapters of the text provide, in addition to teaching strategies and skill sequences, an in-depth discussion of the necessary components of program development in sheltered employment, adapted physical education, recreation, and aquatic therapy with emergency procedures.

This organization of the text provides preservice and inservice professionals and paraprofessionals with extremely practical suggestions for program organization, design, and implementation. It is our hope that you will use this text to establish or reestablish the desire, commitment, and optimism necessary to provide quality educational experiences to severely retarded children and adults.

Allen A. Mori, Ph.D.
and
Lowell F. Masters, Ed.D.

April 1980

Acknowledgments

The writing of a book like this is rarely the sole work of one or two people. Many individuals have assisted us in the completion of this book. To our professors and colleagues we owe special thanks for the many hours of learning, challenging, and discussing that helped us form the foundation for this book. We would also be remiss if we did not note appreciation to all those special children and adults in public and private classrooms and state institutions who taught us the realities of severe retardation, inspired our optimism, and gave us the sheer joy of seeing other human beings achieve, for them, a monumental goal.

To get from idea to rough draft to final manuscript and finally a published book takes not only the firm resolve of the authors, but also the belief, support, and inspiration of a publisher. In our case we owe very special thanks to R. Curtis Whitesel, Aspen's Acquisitions Editor, for believing in this project all the way.

To our wives Barbara Mori and Susan Masters go our deepest love and appreciation for their total support and encouragement in spite of the many hours they spent alone and the things they did by themselves because we were busy with this project. Our daughters Kirsten Mori and Jessica Masters also deserve thanks for being so patient and loving even though their daddies were often too busy or too tired to play with them while this book was being written.

Finally, we wish to acknowledge Karen Bloomdahl who typed and retyped the many drafts of this manuscript.

Chapter 1

Nature and Needs of the Severely Retarded

This book is about people, people who have severe disabilities that seriously alter the manner in which they learn, communicate, move about, and generally react to their world. To help these people better adapt, adjust, and become more functional members of our society, professionals, paraprofessionals, and parents can apply interventional strategies designed to accelerate achievement of important skills. This chapter begins with a discussion of individuals who work with the severely retarded. A description of the need for the right type of person, competencies for workers, salary expectations, and personnel preparation is provided. We sincerely believe that dedicated, well-trained, and knowledgeable individuals are essential to promote skill acquisition in the severely retarded population. After you read these beginning sections, we hope your interest and desire to work with the severely retarded is intensified. If, however, you feel you do not possess the requisite personal characteristics and dedication, or the salary ranges are below your expectations, perhaps you should consider other career possibilities.

The remainder of Chapter 1 includes discussions of the definition and characteristics of the severely retarded, program needs, and program content. This format provides a realistic overview of the many facets regarding the severely mentally retarded and, in doing so, will stimulate your interest and desire in working with this group of people.

THE NEED FOR THE RIGHT PEOPLE

The fact that you are reading this book is testimony that you are interested in the field of mental retardation. Although the severely retarded population is small, there are many opportunities for employment depending upon the individual's interest, motivation, and qualifications.

The next decade will provide more opportunities to work with the lower functioning retarded than ever before. The reasons are twofold: (1) legislative action has improved funding resources, and (2) expectancies have increased for lower functioning retardates; therefore, more and better programs will continue.

There is no magic formula for developing good employees to work with the severely retarded; however, several qualities appear to be extremely important. First is the desire to work with and help others. The employee must be able to gain some sense of satisfaction from performing a service to others who are less fortunate. In addition, feelings of self-worth for doing something others might find distasteful or unpleasant fall into this category.

Second is the positive attitude the employee feels toward the work. Paramount is the belief that working with or teaching the severely retarded is just as important and significant as instructing the nonhandicapped.

The third factor involves money. Individuals who enter the field to make large salaries should explore the earning potential before entering the field. If employees are continually examining and complaining about salary figures, they will seldom yield quality work or remain on the job.

The fourth quality is emotional stability. This trait requires that an individual not overreact to stressful situations or become discouraged or depressed by client regression or small increments of improvement. A fifth and final quality to be mentioned is personal integrity. This means that the individual takes sick time only in extreme circumstances, doesn't falsify claims for injury, and maintains a quality attendance record.

What It Takes to Teach the Severely Retarded

Not all persons who work with the severely retarded are certified teachers; however, most direct caseworkers, teacher aides, or volunteers will most likely attempt to teach basic skills.

Siudzinski and VanNagel (1978) identified and studied thirteen competencies they thought to be important for teachers of the severely handicapped. In their research, they demonstrated that teachers trained with the thirteen competencies brought about significant gains in learner achievement. Although additional research is needed to provide further support, the following competencies have survived an initial validation:

1. *Objectives:* The teacher can construct and implement daily lesson plans complete with objectives stated in observable and measurable terms.
2. *Rapport:* The teacher can establish rapport with the learner.
3. *Motivation:* The teacher is able to identify things that interest the learner and is able to use these interests in daily lessons.

4. *Entering Behavior:* The teacher is able to determine the skills the learner possesses initially using criterion referenced tests.
5. *Modality Assessment:* The teacher is able to identify the learner's strongest modality or modalities and offer instruction through them.
6. *Identified Elicitors:* The teacher can select appropriate instructional methods and materials.
7. *Developmental Lessons:* The teacher understands the hierarchical nature of learner tasks and can accurately order the presentation of objectives.
8. *Achievement Reinforcer:* The teacher can select and use positive reinforcers in the teaching process.
9. *Desirable Behavior Reinforcer:* The teacher appropriately reinforces desirable behavior and doesn't reinforce undesirable behavior.
10. *Schedules and Levels Reinforcement:* The teacher can recognize what reinforcement schedule should be used and where reinforcement should be increased or diminished.
11. *Evaluation:* The teacher can evaluate learner progress or regression in terms of behavior change.
12. *Transfer and Generalization Teaching:* The teacher develops instructional lessons that demonstrate that learning has occurred in various environmental settings and conditions.
13. *Knowledge of Theoretical and Scientific Studies:* The teacher is able to study and apply scientific and theoretical information to the point that it is used in educating the pupil.

Salary of Individuals Working with the Severely Retarded

It may seem inappropriate to include this section here. Regardless, we have found that it is better to state immediately what the financial picture will look like if you choose this field. As professors and administrators, we have had many students and prospective employees vocalize their desire and commitment to working with the severely retarded. The unfortunate results have all too frequently been cries and complaints of low salary, poor fringe benefits, and not enough time off.

In the hope that prospective employees can at least see a portion of the road ahead, a listing of positions and their approximate salary range has been provided in Table 1-1. This table is certainly not meant to discourage anyone from entering this type of work; however, prospective workers should examine their financial aspirations and plan accordingly. Note that the figures are merely ranges ascertained by directly contacting various facilities in different parts of the country; these figures are very rough estimates.

Table 1-1 Employment Position and Approximate Salary Range

Employment Position or Facility	Annual Wage
State Residential Facilities:	
Direct Care Workers:	
Level I	$ 7,200-$ 8,500
Level II	8,500- 9,600
Level III	9,600- 11,000
Supervisory Staff	12,500- 15,000
Specialists:	
Child Developmental Specialists	$11,500-$19,000
Psychologists	13,000- 32,000
Social Workers	10,500- 19,500
Recreational Therapist	11,000- 18,000
Occupational Therapist	13,500- 17,500
Physical Therapist	13,500- 17,500
Speech Therapist	13,500- 17,500
Administrative Personnel:	
Assistant Director	$18,500-$24,500
Director	24,000- 31,500
Superintendent	32,500- 44,500
Public Schools:	
Teacher Aides	$ 5,000-$ 7,000
Teachers:	
Beginning B.A. or B.S.	9,500- 11,000
Beginning M.A. or M.S.	10,000- 14,000
Experienced 10 years plus M.A.	15,000- 25,000
Coordinators	23,000- 32,000
Supervisors	23,000- 32,000
Principals	21,000- 31,000
Private Schools:	
Teacher Aides	$ 3,500-$ 6,000
Teachers:	
Beginning B.A. or B.S.	7,200- 9,000
Beginning M.A. or M.S.	9,000- 12,000
Experienced 10 years plus M.A.	12,000- 15,000
Activity Centers and Sheltered Workshops:	
Director	$23,000-$32,000
Community Day Training Programs:	
Direct Care Workers	$ 6,500-$ 8,900
Specialists	10,000- 13,000
Director	15,000- 17,500

Table 1-1 continued

Employment Position or Facility	*Annual Wage*
State Associations for Retarded Children:	
Specialists	$14,000-$20,000
Directors	22,000- 30,000
State Special Olympics:	
Director	$18,000-$25,000
University Personnel:	
Lecturers	$15,000-$18,000
Assistant Professors	16,000- 19,000
Associate Professors	19,000- 25,000
Professors	25,000- 30,000

Qualifications

Work experience and professional training vary with each employment opportunity. In most cases entry level positions such as direct care workers, teacher aides and community training center staff presently require little or no previous work experience or schooling beyond high school graduation. As responsibility and supervisory duties increase, proportional amounts of training and experience are generally required. For example, Level I residential direct care technicians in Nevada are required to possess a high school diploma and one year of any respectable type of employment experience.

The highest paid positions are in administrative roles such as directors and superintendents. However, the qualifications for positions at this upper level generally require five or more years in the special education field or a related field and a master's, specialist, or doctorate degree.

Teacher Certification

Training programs specifically for the severe and profoundly retarded are not as common as more generic or general training programs. In 1976, Russo and Stark reported that only four states offered a categorical certification in the area of severely and profoundly handicapped. Although the categorical approach to teacher preparation is not always an accepted approach, several states have developed specific certification programs since Russo and Stark's study.

Gilmore and Argyros (1977) reported the following states as having certification for the trainable mentally retarded (T.M.R.):

1. Kansas
2. Maine
3. Kentucky
4. Missouri

5. Wyoming
6. Minnesota
7. South Carolina

Among those claiming to have certification for severely retarded were California and Missouri. Hawaii offers a specialized certification for the severely multiply handicapped.

Teacher Training

In order to teach, the instructor must first expose the student to appropriate materials or the learning situation, and second, provide motivation for the person to learn.

Teaching severely retarded pupils is different. Dever and Knapczyk (1976) describe teaching for this population as both an art and a science—*science* meaning the teacher must know what to teach and *art* the ability to get the learner to reach the goal behaviors that are determined to be appropriate. For the severely retarded, it is certainly a science when the teacher understands what the pupil's behavior means in relation to developmental stages. It too is a science when the teacher can develop a program specific to the learner's unique set of circumstances.

The art of teaching requires determining just how to move the pupil to the goals that have been identified. As pupil behaviors present themselves, the teacher must alter the instructional approach, materials, and possibly the instructional setting.

Successful teachers have a vast repertoire of teaching ideas. They adjust and readjust with each situation. According to Dever and Knapczyk (1976), the teacher orchestrates the environment so that the learner does what the teacher wants and performs what the teacher has decided should be learned.

The teaching-learning act requires the learner to respond in an active and physical manner. Severely retarded pupils learn best by doing. College training programs for prospective teachers attempt to mold, develop, and enhance instructional qualities. Despite the fact that the needs of severely retarded individuals are basically the same throughout the United States, teacher preparation programs vary remarkably.

Following are two university undergraduate training programs. Each provides, upon completion, the certification to teach the severely mentally retarded.

Exhibit 1-1 *Example Program I* (undergraduate preparation in severely mentally retarded)

Academic Component (Part I)	*Semester Credit Hours*

1. Professional Education Courses

Introduction to Teaching	3
Human Development and Learning	5
Principles of Secondary Education	3
	11

2. Introduction into Special Education

Introduction to Special Education	3
Introduction to Mental Retardation	3
Education of Emotionally Disturbed Children and Youth	3
	9

3. Methods and Materials Coursework

Methods for Severely Mentally Retarded	3
Methods for Multiply Handicapped	3
Language Assessment and Methods	3
Assessment and Human Development	3
Behavior Management Techniques	3
Motor Assessment and Methods	3
Reading Methods	3
Math Methods	3
	24
Academic Component Total	44

Practicum Component (Part II)

Junior Year practicum experience includes 20 clock hours per week in four placements, 8 weeks each.

Senior year practicum experience involves 16 weeks of full time student teaching the first semester. A second semester is also available as an option.

Total	26
Total Course Preparation	120 hours

Exhibit 1-2 *Example Program II* (undergraduate preparation in severely mentally retarded)

Academic Component (Part I)	Semester Credit Hours
1. General Education Courses	
School Law	2
Human Growth and Development	3
Psychology in Education	3
Tests and Measurements	3
Multicultural and Sociological Foundations	3
	12-14
2. General Methods Courses	
Contemporary School Math 1&2	6
Psychology in Education	3
Teaching Elementary School Math	6
	15
3. Area of Specialization	
Introduction to Exceptional Children	4
Psychological and Physiological Aspects of Handicapping Conditions	4
Education of the Severely Mentally Retarded	3
Foundations of Motor Skills	3
Communication Disorders of the Severely Mentally Retarded	4
Multimedia Techniques for the Handicapped	2
Adaptive Physical Education and Recreation for the Handicapped	3
Techniques of Classroom Management for the Severely Retarded	3
	26

Practicum Component (Part II)	
Supervised Teaching	6-12
Student Teaching Seminar	2
	8-12
Academic Component Total	69-81

The two programs outlined in Exhibit 1-1 and Exhibit 1-2 do not include the general academic requirements such as humanities, communication skills, science, and social science typically found in bachelor degree programs. In comparing the two programs, the readers should note the number of course credits specifically designed for the severely retarded. Attention should also be given to the emphasis given to practicum and student teaching assignments. Although course titles offer no guarantee of course quality, the student seeking a reputable program should learn to scrutinize program components and offerings carefully.

Seeking Employment

Regardless of whether you are planning to go to work immediately or upon completion of a university training program, you may want to explore the employment market now. The first decision you must make is the geographic location you wish to explore. All states have residential facilities, sheltered workshops, and educational classrooms for the severely retarded. Large residential facilities (institutions) are often near large metropolitan centers; yet with the recent right to education laws, programs of all types exist in both rural and urban settings.

For a listing of educational programs and services available for the handicapped, you may contact: Closer Look Inc., Box 1492, Washington, D.C. 20013, Telephone: (202) 833-4160. State departments of education and mental health services departments can also provide a listing of programs that serve this population.

As a final source for state mental retardation facilities, the National Association of State Mental Retardation Program Directors, Inc. can be contacted: 2001 Jefferson Davis Highway, Arlington, Virginia 22202, Telephone: (703) 920-0700.

If you are planning to receive teacher training in one state, yet anticipate teaching in another, it is advisable to contact the State Department of Education in the state in which you plan to apply for a job. Upon your request, they will send you their teacher certification requirements, which may be quite different from those of the state in which you are receiving your training.

As a final note, it makes good sense to plan for your future employment. A few letters or telephone calls may save you months of time and possibly develop credentials and contacts that will help you obtain employment when you are prepared.

DEFINITION OF MENTAL RETARDATION

Numerous authors (MacMillan, 1977; Hutt and Gibby, 1976; Robinson and Robinson, 1976; Gearheart and Litton, 1975) have noted the difficulty in arriving at a universally acceptable definition of mental retardation. Mental retardation as a concept has eluded precise definition essentially because it is a highly relative and complex sociocultural phenomena (Scheerenberger, 1971).

Gearheart and Litton (1975) suggested four factors that have combined to prevent the development of a single, universally acceptable definition of mental retardation:

1. Mental retardation, regardless of form or cause, is determined primarily on the basis of sociocultural standards of a given society. These standards are often in a constant state of fluctuation.
2. Many disciplines are involved in providing services to the retarded (i.e., medicine, law, education, social work, etc.). Each discipline has developed a definition or definitions to suit its professional area of concern.
3. Mental retardation is an extremely complex concept with different causes and levels of functioning. It is difficult to include such diversity under one rubric.
4. Western civilization prizes intellect very highly. It is difficult to arrive at a definition of mental retardation which does not have negative connotations and is socially acceptable.

Broad disciplinary concern for a widely applicable definition of retardation caused professionals from the American Association on Mental Deficiency to formulate a definition in 1959. This definition, revised in 1961 (Heber, 1961) defined mental retardation as:

> . . . subaverage general intellectual functioning which originates in the developmental period and is associated with impairment in adaptive behavior (p. 3).

The definition contained a psychometric criterion, a social criterion, and established a maximum age by which the condition had to originate. All three criteria had to be present in order for an individual to be diagnosed mentally retarded.

Each criterion was defined, and information explaining how to measure the factors was included. Subaverage intellectual functioning was defined as performance on an individual test of intelligence that was greater than one standard deviation below the mean. The developmental period was established with an upper chronological age limit of sixteen years. Finally, adaptive behavior was defined as behavior that demonstrated the person's ability to meet the natural and social demands of a particular community or society.

From 1961 to 1973 the field of mental retardation underwent significant changes. There were court cases involving the labeling and classification of the retarded. Concerns involving the use of intelligence tests with minority and disadvantaged children surfaced among professional, advocacy, and parental groups.

Shifts in prevailing attitudes involving the use of the term borderline retardation were evident in the 1977 American Association on Mental Deficiency (AAMD) revised definition of retardation. The definition now reads (Grossman, 1977):

> Mental retardation refers to significantly subaverage general intellectual functioning existing concurrently with deficits in adaptive behavior, and manifested during the developmental period (p. 7).

The 1977 revision stipulates that significantly subaverage general intellectual functioning is determined by performance on an individual test of intelligence that is greater than two standard deviations below the mean. Thus, instead of a ceiling IQ of 84 or 85, the revised definition employs a ceiling IQ of 68 or 70 (dependent upon whether the Wechsler Test or Stanford-Binet is used).

Additionally, the developmental period was extended upwards to have an upper chronological age limit of eighteen years. Furthermore, adaptive behavior was more precisely defined in terms of problem areas and age-relevant criteria.

Employing the 1977 AAMD definition of retardation, once the IQ score is determined, an individual is assigned to a level of retardation ranging from mild to profound. Table 1-2 depicts the retardation level and accompanying IQ scores for each level.

The levels are determined by the extent to which the IQ is below the mean in terms of standard deviation units. For the Wechsler tests, a standard deviation is equal to ± 15 IQ points, while the Stanford-Binet has a standard deviation equal to ± 16 IQ points.

Table 1-2 AAMD Levels of Intelligence

Retardation level	Range in S.D. values	Range in IQ scores Stanford-Binet	Range in IQ scores Wechsler Tests
Mild	−2.01 to −3.00	67 to 52	69 to 55
Moderate	−3.01 to −4.00	51 to 36	54 to 40
Severe	−4.01 to −5.00	35 to 20	39 to 25*
Profound	Below −5.00	19 and below	24 and below*

*Extrapolated

CHARACTERISTICS OF THE SEVERELY MENTALLY RETARDED

Just who are the severely mentally retarded? What cognitive, affective, and physical characteristics are present in this population? Some authors (Sontag, Smith, & Sailor, 1977) suggested that attempts to define this population on the basis of intelligence quotients and specific characteristics lack relevance for educational program planning. Instead, they proposed that identification be made in terms of effective educational programming and teacher competencies. This proposed alternative will not be challenged here. The premise here is that precise definition and classification by characteristics or common denominators is necessary for administrative purposes and for preliminary program planning. Even the unfamiliar reader is aware of the wide range of human variability found among individuals in an identified group. A description based upon characteristics of a certain group should not lead to the assumption that the service delivery system would be alike for all members of that group. As would always be the case, specific objectives for educational program purposes must be determined on an individual basis depending upon the needs of the student.

For ease of communication, the term *severely retarded* refers to children with severe and profound retardation (Tawney, 1977), at the risk of program planners' ignoring the widespread heterogeneity in this group in favor of more homogeneous grouping. However, in terms of a range of functional behaviors, the severely retarded may be nonambulatory, health impaired, physically debilitated, or manifest no measurable behavioral repertoire. On the other hand, the severely retarded child could be a high functioning Down's child whose preschool training is geared to enable him to enter first grade (Tawney, 1977). Sontag et al. (1977) suggested that youngsters with severe handicaps are children who are divergent in degree, not in kind. Thus, this group forms an extremely heterogeneous population.

The Bureau of Education for the Handicapped's description of severe handicaps includes the severely and profoundly retarded and suggested that:

'severely handicapped children' 1) may possess severe language and/or perceptual-cognitive deprivations, and evidence abnormal behaviors such as: (i) failure to respond to pronounced social stimuli, (ii) self-mutilation, (iii) self-stimulation, (iv) manifestation of intense and prolonged temper tantrums, and (v) the absence of rudimentary forms of verbal control, and 2) may also have extremely fragile physiological conditions (Federal Register, Vol. 40, No. 35, 1975, p. 7412).

Tawney (1977) suggested a set of descriptions of the functional level of children with severe retardation that included:

1. little or absence of vocal behavior
2. little motor gestural behavior
3. limited self-help skills
4. inconsistent or absent bowel or bladder control
5. no obtained score on standardized tests because none were administered or because these persons were untestable
6. little social interaction with others
7. inability to follow simple directions
8. absence of reciprocal social reinforcement of people in their environment
9. stereotyped behaviors
10. disruptive social behaviors
11. low rates of behavior generally called "constructive play behavior"
12. attendant multiple handicaps

There is a real danger that the reader will conclude that the severely retarded as a group are largely vegetative. Descriptions of the truly severe handicaps this group possesses can cause a great deal of pessimism on the part of both professionals and paraprofessionals who work with this population. The unfortunate result of this pessimism is almost sheer immobilization. Until recently, any person classified as severely retarded had a bleak outlook for even marginal social adjustment. Usually secured away in the back wards of isolated institutions, this group of people has been subjected to the most dehumanizing existence imaginable (Anderson, Greer, & Dietrich, 1976).

The passage of Public Law 94-142, the Education for All Handicapped Children Act of 1975 and other actions taken by the judicial system, started a new era of public concern for the severely retarded. Pioneering efforts by people like Dr. Marc Gold and others have demonstrated that people with severe limitations can be taught to be productive and contributing members of society. Finally, educators are becoming aware that this group "can do" and not that they are totally incapable of even minimal responses. There are so many reasons for professionals, paraprofessionals, and parents to be far more optimistic about what the severely retarded can accomplish with appropriate educational experiences. Because of new technology and teaching methodology, those who work with the severely retarded will be able to see and document real successes in the acquisition of adaptive skills.

Luckey and Addison (1974) noted that an examination of the literature of the past decade revealed that the use of reinforcement techniques can assist the severely mentally retarded to acquire adaptive skills such as self-feeding, independent dressing, toileting, grooming, motor skills, language development, and socialization. We are now at a crossroads in the provision of services to the severely retarded. We can continue to treat adult severely retarded people as children and perpetuate their helplessness and dependency, or we can treat them as physically developed individuals with experience in practicing certain skill patterns. We can abandon previous perceptions that thought this group to be incapable of learning and engage severely retarded persons in daily " . . . meaningful activities that help prevent unnecessary physical and psychological deterioration, and enhance their acceptability in the non-retarded world" (Luckey & Addison, 1974, p. 130). We can begin to train more professionals and parents to work with the severely retarded and become rewarded for their efforts when the child learns to eat solid food, zip a zipper, or work a drill press. It is exciting to be at the forefront of a movement, and those who have chosen to devote their careers to teaching the severely retarded can look forward to a great challenge, but a challenge that could result in deep personal satisfaction for the practitioner.

Cognitive Characteristics of the Severely Mentally Retarded

Piaget described four major stages of intellectual development: sensorimotor operations, pre-operational, concrete operations, and formal operations. These particular stages normally occur in a hierarchical sequence; however, certain developmental anomalies, common among the severely mentally retarded, can cause irregular development (Stephens, 1977).

Using the Piagetian schema to study the cognitive growth of the severely mentally retarded, it is evident that this population rarely proceeds beyond the sensorimotor stage, although it may be possible for some individuals to proceed to the pre-operational level. Thus, discussions of cognitive development would necessarily focus upon the sensorimotor (Stage 1) and pre-operational (Stage II) periods.

The sensorimotor period is normally achieved during the first two to two and one-half years of a child's life. However, a severely retarded individual may never proceed beyond this stage. Briefly, the behaviors associated with the period are characterized by:

1. reflexive actions such as sucking, grasping, visual tracking
2. arm movements, hand waving, hand regard (repeated frequently)
3. eye-hand coordination—often beyond the behavioral repertoire of the profoundly mentally retarded, it still remains a critical skill to be acquired and as such, must be programmed for (see Chapter 4)
4. beginning of certain adaptive behaviors—exploration of new objects, discovery of means differentiated from ends, imitation of motor movements
5. cause and effect and object permanence—the child will attempt to discover new means through experimentation and search for hidden objects
6. simple deductive thinking and simple problem solving through mental operations

During the pre-operational period (from two to seven years) the child makes a transition from direct sensorimotor actions to representative symbolic behaviors. Behaviors associated with this period are characterized by:

1. language development
2. imitative play
3. perceptual confusions
4. thought processes basically egocentric
5. centering (child focuses attention on most compelling attribute of a stimulus situation)
6. irreversability (child cannot move back and forth along a train of thought)

Inhelder's (1968) research demonstrated that the severely mentally retarded adult can be viewed as fixated at the level of sensorimotor intelligence and as exhibiting a viscosity in mental functioning. This viscosity not only retards progress, but causes the learner to remain in a state of transition between stages for a long period of time.

Although there is not a great deal of research, most of Inhelder's observations tend to be confirmed by other researchers. For example, Woodward (1959) was able to match the behavior of severely mentally retarded children with Piaget's six substages of sensorimotor intelligence. Thus, the population of severely mentally retarded learners possesses the characteristics associated with children functioning in the sensorimotor stage.

Personality and Emotional Development

Professionals in special education agree that there is a high incidence of behavioral disturbances among the retarded population as compared to the population of nonhandicapped individuals. Chinn, Drew, and Logan (1975) cite research that indicates that approximately 40 percent of the retarded population may have emotional or personality deviations, compared to about 10 percent for the non-retarded population.

Among children with intelligence quotients below 25, an extremely high percentage show bizarre symptoms that are compulsively repetitive or self-mutilative (Menolascino, 1972). These behavorial patterns are usually more prevalent among institutionalized populations than among children living in home situations. Forehand and Baumeister (1970) indicated that these bizarre patterns were probably related to tension and to a lack of interesting and active pursuits. They are more common in blind retarded individuals than in sighted ones and in the nonambulatory than in the ambulatory (Guess, 1966). Robinson and Robinson (1976) suggested that self-mutilative behaviors can be a form of occupation when normal stimulation is lacking for too long a time period.

Physical and Health Characteristics of the Severely/Profoundly Mentally Retarded

A direct correlation between the degree of mental retardation and the degree of physical defect exists. The more severe the mental retardation, the greater the probability of physically handicapping conditions including problems such as spasticity, athetosis, and hypotonia (these will be defined and discussed in Chapter 4).

In addition to the overall characteristics of too little, too much, or constantly fluctuating levels of muscle tone, most of the severely mentally retarded with physical handicaps have abnormal posture with concomitant difficulty in movement (Utley, Holvoet, & Barnes, 1977). Because changes in posture are made possible by the presence of righting and equilibrium reactions, and these reactions are often absent or delayed in this population, voluntary movement may be severely limited.

Finally, the severely mentally retarded with physically handicapping conditions often have reflexes that persist long after the normal time of inhibition. When these abnormal reflexes persist, they cause abnormal movements, which make more advanced forms of movement impossible (Utley et al., 1977).

A survey of the literature suggests a preponderance of sensory defects among severely mentally retarded children. Chinn et al. (1975) reported the results of numerous research studies that found disproportionate percentages of deafness, hearing loss, and defects of visual acuity in populations of moderately, severely, and profoundly mentally retarded children.

In addition to the physical problems associated with severe mental retardation, the literature strongly suggests that this population has greater amounts of chronic health problems than either the population of nonretarded people or even the mildly and moderately mentally retarded. It is beyond the scope of this text to discuss these chronic health problems in any detail, but it will be noted that these problems can include:

- metabolic disorders
- seizures
- abnormal dermatoglyphics
- congenital heart disease
- respiratory diseases and/or infections
- gastrointestinal disorders
- diabetes

EDUCATING THE SEVERELY RETARDED

Prior to the passage of P.L. 94-142, the severely mentally retarded were systematically excluded from public school programs. Exclusion was usually justified on the basis of lack of resources, lack of facilities, and lack of trained personnel to provide an adequate educational experience for this population. When public education for the severely retarded was being provided, it was usually occurring in special schools or residential facilities. These schools, operated exclusively for the mentally retarded, were isolated from the mainstream school elements. Proponents of the special or residential schools claimed that these arrangements provided for greater numbers of children more efficiently, lessened transportation problems, and allowed for a concentration of professional and ancillary services (physical therapy or speech therapy).

There were, however, many critics of this approach. The central thrust of the criticism was the isolation and stigmatization that occur when children are educated in special schools or residential facilities. Thus, removing children from the educational mainstream deprives them of their basic rights and many valuable experiences.

The current thrust of P.L. 94-142 stressing education in the least restrictive environment may cause a shift away from the special school or residential facility toward the special self-contained classroom in the neighborhood school. While this arrangement is more frequently used for mildly or moderately retarded youngsters, the current pressure to develop programs to fit the needs of the child will probably serve to facilitate greater integration of the severely mentally retarded into the mainstream of public education.

Service Needs

Wilcox (1979) suggested that the service system required to provide comprehensive programming to the severely retarded must contain certain elements including:

- Early identification and intervention—Current efforts in many states are leading to the implementation of high risk registries. In this fashion children may receive continuous follow-along services. Certainly early, continuous, and coordinated intervention will maximize the gains to young severely retarded children and their families.
- Integrated services from many relevant sources, including parents— Described in later chapters of this text, the resources and services of professionals from many disciplines and parents will be necessary to maximize service delivery to this population. Coordination of services is extremely important to ensure that all resources are brought to bear, and little or no program overlap exists.

- Curricula organized around longitudinal skill sequences designed to facilitate acquisition of vital independent functioning skills—Subsequent chapters will present a coordinated sequence of long- and short-range objectives that are consistently integrated to provide a complete curricular framework of the essential skills in motor, communication, self-help, social, personal, vocational, and other areas required for more independent functioning.
- A continuum of educational, vocational, and home-living arrangements that emphasizes and facilitates movement to less restrictive environments—Since it is reasonable to expect that improved service delivery to the severely retarded will result in the development of more advanced skill repertoires, it will be necessary to have less restrictive environments available in educational, vocational, and home-living areas.
- Data-based approach to evaluation of instruction and systems efforts—The total range of services to the severely retarded, including the preparation of personnel to work with this population, must be subject to evaluation for cost effectiveness and benefit.

Educational Program Content

While a number of references exist regarding curriculum for the severely retarded, Luckey and Addison (1974) have prepared a comprehensive summary of these sources with over 100 references. They presented this summary divided into the following areas:

1. Preschool curricula
   a. sensorimotor stimulation including developing sensory responses, enriching the environment, and encouraging exploration behavior
   b. physical development that involves body positioning, movement, and locomotion skills
   c. pre-self-care that suggests passive acceptance to feeding, dressing, bathing, and toileting
   d. language stimulation that includes attentiveness, localization, and vocalization
   e. interpersonal response including recognition of people, object or toy manipulation, and requesting attention from other people

2. School age curricula
   a. sensorimotor development includes identification of objects, sounds, textures, and odors
   b. physical mobility and coordination includes practice in walking, using playground equipment, and advanced motor behaviors such as running, skipping, jumping, balancing, and climbing

  c. self-care development such as self-feeding, appropriate behavior while eating, dressing and undressing, partial bathing, and toileting
  d. language development including recognition of one's name, naming objects and body parts, responding to commands, speech imitation, and the use of gestures, words, or phrases
  e. social behavior involves requesting attention, playing alongside others, and cooperative play

3. Adult curricula
  a. sensorimotor integration involves such skills as sorting, inserting, pulling, folding, response to music and warning signals, making personal choices, and discriminating sizes, weights, colors, and so on
  b. physical dexterity and recreation includes riding vehicles, participating in track and field, arts and crafts, swimming and other aquatic activity, and the use of parks, playgrounds, and other recreational resources
  c. self-care that involves independent eating, dressing, bathing, and toileting
  d. language and speech including listening, using gestures and words, and following simple directions
  e. self-direction and work includes sharing, taking turns, traveling with or without supervision, completing assigned tasks, and working in a work activity center

The obvious optimism evidenced in this selection of educational topics for the severely retarded along with our personal experiences working in various capacities in residential facilities for the severely retarded has inspired us to similarly adopt a positive view regarding the capabilities and potential of that population. The following chapters of this textbook will present an integrated, coordinated series of educational activities that could easily be woven into a total curricular format. The topics chosen coincide with the topics presented by Luckey and Addison (1974), and cover skills from preschool to adult ages.

SUMMARY

This chapter established a positive and optimistic position regarding full educational opportunities for the severely retarded. A discussion was presented of the facilities providing services to this population, and included a discussion of personnel training needs and salaries for professionals.

Mental retardation was defined and the cognitive, personality, emotional, physical, and health characteristics of the severely retarded were presented. The educational provisions for the severely retarded including service needs and curricular content were discussed.

REFERENCES

Anderson, R.M., Greer, J.G., & Dietrich, W.L. Overview and perspectives. In R.M. Anderson & J.G. Greer (Eds.), *Educating the severely and profoundly retarded.* Baltimore: University Park Press, 1976.

Chinn, P.C., Drew, C.J., & Logan, D.R. *Mental retardation: A life cycle approach.* St. Louis: Mosby, 1975.

Dever, R.B., & Knapczyk, D. Indiana School of education undergraduate program for training teachers of moderately, severely, and profoundly retarded individuals, 1976. (ERIC Document Reproduction Service No. ED 159 135).

Federal Register, 40-35, 1975, 7412.

Forehand, R., & Baumeister, A.A. Effect of frustration on stereotyped body rocking: Follow-up. *Perceptual and Motor Skills,* 1970, *31,* 894.

Gearheart, B.R., & Litton, F.W. *The trainable retarded: A foundations approach.* St. Louis: Mosby, 1975.

Gilmore, J., & Argyros, N. Special education certification: A state of the art survey, 1977 (ERIC Document Reproduction Service No. ED 158 447).

Grossman, H.J. (Ed.). *Manual on terminology and classifications in mental retardation.* Washington, D.C.: American Association on Mental Deficiency, 1977.

Guess, D. The influence of visual and ambulation restrictions on stereotyped behavior. *American Journal of Mental Deficiency,* 1966, *70,* 542-547.

Heber, R.F. A manual on terminology and classifications in mental retardation. *American Journal of Mental Deficiency Monograph,* 1961, (Supp. 64).

Hutt, M.L., & Gibby, R.G. *The mentally retarded: Development, education, and treatment* (3rd ed.). Boston: Allyn and Bacon, 1976.

Inhelder, B. *The diagnosis of reasoning in the mentally retarded* (2nd ed.). (W.B. Stephens and others, trans.) New York: Chandler, 1968.

Luckey, R.E., & Addison, M.R. The profoundly retarded: A new challenge for public education. *Education and Training of the Mentally Retarded,* 1974, *9,* 123-130.

MacMillan, D.L. *Mental retardation in school and society.* Boston: Little, Brown, 1977.

Menolascino, F.J. Primitive, atypical, and abnormal behaviors. In E. Katz (Ed.), *Mental health services for the mentally retarded.* Springfield, Illinois: Charles C. Thomas, 1972.

Robinson, N.M., & Robinson, H.B. *The mentally retarded child: A psychological approach.* New York: McGraw-Hill, 1976.

Russo, T., & Stark, N.B. Teacher certification trends. *Mental Retardation,* 1976, *14,* 24-26.

Scheerenberger, R.C. Mental retardation: Definition, classification, and prevalence. In J.H. Rothstein (Ed.), *Mental retardation: Readings resources.* New York: Holt, Rinehart and Winston, 1971.

Siudzinski, R.M., & VanNagel, C. The validation of competencies in special education: A competency based approach, 1978. (ERIC Document Reproduction Service No. ED 158 468).

Sontag, E., Smith, J., & Sailor, W. The severely/profoundly handicapped: Who are they? Where are we? *The Journal of Special Education,* 1977, *11,* 1, 5-11.

Stephens, B. A Piagetian approach to curriculum development for the severely, profoundly and multiply handicapped. In E. Sontag (Ed.), *Educational programming for the severely and profoundly handicapped.* Reston, Virginia: Council for Exceptional Children, 1977.

Tawney, J.W. New considerations for the severely and profoundly handicapped. In R.D. Kneedler & S.G. Tarver (Eds.), *Changing perspectives in special education.* Columbus, Ohio: Charles E. Merrill, 1977.

Utley, B.L., Holvoet, J.F., & Barnes, K. Handling, positioning, and feeding the physically handicapped. In E. Sontag (Ed.), *Educational programming for the severely and profoundly handicapped.* Reston, Virginia: Council for Exceptional Children, 1977.

Wilcox, B. Severe/profound handicapping conditions: Administrative considerations. In M. Stephen Lilly (Ed.), *Children with exceptional needs.* New York: Holt, Rinehart and Winston, 1979.

Woodward, M. The behavior of idiots interpreted by Piaget's theory of sensorimotor development. *British Journal of Educational Psychology,* 1959, *29,* 60-71.

Chapter 2

Defining and Assessing Adaptive Behavior

The concept of impaired adaptive behavior appears in the definition of mental retardation and is considered one of the criteria for determining if an individual is mentally retarded. Early workers in the field suggested that social competency was the ultimate determinant of the diagnosis of retardation. Unfortunately the professionals' need to ascertain information regarding adaptive behavior far exceeds their ability to accurately and reliably measure it.

The difficulties of defining and assessing adaptive behavior will be discussed in this chapter since the evaluation of adaptive behavior is a critical component of a comprehensive diagnosis.

DEFINING ADAPTIVE BEHAVIOR

A major consideration used in the classification of individuals as mentally retarded is adaptive behavior. Its descriptions vary with each author; however, several common components generally prevail. In the work of Nihira, Foster, Shellhass, and Leland (1969) adaptive behavior is defined as the ability to cope. Employing their criteria, three major facets are considered:

1. Independent functioning . . . the ability of the individual to successfully accomplish those tasks or activities demanded of him by the general community and in terms of the typical expectations for specific ages.
2. Personal responsibility .   both the willingness of the individual to accomplish those critical tasks he is able to accomplish . . . and his ability to assume individual responsibility for his personal behavior. The ability is reflected in decision making and choice of behaviors.

23

3. Social responsibility . . . the ability of the individual to accept responsibility as a member of a community group . . . reflected in levels of conformity, socially positive creativity, social adjustment, and emotional maturity . . . some level of civic responsibility leading to complete or partial economic independence (Robinson & Robinson, 1976, p. 356).

A more recent publication contributed by Grossman (1977) describes adaptive behavior as the effectiveness or degree with which an individual meets the standards of personal independence and social responsibility expected for his age and cultural group.

Contained within these aspects of adaptive behavior is the concept of social maturity. This developmental phenomenon takes into account the specific skills and/or behaviors that are considered appropriate for specific chronological ages. Employing this concept, the focus encompasses the general areas of independent functioning, cognitive skills, social behavior, motor development, and communication skills. Of course, once an evaluation of adaptive behavior is completed, those observations must be compared to an established set of age standards for that specific culture, for the domain of motor development observations are compared to expected developmental milestones for individuals of the same chronological age. In doing so the evaluator must have an understanding of "normal" child development. As an example, the motoric development of a preschool aged youngster can be assessed with relative ease if it is known that a child should possess specific reflexes, sit alone at approximately seven months, stand by nine months, and walk at one year (Frankenburg, Dodds, & Fandal, 1970). For many of the individuals that are classified as severely retarded, delayed motor development may be an accompanying characteristic; however, this is not always the case. Impaired motor development can occur independent of mental functioning as in conditions of cerebral palsy and hypotonia. It is this circumstance that creates problems for the determination of intellectual functioning.

Language development is a second area that must receive attention when determining one's adaptive behavior. Delayed speech due to articulation, fluency, and other expressive problems may serve as indicators of retardation (Kirk, 1964; Spradlin, 1963). In addition, receptive and organizational problems involving language may hold the same functions. The assessment of communication levels can be easily achieved through the use of established developmental milestones for normal speech, language skill areas (reading, vocabulary, spelling, and writing), and social conversation. It is not uncommon for severely retarded individuals to exhibit sensory defects (hearing or vision) thus causing depressed language skills. The assessment of adaptive behavior in this area requires careful consideration of each individual's opportunity for language development. Regardless of how remote the chances appear, it just may be possible to improve communication significantly if the appropriate teaching method or equipment is used.

Cognitive skills are the third area of consideration in determining adaptive behavior and the most direct measure of general intelligence. According to Piaget, the level of intellectual development in the retarded person is fixated at a specific level of organization. Concomitant with this idea, Inhelder's (1968) research indicates that the severely retarded do not go beyond Piaget's sensorimotor level of intelligence. Because adaptive behavior is a combination of several aspects of behavior and a function of a wide range of specific abilities and disabilities (Grossman, 1977), cognitive skills give the individual the opportunity to master language, understand the world, and control much of the environment. With the severely retarded, adaptive behavior in this area will primarily reflect the fundamentals of language, knowledge of common objects in the environment, and basic concepts related to health needs and social habits.

The final area for consideration relative to adaptive behavior is social skills. The personality factors such as feelings of adequacy or success, emotional stability, and self-valuation will be collectively influenced by the quality of the individual's interpersonal relationships with family, school, and the community. Social behavior of severely retarded individuals, depending on the chronological age, will generally range between limited recognition of an object or face to spontaneous play for the higher functioning severely retarded.

Adaptive behavior is a complex and dynamic attribute continually changing with maturation and experience. Of course, whether others view an individual as exhibiting appropriate adaptive behavior is governed by a number of cultural and societal factors. The fact that an individual may be viewed by a particular group within a given society as possessing appropriate skills and behaviors certainly does not mean that this same individual will exhibit acceptable performance within different cultural or societal groups. For the severely retarded, adaptive behavior is critical to the determination of appropriate educational programs, economic aptitude, and related services.

ASSESSING ADAPTIVE BEHAVIOR

Kazdin (1978, p. 269) defined assessment as "the collection of information for the purpose of making decisions; the kind of information gathered depends upon the decisions to be made." Obviously this general definition allows each distinct discipline to collect data regarding decisions they consider important or relevant. Salvia and Ysseldyke (1978) listed five reasons for engaging in assessment in educational settings including intervention planning. In planning for intervention, the educator is interested in determining where to begin instruction based upon the learner's current level of functioning.

Assessment Techniques

Salvia and Ysseldyke (1978) discussed three different assessment techniques: observation, judgments, and testing. Each of the techniques will be discussed with a particular elaboration of testing procedures.

Observation

Observation can be considered a basic assessment tool and in point of fact, is really part of all other techniques. Observation may be informal or formal. Users of informal observation record those behaviors they consider significant. Generally, however, there are no predetermined behaviors to be recorded. On the other hand, formal observation is characterized by the observation of prespecified behaviors and the formal recording of the extent to which those behaviors are exhibited (Kazdin, 1978).

Kazdin (1978) described several formal observation techniques including:

- Narrative data—This approach involves the gathering of the totality of an event or sequence of events. Usually this data takes the form of audio or video tapes, photographs, films, logs, diaries, and so on. Once the observer has gathered this type of data, it then becomes necessary to reduce it to some other form of data (i.e., specific behaviors).
- Rating scales—Usually the use of rating scales involves lists of prespecified behaviors rated on the basis of frequency of occurrence. While the use of these scales is considered to be a formal and systematic data collection procedure, rating scales are open to criticism because of the possibility of different interpretations of the behaviors to be rated.
- Formal behavior recording—This approach may be described as the observation and recording of the extent of occurrence of specific predetermined behaviors. Kazdin (1978) noted that behavior recording includes frequency counting, a tallying of the number of times a behavior occurs; interval recording, a recording of whether behavior occurs during a specified time period such as a five minute interval; and duration of response, recording the actual length of time that a response occurs. Chapter 3 contains an in-depth discussion of behavior recording.

Judgments

Often times educators are called upon to use their professional judgment to make a decision relative to the program of a mentally retarded child. In this sense the judgments are considered personal and are often rendered independent of other formal assessment procedures (Kazdin, 1978).

Testing

Typically, the testing of severely retarded learners is an extremely challenging task. Kazdin (1978) noted that tests provide the teacher with two kinds of information: quantitative and qualitative. The quantitative information is usually provided by a score on some instrument (i.e., a social quotient on the Vineland Social Maturity Scale). When teachers gather qualitative information, they are getting data that tells them how the score was derived (i.e., the student consistently failed to discriminate red objects).

Tests may be divided into two major categories: norm-referenced and criterion-referenced tests. The use of one of these categories of tests is often determined by the particular model of assessment the teacher chooses to employ.

PSYCHO-EDUCATIONAL ASSESSMENT

One approach to assessment is often referred to as the psycho-educational or psycho-medical model. Teachers employing this approach make basic assumptions regarding the failure of the student to learn (i.e., something is wrong with the cognitive, perceptual, or motor processes) and attempt to remediate learning problems by changing the student's perceptual or cognitive processes. The most frequently used tests in the psycho-educational model are norm-referenced tests. Norm-referenced tests emphasize that the evaluation of a person is comparison to others who are supposed to be alike. The tests are developed by selecting a series of test items believed to sample a certain behavior and then standardizing the items on a group of individuals. Kazdin (1978) noted that norm-referenced tests yield grade equivalents, age scores, percentiles, quotients, and stanines to express the performance of the learner.

Norm-referenced tests have undergone a great deal of criticism relative to their use with severely retarded students. Perhaps the primary criticism of most of these norm-referenced tests is that the behaviors measured are not in small enough increments to be useful with this population. In addition, the typical norm-referenced test does not usually allow the user to plan a meaningful educational program based upon the results of the test.

Further, the use of norm-referenced tests to assess adaptive behavior is extremely difficult. Grossman (1977) identified the reason for this difficulty as a problem in obtaining information on what a person routinely does do, which is essentially the information needed for determining adaptive behavior. Instruments measuring adaptive behavior cannot be given in offices or laboratories; adaptive behavior must, instead, be determined on the basis of a series of observations in many places over periods of time.

Adaptive behavior is a composite of a variety of behavioral aspects and a function of a wide range of specific abilities and disabilities. Behaviors that have been categorized under the headings intellectual, affective, social, motor, and motivational all contribute to and are a part of total adaptation to the environment. Thus the behaviors sampled by current intelligence tests contribute to total adaptation, and the level of function on measured intelligence will correlate with the level of adaptive behavior (Grossman, 1977).

As is the case with retarded intellectual development, adaptive behavior is categorized into levels of impairment. These levels are scaled from mild (but apparent and significant) deviation from the population norms in adaptive behavior to almost a complete lack of adaptive behavior at the lower extremes—profound (Grossman, 1977). For example, adults at the severe and profound levels of impairment are quite likely to have central nervous system damage that restricts social behavioral responses. These individuals will need training in communication skills and self-care skills and will not profit from academic instruction. Habits of dressing, eating, and finding their way around the neighborhood require systematic and supervised practice extended over long periods of time. Little independent behavior is observed (Robinson & Robinson, 1976).

Profoundly retarded persons are frequently restricted in mobility and are unable to care for themselves. Most having severe central nervous system damage are confined to wheelchairs or hospital beds. While they may learn to walk, vocalize a greeting, feed themselves, and toilet independently, total supervision is necessary (Robinson & Robinson, 1976).

The tentative nature of adaptive behavior levels requires reexamination of individuals at fairly frequent intervals. Adaptive behavior may change due to environmental shifts or training emphasis, thus consideration of these factors is often extremely helpful in evaluating adaptive behavior levels (Grossman, 1977).

Social maturity is closely related to adaptive behavior. Thus as individuals grow older, they must cope with an ever-expanding social environment. A maturity concept suggests age increments. In measurement terms, two competing priorities are presented. The developmental orientation suggests that test items be arranged by age level and be selected to sample socially adaptive responses common of children of that particular age (Robinson & Robinson, 1976). Robinson and Robinson (1976) noted that this was a scale of the Binet type—a few representative items, selected to prevent a statistically balanced series and additionally, to be highly correlated with scores on the total scale. This approach is based upon normal development and measures an individual's adaptive behavior against age norms. In contrast, the concept of adaptive behavior, as broadly inclusive of skills and responsibilities in a number of areas, demands the inventory type of scale with subscales (Robinson & Robinson, 1976).

The inventory approach would appear to be more popular than the developmental approach because of the ease with which important target behaviors can be included and the greater ease in standardization. The majority of inventory scales are tested on institutionalized mentally retarded populations, which limits interpretive possibilities, but facilitates the standardization process.

Robinson and Robinson (1976) suggested a number of scales that have been designed to measure adaptive behavior and/or social competence. The Alpern-Boll Developmental Profile, the Bristol Social Adjustment Guides, and the Vineland Social Maturity Scale are the only ones of this group originally standardized on normal populations, although a standardization of one form of the AAMD Adaptive Behavior Scales has now been accomplished with nonretarded public school children as well as subjects in special classes for the handicapped (Lambert, Wilcox, & Gleason, 1974). The scales and authors are as follows:

- AAMD Adaptive Behavior Scales (Nihira, Foster, Shellhaas, & Leland, 1969)
- Adaptation for Profoundly Retarded (Congdon, 1973)
- 1972 Revision—School Form (Lambert et al., 1974)
- Alpern-Boll Developmental Profile (Alpern & Boll, 1972)
- Balthazar Scales of Adaptive Behavior (Balthazar, 1971; Balthazar, Roseen, & English, 1968)
- Bristol Social Adjustment Guides (Stott, 1963)
- Cain-Levine Social Competency Scale (Cain, Levine, & Elzey, 1963)
- Fairview Behavior Evaluation Battery for the Mentally Retarded (R.T. Ross, Boroskin, & Giampiccolo, 1970-1974)
- Gardner Behavior Chart (Dayan & McLean, 1963; Wilcox, 1942)
- Hospital Adjustment Scale (McReynolds, Ferguson, & Ballachey, 1963)
- Newman-Doby Measure of Social Competence (Newman & Doby, 1973)
- Preschool Educational Attainment Record (Doll, 1966)
- Progress Assessment Chart of Social Development (Gunzburg, 1968)
- Social Competence Rating (Banham, 1960)
- Vineland Social Maturity Scale (Doll, 1964)

These particular scales attempt to isolate the factors usually associated with adaptive behavior. In particular, twelve major areas of adaptive behavior are commonly assessed in the scales:

1. self-help skills, e.g., dressing, grooming, toileting, etc.
2. communication skills
3. socialization of interpersonal skills
4. locomotion
5. self-direction, e.g., initiative, attending
6. occupational skills
7. economic activity
8. neuromotor development

  9. personal responsibility
 10. social responsibility, e.g., care of others' property
 11. emotional adjustment
 12. health (Robinson & Robinson, 1976).

When comparing these major areas to the AAMD definition of adaptive behavior, the deficits in adaptive behavior will be reflected in the following areas
according to age and cultural group.

  1. During infancy and early childhood in the following:
     a. sensorimotor skills development
     b. communication skills (including speech and language)
     c. self-help skills
     d. socialization (development of ability to interact with others)
  2. During childhood and early adolescence in the following:
     a. application of basic academic skills in daily life activities
     b. application of appropriate reasoning and judgment in mastery of the
        environment
     c. social skills (participation in group activities and interpersonal relation-
        ships)
  3. During late adolescence and adult life in the following:
     a. vocational and social responsibilities and performances (Grossman,
        1977, p. 13).

Despite the problems with and criticisms of norm-referenced tests, many school
districts mandate the use of these tests both for placement and educational pro-
grammatic decision making. Therefore, certain norm-referenced tests will be
discussed with the caution that the reader be aware of the deficiencies of norm-
referenced tests in making educationally relevant decisions.

Four instruments are most frequently employed for obtaining adaptive behavior
information: The Vineland Social Maturity Scale; the AAMD Adaptive Behavior
Scale; the AAMD Adaptive Behavior Scale, Public School Version; and the
Cain-Levine Social Competency Scale. Each of these scales will be analyzed in
depth in the following section of this chapter.

Vineland Social Maturity Scale

The Vineland Scale was first developed in 1935 at the Training School at
Vineland, New Jersey, by Dr. Edgar A. Doll. Subsequent standardization resulted
in a second form and a revised manual. The major objective of this scale is the

measurement of the social competence or social maturity of an individual. The scale is not based upon direct observation of performance, but instead employs a method of report. The examiner utilizes specific interviewing strategies to obtain information about the subject from an individual or individuals who are extremely familiar with the subject, i.e., parent or teacher. Using the information provided by the respondent, the interviewer must determine whether the subject *habitually* and *customarily* performs certain acts, not simply if the subject can perform these acts (Salvia & Ysseldyke, 1978). Scoring is similar to the Stanford-Binet ratio procedure in which basal and ceiling ages are determined and a Social Age (SA) is obtained by adding credits to the basal figure. The SA is then divided by the Life Age (LA); and the quotient is multiplied by 100, with the product called the Social Quotient (SQ) (Payne and Mercer, 1975).

Payne and Mercer (1975) noted that the major drawback of using the Vineland Scale as an indicator of adaptive behavior is the variability of the standard deviations within the various age levels. A SQ may indicate marked differences of social competence at different ages.

Additionally, the original standardization sample for the scale consisted of ten normal subjects (male and female) at each age (birth to 30), for a total of 620 subjects. All the subjects lived in Vineland or a nearby suburban area with all data obtained in the 1930s. Doll (1953) recognized the problem of the small standardization sample but pointed out the internal consistency of the scale as a whole.

The Vineland Scale contains 117 items numbered in a hierarchical sequence. The items are separated into 17 age groupings, categorized according to the following areas: self-help general, self-help eating, self-help dressing, self-direction, occupation, communication, locomotion, and socialization. Representative types of items in each of the eight clusters follow:

Self-Help General: The items included in this general heading assess general self-help activities such as sitting and standing unsupported, avoiding simple hazards, and independent toileting.

Self-Help Eating: Items categorized under this heading assess the subject's increasing responsibility in eating. Skills include drinking from a cup with assistance, using a spoon, getting a drink unaided, and being self-sufficient at the dinner table.

Self-Help Dressing: The items under this category assess an individual's responsibility in dress and personal hygiene. Included are such skills as putting on a coat, buttoning, washing, and dressing unaided.

Locomotion: The items under this heading include walking, moving about the house, yard, town, and going to near and distant places alone.

Occupation: The items under this category measure an increasing orientation to gainful employment. Items at earlier ages involve occupying oneself while unattended and doing routine chores. At older ages items include being employed and performing skilled work as well as expert work.

Communication: Items included under this heading measure command of increasingly complex forms of communication beginning with rudiments of language such as imitation of sounds and concluding with items such as reading, writing, using the telephone, and sending and receiving mail.

Self-Direction: The items under this heading deal with using money (i.e., to make purchases, buy for others) and assuming responsibility for oneself (i.e., goes out in day or night without supervision).

Socialization: Items under this category measure interpersonal relationships (Salvia & Ysseldyke, 1978).

Payne and Mercer (1975) noted that although the Vineland Scale was developed more than 30 years ago, the items are still relevant; and it remains one of the better measures of social competency. However, the Vineland's value and accuracy depend on a skilled interviewer with an honest and knowledgeable informant. Salvia and Ysseldyke (1978) suggested that the Vineland was in need of revision and updating including revision of item placement.

AAMD Adaptive Behavior Scale

In 1965, the American Association on Mental Deficiency initiated a project to study adaptive behavior. As a result of the project, two adaptive behavior scales were developed (Nihira, Foster, Shellhaas, & Leland, 1969). One scale was to be employed with children from three to twelve, the other for individuals of thirteen to adulthood. In 1974 the scales were revised and combined to form the AAMD Adaptive Behavior Scale, 1974 Revision (Nihira, Foster, Shellhaas, & Leland, 1974). The current scale is designed to provide objective descriptions and evaluations of a subject's effectiveness in coping with the natural and social demands of the environment.

The AAMD Adaptive Behavior Scale (1974 Revision) is divided into two parts. The first part is organized along developmental lines with individual skills divided into ten behavioral domains related to personal independence in daily living. The ten domains are subdivided into twenty-one subdomains as follows:

I. independent functioning
   a. eating
   b. toilet use
   c. cleanliness
   d. appearance
   e. care of clothing
   f. dressing and undressing
   g. travel
   h. general independent functioning

II. physical development
   a. sensory development
   b. motor development

III. economic activity
   a. money handling and budgeting
   b. shopping skills

IV. language development
   a. expression
   b. comprehension
   c. social language development

V. numbers and terms

VI. domestic activity
   a. cleaning
   b. kitchen duty
   c. other domestic activities

VII. vocational activities

VIII. self-direction
   a. initiative
   b. perseverance
   c. leisure time

IX. responsibility

X. socialization

There are two kinds of items in Ia. The examples given in the manual are shown in Exhibit 2-1.

Exhibit 2-1 Example of AAMD Adaptive Behavior Scale Item

Eating in public (Circle only ONE)

Orders complete meals in restaurants	3
Orders simple meals like hamburgers or hot dogs	②
Orders soft drinks at soda fountain or canteen	1 ②
Does not order at public eating places	0

   Notice that the statements are arranged in order of difficulty: 3,2,1,0. Circle the one statement which best describes the most difficult task the person can usually manage. In this example, the individual being observed can order simple meals like hamburgers or hot dogs (2), but cannot order a complete dinner (3). Therefore, (2) is circled in the example above. In scoring, 2 is entered in the circle to the right . . .

Table manners (Check ALL statements which apply)

Swallows food without chewing	___	8 - number
Chews food with mouth open	X	checked =⑥
Drops food on table or floor	___	
Uses napkin incorrectly or not at all	X	
Talks with mouth full	___	
Takes food off others' plates	___	
Eats too fast or too slow	___	
Plays in food with fingers	___	
None of the above	___	
Does not apply, e.g., because he or she is completely dependent on others. (If checked, enter "0" in the circle to the right.)	___	

In Exhibit 2-1, the second and fourth items are checked to indicate that the person "chews food with mouth open" and "uses napkin incorrectly." In scoring, the number of items checked, 2, is subtracted from 8, and the item score, 6, is entered in the circle to the right. Most items do not, however, require this subtraction; instead, the number checked can be directly entered as the score. The statement "None of the above," which is included for administrative purposes only, is not to be counted in scoring here (Nihira et al., 1969, pp. 1-2).

Part Two represents maladaptive behavior related to personality and behavior disorders. Part Two contains fourteen domains:

  I. Violent and destructive behavior
 II. Antisocial behavior
III. Rebellious behavior
 IV. Untrustworthy behavior
  V. Withdrawal
 VI. Stereotype behavior and odd mannerisms
VII. Inappropriate interpersonal manners
VIII. Unacceptable vocal habits
 IX. Unacceptable or eccentric habits
  X. Self-abusive behavior
 XI. Hyperactive tendencies
XII. Sexually aberrant behavior
XIII. Psychological disturbances
XIV. Use of medications—"Use of medications . . . is not a behavior domain, but does provide information about a person's adaptation to the world" (Nihira et al., 1974, p. 7).

The example given in the manual of a Part Two item is shown in Exhibit 2-2.

Exhibit 2-2 Sample Item AAMD Adaptive Behavior Scale

	Occasionally	Frequently	
Damages personal property			
Rips, tears, or chews own clothing	①	2	
Soils own property	1	②	
Tears up own magazines, books or			⑤
other possessions	1	②	
Other (Specify: _____)	1	2	
___None of the above Total	1	4	

Select those of the statements which are true of the individual being evaluated, and circle (1) if the behavior occurs occasionally, or (2) if it occurs frequently. Check "None of the above" where appropriate. In scoring, total each column on the bottom (Total) line, and enter the sum of these totals in the circle to the right. When "None of the above" is checked, enter 0 in the circle to the right. In the above example, the first statement is true occasionally, and the last two statements are true frequently; therefore, a score of 5 has been entered (Nihira, Foster, Shellhaas, & Leland, 1969, p. 11).

There are three ways to administer the scale: first-person assessment, third-party assessment, or the interview method. The first-person assessment method utilizes an informed observer to complete the scale. The third-party assessment method involves an evaluator questioning an informed individual and then recording the responses. The interview method involves attaining information through interviewing techniques (Payne & Mercer, 1975).

Once the test is completed, a profile can be developed depicting the strengths and weaknesses in an individual's adaptive behavior. To date, the standardization and norms have been established only for institutionalized mentally retarded individuals (Payne & Mercer, 1975).

Salvia and Ysseldyke (1978) noted that estimates of interrater reliability were extremely low, and thus the majority of domains should be considered accurate enough for screening purposes only. Validity data is limited; and at present, the scale does not appear adequate for making critical education-relevant decisions about individuals (Salvia & Ysseldyke, 1978).

AAMD Adaptive Behavior Scale Public School Version (1974 Revision)

Lambert, Windmiller, Cole, and Figueroa (1975) prepared a separate manual for the 1974 revision of the Adaptive Behavior Scale for use in the public schools. Domains, areas, and items that were not school relevant or could not be observed in school were deleted. For this scale, the teacher is the recommended respondent.

The Public School Version of the scale was standardized on 2600 California children in six age groups (seven years 3 months through thirteen years two months) by type of educational placement (regular class, special class for educable retarded (EMR), special class for trainable retarded (TMR), special class for the educationally handicapped, and resource class for the educationally handicapped); by sex; and by ethnic status (white, black, Spanish, other) (Salvia & Ysseldyke, 1978).

Salvia and Ysseldyke (1978) noted that the AAMD Adaptive Behavior Scale Public School Version contains no items that are not found in the institutional version from which it was derived. While the norms appear representative of California, the reliability and validity of the scale are not adequate for placement and program planning decisions.

Cain-Levine Social Competency Scale

The Cain-Levine Social Competency Scale (Cain, Levine, & Elzey, 1963) is an assessment device intended to measure the independence of trainable mentally retarded children between the ages of 5 years and 13 years, 11 months. The scale is administered in a structured interview situation with a respondent who is quite familiar with the subject. The subject is not interviewed nor visually observed; instead the interviewer introduces each item with a general question about the subject's behavior in an area and then probes the respondent's response (Salvia & Ysseldyke, 1978).

There are 44 items in the scale divided into four subscales: Self-Help, Initiative, Social Skills, and Communication.

Self-Help: This subscale contains 14 items assessing skills in dressing, washing, eating, and helping with simple household chores.

Initiative: In this subscale, the ten items assess the extent to which the subject initiates activities or is self-directed in dressing, toileting, or completing tasks.

Social Skills: This subscale has ten items designed to determine the subject's ability to maintain and/or engage in interpersonal relationships. Typical items include playing with and helping others.

Communication: This subscale has ten items designed to assess the degree to which an individual can communicate his needs. Items range from the use of oral language to relating objects to actions.

The items are rated either on a four- or five-point scale with a score of one representing the absence of behavior. Raw scores are summed with males having a constant added to the total score (to compensate for the lower scores typically earned by males). Raw scores are then converted to percentile ranks.

According to Salvia and Ysseldyke (1978), the Cain-Levine is sufficiently reliable for screening purposes. Additionally, it appears to have adequate validity in spite of the fact that the normative sample was limited to children living in California.

TASK ANALYTICAL ASSESSMENT

Another approach to evaluation or assessment is the task analytical approach. The user of this approach assumes that task failure is related to an inability of the student to master certain subtasks within the major task. This particular model uses criterion-referenced tests comprised of validated sequences of skills. The focus then becomes what the student is able or not able to do and educational planning is directly related to a specific sequence of subtasks and tasks that will lead to accomplishment of some skill.

Howell, Kaplan, and O'Connell (1979, pp. 8-9) have developed a description of the task analytical model, which includes premises, products, and skills. This model is presented in Table 2-1.

Table 2-1 Task Analytical Model

Premises

1. The student is behaving improperly.
2. Instruction can change improper behavior.
3. The reason the student has failed to change already is that he has received inappropriate instruction.
4. Instruction is inappropriate when:
   a. It teaches the wrong thing.
   b. It teaches the right thing poorly.
5. Diagnosis answers the questions:
   a. What to teach?
   b. How to teach it?
6. Diagnosis cannot take place in the absence of information about tasks (what is taught) and treatments (how it is taught).
7. Diagnosis is not complete until the student has been placed in a treatment and his progress has been monitored.
8. The model of educational evaluation which is most useful is the model which evaluates variables teachers can control.

Products of Diagnosis

A. What to teach?
A1. Teach the content that the student needs to learn.
A2. Teach only those tasks which are related to the content.
A3. Teach only the essential subtasks of a task.

B. How to teach it?
B1. Use only direct instruction.
B2. Use instruction which is well designed.
B3. Select instruction which is appropriate to the student's characteristics.

Skills Needed for Diagnosis

1. TASK ANALYSIS
   a. able to specify tasks.
   b. able to identify essential subtasks.
   c. able to test essential subtasks.

2. TREATMENT ANALYSIS
   a. able to review relevant research.
   b. able to specify instructional variables.
   c. able to monitor the effectiveness of a treatment.

3. LEARNER ANALYSIS
   a. able to assess students' needs.
   b. able to identify physiological limitations.
   c. sensitivity to individual differences.

Source: From *Evaluating exceptional children: A task analysis approach,* by K.W. Howell, J.S. Kaplan, and C.Y. O'Connell, pages 8-9, © 1979. Reprinted by permission of Charles E. Merrill Publishing Co., Columbus, Ohio.

As can be seen, this model has value because the evaluation component has a direct relationship to the instructional component. Using this approach the teacher will be able to identify behaviors that need to be changed and then match the behaviors to corrective intervention strategies (Howell et al., 1979).

Criterion-referenced tests are an important diagnostic tool in the task analytical model. Howell et al. (1979) noted that the purpose of a criterion-referenced test is to assist teachers in determining whether or not a student has certain skills. Since the idea is not to compare the student to his peers, all items on a criterion-referenced test are at the same or nearly the same level of difficulty. In addition, the criterion-referenced test does not really yield a score in the real sense of the word. Students either pass or fail the test indicating they do or do not possess the skill being measured.

Developing a Criterion-Referenced Test

The development of a criterion-referenced test begins with a decision regarding what you want to know about a student's performance behavior or skill. Once this decision has been reached, the teacher must write a performance or behavioral objective that is descriptive of the testing procedure. These performance objectives should include the following three components:

1. a precise description of what the student must do;
2. the exact conditions under which you expect the behavior to occur; and
3. the minimal acceptable performance the student must demonstrate to pass the test (Howell et al., 1979).

The development of objectives is discussed in more detail in Chapter 3.

Once this step has been completed, the performance objective or objectives become test items and a test. The criterion-referenced test includes directions for administering and scoring the test, the criterion for passing the test, and the various materials needed to administer the test.

Howell et al. (1979) described the final task in the development of a criterion-referenced test as the establishment of a criterion for acceptable performance. This is determined by administering the criterion-referenced test to a preselected group of individuals who already possess the skill being measured. The minimum level of this group's performance on the test would become the standard for passing the criterion-referenced test or the criterion for acceptable performance. For certain behaviors and depending upon the student, this final step may be unnecessary. For example, if self-initiated toileting was the performance objective, then the level of performance expected should be 100 percent accuracy or accident freeness.

Like norm-referenced tests, it is essential that criterion-referenced tests have validity and reliability. Validity, having the test measure what it was supposed to measure, is established in criterion-referenced tests exactly as it is in norm-referenced tests. Thus if a criterion-referenced test is based upon relevant perform- ance objectives, the test has validity. Validity is assured if the test answers the question asked; if it answers a different question, then it is not valid (Howell et al., 1979).

Reliability of criterion-referenced tests is established when the performance objectives are complete and comprehensive. An objective is complete when it contains the previously discussed elements: (1) the behavior; (2) the conditions under which the behavior will occur; and (3) the criterion of acceptable perform- ance. For an objective to be comprehensive, the performance objective must be stated so that no confusion exists when different examiners use the criterion- referenced test. In other words, anyone who administers the test will know exactly what the student is to do and there is no need for the examiner to interpret the components (Howell et al., 1979).

Howell et al. (1979, p. 102) provided an example of a criterion-referenced test that could be used to determine the ability of a severely retarded learner to feed herself. This example is provided as it meets all the conditions for a valid and reliable criterion-referenced test as shown in Exhibit 2-3.

Exhibit 2-3 Example of Criterion-Referenced Test

Task: Able to feed herself

Materials: Glass of liquid, for example, juice or milk; plate containing food already cut for eating; cup containing liquid (e.g., juice or milk); bowl containing cereal or soup; fork and spoon.

Directions (to student): See below

Directions (to examiner): Place glass of liquid in front of the child and say, "Take a drink of _____ from this glass." Put plate of cut food in front of the child and, giving her a fork, say "Use this fork and show me how you eat this food with it." Give the child a bowl of soup or cereal and a spoon and say, "Show me how you eat your _____." Put a cup of liquid in front of the child and say, "Pick up the cup and drink from it." Note: Modeling by the examiner may be used in cases where receptive language is impaired.

Scoring: Count as acceptable if the child is able to transfer liquid and/or solid food from plate, bowl, glass, and cup to mouth without "excessive" spillage. All food must be ingested without aid within one minute of each request.

CAP: 100% accuracy (standardized on four Arizona State University faculty members at the "Dash-in" Restaurant, Tempe, Arizona)

Source: From *Evaluating exceptional children: A task analysis approach,* by K.W. Howell, J.S. Kaplan, and C.Y. O'Connell, page 102, © 1979. Reprinted by permission of Charles E. Merrill Publishing Co., Columbus, Ohio.

Often teachers will ask how the content of a criterion-referenced test is determined. It may be stated that the objectives or content of criterion-referenced tests in the adaptive behavior area should be those subtasks or behaviors necessary for the individual to complete important major task areas. The teacher must determine which subtasks of a skill area are important or essential and then include those in the criterion-referenced tests. Major content areas for the criterion-referenced tests may be determined by examining norm-referenced tests of adaptive behavior, curricula that have been adopted by schools or school districts, or determining through consultation with other special educators and parents what the learners should achieve to enhance their potential for social integration.

SUMMARY

This chapter provided a definition of adaptive behavior, its related components, and the situational and societal aspects that influence its determination. Adaptive behavior remains an elusive concept to both define operationally and measure accurately. A number of assessment devices have been developed to measure adaptive behavior with the scales generally given by report. Thus, the technical adequacy of adaptive behavior assessment methods lags far behind the technical adequacy of good achievement tests.

Four adaptive behavior scales were reviewed extensively: The Vineland Social Maturity Scale; the AAMD Adaptive Behavior Scale; the AAMD Adaptive Behavior Scale, Public School Revision; and the Cain-Levine Social Competency Scale.

The task analytical approach to assessment was presented along with a discussion of criterion-referenced tests and test development.

REFERENCES

Alpern, G.D. & Boll, T.J. *Developmental profile*. Indianapolis: Psychological Development Publications, 1972.

Balthazar, E.E. *Balthazar Scales of Adaptive Behavior, Section I: The scales of functional independence (BSAB-I)*. Champaign, Ill.: Research Press, 1971.

Balthazar, E.E., Roseen, D.L., & English, G.E. *The Central Wisconsin Colony Scales of Adaptive Behavior: The Ambulant Battery*. Madison: Wisconsin State Department of Administration, 1968.

Banham, K. *A social competence scale for adults*. Durham, N.C.: Family Life Publications, 1960.

Cain, L., Levine, S., & Elzey, F. *Manual for the Cain-Levine Social Competency Scale*. Palo Alto: Consulting Psychologists Press, 1963.

Congdon, D.M. The adaptive behavior scales modified for the profoundly retarded. *Mental Retardation*, 1973, 11, 20-21.

Dayan, M.I. & McLean, J. The Gardner Behavior Chart as a measure of adaptive behavior of the mentally retarded. *American Journal of Mental Deficiency*, 1963, 67, 887-892.

Doll, E.A. *Measurement of social competence: A manual for the Vineland Social Maturity Scale.* Circle Pines, Minnesota: American Guidance Service, 1953.

Doll, E.A. *Preschool attainment record* (Research ed.). Circle Pines, Minn.: American Guidance Service, 1966.

Doll, E.A. *Vineland Social Maturity Scale.* Minneapolis: American Guidance Service, 1964.

Frankenburg, W.K., Dodds, J.B., & Fandal, A.W. *Denver Developmental Screening Test.* Denver: University of Colorado Medical Center, 1967, 1970.

Grossman, H.J. (Ed.). *Manual on terminology and classification in mental retardation.* American Association on Mental Deficiency Special Publication No. 2, 1977.

Gunzburg, H.C. *Social competence and mental handicap.* London: Baillere, Tindall, & Cassell, 1968.

Howell, K.W., Kaplan, J.S., & O'Connell, C.Y. *Evaluating exceptional children: A task analysis approach.* Columbus, Ohio: Charles E. Merrill, 1979.

Inhelder, B. *The diagnosis of reasoning in the mentally retarded (2 ed.).* (W.B. Stephens and others, Trans.) New York: Chandler Publishing, 1968.

Kazdin, A.E. Assessment of retardation. In J.T. Neisworth & R.M. Smith (Eds.), *Retardation: Issues, assessment, and intervention.* New York: McGraw-Hill, 1978, pp. 271-295.

Kirk, S.A. Research in education. In H.A. Stevens & R. Heber (Eds.), *Mental retardation: A review of research.* Chicago: University of Chicago Press, 1964, pp. 57-99.

Lambert, N.M., Wilcox, M.R., & Gleason, W.P. *The educationally retarded child.* New York: Grune and Stratton, 1974.

Lambert, N.M., Windmiller, M., Cole, L., & Figueroa, R. *Manual for AAMD Adaptive Behavior Scale Public School Version (1974 revision).* Washington, D.C.: American Association on Mental Deficiency, 1975.

McReynolds, P., Ferguson, J.T., & Ballachey, E.L. *Hospital adjustment scale.* Palo Alto, CA: Consulting Psychologists Press, 1963.

Newman, H.G. & Doby, J.T. Correlates of social competence among trainable mentally retarded children. *American Journal of Mental Deficiency,* 1973, 77, 722-732.

Nihira, K., Foster, R., Shellhaas, M., & Leland, H. *Adaptive Behavior Scales: Manual.* Washington, D.C.: American Association on Mental Deficiency, 1969.

Nihira, K., Foster, R., Shellhaas, M., and Leland, H. *A.A.M.D. Adaptive Behavior Scale (1974 Revision).* Washington, D.C.: American Association on Mental Deficiency, 1974.

Payne, J.S., & Mercer, C.D. Adaptive behavior and behavioral characteristics. In J.M. Kauffman & J.S. Payne (Eds.), *Mental retardation: Introduction and personal perspectives.* Columbus, Ohio: Charles E. Merrill, 1975.

Piaget, J. *The language and thought of the child.* New York: Harcourt, Brace, 1926.

Piaget, J. *The origins of intelligence in children* (2nd ed.). New York: International Universities Press, 1952.

Robinson, N.M., & Robinson, H.B. *The mentally retarded child: A psychological approach* (2nd ed.). New York: McGraw-Hill, 1976.

Ross, R.T., Boroskin, A., & Giampiccolo, J.S., Jr. Fairview Behavior Evaluation Battery for the mentally retarded (5 scales). Costa Mesa, CA.: Fairview State Hospital, Research Department, 1970-1974.

Salvia, J., & Ysseldyke, J.E. *Assessment in special and remedial education.* Boston: Houghton Mifflin Co., 1978.

Spradlin, J.E. Language and communication of mental defectives. In N.R. Ellis (Ed.), *Handbook of mental deficiency.* New York: McGraw-Hill, 1963, pp. 512-555.

Stott, D.H. The social adjustment of children: Manual to the Bristol Social Adjustment Guides. London: University of London Press, 1963.

Wilcox, P.H. The Gardner Behavior Chart. *American Journal of Psychiatry,* 1942, 98, 874-880.

Chapter 3

Planning Educational Activities for Adaptive Skills Training

The design of appropriate educational programs for the severely retarded is a challenging task for educators. Schools have experienced great difficulty in educating children with special needs—particularly those children for whom "education" implies a total range of services, only one of which is the interaction between the teacher and learner.

Maximizing learning experiences for severely retarded individuals is made possible by applying basic principles of precise teaching technology. Haring, Hayden, and Beck (1976) described the process as:

1. measuring entering behavior (developmental level)
2. specifying terminal behavior (that is, a particular target skill or set of skills)
3. requiring an active response by the learner
4. arranging small, sequential steps to achieve the target behavior in order to maximize possibility for success (task behavior)
5. designing purposeful review of acquired skills (perhaps utilizing drill and practice)
6. removing discriminative stimulus systematically by shaping generalization and differential discrimination skills
7. collecting data to measure progress throughout the program

Essentially this process involves using assessment data to determine skills the learner has and has not mastered and targeting priority areas for instruction. Instruction involves breaking a target skill into small and precise enough steps for the learner to achieve success and then collecting data to verify the achievement of the target skill.

This chapter will examine the basic steps involved in precise teaching technology including: assessment, targeting behavior, writing objectives, skill sequencing, task analysis, reinforcement procedures, techniques for decreasing inappropriate behavior, focusing learner attention, and the evaluation of progress.

45

ASSESSMENT—THE ESTABLISHMENT OF ENTERING BEHAVIOR

In the process of precise teaching technology the starting point is the establishment of the learner's present level of functioning. For the area of adaptive behavior the learner's present functional level is determined through observation and the use of instruments designed to measure the learner's ability to cope with the natural and social demands of the environment. Chapter 2 provided an in-depth description of instruments used to measure adaptive behavior. Using these or other tools would lead the teacher to determine which of the most adaptive and useful behaviors the learner has either mastered or not mastered; thus the teacher could develop a profile of the learner's skill-acquisition levels in the areas of adaptive behavior.

In addition to the scales discussed in Chapter 2, various developmental checklists may be utilized to measure the learner's skill level. Often, however, these checklists designed by others may not measure behavior in increments small enough for a teacher's needs. In such cases the teacher may need to develop new checklists or to add to existing checklists. Two assessment instruments that have finely sequenced behaviors and may be used to effectively measure the learner's present functional level are the Uniform Performance Assessment System (UPAS) or the Pennsylvania Training Model: Individual Assessment Guide (Sommerton & Turner, 1975).

SELECTING AND SPECIFYING TARGET BEHAVIORS

Teachers employed in a residential facility, school, or training center for the severely retarded spend much of their time identifying and recording behaviors. The first step in this process is to identify a behavior that requires alteration. In most cases the critical behaviors are obvious and take the form of failure to comply, aggressiveness toward others, and tantrums. However, any behavior that needs altering can be called a target behavior.

In its written form, a target behavior should communicate the observable behavior. For example, the statement, "Johnny is aggressive to others," is not sufficient. A more complete description would be, "Johnny scratches others with his fingernails and yanks on their hair." When the behavior is clearly defined, it can be observed and recorded by various individuals and still yield accurate data. Once the target behavior has been identified, its occurrence must be measured. The information to be recorded should reflect (1) the situation where the behavior occurs and (2) the number of times that it occurs. Those recording the behavior must identify where, when, and how frequently their observations will take place.

Take, for example, Johnny's scratching and hair pulling behavior. Its accurate measurement requires that previous to recording, the following will be determined:

1. where he will be observed
2. the time observations will occur
3. the length of each observation period
4. the written style to be used when recording the data

There are basically eight methods for recording an individual's behavior; each will be briefly outlined. For more complete source information see *The Power of Positive Reinforcement: A Handbook of Behavior Modification* (Favell, 1977).

Narrative Recording

Longhand recording requires documentation of all client behaviors including the observer's starting and ending times, client actions, the environmental situation, and actions of others present. Table 3-1 provides an example of the narrative format.

Event Recording

If target behaviors have been previously identified and staff are expected to record them, the tally sheet is often used. This instrument allows staff to record the number of times a behavior occurs while continuing to perform various work duties.

Table 3-1 Example of Narrative Recording

Time	Client Behavior	Other's Behavior
2:00	1. Sits on floor patting hands on knees and opening and closing mouth.	2. Cottage parent approaches.
2:01	3. Looks up and smiles, gets up, lifts arms.	4. Cottage parent walks away.
2:02	5. Jumps up and down, yells, runs, and holds arm.	6. Cottage parent holds his hand.
	7. Smiles, grasps, jingles keys, and looks around.	

Source: From *The power of positive reinforcement,* by J.E. Favell, p. 12. © 1977. Reprinted by permission of Charles C. Thomas, Springfield, Illinois.

Documenting Products of Behavior

It is not always necessary to observe every behavior at the exact time it occurs. Some behaviors have products that prove a behavior or event has taken place. One example is soiling oneself. The behavior does not have to be witnessed because stained clothing or a foul smell generally provides all the evidence that is required. Bruises on the body, gaining weight by overeating, and assembling piece goods are just several examples of natural products that provide evidence that a behavior has taken place.

Artificial products can also be used to record behaviors without direct observation. Hyperactivity or excessive movement can be recorded by mechanical seat cushions or counting devices strapped to the legs or arms. Thumb sucking can be detected by painting a dye solution on the thumb that transfers to the lips when the thumb is placed in the mouth. The use of products of behavior as the measuring tool does restrict the type of data that can be obtained. In the case of gaining weight by overeating, the recorder has only a measure of the weight gained and not what foods were eaten, size of the portions, or amount of physical exercise the client receives. Another shortcoming of this technique is that in some cases, clients can conceal the fact that the behavior occurred by hiding or destroying the products before the observer has an opportunity to record it.

Duration Recording

There are times when a behavior itself is desirable but the length of time is not. Dressing is an important self-help skill; however, if a client takes one hour to complete the morning task, the behavior may present a serious problem. The use of an electric timer to record when the behavior begins and ends or writing the start and completion times while observing a clock are examples of duration recording.

Interval Recording

This method is used to record one or more behaviors within specified time blocks. The selection of prearranged time intervals will depend upon the type and frequency of the behavior(s) to be monitored. Five seconds is usually the shortest suggested interval for recorder reliability reasons and several minutes the longest.

When a behavior occurs only one notation is made within a time block. (See Figure 3-1.) If the behavior occurs a number of times within an interval, this is an indication that the time interval is too long. Also, if the behavior occurs in time interval number one and continues into interval two, the behavior is recorded in each. Finally, if the behavior occurs more than one time within the same interval, only one notation is made.

Figure 3-1 Example of Interval Recording

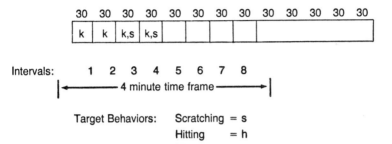

Seconds:

30	30	30	30	30	30	30	30	30	30	30	30	30
k	k	k,s	k,s									

Intervals: 1   2   3   4   5   6   7   8

|←————— 4 minute time frame —————→|

Target Behaviors: Scratching = s
                     Hitting   = h
                     Kicking   = k

Time Sampling

A method often used in conjunction with interval recording is time sampling. Here observations are taken after a predetermined time period. Generally, a timer is set for 5 or 10 minutes; when that time period has elapsed, the observer records the behavior the client displays at that time. Immediate behavior or products of behavior can be recorded for predetermined lengths of time.

Test Method

This technique measures "how well" a behavior is performed. Initially, a target behavior must be identified and followed by observing and recording how well the task is performed. Self-help skills (e.g., brushing teeth, dressing, and toileting), prevocational skills, and academic tasks are only a few of the many behaviors that can be evaluated by the test method. Scoring systems vary according to the type of measurement desired. For example, a client's ability to sort six different colored chips into separate containers could be evaluated by a yes/no checklist using a pass/fail criterion and, if necessary, the inclusion of a stopwatch to gain a time measure.

Automatic Recording

Recorder observations with pencil and paper are generally the most widely used measurement techniques outside the clinical setting. However, a number of mechanical devices do exist that measure numerous behaviors. Electrical counting apparatuses exist for measuring increased heart rate, body movement, perspiration, and many other human behaviors. Through modern electronic technology, machines are available that measure rocking and striking, verbalization, head banging, hyperactive movements, body tension, and many more physical as well as mental behaviors.

Once the target behaviors have been identified and recorded accurately, the next step is to write the target behaviors as instructional objectives.

WRITING INSTRUCTIONAL OBJECTIVES

Instructional objectives are the means through which expected student behaviors are identified and measured. The needs of the students are translated into educational objectives by specifying behaviors the students must acquire. The objectives are always pupil oriented or learner centered and reference to teacher behavior and method are strictly avoided.

Meaningfully stated objectives are those that succeed in communicating to the reader the writer's instructional intent. Mager (1962) indicated three steps to follow in making objectives more specific. First, identify the terminal behavior by name so that the reader can identify the acceptable behavior and also know when the learner has achieved the objective. Since learning can be inferred only by observing some aspect of performance, it is critical to specify exactly what the learner must be able to do to demonstrate mastery of the objective (Mager, 1962). For example, when teaching a child form discrimination, the terminal behavior might be: the child will be able to identify a circle, square, and rectangle by correctly pointing to the picture of each shape. In the area of gross motor skills an appropriate objective could be: the child will be able to stand up from a prone or a sitting position unassisted. In both cases, the objectives meet Mager's first criterion because they tell exactly what the learner will be doing when demonstrating achievement of the objective.

The second criterion suggested by Mager (1962) is the further definition of the desired terminal behavior by describing the important conditions under which the behavior will be expected to occur. This statement of conditions often helps to avoid confusion or eliminate the possibility that other behaviors would be mistaken for the desired behavior. Thus the conditions the instructor imposes upon the learners when they are demonstrating mastery of the objective are specified. For example, when teaching a child toileting skills it becomes critical to describe the conditions under which the teacher expects the child to demonstrate mastery of this objective. Do we expect the child to eliminate when placed on the toilet or do we expect him to self-initiate the action? If this qualification is not stated, an independent observer could misinterpret the objective. To meet Mager's criterion it would be necessary to state the objective as follows: Given the child has been placed on the toilet, he will urinate or have a bowel movement. . . . By stating the objective in this fashion and meeting two of Mager's criteria, the target behavior would be easily recognized by another competent person, and is detailed enough so that other possible behaviors would not be mistaken for the desired behavior.

Finally, the third criterion (Mager, 1962) communicates the level of acceptable performance or how well the learner is able to perform the objective. Thus if the instructor specified a minimum acceptable performance for each objective, a performance standard can be established. The instructor then has a means for determining whether the instructional program has been successful.

Mager (1962) suggested some ways of specifying minimum acceptable performance. One method is to indicate or specify a time limit where one is appropriate. For example, if the instructor is teaching the student to place various shapes into a formboard and this objective will not be considered as being achieved unless it can be done in one minute, then it should be stated as: to be able to place seven geometric forms into the formboard within a period of one minute.

Another way to indicate an acceptable minimum criterion is to specify the minimum number of correct responses you will accept. For example: Given a picture of 15 commonly used dinner utensils, the student will be able to correctly identify at least 8 utensils. An alternative to indicating number correct is to indicate percentage or proportion. Thus the instructor may specify: the student will be able to name correctly at least 80 percent of his body parts.

In summary then, if you can write objectives that:

1. identify what the learner will be doing when demonstrating his achievement;
2. define the important conditions under which the behavior is to occur; and
3. define the criterion of acceptable performance;

then you have an excellent chance of having your educational intent made clear.

In order to achieve teaching success, the teacher's next step should involve the identification of skill sequences for instruction.

SKILL SEQUENCING

A skill sequence is an organizational tool that can provide a structure of tasks or objectives within which varying instructional materials and methodologies may exist. As suggested by Williams (1975), a skill sequence does not tell how to teach, but provides a statement of what should be taught and in what order. The development of this framework for instruction can be time consuming; however, a number of resources such as curriculum guides, systematic teacher observations, and instructional research are currently available and provide ready assistance. Employing information from each of these resources, skill sequences tie related isolated activities to future competencies into sequenced instructional programs.

A characteristic of skill sequences is that they should never be considered finished products (Williams, 1975). They must remain flexible to accommodate change such as those involving societal values or expectations, increased knowledge of mental retardation, and human behavior.

Once the components of instruction and their sequence have been designated, lessons within this framework become the instructional focus. At this point it is important to remember that training should not become specific to one area, for example, gross motor, because people are seldom called upon to perform skills that involve one isolated area. Gross motor training, if educationally relevant to a specific individual, would, therefore, be coordinated or related instructionally to other relevant areas such as language, social behavior, and academic concepts.

In programming for the severely mentally retarded, it is often difficult to find commercial curricular materials or available school district products that meet all of this group's training needs. Through necessity, interested teachers, administrators, and client care workers in the past have relied heavily upon curricular materials and instructional skill sequences they have developed.

The field is becoming increasingly more productive as exemplified by the guides developed by Fredericks, Riggs, Furey, Grove, Moore, McDonnell, Jordan, Hanson, Baldwin, and Wadlow (1976); Popovich (1977); Bender and Valletutti (1976); Project MORE (1975); and the Murdoch Center C & Y Program Library (Wheeler, Miller, Duke, Salisbury, Merritt, & Horton, 1977).

With curricular areas identified and appropriate skill sequences developed, the next step is to break skills into small learner steps. This instructional planning technique is known as task analysis.

TASK ANALYSIS: GENERAL FORMAT

Task analysis has been defined as a ". . . problem-solving strategy for determining what to teach and for developing the proper sequence that will enhance student mastery of the objective" (Williams, 1975). Just as a skill sequence aids in determining instructional content and sequential order, task analysis breaks each instructional skill into small teaching components following an order from the first to the final step that demonstrates performance of the stated behavioral objective.

According to Williams (1975, p. 229), the development of task analysis generally requires seven steps:

1. Delineate the behavioral objective.
2. Review instructionally relevant resources.
3. Derive and sequence the component skills of the objective.
4. Eliminate unnecessary component skills.

5. Eliminate redundant component skills.
6. Determine prerequisite skills.
7. Monitor student performance and revise the sequence accordingly.

Delineating Behavioral Objectives

Before any task analysis is initiated, each student's present level of performance must be evaluated. (For further discussion see Chapter 2). Once present performance has been established, appropriate behavioral objectives can be formulated.

Reviewing Instructionally Relevant Resources

In order to determine how a skill develops or should be taught, teachers should consult a number of resources such as curriculum guides, resources on child development, and commercial materials developed for specific areas. Often several of the most useful resources are instructional materials centers and task analyses developed by other professionals.

Deriving and Sequencing the Component Skills

After the essential component skills have been determined from available resources, the instructor's task is to determine the essential steps leading to completion of the behavioral objective. Often instructors will find it helpful to watch others perform the skill or complete it themselves step by step in order to determine component skills and their sequence.

Eliminating Unnecessary Component Skills

There are many instructional tasks employed in training that are related to completion of a specific behavioral objective; however, not all are "necessary" to the accomplishment of the objective. As an example, the task of collating three different colored sheets of paper may be related to the objective of teaching a child to sort different colored plastic chips; but its mastery is not "necessary" to meeting the objective. Many lessons that are taught daily may be related to a specific objective and help facilitate skill generalization, yet they are not "necessary" to completing the objective.

Eliminating Redundant Skills

Task analysis usually reflects small steps; therefore, each must build upon its precedent. Skills that require the same performance as another step in the sequence must be eliminated if only to reduce instructional time.

Determining Prerequisite Skills

Full consideration should be given to the skills the student must possess before entering that first step that leads to the behavioral objective. Determining prerequisite skills may require arbitrary decisions as to what is and is not essential to learning the task.

Monitoring Performance and Revision

Student progress depends heavily on the use of ongoing evaluation. Since skill sequences are not finished products, they may require revision in order to best meet the needs of individual students. A responsibility of the instructor is to continually modify skill sequences according to current research, updated materials, and student observation.

Selection of a written format for task analysis is a matter of personal preference. Of course, the format selected must incorporate the basic principles of first stating the teaching objective in behavioral terms and, second, following an orderly sequence from the first step of the task to its final step. It is often appropriate to label a skill such as the example in Table 3-2 as a milestone. Therefore, putting a stocking cap over the ears becomes the milestone to be accomplished.

Once the steps for completing a milestone are determined, written, and numbered, it is helpful to devise an accounting system that provides a measure of the student's attitude or performance level.

In Table 3-3 student behavior is divided into four groups: physical assistance, physical prompt, verbal cue, and completes unassisted.

TASK ANALYSIS: STRUCTURE

The preceding paragraphs provided a basic description of task analysis, its design and components.

A system of task analysis labeled *task analysis structure* (often referred to as the try-another-way approach) has been used in teaching the severely and profoundly retarded, deaf, blind, and multiply handicapped—so successfully that discussion of its components is warranted.

Table 3-2 Example of Task Analysis

Student Name_____

Stocking Cap

Functional Task Analysis*   *Attitude*

Objective: The pupil will put on a stocking cap over the ears.

The Student Will:	Date	Physical Assistance	Physical Prompt	Verbal Cue	Unassisted
0. Hold cap in both hands					
1. Position in front of stomach					
2. Position hands on opposite sides of cap					
3. With both hands roll cap about 3 inches from its top					
4. With both hands on opposite sides of cap bring over head					
5. Position cap on top back portion of head					
6. Place left hand on cap at back					
7. Place right hand on cap at front					
8. Hold cap with left hand					
9. Pull front of cap down over top of forehead					
10. Place right hand on cap above right ear					
11. Place left hand on cap above left ear					
12. Slowly unroll cap with both hands to cover the ears					
13. With right hand push front of cap up on forehead above eyes					

Table 3-3 Example of Task Analysis

Student Name_____

Gloves

*Functional Task Analysis**   *Attitude*

Objective: The pupil will put one glove on each hand with the fingers in the correct spaces.

	Date	Physical Assistance	Physical Prompt	Verbal Cue	Unassisted
0. Hold left hand glove in right hand, directly in front of stomach					
1. Position glove with thumb pointing up					
2. Slide left hand into glove until ends of fingers reach the beginning of glove fingers					
3. Turn left thumb to up position					
4. With right hand work little finger of glove half way on to little finger					
5. With right hand push glove half way on to ring finger					
6. Push glove half way on to middle finger					
7. Push glove half way on to index finger					
8. Push glove half way on to thumb					
9. Pull glove at base with right hand while partially opening and closing fingers of left hand					
10. With right hand fingers push between fingers of the glove hand					
11. Hold right hand glove in left hand, directly in front of stomach					
12. Position glove with thumb pointing up					

Table 3-3 continued

	Date	Physical Assistance	Physical Prompt	Verbal Cue	Unassisted
13. Slide right hand into glove until ends of fingers reach the beginnings of glove fingers					
14. Turn right hand thumb to up position					
15. With left hand work little finger of glove half way on to little finger					
16. With left hand push glove half way on to ring finger					
17. With left hand push glove half way on to middle finger					
18. With left hand push glove half way on to index finger					
19. With left hand push glove half way on to thumb					
20. Pull glove at base with left hand while partially opening and closing fingers of right hand					
21. With right hand fingers, push between fingers of the glove hand					

Task analysis structure contains a seven-phase decision-making process. The process requires the instructor or trainer to make the following decisions:

Phase 1. the method or way that task will be performed
Phase 2. how to construct the content task analysis, determine the steps in which the instruction is to be divided
Phase 3. the way to instruct the child by thinking through the process task analysis
Phase 4. after training has taken place, decide if the task analysis needs revision
Phase 5. redo the process task analysis; if it fails to produce the end result, then
Phase 6. redo the content task analysis; if progress continues to lag, then
Phase 7. redo the method and return to Phase 2.

It is through the implementation of the outline that Gold (1976), Gold and Barclay (1973) found success in teaching the severe and profoundly retarded to perform skills that were once thought to be far beyond their capabilities. Due to the importance of this pioneer effort, a closer look into its fundamental ingredients (method, content, and process) follows.

Method

Most skills or tasks can be performed in more than one way. For example, a child can be taught to put on a coat using the method of holding onto the collar with the left hand while placing the right arm through the sleeve; then with the coat fixed on one shoulder, the left arm can be placed in the opposing sleeve. An alternative is to place the coat on a table upside down and on its back. The learner then slides both arms into the sleeves simultaneously and lifts the coat over the head.

Performance decisions of this type must be made prior to teaching. Therefore, careful consideration must be given to such factors as: mental and physical limitations, maturity, equipment, materials, and time. For the sake of accurate record keeping, it is also a good idea to include a statement in the task analysis describing the method to be used. Of course, statements of this type are only necessary when their omission might lead to confusion or misinterpretation. Gold (1976) illustrates this point:

> a task analysis on the use of a knife and fork might include a statement that the "European method" will be used. Anyone knowing the European method will immediately know how the knife and fork are to be positioned (p. 2).

Content

Once the method has been chosen, the action or skill is divided into teachable steps. The teacher must decide how many steps will be included, their size, sequence, and the required prerequisite skills.

The format for the content portion is quite simple. Each instructional step is sequenced and numbered much in the manner that you find simple assembly directions for model cars or electronics kits. The following list is a portion of the content phase for washing hands:

0. Stand facing the sink.
1. Pull up right sleeve.
2. Pull up left sleeve.
3. Put hand on cold faucet.
4. Turn the faucet counterclockwise until a steady stream of water appears.

Up to this point the trainer's decisions have been to determine: (1) the skills to be taught; (2) the teaching sequence for each skill; (3) the method the performer is to use; and (4) the steps and sequence instruction will take. Remaining is the manner in which the learning environment will be arranged and how instruction is to be conducted. This final component is referred to as the *process*.

Process

When actions, tasks, or skills are taught, the process or strategies for teaching the content are critical to learner success. The process phase of task analysis contains the subcomponents of format, feedback, and procedure. Within these important subcomponents lie the strategies and intricacies of teaching.

The term *format* refers to the manner in which the content is presented—its instructional design. Selection of an appropriate instructional design depends first upon the number of pieces (items) that must be learned in order to complete the assigned task. For example, in a visual discrimination task, if a single piece of data is to be learned (e.g., selecting a one-inch yellow cube from a group of different colored one-inch cubes) two basic designs are often used: match-to-sample and oddity.

In the match-to-sample design, the learner must select from two or more objects the one that corresponds to the model object presented by the trainer. Oddity in contrast requires the learner to select from a group of objects the one that is different.

When teaching tasks that involve a number of steps such as dressing, feeding, or assembling objects, backward or forward chaining designs are used. Forward chaining follows the traditional progression beginning with the first step of the task and moving to each successive step until the entire sequence is completed. In backward chaining (see section on ". . . Teaching Independent Dressing Skills" in Chapter 6) instruction begins on the step that the learner fails to perform independently or without assistance from the trainer. A prompt sequence and fading process is used to allow the learner to perform the step independently. Of course, any steps the learner had performed independently before would be carried out without a prompt. Table 3-4 illustrates the backward chaining sequence for drinking from a glass.

Table 3-4 Example of Backward Chaining Sequence for Drinking from a Glass

GOAL OR STEP (Student Behavior)	METHOD (Trainer Behavior)
6. Picks up glass	6. Give command, "_____, drink." If necessary, guide student's hands to locate and pick up glass. Fade physical guidance gradually.
5. Lifts glass from table, half way to mouth	5. When fading guidance, be ready to resume physical contact immediately in order to prevent spilling, dropping, or turning over glass.
4. Lifts glass from half way to mouth	4. Same as Step #5.
3. Drinks from glass	3. Same as Step #5. Initially, trainer may have to help student tilt glass. Fade gradually.
2. Lowers glass half way to table	2. Same as Step #5.
1. Lowers glass from half way down to table and sets glass down	1. Same as Step #5. After student replaces glass, reinforce with edible (preferably a salty food).

Source: Adapted from *Murdoch Center C and Y Program Library,* by A. Wheeler, R. Miller, J. Duke, E. Salisbury, V. Merritt, and B. Horton, © 1977, reprinted by permission.

In backward chaining training usually begins near the last step of the task. The student could be quickly guided through all the steps with instruction beginning on the training step that has been identified through baseline assessment, or the trainer could start with the training step. For example, if a student could perform Step 2 in Table 3-4 independently (lowers glass from half way to table), training would begin on Step 3 (drinks from glass). The trainer would have the option of beginning all instruction with Step 3 and allowing Steps 2 and 1 to be performed independently or begin with Step 6, quickly guiding the student through Steps 6, 5, and 4, and really training on Step 3. Steps 2 and 1 would follow, being performed independently.

In select instances, a total task format can be used. This technique requires the teacher to model the entire task sequence from start to finish. Once completed, the student imitates the entire sequence of behavior.

A second subcomponent termed feedback refers to how the trainer provides information to the learner prior, during, and after a task has been performed. Examples of feedback methods include: (1) stimulus control procedures, where the learning setting and materials are prearranged to evoke a specific set of responses and (2) reinforcement control procedures that include the use of positive or negative reinforcers and aversive techniques.

Since feedback is communication between the learner and the environment, not all modes of presentations are appropriate. For many severely retarded individuals, verbal or written directions and instructions are difficult, if not impossible, to comprehend. For this reason, methods of instruction must be presented through the learner's sense modalities that are intact. Instruction should also be designed to insure that the learner's thoughts and actions are shaped or focused toward a point where the desired response will have the highest probability of occurring.

Effective teachers may not realize it, but their choice of instructional strategies and materials forces the learner to focus on the most relevant aspects (dimensions) of the task. They also apply the principles of redundancy in discrimination tasks and the effects of fading when teaching new behaviors. Due to the importance of these and other feedback techniques, they are discussed further in this chapter in the section on focusing learner attention.

The final subcomponent labeled *procedure* refers to a description of the training plan to be used. This written statement spells out how the instruction will be conducted. Gold (1976) provides the following example:

> The trainer points to the first part; if the learner does not reach out and take the part, the trainer takes the learner's left hand and places it on the part (p. 4).

A short narrative such as this describes the trainer's instructional procedure, thus providing documentation on the "how" of instruction.

REINFORCING BEHAVIORS TO PROMOTE CHANGE

Assessing student behavior, identifying target behaviors, writing objectives, and compiling skill sequences in the form of task analysis are all essential to systematic teaching; however, altering and improving behavior requires a workable treatment technique.

For the severely retarded, acceptable or desired behaviors can be overshadowed by less appealing activities such as masturbation, throwing food, vomiting, biting, spitting, soiling, and the near absence of meaningful activity. To amend this behavior and increase the probability of more acceptable responses, a behavior management system that employs the principles of behavior modification has been found successful.

The Underlying Principle

Actions that can be observed, measured, and evaluated are called behaviors (Neisworth & Smith, 1973). A behavior is learned and is a function of its consequences (Stellern, Vasa, & Little, 1976); therefore, behavior can be altered and/or regulated by environmental stimuli. In this theoretical framework the psychological functioning of man involves a joint interaction between behavior and its controlling environment (Bandura, 1969).

Behavior modification is an application of this underlying principle and provides a method in which behaviors are learned, manipulated, and changed through the systematic control of consequences after a behavior has occurred.

B.F. Skinner (1968) applied this principle in his operant conditioning model in which a response (R) is followed by a reinforcer (Rd). This model with the formula R-Rd can be quite troublesome for the educator because the desired response or behavior must precede the reinforcement, forcing the teacher to wait for the desired response to occur.

A model proposed by Thorndike (1913, 1932) and later applied by Hilgard (1966) is far more realistic for the educator. In this formula S-R-Rd, the stimulus (S) is created by the teacher. The stimulus is followed by the student's response, which is then followed by a reinforcer. In teaching a severely retarded individual to lift his head, the Thorndike model can be exemplified as such:

S = While assisting the student to lift his head, the instructor says, "Gaylen, head up."

R = Gaylen responds by lifting head with teacher's assistance.

Rd = Once the head is raised, the teacher reinforces Gaylen by squeezing an eye dropper of metracal into Gaylen's mouth and simultaneously saying, "Good, Gaylen. Your head is up."

Using the S-R-Rd paradigm, the stimulus becomes anything within the environment that signals desired response. The response is the specific observable behavior and the reinforcement is the rewarding consequence for the desired observable behavior.

Positive Reinforcers

A positive reinforcer is any object or event that when presented after a specific behavior has occurred increases the probability that the behavior will occur again. For example, if a child screams at the top of his lungs, and the teacher looks at him saying in a harsh tone, "No! Don't do that," the attention the teacher has shown by scolding may increase or maintain the screaming. If the screaming was, in fact, maintained or increased by teacher attention, the comments are the positive reinforcer. Edibles, praise, and freedom are more commonly associated with the term *positive reinforcers;* however, they may only be considered such if they increase or maintain a particular behavior.

Food, one of the most widely used reinforcers, is the group known as edibles. Cookies, raisins, M & M's, and the like are often the initial reward supplied for appropriate behaviors. A positive function of edible reinforcers, as suggested by Thompson and Grabowski (1977), is their relationship to improving social responsiveness, for it is usually through direct contact between student and instructor that edibles are administered.

Attention is one of the most powerful reinforcers. Attention-seeking behavior can easily be overlooked as a possible reward for some individuals. Scoldings, a raised voice, or a firm shake can produce just the opposite of what the teacher is intending to achieve, providing the attention the student is seeking. In this vein, many bizarre and disruptive behaviors are carried out for the sole purpose of the attention or shock value they bring. A student who makes grunting sounds, exposes himself, or urinates on classroom articles may find the teacher's or peers' behavior far more rewarding than any edible reinforcer or praise. When this situation exists, the teacher must create appropriate attention-gaining avenues for the student and use techniques to extinguish inappropriate behavior.

The knowledgeable educator must recognize the power attention holds as a reinforcer. Remarkable gains have been made by simply giving the student teacher-attention through physical contact such as a pat on the back, a firm squeeze, or kind words and a caring attitude at appropriate times.

Idiosyncratic Reinforcers

It is not unusual to find that a simple toy, color, record, or sound is extremely pleasurable, and therefore reinforcing. A particular student may even display enjoyment when a word or words such as "Sam Drucker" are spoken by himself or others. Another may find delight in an Elvis Presley record, and still another may clutch emphatically to a ragged toy poodle. The fact that idiosyncratic reinforcers exist often provides the teacher with an effective treatment device.

Games and Special Activities

Not to be overlooked as strong reinforcers are the numerous activities students may find pleasurable. Sitting in an old rocking chair, kicking a ball, going for a walk, or standing alone are just a few examples. The teacher who recognizes the reinforcement value of activities to various individuals can use them as positive reinforcers, and thus gain some control over preceding behavior.

Tokens

There are several advantages to a token system that are not generally met with other reinforcers. First, they do not disrupt instruction as primary reinforcers do, for they can be administered and later exchanged for edibles or special activities. Second, they can be exchanged for varying rewards, which prevents the possibility of satiation (a point where the payoff is no longer reinforcing). Third, the token system is the closest approximation to the real world; a student operating for chips is much like someone working for a weekly paycheck.

Selecting Reinforcers

The most practical method of determining if something is reinforcing is through observation or interview. Generally a visit with the client, parent, or care-giver will supply an accurate starting point. The following guidelines are useful in selecting appropriate reinforcers:

1. Determine what the individual plays with or talks about.
2. Look for foods that appear to be favorites.
3. Observe the student's reaction to praise, smiles, or affection.
4. Determine the student's preferences during unrestricted activity time.

Dispensing Reinforcers

Once an effective reward or reinforcer has been identified, it must be administered in a predetermined manner in order to be effective. When initially attempting to alter the behavior of the severely retarded, rewards must be dispensed immediately after the desired response as few retarded, not to mention young children, can initially delay the gratification reinforcers may bring. As the student begins to demonstrate the desired behavior with more consistency, the payoff can be administered on a frequent intermittent schedule and later, on an occasional basis. Once the desired behavior occurs uniformly over time, the previously extrinsic reinforcer may no longer be necessary.

Rates of Reinforcement

Immediate reinforcement or payoff for each response may be necessary in the beginning stages of training; however, if continued once the behavior has been learned, the one for one ratio will have a weakening effect. Once the desired response is occurring, the trainer should begin intermittent payoffs by skipping reinforcement for two or three responses. Intermittent schedules are generally ratio or interval in design. Ratio schedules are either fixed to pay off on a predetermined rate (i.e., following the second, third, fourth, or fifth time the response occurs) or variable by which the payoff follows no particular order (random reinforcement). Interval types may also follow a fixed pattern where a reinforcement is delivered on a predetermined time—i.e., every five, ten, thirty seconds or on a variable nonscheduled basis.

Reinforcement Decisions

Determining the reinforcement schedule depends on the type of behavior to be reinforced, personnel and equipment available, and the student contact time. Generally our experience has led us to prefer a fixed ratio schedule when teaching a behavior, and after a short period of time changing to a fixed interval, and finally to a variable interval to maintain desired performance.

One of the most critical factors related to program success is consistency. The instructional personnel should follow identical procedures, and training must be carried out on an hourly, weekly, and monthly basis in the educational setting, home, and community. Thus all individuals who are in direct contact, (teachers, siblings, parent) must cooperate with the contingencies of the individually designed program.

Another important decision involves getting the student to maintain the desired behavior on his own without the continued use of primary reinforcers. This decision encompasses the fundamental goal of behavior modification — to effect self-maintaining desirable student behavior (Stellern et al., 1976).

With higher functioning individuals, the intent of behavior modification is often to restructure the value system by altering existing values and establishing new values relative to a specific behavior. Attempts to this end are carried out through a process that moves from primary to secondary to tertiary reinforcers.

For the severely retarded, tertiary reinforcers or feelings of accomplishment and self-praise are extremely desirable but highly unrealistic. The reason for such a statement is simple—a tertiary reinforcer requires a change in values, meaning that the payoff comes from the feeling that one gets from knowing that it was done well or correctly. In practice the teacher of low functioning students finds this behavioral level highly impractical and therefore relies heavily upon primary reinforcers, pairing these with slightly higher order reinforcers. Through the continual association of the two levels of reinforcers, the higher order level gradually assumes the same payoff value as the original lower level reinforcer. This can be demonstrated easily by pairing an edible (juice) with praise (saying "good job").

While behaviors can be strengthened through reinforcement techniques, there are other methods that change behavior and complement positive reinforcement strategies.

DECREASING INAPPROPRIATE BEHAVIOR

Positive reinforcement techniques are designed to reward and encourage appropriate behavior. But sometimes an individual will demonstrate appropriate behaviors that are increased by positive reinforcers and almost simultaneously exhibit inappropriate behaviors that must be extinguished. For example, a student could be working quite well in an instructional feeding program, where the use of utensils is the major focus, while continually hitting others who sit nearby. In this instance, it may be appropriate to continue the positive reinforcement schedule for the use of utensils, but initiate a strategy to decrease the hitting behavior.

The techniques employed to change behavior are numerous and varied. The most common methods employed to decrease unwanted behaviors are organized into three levels. Level I begins with techniques that are least restrictive. Level II progresses to more unpleasant, distasteful measures, and Level III culminates with punitive and extremely aversive devices.

Level I

Techniques in this group are quite mild and generally paired with positive reinforcement techniques. Due to their nonrestrictive nature, permission to employ them is not required by the parent, guardian, or a human rights committee.

Ignoring Specific Behaviors

The first method, ignoring, can reduce some types of undesirable behavior; however, success with this technique depends on two critical points—the type of undesirable behavior and the consistency with which ignoring is maintained. It is impractical to believe that all behaviors can be extinguished by mere ignoring as many responses exhibited by severely retarded students are highly reinforcing, thus providing self-gratification, stimulation, or contentment. Finger waving, rocking, masturbation, grunting, and screaming sounds are seldom reduced by ignoring their presence. Attention-gaining behaviors such as pounding on a table or snorting have a higher probability of being reduced or eliminated by ignoring;

however, to insure any degree of success, ignoring must be ongoing by all individuals within daily contact.

Counterconditioning

A second extinguishing technique, counterconditioning, often referred to as differential reinforcement of incompatible behavior, can also be useful with the severely retarded. It is carried out by reinforcing a desired behavior which in turn makes it next to impossible for the undesired behavior to occur. Its operational success requires the staff to select activities that are antagonistic or opposing to the undesirable behavior, thus taking away the student's opportunity for inappropriate action. As an example of this procedure, Ronnie continually displayed a behavior of picking his wrists, digging deeply into the skin. In an effort to curb this self-abusive behavior, Ronnie was first rewarded with small amounts of Metracal for wadding balls of newspaper. Later his program was changed, and only sitting with his hands folded was reinforced. Pairing opposing behaviors is a challenging task; however, through careful selection, undesirable responses can be replaced with activities that do not permit the unwanted behavior to be carried out. Of course the child will also receive reinforcement for the desired behavior.

Level II

Techniques within this level attempt to limit or restrict an individual's freedom, cause the loss of objects or privileges, and/or force a behavior against the individual's will. Level II techniques are considered aversive; therefore, they generally require approval by the parent, guardian, and/or psychologist before they can be implemented.

Satiation

Satiation is a method that requires the student to continually repeat the undesired behavior until it becomes boring and is extinguished or the student becomes physically fatigued and terminates the inappropriate response. For example, if a student cries because he is dissatisfied the teacher would encourage continual crying until the child eventually stopped.

Desensitization

Desensitization is a procedure used to eliminate fear-producing stimuli. It operates on the concept that fear will be reduced or extinguished if a positive or pleasant reinforcer is presented during a gradual program of exposure to the fear stimulus.

Reward Removal or Response Cost Punishment

Another method used to reduce an undesirable behavior utilizes removal of a reinforcer. When this technique is truly effective, rewards (reinforcers) have been previously administered on a regular and consistent basis. For example, if the student is using a token economy program and receiving plastic chips for the performance of various tasks, several can be taken away for inappropriate behavior.

In order for this technique to be effective, the student must possess some degree of anticipatory sense. Also the teacher must place more emphasis on the delivery of the positive reinforcer (i.e., tokens or food) than on their removal.

Nonisolated Time Out

Moving an individual to a designated area within a room can be called time out. In such cases, the individual is removed from the group and directed to remain in a predetermined area for a brief period of time. This consists of standing in a corner or within a space marked on the floor. In other instances, the individual could be asked to sit in a corner, thus unable to participate in a meaningful activity.

Limited Time Out

Another form of time out utilizes a netting or mesh which is used to divide or section a room. When time out is required, the individual is placed away from the group on the opposite side of the net and told to stay. In this procedure, the individual is allowed to view the positive group activities that are occurring with other students.

Overcorrection

This is a procedure in which an individual who disrupts a social or physical situation is required to restore, clean up, or repair damaged articles. An individual who throws his dinner on the floor may be verbally requested to clean up the mess and/or shown how. A more punitive method is to physically prompt the individual and, through contact, force student participation by moving the arms and hands in cleaning up the mess.

Overcorrection techniques are generally paired with relaxation or self-monitoring strategies. In such instances if the individual were to make a mess by first throwing his food at the dinner table and then throwing chairs, the teacher would initially help the individual gain self-control.

The first step would be to remove the individual from the area and place him on a soft mat or bed. In this relaxation phase the individual's movements are restricted as the teacher holds the person in a prone position. Once the tantrumming individual gains full control and acts calm (lying quietly on the mat for a predetermined time period), that individual can be returned to the dinner table and physically assisted to the point that all messes are cleaned up. Extra chairs and food are also picked up, thus emphasizing to the individual the work that goes with cleaning up a mess.

Positive Practice

A technique similar to the previous overcorrection procedure requires that after an inappropriate behavior has taken place, the individual is encouraged to practice an alternative behavior. For example, if a male individual were to self-stimulate by zipping his trousers up and down, the trainer might offer intense instruction in holding the hands still and at the sides or in the pants pockets.

Level III

Procedures within this group are considered aversive, therefore, unpleasant for the recipient. In facilities for the mentally retarded, the use of such measures generally necessitates permission by a psychologist, principal, staffing team, and when possible, the parent and/or guardian.

Punishers

Spanking, pinching, and slapping are common punishers; however, they are not permitted in most mental retardation programs. More acceptable punishers are sounding a loud noise (horn, bell, buzzer), presenting sour tastes, blowing air in the face, and squirting a water mist in the face.

The presentation of a punisher should always be preceded by a conditioned punisher. In effect, this conditions a more socially acceptable punisher such as saying the word "no" to accomplish the same result as the aversive stimulus (squirting water mist in the face). The training sequence might be as follows.

Target Behavior: Child slaps others when they are near.

1. Child is placed in a stimulating activity and reinforced for appropriate behavior.
2. Child slaps another student.
3. Trainer immediately says, "No, John!" (NOTE: If the child continues to slap others at various times, then it can be assumed that the words "No, John" are not punishers and an effective punisher should be paired.)
4. If the child slaps another child, the trainer immediately says, "No, John!" and squirts water mist in the child's face. (NOTE: Water mist squirted in the child's face has been predetermined as a punisher and approved by administrative policy.)

5. The next time the child slaps someone, only the words "No, John!" are given.
6. Immediately after the next slapping episode, the words "No, John!" are followed by the mist spray.
7. For the next few episodes the words are presented and followed by the mist spray.
8. As slapping behavior decreases, the mist spray can be faded and only periodically paired with the words "No, John!" to restore their effectiveness.

Isolated Time Out

Isolated time out employs a room or area that physically contains the individual. Isolation rooms should be constructed to federally approved specifications and employed for periods not to exceed 30-minute intervals. Specific monitoring procedures generally include continuous observation on a minimum of 5-minute intervals including precise written documentation.

Electric Shock

"Hot shots" often referred to as cattle prods and electric shock vests are highly controversial, yet sometimes a necessary measure for behavioral control. Before any punitive technique of this magnitude is employed, attempts to modify behavior through previous methods described in levels I, II, and III should be exhausted.

Chemical Intervention

Tranquilizers, sedatives, and other drugs are often prescribed to decrease inappropriate behavior. Although medications often restrict some behaviors, they sometimes possess potential dangers due to undesirable side effects. Careful observation, documentation, frequent check-ups, and continuous communication between physician and staff help insure proper dosage and positive behavior change.

Physical and Equipment Restraints

Physical body restraint or equipment restraints are sometimes necessary in order to keep an individual from harming himself or others. If arm restraints and/or straightjackets are used, they should be paired with a conditioned punisher (see section entitled punishers) so that their use can be faded within a short time period. As with other techniques, success will depend on the following:

1. whether the restraint is considered by the abusive client as a punisher.
2. whether aggressive behavior (inappropriate) is first followed by a stimulus to be conditioned and secondly, the restraint.
3. whether the restraint program is followed faithfully by all staff.

Level I, II, and III Techniques: A Summary

Regardless of the type of aversive stimulus used to modify or extinguish behavior, its application must occur immediately after the inappropriate response. The effectiveness of aversive methods depends upon several factors: (1) the stimulus presented must be aversive to the subject and to the degree that it will reduce inappropriate behavior; (2) the teacher should issue a warning to the student that the punishment is forthcoming unless the undesirable behavior is stopped; and (3) the warning and punishment must consistently precede and follow, respectively, the undesired behavior each time it occurs.

The continued application of these techniques again demands appropriate use of operant principles. Just as with primary and secondary reinforcers, the aversive stimulus must be faded until only the warning is necessary and finally memory itself or the new habit is enough to extinguish the undesirable act.

These techniques, like all methods mentioned, can be effective given specific individuals and situations. Generally, the most effective results are gained through a combination of two or more of the decreasing behavior techniques. In one instance, a child who throws things in response to doing constructive seat work activities may be placed on a combined program employing counterconditioning and reward removal.

Punishment techniques are often the first methods that come to mind when overt behavior becomes a problem for staff or clients. It is important to remember that: (1) inappropriate behavior will generally continue if the behavior is periodically reinforced even where punishment follows; (2) inappropriate behavior will continue if immediate positive reinforcement follows a punisher; (3) punishment will be more effective if appropriate behaviors, which are displayed throughout the day, are positively reinforced; and (4) undesirable side effects may be produced with the use of punishment.

The fact that human lives are potentially affected through the use of decreasing behavioral techniques requires that caution and sincere consideration be taken before such programs are implemented. Decisions to use Level II and III procedures should be made through collective agreements among client (when appropriate), professional staff, direct care workers, the parent and/or guardian, and only when level I procedures prove ineffective. A level II or III procedure is often used in conjunction with positive reinforcement techniques and/or another decreasing behavioral technique which proves compatible.

FOCUSING LEARNER ATTENTION

Throughout this chapter, the authors have stressed the sequence and content of the teaching process from assessment through methods of decreasing inappropriate behaviors. All of this dialogue has been provided to help the teacher focus the students' attention on the bit of information to be learned. Positive reinforcement techniques are one strategy used to engineer the students' attention; however, just as important are the teaching materials and the way they are presented.

Research compiled by Zeaman and House (1963) and Gold (1972) demonstrates that through systematic presentation of information, retarded individuals can focus their attention on relevant aspects of the learning task and in turn be taught to complete rather complex assembly tasks.

Utilizing Zeaman's principles, Gold and Scott (1971) arranged teaching materials so that their students could focus their attention on the relevant dimensions of the problem. Several basic components that are helpful in teaching severely retarded learners follow.

Dimensions

When teaching a particular piece of information, it is often useful to consider its characteristics. Any piece of information is generally related to other similar pieces of information and is, therefore, said to have dimensions. Color is a dimension; so are shape, size, and texture. Whenever individuals attempt to learn a piece of information, they must first focus upon the dimension that is relevant.

For example, when teaching an individual to be able to point to a yellow block when presented simultaneously with a green block, the relevant dimension would be its color, not its size, shape, or other dimensions.

Once an individual focuses his attention and comprehends the dimension to be learned, the correct response soon appears. In conjunction with this behavioral pattern, any new pieces of information within the same dimension that are presented immediately will be learned at a much higher rate. Thus, in teaching the color yellow, it is best to continue teaching additional colors rather than "shift" to another dimension such as shape.

Redundancy

When severely retarded individuals attempt to solve a problem, they will most likely experience the greatest success when more than one dimension is used to make a correct decision. Redundancy is that condition whereby more than one dimension is used to solve a problem. For example, if a child were asked to point to a large yellow triangle when another choice of a small red cube was also presented, the correct response could be achieved in several ways:

1. by choosing the largest
2. by choosing the yellow one
3. by choosing the triangle
4. by a combination of the above

Redundancy provides more information for the learner to draw from before making a choice. With this in mind, teachers should first provide a number of dimensions to insure the highest probability of a successful choice, then reduce the number of dimensions to focus upon the one or two that are the most relevant.

Fading

The act of changing the stimulus or reducing the number of stimuli is called fading. If the number of dimensions is gradually reduced, an individual can be taught to focus upon one dimension. Gold and Scott (1971) provide this example that utilizes redundancy and a fading schedule:

> . . . let us suppose that a child can already distinguish between a red and yellow stimulus but cannot do this for a circle and an ellipse. At the start of training both colors and forms are made redundant. That is, the circle is always yellow and the ellipse always red. This problem could be solved either by the use of color or form. At first, knowing the color discrimination, the child will use it to solve the problem. Gradually, through the course of training, the difference between the red and yellow is decreased until both are orange while the forms remain constant (p. 4).

The rate at which fading takes place is critical. If the procedure is too slow, it may become laborious; if it is too fast, learning will not be achieved.

Prompting and Cuing a Behavior(s)

The performance of a behavior requires that it is preceded by antecedent events (stimuli) that prime or trigger a response. Teachers use a number of methods to prompt their students when new skills are taught. For instance, the verbal instruction of "No" may be sufficient to keep a child from touching a hot stove. In other learning situations, physical guidance, a nod of the head, or a demonstration of the desired behavior may be required before the student will perform as desired.

Lent and McLean (1976), directors of Project MORE, have successfully used a prompting system that gradually increases the amount of instructor assistance when the student fails to respond or perform a step or task correctly. Their sequence is described as follows:

1. Student attempts to perform task independently. If he does not respond appropriately, go to step 2;
2. Verbal cue is used as student is told what to do. If correct response is not given, go to step 3;
3. Verbal cue is given with visual cue. (Student is told what to do and shown through gestures or demonstration.) If correct response is not given, go to step 4;
4. Verbal, visual and physical cues (student is told, shown, and given physical assistance) are used.
5. If student fails to respond correctly, step 4 is repeated on the same task. If student still fails to respond, stop and identify a more elementary task.

The number of ways that a student can be guided or primed to respond are limited; however, if these resources are used appropriately and in conjunction with positive reinforcement techniques, tremendous individual gains can be made.

Oral Directions

Oral directions or verbal cues are often the first strategy used to attain a desired response. The major key to their success lies in the student's ability to understand them. With severely retarded learners, spoken directions must be given slowly using a simple vocabulary and with appropriate intonation.

Gestures, signs, and pictures should also be used to facilitate learner comprehension when verbal cues alone do not appear adequate. As a final note, directions, verbal or visual, must be presented at the learner's language level; therefore, the teacher must take into account the number of steps to be remembered and the complexity of the request.

Modeling

In addition to telling individuals what performance is expected, the teacher may also show them through demonstration. Modeling can involve the teacher or another student demonstrating a step of a task or an entire sequence of steps from start to finish. Utilizing visual input, the student can attempt to imitate or repeat the behavior.

It is often difficult to hold the severely retarded individual's attention, even when a visual demonstration is paired with verbal requests. When this occurs, attending behaviors such as sitting in a chair and eye contact must be taught.

Physical Prompts

Telling the individual what to do (verbal prompts) and visual demonstration may not at first provide enough input to elicit the desired response. When this occurs it may be helpful to use the additional sense modalities of body movement (kinesthetics) and touch (tactile). In this approach, verbal directions are offered as the student's limbs are physically guided through the task or series of tasks.

When using physical prompting as a response priming mechanism, a fading process must also be used. If not, it won't take long for the student to learn that if he stalls or hesitates, the teacher will do it for him. A fading sequence may appear as follows:

1. Hold the individual's hands and guide them through the full task sequence while offering verbal directions.
2. Hold the individual's hands and guide them through a part of the sequence where difficulty occurs and give verbal directions.
3. Touch the individual's arms lightly as they move through the task and give verbal directions.
4. Tap the individual's arm to initiate movement and give verbal direction.
5. Give verbal directions.
6. Fade verbal directions.
7. Time of day; seeing an action or object becomes the natural stimulus for behavior to occur (e.g., waking up in the morning triggers putting on clothes).

Many teachers have found more success by only initially giving a verbal command for what is to be performed (target behavior). From this point on, no verbalization is given until the task is completed. Gestures, physical prompts and manipulation are used to obtain the desired learner action without any intermediate verbal directions because verbalization is difficult to fade.

There are several things to remember when determining the type of prompting procedure or cue to be used. First, physical prompting is the most fundamental response primary procedure. Paired with it are verbal and/or gestural directions. Second, imitative skills must be present before modeling can be used effectively. Third, a fading procedure must be used with all prompting techniques including verbal directions. The situation, time, or sight of an object or action should eventually trigger the desired behavior. Fourth, absence of or slow progress by the learner may be due to any one or a combination of difficulties as presented in Table 3-5.

Table 3-5 Problems Resulting in Lack or Slowness of Learner Progress

Prompt	Possible Difficulty
Oral Directions	commands may be too complex and vocabulary too high
	may be unable to comprehend verbal directions or remember entire sequence
	auditory input may not be enough to accomplish understanding at this point
	other prompts may be required
Gestural Directions	may need verbal as well as gestural cues
	may not comprehend gestures used
	visual input may be confusing
	other prompts may be required
Physical Prompt	sequence of steps may be too long
	may need more manual guidance than you are giving
	may need training in simple attending to task behavior (eye contact)
	may not respond to physical touch
Modeling	may not possess imitative skills
	may have trouble attending to demonstration
	task may be too complex and needs to be broken into small, simple segments
	student may not be able to interpret visual directions due to directionality problems (child standing in front of instructor may mirror image movements, e.g., each time instructor's left arm moves, student moves right arm)
	visual input may be distracting or confusing

EVALUATING STUDENT PROGRESS

Evaluation is the most overlooked component of any educational program. Huberty and Swan (1977) maintain that little effort is expended for evaluation because: it is not generally expected or mandated; it is difficult to do because of assessment problems; no one is committed to it; no one perceives it as beneficial, and few individuals have the expertise to conduct evaluation. Of course, the passage of Public Law 94-142 has changed the profession's outlook on evaluation. Because it is now mandated, classroom teachers of the severely retarded must be ready to provide empirical evidence of the success or lack of success of educational intervention programs.

The evaluation of student progress can be greatly facilitated if evaluation is visualized as a continuous or ongoing process with constant input and modification occurring on the basis of the input received.

In order to select an assessment strategy, the instructor should consider the number of students involved in the assessment, the criteria against which the adequacy of behavioral change will be measured, and the frequency with which data will need to be gathered (White & Liberty, 1976).

Because of the specific mandates in P.L. 94-142 for an individual educational plan, the teacher's emphasis will need to be upon the collection and analysis of individual assessment data. Second, the adequacy of behavioral change should be established as a criterion for minimum acceptable performance. White and Liberty (1976) suggest that minimum acceptable criteria are those that facilitate the learning of the next step in a sequential task hierarchy and are required for maintenance or improvement in the learning environment. Finally, evaluation of progress must be done on a daily basis in order for the instructor to react to the needs of the student relative to shifts in program emphasis.

After establishing that evaluation must be individual, criterion referenced, and daily, it is necessary to decide exactly what instrumentation should be used to record behavior change. The most frequently employed classroom assessment instruments are checklists. Yes/no statements are often used to reduce the complexity and facilitate the teacher's role in the gathering of daily assessment information. These checklists may be constructed by listing the critical elements of the program or objectives from the curriculum and then checking these off as the elements or skills are achieved.

White and Liberty (1976) noted that checklists of this type were a valid measurement instrument for skills that are essentially permanent. That is, once a child learns to sit he will continue to do so unless he becomes ill or injured. Thus sitting is a skill that is amenable to assessment with a yes/no checklist. These checklists may be utilized to determine even more complex behaviors by adding elements to the criteria for success. (i.e., a time criterion may be added such as "sits alone for 30 seconds.")

Yes/no checklists can be used for all types of programs for the severely retarded provided the behaviors on the list represent small enough sequential learning steps. The steps must be small enough so that the checkmarks are made frequently enough to provide information appropriate for program modifications. If skills become too complex and require a great deal of time to acquire, then information provided by yes/no checklists will not be adequate for program review and modification (White & Liberty, 1976). However, the majority of skills or behaviors to be taught to severely retarded students could easily be assessed with this format.

Another methodology, which could be used to evaluate child progress, is trials to criterion with levels of assistance (Haring, 1977). With this approach, each skill or objective is task-analyzed into sequential steps. At each level, a student may require one of four levels of assistance:

1. unassisted or independent
2. verbal cue
3. physical prompt
4. physical assistance

In Table 3-2, the task analysis of putting on a stocking cap, the first step is "holding the cap in both hands." The teacher directs the pupil, "It's time to put on your stocking cap." The student may need to have the cap placed in his hands and then physically assisted through the sequence of putting the cap on his head. Physical assistance is gradually faded to physical prompting, then to a visual cue alone, and, finally, the student should be able to respond independently to the suggestion, "It's time to put on your stocking cap." A criterion of 80 or 85 percent is generally set and once the student can achieve the task 80 or 85 percent of the time at a set level of assistance, for three consecutive days, he is moved on to the next higher level (Haring, 1977).

The Murdoch C & Y program offers the fundamental components for an instructional curriculum including a method for collecting baseline data, tasks to be taught in a task analytical format, and a data collection/recording system. Although the number of published texts and curriculum guides is increasing, few meet the total training needs for the severely retarded to the level achieved by the Murdoch Center staff.

SUMMARY

A systematic instructional framework to facilitate the classroom learning process has been presented in this chapter. In planning educational activities for the severely retarded, the teacher must gain useful assessment data and specify critical target behaviors. Written instructional statements in the form of behavioral objectives and an understanding of how those behaviors fall into the skill sequence insure that appropriate activities will be taught.

Successful instruction requires that each task is broken into small, teachable steps and that consideration is given to the method of task performance, instructional content, and the teaching process.

Shaping procedures utilizing reinforcement principles and methods of decreasing inappropriate behavior serve as tools for behavioral change. Such methods are used in conjunction with instructional strategies and prompting techniques.

A terminal step is the documentation of learner progress. These data can be gathered through numerous methods generally involving data sheets, yes/no checklists, and task analysis forms.

REFERENCES

Bandura, A. *Principles of behavior modification*. New York: Holt, Rinehart and Winston, 1969.

Bender, M., & Valletutti, P. J. *Teaching the moderately and severely handicapped* (Volumes I, II, and III). Baltimore: University Park Press, 1976.

Favell, J. E. *The power of positive reinforcement: A handbook of behavior modification*. Springfield, Illinois: Charles C. Thomas, 1977.

Fredericks, H.D., Riggs, C., Furey, T., Grove, D., Moore, W., McDonnell, J., Jordan, E., Hanson, W., Baldwin, V., & Wadlow, M. *The teaching research curriculum for moderately and severely handicapped*. Springfield, Illinois: Charles C. Thomas, 1976.

Gold, M.W. Stimulus factors in skill training of the retarded on a complex assembly task: Acquisition, transfer and retention. *American Journal of Mental Deficiency*, 1972, *76*, 517-526.

Gold, M.W. Task analysis: A statement and an example using acquisition and production of a complex assembly task by the retarded blind. *Exceptional Children*, 1976, *43*, 78-84.

Gold, M.W., & Barclay, C.R. The learning of difficult visual discriminations by the moderately and severely retarded. *Mental Retardation*, 1973, *11*, 9-11.

Gold, M.W., & Scott, K.G. Discrimination learning. In W.B. Stephens (Ed.), *Training the developmentally young*. New York: John Day, 1971, 420-444.

Haring, N.G. Measurement and evaluation procedures for programming with the severely and profoundly handicapped. In E. Sontag, J. Smith, & N. Certo (Eds.), *Educational programming for the severely and profoundly handicapped*. Reston, Virginia: The Council for Exceptional Children, 1977.

Haring, N.G., Hayden, A.H., & Beck, G.R. General principles and guidelines in "programming" for severely handicapped children and young adults. *Focus on Exceptional Children*, 1976, 8.

Hilgard, E. *Theories of learning* (3rd ed.). New York: Appleton-Century-Crofts, 1966.

Huberty, C.J., & Swan, W.W. Evaluation of programs. In J.B. Jordan, A.H. Hayden, M.B. Karnes, & M.M. Wood (Eds.), *Early childhood education for exceptional children*. Reston, Virginia: The Council for Exceptional Children, 1977.

Lent, J.R., & McLean, B.M. The trainable retarded: The technology of teaching. In N.G. Haring & R.L. Schiefelbusch (Eds.), *Teaching special children*, New York: McGraw-Hill, 1976.

Mager, R.F. *Preparing instructional objectives*. Belmont, California: Fearon, 1962.

Neisworth, J., & Smith, R. *Modifying retarded behavior*. Boston: Houghton Mifflin, 1973.

Popovich, D. *A prescriptive behavioral checklist for the severely and profoundly retarded*. Baltimore: University Park Press, 1977.

Skinner, B.F. *The technology of teaching*. New York: Appleton-Century-Crofts, 1968.

Snell, M.E. (Ed.). *Systematic instruction of the moderately and severely handicapped*. Columbus, Ohio: Charles E. Merrill, 1978.

Sommerton, E., & Turner, K. *Pennsylvania training model: Individual assessment guide*. Harrisburg, Pennsylvania: Pennsylvania Department of Education, 1975.

Stellern, J., Vasa, S., & Little, T. *Introduction to diagnostic-prescriptive teaching and programming*. Glen Ridge, New Jersey: Exceptional Press, 1976.

Thompson, T., & Grabowski, J. *Behavior modification of the mentally retarded* (2nd ed.). New York: Oxford University Press, 1977.

Thorndike, E.L. *The psychology of learning.* New York: Teachers College Press, 1913.

Thorndike, E.L. *The fundamentals of learning.* New York: Teachers College Press, 1932.

Uniform Performance Assessment System. Seattle: University of Washington, date unknown.

Wheeler, A., Miller, R., Duke, J., Salisbury, E., Merritt, V., & Horton, B. *Murdoch Center C & Y Program Library: A collection of step by step programs for the developmentally disabled.* Butner, North Carolina: Murdoch Center, 1977.

White, O.R., & Liberty, K.A. Behavioral assessment and precise educational measurement. In N.G. Haring & R.L. Schiefelbusch (Eds.), *Teaching special children.* New York: McGraw-Hill, 1976.

Williams, W. Procedures of task analysis as related to developing instructional programs for the severely handicapped. In L. Brown, T. Crowner, W. Williams, & R. York (Eds.), *Madison's alternative for zero exclusion: A book of readings.* Madison, Wisconsin: University of Wisconsin, 1975.

Zeaman, D., & House, B.J. The role of attention in retardate discrimination learning. In N.R. Ellis (Ed.), *Handbook of Mental Deficiency.* New York: McGraw-Hill, 1963.

Chapter 4

Motor Skills Training

Earlier chapters of this text have been devoted to describing the nature of the severely retarded learner, techniques of assessment, the application of instructional and environmental alterations, and the process of reinforcement. This chapter will place special emphasis on describing general patterns of motoric development and the relationship between gross motor development and later acquisition of critical skills. Many severely retarded learners present problems in the classroom due to their immobility, which may be caused by severe postural deviations, abnormal movement, other forms of muscular impairment, or lack of opportunity to practice motor skills. In many of those individuals, critical body righting and equilibrium reactions are either absent or greatly delayed. Since postural adjustments are made possible by these reactions, these individuals will be severely limited in their voluntary movements. Finally many of these learners will exhibit abnormal reflexive behavior. Some of these reflexes are present in normal infants at various ages, but primarily before one year. Usually reflexes disappear and are later replaced by more voluntary muscular actions. Within the population of severely retarded individuals, those reflexes tend to persist long after normal suppression occurs, making voluntary muscle movement difficult, if not impossible.

This chapter will discuss activities involving righting and equilibrium reactions, the elimination of abnormal reflexes, the acquisition of locomotor movement patterns, and the development of fine motor skills.

RIGHTING AND EQUILIBRIUM REACTIONS

Weisz (1938) described righting reactions as compensatory movements that make balance possible. These reactions consist of two main parts: (1) a state of readiness sufficient to bring the legs and arms into a position of balance; and (2) a necessary amount of support tonus. Body righting and equilibrium reactions are activated by a change in either body spatial position or its supporting parts or by a change in the position of the limbs in relation to the trunk.

Generally these reactions can be elicited by quickly tipping the supporting surface when the individual is prone, sitting, or standing (see Table 4-1). Weisz (1938) first found the equilibrium reaction to occur at six months and to appear first with changes in the lying, sitting, and standing position in the order listed. Thus it may be maintained that there is a definite relationship between the equilibrium reactions and the learning of sitting, standing, and walking.

Schaltenbrand (1928) concluded from his studies on the development of posture and locomotion that getting to an upright position is the result of a successive changing of the body righting reflexes. Apparently the body righting reflexes do not totally disappear in adulthood but may be somewhat suppressed.

But these reactions may be delayed or absent in the severely retarded learner. Since those reactions are requisite to the more advanced motor actions, the necessity of stimulating the acquisition of these reactions is evident.

Prior to beginning any motor program, the severely retarded learner should be thoroughly evaluated by a physical therapist. It is expected that any intensive work done with this population will require that the physical therapist remain a pivotal member of the treatment team.

It will be necessary for the teacher to "test" each student for the presence of these reactions, which may be done simply by employing the suggestions for eliciting the reflex in Table 4-1. For those reactions that the teacher is unable to elicit, the following activities are presented as suggestions to exercise and strengthen or, in some instances, develop these reactions.

In handling or positioning the student with severe muscular involvement, it is critical to avoid applying great pressure to limbs or muscles with spasticity or athetosis. Rather the teacher should exert gentle pressure or support to key points such as the neck, spine, shoulder girdle, and pelvic area (Bobath, B., 1969). These particular support points, because of their location on the body, control the amount of muscle tone present in the extremities (Utley, Holvoet, & Barnes, 1977). However the reader should be aware that individuals with severe muscular involvement require careful handling in any positioning activities; see Finnie (1975) for further information on positioning and handling the severely physically involved.

Table 4-1 Righting and Equilibrium Reactions

Reflexes and reactions	Age of appearance and inhibition in normal development	Stimulus that elicits reflex	Description
Neck righting reflex	Present from birth to 4 months, then gradually diminishes.	Place the student on his back and turn the head to one side.	The body rotates as a whole toward the side to which the head is turned.
Body righting reflex acting on the body	Emerges between 6 to 8 months and is present until 3 years of age.	Place the student on his back and turn the head to one side.	This reflex modifies neck righting by the addition of rotation of trunk between the shoulders and pelvis. (Rather than the body turning as a whole unit, the head turns to one side, then the shoulder girdle and finally the pelvis.)
Body righting reflex acting on the head	Emerges between 4 to 6 months and inhibited between 1 to 5 years.	Place the student's feet on the ground or lay the student on either side on a hard surface.	This reflex "rights" the head in space by bringing it into alignment with the trunk of the body.
Equilibrium reaction in lying on abdomen and back	On abdomen, this response emerges between 4 to 6 months; on the back, between 7 to 10 months. Normal throughout life.	Place the student on a tilt board on the abdomen or back and tilt to one side.	The head bends and the body arches toward the raised side. The arms and legs straighten and come out from the midline of the body.
Quadrupedal equilibrium reaction	Appears between 10 to 12 months. Normal throughout life.	Place the student on hands and knees and tip gently to one side.	The arm and leg on the raised side straighten out from the midline; the opposite arm also extends out from the midline as a protective reaction.

Table 4-1 continued

Reflexes and reactions	Age of appearance and inhibition in normal development	Stimulus that elicits reflex	Description
Sitting equilibrium reaction	Appears between 12 to 14 months. Normal throughout life.	1. Place the student in a sitting position and push gently to one side.	The head moves to the raised side; the arm and leg of the raised side straighten out from the midline of the body as do the opposite arm and leg.
		2. Push the student backward from a sitting position.	The head, shoulders, and arms move forward and the legs straighten.
		3. Push the student forward.	The legs flex, the spine and neck extend and the arms move backward.
Standing equilibrium reaction	Appears between 12 to 18 months. Normal throughout life.	1. Place the student in a standing position, straighten and pull outward on either arm.	The opposite arm and leg straighten outward and the head "rights" itself to maintain the normal position in space.
		2. Hold the student under the armpits and tip him backward.	The head, shoulders, and arms move forward and the feet point upward bending at the ankles.

Source: Handling, positioning, and feeding the physically handicapped, by B.L. Utley, J.F. Holvoet, and K. Barnes. In E. Sontag (Ed.), *Educational programming for the severely and profoundly handicapped,* p. 280, ©1977. Reprinted by permission of the Division of M.R., CEC, Reston, Va.

Table 4-2 Activities for Exercising and Strengthening Body Righting and Equilibrium Reactions

Neck Righting Reflex

1. Place student in the supine position.
2. Gently turn the student's head to one side, attract student's attention with a brightly colored object or sound toy.
3. Repeat to the other side.
4. Continue these activities until the student's body follows the direction of the head turn.

Body Righting Reflex Acting on the Body

1. Repeat the same activities above, but this time note that the shoulder and then the pelvis follow the direction of the turn instead of the whole body moving as in the neck righting reflex.

Body Righting Reflex Acting on the Head

1. Place the student on his left or right side on a flat surface.
2. Gently position the student's head by applying support to the neck. This action should bring his head into alignment with his body.
3. Repeat to the other side.
4. Encourage him to make these movements voluntarily.

Equilibrium Reaction in Lying on Abdomen and Back

1. Place the student on a tilt board in either prone or supine position.
2. Gently tilt board to one side or the other.
3. Apply support to both head and shoulders causing the head to bend and shoulders to arch toward the raised side.
4. Repeat until this can be accomplished without assistance.
5. Repeat step 2; this time place arms and legs into a state of extension from the body midline.
6. Again continue to repeat the positioning until all reactions occur without teacher assistance.

Quadrupedal Equilibrium Reaction

1. The student should be placed on his hands and knees on a level surface.
2. Gently tip him to one side or the other.

Table 4-2 continued

3. The arm and leg on the tipped side should straighten out from the midline with the opposite arm extending in a protective reaction.
4. The teacher may apply support to the limbs to cause them to extend outward from the midline.
5. Repeat to the other side, giving as much assistance as necessary.
6. Gradually fade support as the student becomes capable of demonstrating this reaction.

Sitting Equilibrium Reaction

1. Place the student in a sitting position with pillows in the back and to the sides.
2. Gently push him to the side noting if he can straighten his arms and legs to prevent falling over. If not, gently straighten the legs downward at the hips and the arm at the shoulder and elbow.
3. Repeat to the other side and continue this pattern of movement until the reaction is firmly established.
4. Gently push the student backwards, noting if the head, shoulders, and arms move forward with the legs straightening out. If not, apply support to the key points (neck, spine, and shoulders) causing the head to come forward slightly with the shoulders in a slightly rounded forward position and the arms extended outward (see number 2). Repeat this activity until the reaction is firmly established.
5. Gently push the student forward; the response should be the opposite to that in number 4. Continue positioning as in number 4 until the reaction is established.

Standing Equilibrium Reaction

1. With the student in a standing position (with support if necessary), straighten and pull outward on either arm. Note if the opposite arm and leg extend out with a head righting reaction. If not, the teacher can apply support or gentle pressure to "cause" the reaction to occur. Repeat until the reaction is firmly established.

POSTURAL REFLEXES

According to Semans (1967), preliminary assessments of students should determine:

1. the normal postural and movement patterns the students possess and those they lack
2. which abnormal postural patterns block or distort movement and so interfere with normal function

Table 4-3 provides a description of some postural reflexes that, when they are not inhibited, cause abnormal movements and make advanced forms of movement impossible.

One type of treatment for the problem of abnormal reflexive behavior is a technique developed by Bobath and Bobath (1966). Their opinion is that the essential deficit is the derangement of a normal postural reflex mechanism. This mechanism comprises the integrated activity of all those automatic reactions (including righting, protective, and equilibrium reactions) that develop sequentially in the child and serve to coordinate movements and control postures with respect to space, gravity, and nearby objects (Semans, 1967). Abnormal postural patterns are related to abnormal postural tone. By changing the pattern, more normal postural tone can be obtained. Thus, if the relationship of parts of the body is changed, abnormal reflex activity can also be changed. Semans (1967) noted that the student is handled in such a way that abnormal patterns are blocked, thereby changing the tone and allowing the student to move with greater ease and in directions and ranges previously precluded by the abnormal patterns.

The aspect of normalizing tone is considered sensorimotor learning. The learner is given the experiences with varied movements combined with postural adjustments. At first the therapist controls the abnormal postural patterns by inhibiting the reflexes at the key points with a gradual fading of control until the learner is able to exert at least partial movement (Semans, 1967).

Generally, classroom personnel working with severely retarded individuals will also encounter students who have had insult to the developing nervous system and a resulting retardation of motoric development. The child with severe muscular involvement may exhibit certain movement-inhibiting characteristics singly or in combination. These include:

- spasticity, in which voluntary movement is difficult because of simultaneous contraction of both flexor (bending) and extensor (straightening) muscles. Limbs tend to be rigid and movement is jerky and spasmodic. When the spastic individual stands, there may be trembling, unsteadiness, or irregular movements (Baroff, 1974).

Table 4-3 Postural Reflexes

Reflex	Age of appearance and inhibition in normal development	Stimulus that elicits reflex	Description	Detrimental effects
Asymmetrical	Birth to 4 months, then gradually diminishes.	Turning the head to either side while student is lying on his back.	When the head is turned to the side, there is extension of the arm and leg on the face side and flexion of the arm and leg on the opposite side.	1. Makes rolling over difficult or impossible. 2. Causes the student to collapse while in all-fours position if the face turns to either side. 3. May prevent child from getting both hands to midline for hand activities. 4. Makes establishment of self-feeding and ambulation difficult because of alternative flexor and extensor tone.
Symmetrical tonic neck reflex	2 to 4 months, gradually diminishes.	Raising and lowering of the head while the student is held over the knees or in an all-fours position.	When the head is extended (raised up) extensor tone in the arms and flexor tone in the hips and legs increase. Lowering (bending toward the chest) of the head produces increased flexion in the arms and extension in the hips and legs.	Interferes with normal posture while sitting. Bending the head forward to look at an object increases extension of the hips causing the student to sit with rounded back, the hips sliding forward in the chair.

| Tonic laby-rinthine reflex | Appears during 1st and 2nd months and is normal up to **4** months of age. | Place the student:
1. On his stomach.
2. On his back. | 1) On back—extensor tone becomes dominant throughout the body (back arches, legs and arms straighten, head pushes back).
2) On stomach—flexor tone becomes dominant throughout the body (arms, legs and hips bend, head is tucked to chest). | 1. On back—difficult to raise the head, roll over or move from this position due to the inability of the student to flex.
2. On stomach—difficult to raise the head or maintain an all-fours position due to overall flexion. |
| Startle reflex | Normal from birth. | Place the student in supported sitting and push him backwards past the balance point or make a loud noise. | The arms are straightened and are thrown out and up. | Interferes with use of the arms for support in sitting. |

Source: From Handling, positioning, and feeding the physically handicapped, by B.L. Utley, J.F. Holvoet, and K. Barnes. In E. Sontag (Ed.), *Educational programming for the severely and profoundly handicapped,* p. 281, © 1977. Reprinted by permission of the Division of M.R., CEC, Reston, Va.

- athetosis, in which movement is extremely slow and uncontrolled or involuntary. Movements may be in a circular or random pattern. As is the case in spasticity, attempts to gain control of motor movements may actually aggravate the incoordination (Baroff, 1974).
- ataxia, in which balance is extremely poor and the person's gait is staggering and awkward (Baroff, 1974).
- hypotonia, in which decreased muscle tone causes flaccidity and lack of muscular strength (Utley et al., 1977).

Other treatment approaches for severely motorically involved individuals can be and are employed to facilitate motor development in this population. One such approach, the proprioceptive neuromuscular facilitation (PNF) method described by Voss (1974), involves:

1. the concept of human motion. Patterns of facilitation are specific movements wherein each joint of a body segment contributes three types of motion—flexion and extension combined with abduction (movement away from the body midline) and with adduction (movement toward the body midline), and with external or internal rotation.
2. training of coordination which is facilitated through the use of timed sequence of muscle contraction.
3. use of maximal resistance and adjusted resistance to promote irradiation of impulses in a pattern.
4. battery of techniques or procedures which are superimposed on the movement or posture to facilitate performance and promote motor learning.
5. use of tone of voice to increase or decrease the stress on the student.

Stockmeyer (1974) views the sensorimotor approach to treatment as the blending and interaction of two fundamental reaction systems. One system is represented by the sensorimotor mechanisms that provide the learner with the means to change position and exhibit movements free of weight bearing. The second system involves the sensorimotor mechanisms that enable the student to maintain contact and body posture. Working together, first in weight-bearing and then in non-weight-bearing activities, these two systems bring the student to a level of fine manipulative and articulative skills.

DEVELOPMENT OF GROSS MOTOR SKILLS

Smith (1974), in summarizing the results of research dealing with motor skills of the retarded, concluded that this population is deficient to varying degrees in the performance of motor tasks that involve strength, body flexibility, precision, balance, finger dexterity, and some forms of hand manipulation. Of course, with the more severely involved, the problem of gross motor development may be intensified by central nervous system involvement.

Initially the teacher will want to determine the student's present level of performance in the major gross motor developmental milestones. Most of the gross motor tests are simply not adequate to assess the skill level of the severely retarded learner. The behavioral increments are usually too large, thus rendering such instruments worthless. Fredericks, Baldwin, Doughty, and Walter (1972) have developed a motor development scale that is a downward extension of the Lincoln-Oseretsky Motor Development Scale. Its authors present 51 activities or items covering a broad sample of gross motor items. The activities are described according to the equipment needed, the number of trials allowed, the directions, scoring criteria, and points. Not all activities would be relevant for the individual severely retarded learner and the norms should not be used; however, the teacher may evaluate at lower skill levels and develop a profile of the learner's skills.

The Wabash Guide (1977) also provides a number of checklists that can be used to determine an individual's abilities in balance and posture and the acquisition of perceptual motor skills. These checklists may be utilized to determine a learner's actual performance level and from this, goals and objectives can be formulated. Activities to meet the goal may be selected from the Wabash Guide or other curricular formats.

Depending upon the degree of physical involvement, the teacher may find that instruction must begin by teaching the student head control. Since development occurs according to the cephalo-caudal growth principle, the establishment of head control is crucial to more advanced forms of motor movement. The next section of this chapter will describe the *major* gross motor developmental milestones beginning with the establishment of head control and concluding with the ability to jump. For these and all other "milestones" in this chapter, the major heading becomes the target behavior for the learner. For example, head control appears as the first specified target behavior. Head control refers to the learner's ability to hold his head erect in a sitting position (this skill is described in the Wabash Guide Checklist). If the learner cannot hold his head erect and steady in this position, this becomes the specific objective for the learner to accomplish. Within the scope of the activity the teacher may be required to task analyze the skill into smaller steps as described in Chapter 3. The next step involves presenting activities designed to facilitate the achievement of these milestones with the severely mentally retarded. With this criterion-referenced approach the assessment of progress can easily be determined by the level of performance, ranging from acceptable performance with maximal assistance to performance unassisted or a percentage of correct response, i.e., the learner can perform the skill accurately 80 percent of the time or even a yes/no format. Chapter 2 presented a number of different possibilities for designing such evaluative checklists.

Head Control

Interesting age-appropriate activities paired with positive reinforcement techniques facilitate learning. For some individuals the first milestone for gross motor control is the establishment of head control, which can be facilitated through a number of activities.

Head Roll: According to Hart (1974) the student should be placed on the back with her legs extended straight and the hands placed to the side. The instructor then gently rotates the head from side to side, alternately touching each ear to the mat. Rotation is accomplished without movement of the shoulders or extremities. The instructor should talk to the student as the head is rotated stating, for example, "turn this way, and that way, and this way," all in a rhythmic manner. As control improves the instructor begins to fade out the amount of assistance until independent rotation is reached.

Bender and Valletutti (1976) combine the actions of head lifting and rotation with the student in a sitting position. The instructor assists in the rotation and lifting of the head by placing an arm or hand under the neck and head as it is turned.

Head Lift: In order to stimulate the lifting action, a noisemaker of some type (bell, rattle, shaker) should be placed directly in front of the student's head as he lies in a prone position. Assist the student to raise the head and turn to find the noisemaker. If the head cannot be held erect independently, the instructor should offer assistance long enough for the student to see the noisemaker.

Another activity utilizing a padded table cited by the Wabash Guide (1977) requires the student to lie prone with the head extended over the edge of the table. The student is assisted in lowering the head in order to apply stretch to the neck muscles. Assistance is again offered as the student is instructed to lift the head. Several repetitions are generally used. Head lift remediation as described by Hart (1974) can occur with the student lying face down with the legs extended. As the instructor places one hand on the back of the neck and the other under the chin, the student's head is gently lifted off the mat. Movement of the shoulders and chest should not be noticeable. A similar lifting action can be accomplished with the student lying on his back as the instructor gently brings the chin toward the chest. In addition to these activities, remediation may include head circle imitation (Bender and Valletutti, 1976). In this activity the student follows the instructor's head movements from a sitting position as his own head is slowly pulled through a circular range of motion.

Steadying the Head: As lifting the head is achieved, assistance may be required to steady the head. This steadying may be accomplished with the instructor placing her arm or hand behind the neck and head. Support can be added with pillows or headrests. The duration of the head lift may be increased by having the student raise his head to see numerous objects such as his toes, colorful pictures, or the face of a friend (Bender and Valletutti, 1976).

Rolling

Sherrill (1976) described rolling, the ability to turn the body from side to side, as the first locomotor movement pattern children achieve in their development. In the execution of this movement, children turn their heads first, then the shoulders, then the pelvis, and finally their legs. This section will describe activities to facilitate the development of the roll; however, note that the more severely motorically involved may be able to execute only variations of the basic log roll.

Rolling Side to Back: The student should be placed on her side. The instructor may place a toy or other attractive object just out of reach, level with the top of the head, while encouraging or positioning the upper arm to reach for the toy. In reaching for the toy or object, the student should roll onto her back. Encourage the child by rewarding or praising her efforts as described in Chapter 3. Reverse sides so that the student has equal practice rolling from each side.

Rolling Stomach to Back: The student is placed face down on a mat or on a carpeted floor. The instructor should turn the student's head to the right while gently pulling the left hand across the body at shoulder level while tipping the face upward. Reverse this action to the other side. In the next phase, turn the student's head to the right with his hands next to his shoulders. Push the floor with the student's left hand and assist by applying a gentle push at the shoulder until the roll is completed. The third phase is an "activity assisted" roll in which the instructor passes a toy or other attractive object over the student's head and shoulders encouraging him to reach for it and allowing gravity to assist the roll. Finally, the teacher should sit to the right or left of the child and say "roll over" with encouragement and arms outstretched until the child is equally adept at rolling left and right on request (Hart, 1974; Wabash Guide, 1977).

Rolling Back to Stomach: The student is placed on her back on a mat or carpeted floor. In the initial stage, the instructor may assist the roll by turning the student's head in the direction of the roll and lifting the student's right (or left) leg with the knee bent and crossed to the other side. The hip will raise and the instructor may gently rotate the hip until the roll is completed. In the next phase, the instructor passes a toy over the student's head and verbally encourages the student to roll over. Finally, all assistance is faded until the student will roll on command or on her own (Hart, 1974; Wabash Guide, 1977).

Note that rolling over can be detrimental to some students, particularly if they have an asymmetrical tonic neck reflex and/or a neck righting reflex. The positions described above may elicit these abnormal patterns; therefore, the instructor should consult a physical therapist before attempts are made to facilitate rolling (Utley et al., 1977).

Sitting

The student must establish head control before independent sitting can be achieved; however, sitting activities can be encouraged in conjunction with earlier tasks.

Sitting Position from Lying on the Back: In moving to a sitting position the first action by the instructor is to bend the student's head forward at the same time the shoulders and arms are brought forward. This rounds the top of the spine and initiates the posture necessary for sitting (Finnie, 1975). A useful device suggested by Hart (1974) in practicing the "pull to sit" action is an inner tube. The student locks his arms around the inner tube and is encouraged to pull himself up.

Sitting Without Support: Activities for this action might include placing the student on a mat in a corner with additional padding placed on the walls for protection. Assistance is offered by the instructor to maintain the sitting position if balance is lost. Bender and Valletutti (1976) suggested progressing from back support furniture to low back chairs and finally to a low backless stool or bench.

Hitching, Crawling, and Creeping

Sherrill (1976) notes that the first locomotor movements children make with any degree of intention or purpose are hitching, crawling, and creeping. The author (Sherrill, 1976) described hitching as a backward scooting along the floor in which one leg scoots and the other is kept under the child or extended to maintain balance. Since hitching is employed as a travel mode for such a short period of time, it is usually excluded from lists of locomotor movements.

The terms crawling and creeping are sometimes used interchangeably, but there is a definite distinction between the two patterns. Crawling is primarily an arm action in which the body is pulled across the floor with the abdomen and legs dragging behind. On the other hand, creeping is a locomotor pattern in which the body weight is equally distributed on the hands and knees (Sherrill, 1976).

To promote crawling, place the student on her stomach on a mat or carpeted floor. Put a toy about three feet in front of her and call her attention to it. Encourage her to reach for the toy, noting if one leg moves upward. If so, the instructor can place a hand against the sole of the foot and hold it to the floor. When the student straightens her leg, she will push herself forward. If the student requires more assistance than would be given in this activity, the instructor can apply pressure and support by lifting the student's pelvis, alternating between the right and left sides and then applying pressure to the sole(s) of the feet as described above (Wabash Guide, 1977).

Crawling activities should not be utilized with children who are spastic since the activities may strengthen abnormal patterns. Also, athetoid children are often unable to crawl because of inadequate head control. An alternative to crawling is the use of a scooter board (Utley et al., 1977).

Creeping can be introduced once the child has learned alternating movements of his arms and legs and has enough head control and balance to sit (Hart, 1974). Initially, the instructor may use a long towel wrapped around the student's middle and provide the support to raise the student up on his hands and knees. With a brightly colored object placed about three or four feet in front of the child, the instructor should encourage the child to crawl toward the toy, providing as much assistance as necessary. The instructor may also wish to employ an adjustable crawler or provide assistance by pulling up on the waistband of the student's pants. Once the student masters independent crawling, fade out all assistance and provide practice in crawling utilizing obstacle courses, tunnels, inner tubes, and cut-out hand prints along the floor (Wabash Guide, 1977; Bender & Valletutti, 1976).

Standing

Leg Extension: Before training is initiated for standing, two considerations are suggested by Utley et al. (1977):

1. Does the student possess any disabling conditions that might be further complicated by weight bearing activities?
2. Does weight bearing in a standing position elicit an abnormal walking reflex?

Both of these considerations may require consultation with a physical therapist or a physician before the training process begins.

Once clearance has been established with the appropriate medical personnel, weight bearing activities can begin. For some individuals leg extension activities should precede standing posture. In such cases pressure can be applied to the bottoms of the feet from the student's sitting or lying position. With the knees bent and lying on his back the student can also be encouraged to extend his legs against the instructor's resistance. The value of strengthening the legs will soon be witnessed as the student is placed in a standing position and required to maintain a degree of balance.

Standing with and without support: Remedial standing activities generally require the instructor to provide supportive assistance by pulling or lifting the student to a stand. Utley et al. (1977) encouraged the utilization of a standing table. This table or sturdy box is designed with its top surface meeting the student at midchest height. Placing the table 4 to 6 inches in front of the student will allow her to lean slightly forward and rest her arms on the surface. Once in position a pillow or small roll is placed between the legs to separate the feet. With the student in standing position the instructor must provide support by placing his legs or knees around the student's, and at the same time the hands are placed firmly on the hips. As standing time improves a number of activities can be introduced. Bender and Valletutti (1976) suggest "Simons Says" and other games that require pretending. (Example: Pretend you are a "tree" bending in the wind.) Music can also be employed and students required to sway with the rhythm. At this point the success of the above-mentioned games will depend entirely on the student's cognitive level. If the student is unable to pretend, actions can be assisted by the teacher or imitated.

Cruising

Cruising may be defined as a purposive locomotor movement pattern in which the student uses furniture for support and moves along with a sideward step. To promote this movement the instructor may place the child in a standing position (remember, some students will not be physically capable of standing) next to a table with an attractive object just out of hand's reach. Encourage the student to secure the toy or food by taking a sideward step. Eventually the student should begin to cruise voluntarily around the table or other objects in the classroom. The instructor will also want to encourage the student to transfer support to a nearby object once cruising has been well established. This may be accomplished by placing two tables within one or two feet of each other and encouraging the student to transfer by providing minimal support or assistance. Gradually the student should be able to achieve the transfer unassisted (Wabash Guide, 1977).

Walking

In a normal child the skill of walking is generally not perfected until nearly three years after the first step is taken (Sherrill, 1976). Therefore, the "normal" child fully achieves walking skill at approximately age four years. Teaching any individual to walk independently first requires the mastery of balance and protective extension of the arms. The latter is certainly not necessary for mobility; however, the ability to catch oneself during a fall is an essential safety factor.

Once the prerequisite skills are accomplished, walking assistance is usually required to encourage the stepping action. Assistance to smaller individuals can be facilitated with the instructor standing behind the student, grasping the elbows, and straightening the arms as they are rotated outward. This action will not only elevate and push the shoulders forward, but also help straighten and separate the legs in addition to straightening the head, spine, and hips (Finnie, 1975).

Many assistive devices for walking are available; however, they should be prescribed and measured by appropriate medical personnel. For children from one and a half to four years of age "infant walkers" are appropriate. "Child walkers" are designed for children two to eight years and generally have adjustable handrails. "Adult walkers" provide assistive balance and support for the older student. A number of remedial activities and games are suggested in Bender and Valletutti (1976). For some students the use of walkers will be inappropriate; therefore, crutches and canes might provide a functional alternative.

As walking is achieved, "gait" becomes an important factor. Gait, which includes one's carriage, rhythm, and speed of walking, is often determined by watching others. For many severely retarded, "shuffling" is an acquired pattern often observed. It is characterized by slow small steps due to laziness, poor concept formation, or inadequate muscle tonus (Sherrill, 1976). Remediation for the "shuffle" can include strengthening activities for the hip flexors if the latter is thought to be the cause. Proper walking can be initiated through stepping activities requiring imitation of the instructor or stepping over and through obstacles such as the rungs of a ladder lying flat on the ground, ropes, tires, and snap rings, to mention just a few. The student may need to be shown or have his feet manipulated manually to convey the proper heel-toe weight transfer essential to making each step. This sequence requires the heel to touch the surface first, then the body weight is transferred across the outer border of the foot to the toe area. The entire step concludes with a push-off made by the muscles of the big toe. Although this action appears very simple, strengthening exercises such as curling the foot, tapping the toes, and stretching exercises often used by physical therapists may be necessary to accomplish this action.

The skill of walking is a complex task requiring balance, muscular agility, rhythm, and strength. For many individuals extreme deficits in one or all of these components exist; therefore, the training environment must be altered. Besides the array of fitness, exercise, and assistive devices (walkers, crutches, canes) available, teachers should not overlook the merit of a water environment or therapeutic pool. For further information on this topic, consult Chapter 13 of this text.

Running

Severely and profoundly retarded individuals who lack the concept of running can be introduced to it by walking down hills steep enough to quicken the pace to a run (Sherrill, 1976). For example, the instructor and the student can stand at the top of a grassy slope, and the instructor can roll a ball down the slope, take the student's hand, and run down after the ball. The instructor can gradually reduce assistance as the student becomes more adept at this skill. Additionally, the instructor may wish to employ games to refine the skill of running including:

- follow the leader
- obstacle course
- relay races
- running with a partner
- hide and seek

At first most students will not only run stiffly but often show reluctance to running. Constant practice in running games will enhance the students' ability to run to the point that they will feel successful and be able to change speed and direction, and participate in more advanced types of running games.

Jumping

Sherrill (1976) noted the confusion in the literature surrounding the definitions of jump, hop, and leap. The jump is defined as a motor act in which there is a one- or two-foot take off, with the body weight transferred to the two feet during the landing (Sherrill, 1976). With the more severely involved individual, Hart (1974) recommends the use of the two feet on takeoff. The individual should use and control her entire body as she leaves the ground, swinging her arms back as the legs bend, and bringing them up as the legs extend. For the student to maintain the best control upon landing, the legs should be a shoulder width apart and the knees slightly bent so the legs absorb the impact of the landing (Hart, 1974).

The instructor may begin teaching the student to jump by placing her on the bottom step of a flight of stairs or on a box about eight to ten inches high, taking the student's hand (or if necessary, the instructor can provide more support by placing his hand under the student's elbow with the other hand and arm around her waist), and encouraging her to jump to the floor. Gradually the instructor fades his assistance as the student displays greater skill at jumping. Eventually games may be employed to strengthen this skill including:

- trampoline jumping
- jump over the rope (begin by skipping over the rope)
- kangaroo jump
- jumping board activities
- airflow mat

DEVELOPING FINE MOTOR SKILLS

The acquisition of fine motor skills is critical to the optimal development of the severely mentally retarded. Instruction in other areas including self-help, recreational or leisure time pursuits, and occupationally related skills is significantly related to the ability to use the eyes, fingers, and hands to explore and manipulate objects.

This section will present broad areas of fine motor development focusing upon the key milestones and activities to facilitate their development.

Visual Fixation

The ability of the learner to get a "visual fix" on an object is vital to later fine motor development. The instructor may teach this skill with the learner either on his back or preferably in a sitting (supported if necessary) position. The instructor should get the student's attention by ringing a bell and placing his face close to the learner's face while encouraging the student to look at his face. Gradually the instructor should move his face to different positions further and further away from the learner once fixation for two or three seconds has been established. This activity should be repeated using different objects in the room until a firm pattern of visual fixation has been established.

Visual Tracking

Visual tracking may be simply defined as the ability to follow a moving target for three to five seconds with smooth and easy eye movements. These activities should not be attempted until the learner has mastered visual fixation.

Initially the instructor should place the student either on her back or sitting and begin by slowly moving a visually attractive (and sound-making) toy or pen light in lateral, vertical, diagonal, and circular directions. The instructor should make sure that only the student's eyes move, holding the head, if necessary, to prevent head movement. The instructor should observe the learner's eyes carefully; if she loses fixation, he should stop, and ask the student to look at the target. Initially the instructor may have to perform activities for monocular tracking (one eye) until the student is capable of binocular tracking (coordination of both eyes).

Other tracking activities may be employed to enhance this skill including: following a swinging or rolling ball, following rolling or battery-operated toys, watching a balloon tossed in the air, and following a bead on a string. Note that all tracking activities involve complex neuromuscular actions and will cause the learner to become easily fatigued. Thus, at first, visual tracking activities should be practiced for periods of 15 to 20 seconds several times each day, rather than in one concentrated time span (Wabash Guide, 1977).

Hands to Midline, Attempted Grasp

The instructor should place the learner in a sitting position with support if necessary. Rub each of his hands briskly, opening them if necessary, and bring them together, rubbing the palms together as the hands touch. Once the learner attempts to bring his hands together at the midline, the instructor may dangle or hang a toy or other attractive object directly in front of him at the midline. The instructor should encourage the student to reach for it with both hands, giving as much assistance as necessary. If the learner secures the object, allow him to play with it momentarily before continuing the activity (Wabash Guide, 1977).

Tactile reception can be intensified by placing a sticky substance on the student's hands (honey, peanut butter) causing the student to look at his hands. Additionally the instructor can place textured squares of cloth, sandpaper blocks or toys in the learner's hands at the midline position (Wabash Guide, 1977). Remember, however, the intent of these activities is to have the hands engage at the midline; reaching and grasping will be developed in the next stage.

Reaching and Grasping

The instructor may begin teaching these skills by placing some brightly colored toys or blocks in front of the student, demonstrating reaching and securing the object for the learner, and encouraging her to do the same. If the student does not perform the skill, the instructor should sit or kneel behind her, place his hands over hers, and put her through the movement. This form of assistance should be continued until the student is able to reach for the object without assistance. This skill of reaching can be taught in tandem with that of grasping by encouraging and reinforcing the securing of small objects. If the student employs a palmer grasp (fingers pressed to the palms) rather than a pincer grasp (index finger and thumb), the instructor should encourage and facilitate the development of the latter. Beads, small pebbles, small bolts, raisins, and peanuts are all small enough to require the fine motor coordination necessary to practice grasping with a pincer grasp. These activities should be practiced thoroughly until the student has mastered reaching for and grasping small objects (Hart, 1974; Bender & Valletutti, 1976).

Voluntary Release of Objects

With the student in a sitting position, the instructor should first place a small object in one of his hands, and then take a similar object and let it fall saying the words, "Drop it" or "Let it go," thus encouraging the student to imitate the action. If the student does not release the object, the instructor should gently separate his fingers until the object falls, praising his efforts as the object drops to the floor (Bender & Valletutti, 1976).

This skill can be greatly facilitated by having the student drop objects in a container, sand box, or water table. The added motivation of filling the container or seeing the water splash coupled with reinforcement and praise will reduce the amount of time required to teach the skill.

Eye-Hand Coordination and Hand Dexterity

The integration of hand and eye coordination is a crucial foundational skill for later types of training activities. The student should have the opportunity to explore and manipulate a wide variety of objects of different colors, shapes, sizes, and textures. Objects that are particularly good for this activity include those with holes in which a child can explore with her fingers (sandpaper-covered blocks, felt-covered letters, toys with strings attached, and objects that make noise when squeezed or banged together).

Once reach, grasp, and release have been sufficiently developed, the student can practice eye-hand coordination and hand dexterity by placing objects in form boxes or boxes with thin slots cut in the top. Playing with pegs and pegboards also provides excellent eye-hand movements for the child. Large pegs with large holes should be used for initial instruction with later activities employing smaller pegs and holes.

Bead stringing is another activity that facilitates good eye-hand coordination and hand dexterity. The student can learn to string beads by patterns of different colors, shapes, and numbers. For the student who lacks good hand dexterity, initial stringing activities could be employed using a wire rather than string, thus providing an easier means of control for the student (Hart, 1974).

Catching and throwing a ball in various games is an excellent means of developing eye-hand coordination. Beginning with a large ball, the instructor can teach the student to roll and catch the ball. As the student becomes more proficient at this skill, various games such as catching a swinging tether ball or bounce and catch can be employed to enhance the skill (Wabash Guide, 1977).

Building blocks can be utilized to build towers, make trains, place into containers, build fences, and make patterns. Initially the instructor should employ large blocks and gradually decrease the size until the student is able to perform the activities with one-inch cubes.

Nesting boxes, cups, or bowls, with intermediate sizes removed, are an excellent means of providing practice for eye-hand coordination and hand dexterity. The instructor should provide nesting opportunities (assembling containers of gradually increasing sizes), adding intermediate sizes as the student learns to complete the task (Wabash Guide, 1977).

Copying

Prior to instruction in copying simple shapes, the student should have mastered tracing, cutting paper, pasting, and coloring. A simple procedure for teaching copying involves drawing simple shapes (including diagonal lines, circles, squares, and triangles) on oaktag, posterboard, or newsprint. The instructor tells the student to look at the design carefully and draw it on his paper. If the student encounters difficulty in performing this activity, the instructor should guide his hand through the necessary movement, gradually fading assistance until the student is able to complete it by himself. This activity should continue until the student is confident in his ability to copy shapes. Next the instructor should show him the shapes, but remove them from sight, and ask him to reproduce from memory the design he has just been shown. At this level of skill the student needs plenty of cues to help him retain the memory of the requested design.

Sorting

The instructor should utilize sorting activities that require both visual and haptic discrimination. In activities requiring visual discrimination, the instructor should present the student with a variety of objects and demonstrate to the student activities requiring sorting by size, form, color, classification, and association. Objects that may be sorted include: paper clips, rubber bands, beads, nails, poker chips, pictures of dogs, cats, and other animals, geometric shapes, nuts, and bolts. The student should be provided with the opportunity to practice sorting skills in a variety of different situations.

To develop skills in sorting by haptic discrimination, the student can sort by feeling squares of sandpaper, velvet, satin, flannel, wool, and marbles. To enhance motivation, the instructor can construct a "mystery box," which may be a cardboard carton with the top taped shut and a hand hole cut on each end. The instructor can place various objects in the box and ask the student to identify certain objects by feel. If the student cannot explore and feel objects, the instructor can take his hand and demonstrate. The student's first feeling experiences should be everyday objects like a cup or spoon (Wabash Guide, 1977).

Eye-Foot Coordination

To develop good eye-foot coordination it is necessary to have the student's eyes follow what his feet are doing. The instructor may employ a variety of activities to teach this skill. A wide strip of masking or colored plastic tape can be stretched across the floor with the student walking across the tape, touching it with each step. This activity can be duplicated by taping off shapes (circles, squares, triangles), or taping footprints to the floor and having the student walk and touch the tape with each step (Hart, 1974). As a caution, any object taped to the floor runs the risk of getting torn off before the activity is completed. For the best results, initially use painted objects on the floor until the participants learn to use them appropriately. Kicking a ball and various kicking games are also an excellent means of developing eye-foot coordination.

SUMMARY

Remember that a motor program for the severely retarded population is critical for the acquisition of later skills. This chapter presented a systematic developmentally based approach to teaching the key milestones in both gross and fine motor development. The major milestones were presented to show the developmental sequence of skills that can lead from simple to complex motor skills. Further analyses of these skills into smaller sequential steps may be required for the severely retarded to accomplish these major milestones. The classroom teacher must be cognizant of both the needs of the student and the need for consultation with occupational and physical therapists in performing the necessary task analyses to teach the requisite skills to this population.

REFERENCES

Baroff, C.S. *Mental retardation: Nature, cause, and management.* Washington, D.C.: Hemisphere, 1974.

Bender, M., & Valletutti, P. *Teaching the moderately and severely handicapped.* Baltimore: University Park Press, 1976.

Bobath, B. The treatment of neuromuscular disorders by improving patterns of coordination. *Physiotherapy,* 1969, *55,* 18-22.

Bobath, K., & Bobath, B. Seminar and workshop on the Bobath approach to the treatment of cerebral palsy. Marquette University, Milwaukee, Wisconsin, June 20-23, 1966.

Finnie, N.R. *Handling the young cerebral palsied child at home* (2nd ed.). New York: E.P. Dutton, 1975.

Fredericks, H.D., Baldwin, V.L., Doughty, P., & Walter, L.J. *The Teaching Research Motor-Development Scale for moderately and severely retarded children.* Springfield, Illinois: Charles C. Thomas, 1972.

Hart, V. *Beginning with the handicapped.* Springfield, Illinois: Charles C. Thomas, 1974.

Schaltenbrand, G. The development of human motility and motor disturbances. *Archives and Neurological Psychiatry,* 1928, *20,* 720.

Semans, S. The Bobath concept in treatment of neurological disorders. *American Journal of Physical Medicine,* 1967, *46* (1), 732-785.

Sherrill, C. *Adapted physical education and recreation: A multidisciplinary approach.* Dubuque, Iowa: Wm. C. Brown, 1976.

Smith, R.M. *Clinical teaching: Methods of instruction for the retarded.* (2nd ed.). New York: McGraw-Hill, 1974.

Stockmeyer, S.A. A sensorimotor approach to treatment. In P.H. Pearson & C.E. Williams (Eds.), *Physical therapy services in the developmental disabilities.* Springfield, Illinois: Charles C. Thomas, 1974.

Utley, B.L., Holvoet, J.F., & Barnes, K. Handling, positioning, and feeding the physically handicapped. In E. Sontag (Ed.), *Educational programming for the severely and profoundly handicapped.* Reston, Virginia: The Council for Exceptional Children, 1977.

Voss, D.E. Proprioceptive neuromuscular facilitation: The PNF method. In P.H. Pearson & C.E. Williams (Eds.), *Physical therapy services in the developmental disabilities.* Springfield, Illinois: Charles C. Thomas, 1974.

Wabash guide to early developmental training. Boston: Allyn and Bacon, 1977.

Weisz, S. Studies in equilibrium reaction. *Journal of Nervous and Mental Disorders,* 1938, *88,* 150.

Chapter 5

Communication Skills Training

The ability to communicate with others is an especially crucial skill for severely retarded learners. Obviously, communication is the process through which learners' educational, vocational, and social competence skills are measured. It is only through the learners' abilities to communicate that their acquisition and development of learning skill can be measured and effective programs developed (Harris-Vanderheiden & Vanderheiden, 1977). In fact, Hollis, Carrier, and Spradlin (1976, p. 268) noted that regardless of the handicapping condition, ". . . in order for teachers to be effective they must be able to locate or develop at least one functional communication channel; that is, functional reception (sensory input) and expression (motor output)."

While speech is obviously the most effective means of communicating and should be taught to all children who demonstrate potential for it, some severely retarded learners will never be able to acquire effective, functional communication through speech. For this population, augmentative nonspeech or nonvocal communication will need to be explored (Harris-Vanderheiden & Vanderheiden, 1977).

Regardless of whether speech or nonvocal communication is chosen as the primary mode of communication, the process of instruction is a long-range one requiring the cooperative interaction of various professionals and parents.

THE DEVELOPMENT OF LANGUAGE

There are several theories or models with respect to how humans develop language. The psycholinguists maintain that language develops as a natural innate process (Chomsky, 1965). Thus as children begin to acquire language, certain innate linguistic universals allow them to build a theory of grammar. From there children can comprehend and produce an infinite number of sentences.

A second model belongs to those with a medical perspective. The etiology or cause of slow language development is sought so that the source can be treated or cured. Language has a biological basis and is acquired by the developing child as the brain matures neurologically (Lenneberg, 1967). It is Lenneberg's contention that environment is unimportant to language development except that it provides the child with the raw material to be used for communication.

A third model relies on data gathered from many developing children. Norms are determined and language acquisition is identified by steps, stages, and/or milestones. Developmentalists have determined what a child should be able to do at what age. For example, research has shown that at two years of age, children begin to put two words together. Vocabularies total between 200 and 900 words and consist mostly of nouns and verbs.

Finally, the behavioral approach maintains that language acquisition is a process of reinforced imitative behavior (Skinner, 1957). Language as described by Skinner is a learned behavior, which may be observed. Proponents of this philosophy believe that if a child does not learn language through a natural means within the environment, a structured controlled learning environment must be arranged so that learning can take place. While most teachers, care-givers, and parents are interested in language intervention, few generally feel as though they can or should teach it. Speech pathologists and language specialists are often called upon to supply evaluations, consultation, inservice training for staff and, more commonly, direct therapy.

The instructional process for teaching language skills to the severely retarded will be presented here. The process will include initial assessment, basic skills, skill sequence, and instructional programs.

Assessment

The 1980s are the age of accountability, as the public rightfully wants and deserves something for its tax dollar. As in all major instructional areas, teaching is preceded by a measure of what the student can and cannot do. This measurement requires some form of baseline data collection before the intervention program begins, periodic measures during intervention, and at minimum an annual assessment.

There are many types of assessment tools available. Ultimately, the one(s) selected will depend on the personal bias of the user and possibly the type of intervention program that is to follow. It is important for anyone working with the severely retarded to have a general knowledge of the types of evaluative methods that are available. The following paragraphs provide a brief description of those frequently used with this population.

Mean Length Utterance (MLU)—A simple and frequently used measure of language acquisition is mean length utterance (MLU). This measure is obtained by first recording the individual's speech or attempts to communicate when shown various pictures, objects, or questions. Using the MLU guidelines, the first 100 utterances are recorded and the morphemes (the smallest linguistic units that carry meaning) are counted. The average number of morphemes is calculated by dividing the number of morphemes used by the number of utterances (Brown, 1973). The MLU provides an indication of the type of speech errors the individual makes, thus providing direction for intervention.

Test of Language Comprehension and Test of Elicited Language—Both of these instruments are based on normative data and constructed by Carrow (1973, 1974). Measures of the individual's ability to understand his language are determined using the comprehension test while speech production (expression) is identified in the test of elicited language.

Utah Test of Language Development—This formal instrument consists of 51 items that probe the individual's functional communicative performance. The subject is asked to point to pictures of nouns and actions as they are named or described, repeat digits and sentences, draw common geometric shapes, and name the days of the week. Although the authors (Mecham, Jex, and Jones, 1967) suggest that the test has particular value in evaluating brain-damaged children, its use with the severely retarded is limited. The instrument can provide a general level of language ability that is transformed to a language age equivalent score; however, communicative skills such as imitations, gestures, signs, and individual speech sounds are not assessed.

There are numerous formal language tests on the market today. Each test reflects the personal bias of the author(s) as to the makeup of normal language development (Gray & Ryan, 1973). Tests commonly used are portions or all of the Illinois Test of Psycholinguistic Ability (Kirk, McCarthy, & Kirk, 1968), the Peabody Picture Vocabulary Test (Dunn, 1965), the Northwest Syntax Screening Test (Lee, 1969), the Houston Test of Language Development (Crabtree, 1958), and subtests from the Stanford-Binet (Terman & Merrill, 1973) and the Wechsler Intelligence Scale for Children-Revised (Wechsler, 1974).

There are many additional tests other than those mentioned above. However, it is suggested that when selecting an instrument, it is best to determine first the type of information desired and second, the type of intervention that will be used.

Some instructional language programs have their own pre-and post-test assessment and/or screening instruments. One example is the Programmed Conditioning for Language Curriculum by Gray and Ryan (1973). The assessment device in this program attempts to identify grammatical forms the individual possesses plus those forms the individual uses that are not totally correct. Once grammatic forms have been pinpointed, the individual is placed in the Programmed Conditioning lessons to remediate deficits that have surfaced. Other programs that include assessment devices are the Language Training Program by Bricker, Ruder &

Vincent (1976); Systematic Language Instruction: the Illinois Program by Tawney and Hipsher (1972); and G.O.A.L. by Karnes (1972).

Criterion Tests—Some tests are of a criterion nature whereby the students are presented with questions or tasks that attempt to measure their competency in a particular language area. If the response reaches the outcome previously determined by the examiner, the individual is said to have met criterion. The Programmed Conditioning for Language Curriculum by Gray & Ryan (1973) provides tests for each separate grammatical program. A student who meets the predetermined criterion level (e.g., 10 consecutive correct responses) is moved into the next program area. A second example that contains a similar retention inventory is the Language Acquisition Program for the Retarded or Multiply Impaired (Kent, 1977).

BASIC SKILLS IN SPEECH ACQUISITION

The development of speech can be viewed as occurring in three distinct phases: inner language, auditory receptive language, and auditory expressive language.

Inner Language

It has been suggested that word meaning must be acquired before words can be used as words (Johnson & Myklebust, 1967; Wallace & McLaughlin, 1975). If a word is to have meaning, it must represent a given unit of experience. Inner language processes are those that permit the transformation of experience into symbols, thus inner language is the internal language that individuals use to think or communicate with themselves.

Disturbances in inner language are not well understood, nor are there accurate techniques for determining degrees and types of inner language disorders. Additionally, programs for developing or remediating deficiencies in inner language need further research to justify their use with this population.

Auditory Receptive Skills

The second facet of language to be acquired is auditory reception or the ability to comprehend the spoken word. Johnson and Myklebust (1967) suggested that receptive language also encompasses reading and, therefore, consists of two basic types—auditory and visual. Since the ability to read is often beyond the capability of severely retarded individuals, only auditory receptive language will be discussed here.

When analyzing auditory receptive skills, it is important to remember that there is a reciprocal relationship between reception and expression. That is, input precedes output—suggesting that understanding must be attained before a word can be used meaningfully in communication. The major subskills of receptive language include perception of sounds, understanding syntactical and grammatical structure, and following directions (memory and sequence) (Johnson & Myklebust, 1967; Wallace & McLaughlin, 1975).

Auditory Expressive Skills

When children reach the developmental level where they have acquired meaningful units of experience and when comprehension is established, communication with others—auditory expressive language—is possible. Again, since input precedes output, their ability to use receptive language can only be measured by the way they express themselves. The most common ways are pointing, signing, speaking, and gesturing. Reception can, however, be basically intact with expression alone being affected. The input and output systems of the brain are only partially interdependent (Johnson & Myklebust, 1967). The major subskills of auditory expressive language are expressing speech sounds, formulating words and sentences, and selection.

A SKILL SEQUENCE FOR LANGUAGE

It is difficult to identify one teaching sequence for language that has proven more successful than all others. Research reviews by Snyder, Lovitt & Smith (1975) indicate that most language programs utilize various types of imitation in order to teach communication. Garcia and DeHaven (1974) reported that teaching methodology employing operant techniques can be used effectively in teaching expressive speech communication.

Although research studies have been conducted relative to various instructional sequences and methodologies, the number of subjects used has been small. Future efforts are needed to offer more conclusive evidence. Despite rather limited information as to program effectiveness, the following components to some degree appear to be consistent within the programs by: Bricker, Ruder, & Vincent, 1976; Kent, 1977; Gray & Ryan, 1973; Dayan, Harper, Molloy & Witt, 1977; and Hart, 1974:

1. attending skills
   a. sitting in a chair
   b. looking at the clinician
   c. performing simple tasks
   d. sensory motor activities
   e. fundamental gross motor skills
   f. body movements and parts

2. receptive language training
   a. naming nouns (pointing to those named)
   b. body parts
   c. performing actions
   d. responding to commands
   e. verbal imitations
      1. consonants-vowels
      2. gestures-actions
   f. performing gross motor actions and skills of daily living
   g. room and environmental objects

3. expressive language training
   a. tongue, jaw, and lip exercise
   b. consonants-vowels-number concepts
   c. prepositions
   d. chaining speech parts to form sentences, build in new parts of speech
      (one-word vocalizations—multiword vocalizations)
   e. work recognition
   f. naming actions, objects, colors, and counting

While many of the components of the Gray and Ryan program are covered by this list, all elements of their curriculum are contained in Table 5-1.

INSTRUCTIONAL PROGRAMS

A number of language programs have been used with the severely retarded; there is not one perfect or final solution for teaching language. Debate is quick to surface whenever various language program authors discuss their instructional components, sequence, or methods of presentation. In comparing common language programs, similarities exist; however, there are a number of basic differences. The first significant difference is in the basic philosophical approach—

Table 5-1 Language Curriculum

A. Core
1. identification of nouns
2. naming nouns
3. in/on
4. is
5. is verbing
6. is interrogative
7. what is
8. he/she/it
9. I am
10. singular noun present tense
11. plural nouns present tense
12. cumulative plural/singular present tense
13. the

B. Secondary
14. plural nouns are
15. are interrogative
16. what are
17. you/they/we
18. cumulative pronouns
19. cumulative is/are/am
20. cumulative is/are/am interrogative
21. cumulative what is/are/am

22. cumulative noun/pronoun/ verb/verbing
23. singular and plural past tense (t and d)

C. Optional
24. was/were
25. was/were interrogative
26. what was/were
27. does/do
28. did
29. do/does/did interrogative
30. what is/are doing
31. what do/does/did
32. negatives not
33. conjunction and
34. infinitive to
35. future tense to
36. future tense will
37. perfect tense has/have
38. adjectives
39. possessives
40. this/that/a
41. articulation

Source: A language program for the nonlanguage child, by B. Gray and B. Ryan, p. 27.
©1973. Reprinted by permission of Research Press, Champaign, Illinois.

---

some programs are behavioristic in that their intervention plans are based on the premise that language is a reinforced behavior (Bricker et al., 1976; Gray and Ryan, 1973). A second difference is in the sequence or order that language components are taught. One method may alternate between teaching receptive and expressive skills (Kent, 1977); another may work for only a short time on receptive skills before moving to expressive skills (Gray and Ryan, 1973); and still another may spend a much greater amount of time in teaching receptive skills (Dayan et al., 1977; Hart, 1974; Myklebust, 1957; McCarthy, 1954; Lee, 1970).

Table 5-2 presents the basic curricular components for four language programs. These programs possess sequential similarities and methodological differences. One significant similarity is that all have been used with severely impaired children with reasonable success. Each curriculum has noted the difficulty of language generalization or the carry-over of language skills to other settings.

Table 5-2 Comparison of Basic Instructional Components for Four Language Programs

Programmed Conditioning for Language (Gray & Ryan, 1973)	Language Acquisition Program for the retarded or multiply impaired (Kent, 1977)	Total Body Activity (Dayan, Harper, Molloy, & Witt, 1977)	Language Intervention Program (Bricker, Ruder, & Vincent, 1976)
Contains 41 detailed instructional programs	Focuses first on attending behavior	Physical education movement program	Behavior control
Moves from simple single word responses to complex complete sentences	look at objects, clinician's face	Phase I — What we move	sitting in chair
The variables of response, stimulus, reinforcer, criterion, reinforcement schedules, response modes, stimulus modes, and model are controlled and programmed.	motor imitations	body image	looking at trainer
Uses a prompt sequence that is unique to language programming	Receptive language skills	moving body parts	working on task
Contains a branching procedure, meaning that an individual who is unable to complete an instructional step moves to other steps that foster acquisition of a previous step.	Phase I	sensory stimulation and gross motor training	Part I. Training agent-action-object structure
(Available in complete form to those completing workshop training)	body parts	Phase II — Where we move	Functional use of environmental objects is trained (ex. stirs with spoon)
(Structured behavioral approach)	objects	teaching body position and location of the body in relation to other objects	Verbal imitation
	concealed objects	teaching words such as in, out, over, under, etc.	imitation of vocal sounds produced by model to imitation of a 3-word sequence (ex. /a/ to single words)
	room parts	Phase III — How we move	Comprehension
	performance of actions related to body parts, to objects, and room parts	teach basic motor movements of run, walk, skip, etc.	point to object as word is produced by model and the correct action is given by student (ex. show me fill)
	Phase II	respond to commands	
	discriminating possession	receptive language is expanded	
	prepositional relationships		
	giving related object pairs		
	sorting colors		
	Phase III		
	verb-plus-adverbial plan		
	commands		
	vocabulary expansion for nouns		

finding objects named
sorting big and little objects
pointing to colors named

Phase IV
verb-plus-noun commands using new nouns
pointing to relatively sized objects
number concepts one through five
color-plus-object identification

Phase V
vocabulary expansion for nouns
finding objects' names
pointing to relative sized objects
number concepts 1-5
activities on objects
Expressive language skills
vocal imitation
naming body parts, objects, concealed objects and room parts
Expressive expansion:
Phase I
naming whose body parts
naming objects in prepositional relationships to room parts

more detailed body parts are taught using simple games and activities
word identification involving objects in the immediate environment
identification of pictures
daily living and self-help words
Expressive language skills
tongue, lip and jaw exercises
vocal imitation
lip and tongue placement exercises and vocalization
sound vocalization
one word vocalization
multiword vocalization

Begins by demonstrating comprehension of one word utterances and terminates with three word sequences

Production
Ranges from single word production to three word constructions (ex. boy push car)

Part II. Training modification of the agent-action-object structure

Imitation is optional in Part II depending upon behavior of the student

Comprehension ranges from comprehension of modifying nouns-adjectives of size, color, and number (ex. "show me 'red car'")

Table 5-2 continued

Programmed Conditioning for Language (Gray & Ryan, 1973)	Language Acquisition Program for the retarded or multiply impaired (Kent, 1977)	Total Body Activity (Dayan, Harper, Molloy, & Witt, 1977)	Language Intervention Program (Bricker, Ruder, & Vincent, 1976)
	naming missing objects and actions using verb-noun combinations Phase II naming colors, concealed objects, two objects, object plus a room part in a prepositional relationship and counting to five Phase III vocabulary expansion by naming nouns, objects that are missing, actions which include "verb plus noun with new nouns" naming colors plus objects counting disappearing objects (one through five) Also includes information on sign language or total communication Program alternates between receptive and expressive skills		to responding to "wh" questions and terminating with negation training (ex. introduce "no" to the sentence "boy push truck"). As training continues change to "no, boy push truck," and in the later stages, "boy no push truck." The final step is to teach "boy is not pushing truck." Production ranges from production of adjective and noun phrases (ex. "red car") to responses in single word utterances to who, what question and terminates with utterances using a negative marker within a sentence. (ex. boy is not pushing truck)

Programmed Conditioning for Language

A rather strict procedure is required throughout the training process for the Programmed Conditioning for Language approach (Gray & Ryan, 1973). Operant conditioning is used to encourage more complex grammatical skills in the 41 curricular areas. A unique part of the program is its use of a five-phase prompt sequence to initiate the learner's response. First, the learner is presented the entire model of what is to be said just as he begins to say it. Second, a "delayed complete" model is given that requires the learner, after hearing the entire model, to wait momentarily before responding. A third prompt called "immediate truncated" requires the learner to respond after only a portion of the model he is to say is given. The fourth prompt, "delayed truncated" requires the learner to first listen to a portion of the model, wait briefly, then respond. In the final prompt phase, no model is presented. The original stimulus is faded until the learner demonstrates the ability to produce words or sentences when no model is given of what is to be said.

Language Acquisition Program for the Retarded or Multiply Impaired

A criterion retention inventory follows ten training sessions for each part of this curriculum. The programs are characterized by positive reinforcement techniques such as food, tokens, and praise.

The attending behavior shaping program is a strong component of this program (Bradley, 1978) and is followed by receptive and expressive training components that adhere to a traditional developmental approach. Included are instructions in signing for those individuals who fail to respond to verbal language intervention.

Language Intervention Program (Bricker et al., 1976)

This program also presents in its initial stages a fundamental sensorimotor approach. This phase is followed by a developmental sequence of training activities that moves the learner from simple to more complex language skills.

The general training procedures focus first on what its authors refer to as training prerequisites that eventually lead to formal language.

Two assessment procedures are used in conjunction with this program. First, a measure of the learner's general language level is determined before instruction begins. Classroom observations and adaptive or behavioral measures help obtain the individual's general functional level. The second evaluative measure consists of gathering baseline data before training and periodic assessment called "probes" throughout the instructional program. Each probe measures performance using a criterion procedure. If, for example, ten training trials were given, the learner would be required to complete eight trials correctly for three consecutive days before mastery of the task was confirmed.

The instructional format includes giving instructions, modeling the desired response, prompting with a fading sequence, and reinforcement. When the learner gives an appropriate response, it is followed by praise and/or affection and initially paired with edibles such as soda pop, fruit, and candy.

A shaping procedure is used with new or reluctant learners. Reinforcement is given for behaviors that approximate the desired response gradually moving the individual to the terminal response.

Table 5-3 contains the prerequisite skills and the first 14 phases of the Bricker et al. (1976) language program. These phases illustrate the content and cueing procedure for some of the key programs.

Table 5-3 Summary of the Bricker Language Program: Prerequisite Skills and First Phases

Phase	Cue
Prerequisite 1. Sitting in a chair	"S, sit in the chair."
Prerequisite 2. Attending	"S, look at me."
Prerequisite 3. Motor imitation	"S, do this."
Phase 1. Functional use of objects	"S, show me what you do with this."
Phase 2. Verbal imitation of sounds	"S, say _____."
Phase 3. Comprehension of nouns	"Give me (show me, touch, etc.) the _____."
Phase 4. Verbal imitation of nouns	"S, say _____."
Phase 5. Production of nouns	"What's this?"
Phase 6. Verbal imitation of verbs	"S, say _____."
Phase 7. Comprehension of verbs	"Make it _____." or "Make her _____."
Phase 8. Production of verbs	"What's it doing?" or "What's going on?"
Phase 9. Imitation of two-word phrases	"S, say _____ _____."
Phase 10. Comprehension of two-word phrases	"Fill truck," or "Push car."
Phase 11. Production of two-word phrases	"What am I doing?" or "What's happening?"
Phase 12. Imitation of three-word phrases	"S, say _____ _____ _____ (agent) (verb) (object)"
Phase 13. Production of three-word phrases	"What's going on?" or "What am I doing?"
Phase 14. Comprehension of modified nouns	"Give me (Show me, touch, etc.) the _____ _____." (red) (car)

Source: From *Curriculum design for the severely and profoundly handicapped,* by P. Wehman, p. 213, ©1979. Reprinted by permission of Human Sciences Press, New York.

It is recommended that training sessions occur once a day for each child. Their length is an individual matter as interest and motivation will vary among learners. One instructor to one learner is the preferred teaching ratio; however, with appropriate grouping, one instructor to two or one to three ratios are workable.

General Instruction and the T.B.A. Approach

Up to this point the curriculums described have provided rather precise instructional directions, explicit components and definite progressive sequences. The procedures to follow provide various instructional components designed to assist severely retarded individuals to communicate—both vocally and nonvocally. Although the authors firmly believe that the more severe the language disability the more structured the intervention program must be, it is not essential to use a predesigned program such as those already described.

Some teachers enjoy and profit from planning their own language intervention programs. Instructional principles and content selected from various programs can be compiled into a workable instructional system.

The curriculum to follow represents several language intervention strategies that generally depict a developmental philosophy and fundamental instructional components.

According to Hart (1974), there are three basic levels of communication: nonverbal, preverbal, and verbal. Each level has specific characteristics and dictates a different teaching approach. Before any language training is initiated with severely retarded learners, the instructor should determine whether there is a hearing loss (Smith, Neisworth, & Greer, 1978). This is a critical issue since hearing defects are more common among this population, and maladaptive behaviors and general unresponsiveness often hinder a thorough hearing acuity evaluation.

At the level of nonverbal communication learners do not possess the ability to react to words or their meanings. Learners are not able to satisfy their needs because they are not aware of how to use language. Generally, these individuals will cry or scream to indicate they want something while leaving the task to identify what they want to the frustrated parent or teacher.

Individuals who are functioning on the nonverbal level need to be taught that their needs can be communicated to others. Of course, these learners will have only a limited understanding of words at this time, but those interacting with them should continue to talk to the learners mainly as a stimulation activity. The instructor must integrate physical movement (gestures and actions) with words so that the learners will develop the concept and meaning of various words.

At this stage, communicating their needs has priority in the training program. The learners' daily routines—eating, sleeping, toileting, etc.—can all become meaningful content in the training program. Hart (1974) notes that learners who have various physical activities—a diaper change, going to the toilet, eating, sleeping—paired with certain physical comforts—bladder relief or a full stomach—often become capable of anticipating what will happen by the physical feelings they have. Hopefully, when the learners become hungry, they will climb into their chairs or bring their dishes to the teacher or their parents.

Tugging, pushing, or pulling are also signals that nonverbal learners can employ to make their needs known. The learners may tug at the instructor to show him that they are thirsty or hungry. At this point the learners should be rewarded for their efforts, but also taken to the refrigerator while the liquid is poured to facilitate the development of associations. Initially, this form of gross signalling will be replaced by more sophisticated signals and even by actual pointing to the desired object.

The next stage, preverbal, involves the ability to understand basic concepts and the relationship specific sound combinations have to them. Learners in the preverbal stage can be distinguished from the nonverbal learners in that the preverbal individuals can understand that a symbol or word can stand for an action or an object (Hart, 1974). Additionally, individuals at this level will mix verbalizations with gestures (pulling or tugging). The preverbal learners will not be ready for complete verbal communication, but can be encouraged to gesture more abstract concepts such as going to the store or riding in a car. At first the learners' gestures will communicate one word, but training and encouragement can lead to the "stringing together" of more than one word representative gestures.

Dayan et al. (1977) described an approach called total body activity (TBA). In TBA the learners become involved in a physical education movement program designed to teach what they move, where they move, and how they move.

The program begins with the students learning body image. Body image, the knowledge of one's body parts and the manner in which they fit together, is developed by teaching the names and locations of body parts. Dayan et al. (1977) call this portion of their program "What We Move." Before children can understand, "Put your foot in your shoe," they must first know the concept of foot, then shoe, and then to "put in." Teaching such concepts, according to Dayan et al. (1977) depends heavily upon daily training sessions conducted on an activity area large enough to accommodate a solid colored mat or pad and partitioned to separate the one-to-one interaction from other group language and motor activities conducted by a teacher-aide or volunteer.

The learners must be taught the names of the most important body parts. Among these, Hart (1974) recommends ear, eye, face, hair, head, mouth, nose, arm, hands, and leg. The instructor teaches "what we move" by mat work, a whirling brush on a mixer, or a vibrator. The instructor begins with "hands" and works to other parts, brushing the muscles that will cause the body part to move. Thus, if the instructor wants the learners to move their arms and hands away from the body, she should brush the muscles on the outside of the upper arm and shoulders. This will become particularly important to learners who are attempting to use signals (pulling, etc.) to communicate needs and may lack the muscle tonus or control to utilize the muscles to pull, point, or tug. At this level of instruction frequent repetition and continuous reward are critical. As the learners begin to demonstrate their ability to do what was requested, reward should be intermittent.

The next step, teaching "where we move," involves teaching words such as in, out, through, over, and under (Dayan et al., 1977). The instructor employs barrels, hoops, steps, and the balance beam in an effort to teach severely retarded learners the position or location of their bodies in relation to other objects.

Finally, learners are taught motor planning, the ability to control and direct the body. Dayan et al. (1977) referred to this stage as teaching the student "how we move." The basic motor plan involves teaching learners to walk, run, hop, and skip. The learners begin to respond to "come to me" by walking or running to the teacher. Once learners respond to this command, the instructor adds more specific directions such as: "Come to me, run" or "Come to me, march."

As the learners progress in this program, they are learning to listen, respond to directions, and associate words to body parts. As words and names become more meaningful, the learners begin to respond to those signifying position such as "in," "out," and "over."

As their receptive language increases learners should be exposed to the names of more detailed body parts. Hart (1974) suggested that the following list of body parts be taught with the starred items first and the more detailed parts taught after the learners master the more common parts:

head*	eye*	forehead
beard	eyebrow	hair*
chin	eyelash	mouth*
cheek	eyelid	gums
ear*	tears	lips
teeth	face*	ankle
throat	wrist	foot
tongue	back	heel
nose*	spine	nail
nostril	breast	toe
neck*	bottom	
throat	chest	
arm*	anus	
elbow	penis	
forearm	vagina	

hands*	hip
fingers	rib
knuckle	shoulder
nail	side
palm	skin
thumb	stomach
	waist
	leg*

The names of the body parts may be taught using a number of simple activities and games. The following section describes activities for teaching a few of the parts on the preceding list.

In teaching the participants "head," the instructor should attempt to focus the learners' attention on their heads. One way to do this is to attach a brightly colored piece of yarn with bells to the students' heads. By encouraging them to shake their heads while you say "head" the instructor can increase the total sensory awareness of the body part. Other activities to teach the word "head" include:

- rubbing a cotton ball or yarn ball over the students' heads
- have the students try on different hats while looking in the mirror
- have learners imitate actions like shaking their heads or nodding their heads
- use a mannequin or a styrofoam head (such as the type used to display hats or wigs). Both the mannequin and head will come in handy for instruction of other body parts.
  (All of these activities are coupled with the teacher saying the word "head.")

To teach the learners the word "face" use the following activities:

- tickle the learners' faces with a feather duster
- "fingerpaint" the participants' faces with food coloring
- have the students' faces made up as clown faces
- use the mannequin or styrofoam head and have the participants paint or attach cut-out faces on them

When teaching the body parts like hand, foot, arm, leg, fingers, and toes, the following activities may be used:

- Play tickling games.
- Stick pieces of colored scotch tape or masking tape to body parts. The learners should be encouraged to pull them off.

- Have the learners spread paint with the various body parts. For example, spread a large piece of newsprint on the floor. Pour a puddle of water-base paint on the paper and then have the student spread the paint with his hands or feet.
- Trace the student's body on large butcher paper or brown wrapping paper. While you trace, be sure to name the body parts.
- Play "Simon Says" using parts of the body.
- Use the mannequin and have the students point to (and later name) the various parts.

These activities are only suggestions for instructors to build upon until they have developed a series of activities to teach body parts. Once the participants have mastered the list of body parts, instruction should focus upon large objects in the immediate environment.

Word identification activities involving objects in the classroom or home would be a good starting point. Common classroom words would include:

bookcase	door
bulletin board	floor
calendar	pencil sharpener
chair	sink
chalkboard	table
desk	window

Common household words would include:

bed	sofa
blanket	stereo
carpet	stove
chair	table
curtain	television (T.V.)
radio	telephone (phone)
refrigerator	toilet
sink	window

When teaching these objects (one at a time), the instructor should take the students to the object, touch it or pat it, and say the name "desk." In the initial instruction, only the word "desk" should be used. Once the learner has mastered "desk" and can point to the object on command, a second object can be taught in the same fashion. When the instructor has done this several days in a row with two objects, she should begin to request identification by saying the word and having the learners demonstrate that they know what it means, or saying "show me" or "put your hand on the. . . " (bed, desk, etc.). Successes should be rewarded immediately. The instructor should continue to do this, two objects at a time, adding things that are most likely to bring success and that are very familiar to the students (Dayan et al., 1977).

Hart (1974) has suggested several activities to teach common household and schoolroom items:

1. Describe the item while the learner feels it.
2. Name the object and describe its use.
3. Talk about objects that go together.
4. Place doll furniture or pictures of furniture in rooms according to the use of the furniture.

Once learners have mastered identification of the actual objects, the instructor should require identification of pictures of objects. The pictures should be of good quality (photos are best, but pictures cut from magazines and laminated will do fine), and in color. The pictures should be mounted on posterboard or oaktag and covered with clear contact paper. Have the learners point to the objects as they hear the words.

The next area of instruction in receptive language should be words that are important to daily living and self-help skill development. The words essential to these processes could form a basic word list or instructional core. Additionally, the words could be grouped by their major unit or self-help area, i.e., eating (food, utensils), grooming (bathing), or dressing.

The following lists are presented as suggestions and represent adaptations of Hart's (1974) suggestions and those of the authors:

Eating

Food

Fruit
  apple
  banana
  grape
  peach
  pear
  strawberry
  watermelon
Vegetables
  asparagus
  beans
  beets

Eggs, dairy products
& breads:
  bread
  butter
  cheese
  cookies
  crackers
  cream
  eggs
  ice cream
  oatmeal
  rice

	Meat & fish:
broccoli	beef
carrots	bologna
cauliflower	hamburger
celery	hot dogs
corn	steak
lettuce	veal
onion	Fish:
peas	cod
potatoes	haddock
radishes	scallops
spinach	Lamb
squash	Pork
tomatoes	ham
	sausage

Utensils

bowl	napkin
cup	plate
dish	saucer
fork	spoon
glass	tray
knife	

For the items in these lists, the ideal teaching time is lunch or dinner. At this time, foods can be named while the learners eat them. As with common objects, foods should be introduced one at a time until the learners are able to identify and discriminate one from another upon request. Additionally, naming as the students eat the foods will help them to associate different tastes with different foods.

When teaching utensils, the instructor should identify each one (one at a time) as the students use them. Other suggestions for teaching the identification of utensils include (Hart, 1974):

- Show the learner how to set a table and name each utensil as it is placed.
- Match utensils to the foods they are used for (i.e., you eat soup with a spoon, etc.).
- Describe the function of a utensil as you point to it.

Word lists for the grooming area are as follows:

Grooming

Bathing
  bathtub
  brush
  comb
  deodorant
  nail clipper
  nail file
  perfume
  shampoo
  shower
  sink
  soap
  talcum powder
  towel
  washcloth

Brushing teeth
  teeth
  mouthwash
  toothbrush
  toothpaste

Shaving
  after-shave lotion
  razor
  scissors
  shaving cream
  sink

Dressing
  belt
  blouse
  boots
  bra

bracelet
buttons
coat
dress
earmuffs
gloves
hat
jacket
jeans
nightgown
pajamas
pants
panties
purse
raincoat
robe
rubbers
scarf
shirt
shoes
shorts
skirt
slacks
slippers
socks
sweater
swimming suit
swimming trunks
trousers
undershirt
underwear
zipper

The items from these lists are best taught during the actual act of grooming, dressing, or bathing. As the participants are dressing or being dressed, the instructor should name each item of clothing. Additionally the instructor may:

• Dress the mannequin, naming the various articles of clothing.
• Describe the type of clothing appropriate for weather conditions or activities such as swimming.

- Match clothing which goes together, i.e., shoes and socks.
- Lay out all the articles of clothing and have the student identify them as you name them.

As the students master the words that are most necessary in their daily lives, additional words may be added in areas such as: sensory awareness (smells, tastes) shapes, directions, measurements, time, manners, and social roles (Hart, 1974).

Signing

In spite of teachers' efforts to teach youngsters expressive or verbal communication, some learners will remain at the preverbal level. Because of the severity of the handicap, the presence of brain damage, difficulties in auditory acuity, or deformities of speech mechanisms, practical speech may be impossible for some severely retarded individuals. While gesturing is useful for communicating needs, it often lacks generalizability to people other than parents, teachers, or direct care workers. For this reason, a basic sign language should be taught to these students so that they may communicate with each other and others who have knowledge of the sign system.

A number of formal signing systems have been developed for use by populations of deaf retarded, autistic, and physically handicapped individuals. One of these, the Bliss Symbol System, is composed of some 340 visual symbols that convey word meaning. The students learn the symbols and indicate their use in communication by pointing to the characters on a communication board.

Topper (1975) reported on the program at the Denton State School. Their program uses gestures, which are a combination of Indian sign language and sign language of the deaf. There is more emphasis on gross motor as opposed to fine motor gestures. In this way a more simple and concrete gesturing system is achieved with closer relationship to the natural action (Stremel-Campbell, Cantrell, & Halle, 1977).

Other signing systems using hand and body signs and gestures include:

- American Sign Language (ASL or Ameslan)
- Ameslish (pidginization of Ameslan and English)
- Seeing Essential English
- Signing Exact English
- Linguistics of Visual English
- Signed English
- Manual English
- Systematic Sign Language

It is beyond the scope of this text to pursue in depth the actual strategies involved in teaching the signing systems listed above. A wide variety of systems is available, and the selection of the system should be made by taking into account the abilities and needs of the individuals as well as the attributes and shortcomings of the system.

Communication Boards

A communication board is a device on which pictures, words, or letters have been placed. Communication boards range from relatively simple nonelectric and teacher-made devices to more sophisticated electronic apparatuses. The learners indicate needs and respond to questions by finger-pointing, head pointer (a pointer attached to a head band), hand extension or adapted aid, or switches that can be activated by the action of the extremities, blowing from the mouth, moisture from the tongue, or by the proximity of the body to the control switch (VonBruns-Connolly & Shane, 1978; Duffy, 1977). The choice of response mode depends entirely upon the physical abilities of the learner.

VonBruns-Connolly and Shane (1978) described the content of the teacher-or therapist-made communication board. The content should represent those items and concepts needed for situations related to daily living. The content must be appropriate to the learners' educational or functional levels. For the severely mentally retarded learner, symbols would seem to be the most appropriate content, although the name of the object may be printed under the picture. The critical factor is that learners begin using a board that is on a level commensurate with their ability. As the students' communication abilities change and develop, more sophisticated boards may be employed.

Two major considerations determine the physical layout of the communication board. First, the board's placement must be appropriate to the learners' ranges of movement and coordination. Second, the material must be organized in specific ways that help the students to develop more complex kinds of communication (VonBruns-Connally & Shane, 1978).

Vanderheiden and Grilley (1975) have done an excellent, extensive review of nonvocal communication aids, which includes a comprehensive treatment of commercially available aids for the nonvocal student.

The major restrictive factor regarding the use of the communication board is that as the level of intellectual functioning decreases, the value of the communication board as a substitute expressive system also decreases (Vicker, 1974). Duffy (1977) suggested that another limiting factor regarding the communication board is the small number of responses available to indicate. Possible communications are restricted by the size of the boards. Where design features have overcome these limitations, excessive cost may also be a prohibitive factor in widespread adoption of these devices.

Developing Expressive Language

When learners reach the point of correctly and consistently identifying objects and using some method (gestures) to indicate that the words have meaning, they are expressing an idea that has utility for them. If they can also move and control the tongue and lips in separate, distinct movements while making sounds, they are ready to express words. If, however, students are not capable of these fine tongue, lip, and jaw movements, the instructor will need to devise an exercise program to improve the use of these body parts as their proper functioning is necessary in developing communication.

Dayan et al. (1977) recommended that all tongue, lip, and jaw exercises be limited to five- or ten-minute sessions. They (Dayan et al., 1977, p. 35) suggest the following order of training:

1. Move tongue in and out of the mouth.
2. Move tongue from one corner of the mouth to the other.
3. Move tongue tip to upper lip and teeth.
4. Move tongue to lower lip and teeth.
5. Move lip, starting with large movements and developing small movements.
6. Change from tongue movement outside the mouth to tongue movement inside the mouth.

Blowing is the easiest lip exercise. Students can play blowing games in which they have to blow bits of colored tissue paper, blow a whistle or horn, blow a Ping Pong ball on a table, or blow bubbles in water with a straw (Dayan et al., 1977).

A food substance the learner enjoys aids in teaching tongue exercises. The instructor should hold peanut butter on a spoon near the student's tongue so he can lick it, and move the food substance around the outside of the student's mouth until he is capable of licking it. Then the instructor can use the same technique to teach movement inside the mouth—placing sticky food (peanut butter, honey, caramel, or marshmallow) on the inside lip corners and behind the upper teeth to encourage tongue movement (Dayan et al., 1977).

Chewing and sucking are also excellent exercises for developing tongue control and jaw muscle movement. Thus, the instructor should encourage students to chew coarse foods and use a straw to improve their ability to chew and swallow food and take medication orally.

Dayan et al. (1977) recommend that tongue, lip, and jaw exercises should be continued until the learners can chew, swallow, suck through a straw, keep their tongues in their mouths, drool less, and have enough voluntary control over their tongue, lips, and jaw to make speech sounds.

Expressive training should be closely related to the learner's daily living activities. Exercises can be incorporated easily into breakfast, snacktime, lunch, and dinner. Whenever grooming, gross motor, recreation, and chores occur, the opportunity must be taken to work on the basic functional words through expressive activities.

One method of teaching spoken language involves visual cues. The learners study the speaker's lips to actually see how a word is formed. To employ this approach, the instructor must first determine whether the learners can imitate fine movements of the lip, tongue, and jaw outlined earlier. If the learners can successfully and consistently imitate these movements, sound is introduced. The learners are told to open and close their mouths while imitating a sound. The resultant sound should be something like ma-ma-ma or whatever sound is to be imitated. The instructor should reinforce this production and attempt to convert it into a meaningful symbol.

Once several basic words can be spoken, other words selected from the lists should be developed following the same general procedure:

1. establish the general and specific motor pattern
2. introduce sound
3. reinforce successive approximations to that sound
4. convert the sound into a word

Some severely mentally retarded learners will not be able to profit extensively from imitation using visual cues. In this case and for many of the words to be taught, the instructor will have to provide simple detailed verbal instruction for proper tongue and lip placement. For example, "Lift your tongue," as a command may be used to get the learners to successfully complete the movement.

A third method of teaching expressive language involves actually guiding the learners' tongues and lips or jaws into position. The actual placement of these body parts allows the learners to "feel" the motor pattern and reinforces its development through repetition. As suggested earlier, the teacher may use a lollipop to indicate where the learner should place his tongue or a sticky substance (peanut butter, honey) can be placed at various locations in the mouth to show where the tongue should touch.

When teaching the blending of sound combinations, the combinations should constitute meaningful words. Goldstein (1948) indicated that the learning of senseless combinations of syllables did not aid in the development of language. Thus all efforts must be on the provision of words for purposeful communication. The chances for success will be greatly enhanced if the words are selected on the basis of ease of production and importance to the students' daily life activities so that they have ample opportunity to practice what they have learned.

The instructor should begin with sounds made with the lips such as /b/, /p/, /m/, /ch/, /j/, and /w/. Words attempted at this stage should be ones that the learner has already mastered during receptive language training. The instructor should reward successive approximations of words being taught. "/b/" is a good start for the word "bed" or "ball" and should be accepted and rewarded as the instructor shapes the proper expression of the word.

The method of teaching one word at a time employing the actual object is repeated during expressive language instruction. As the students master this word, the instructor moves on to another from the basic word lists presented earlier.

Quite often learners will use words (or actually approximations of words) spontaneously. The instructor should quickly determine what it is that has meaning for them and reward them for their efforts.

The entire process of teaching language to the severely mentally retarded is a difficult and time-consuming effort. Patience is the byword—an instructor may have to say a word many times before students will repeat it and later use it appropriately. However, once the students use a word appropriately, are reinforced for it, and recognize that their needs or ideas are being understood, they will want to continue to use words for communication purposes.

SUMMARY

This chapter provided a brief overview of four theories of language development, assessment procedures, basic language skills, skill sequence, and several contemporary instructional programs. Various activities for teaching communication skills to the severely retarded were also presented. While no consensus can be reached to date as to the best language program, many professionals agree that the greater the language deficit, the more structured the language curriculum needs to be.

Regardless of the area of language to be taught (basic vocabulary, gestures, or signs), the greater the language problem, the larger the amount of practice or trials are required coupled with increased teacher patience. As a final note, greatest learner success appears to be made when the following are used:

1. operant techniques
2. structured curriculum
3. consistent training methods
4. numerous opportunities for practice and review
5. training in varying settings and situations to enhance language generalization

REFERENCES

Bradley, D. *Language intervention*. Chapel Hill, N.C.: Technical Assistance Development System, 1978.

Bricker, D., Ruder, K., & Vincent, B. An intervention strategy for language deficient children. In N. Haring & R. Schiefelbusch (Eds.), *Teaching special children*. New York: McGraw-Hill, 1976, pp. 300-341.

Brown, R. *A first language*. Cambridge, Mass.: Harvard University Press, 1973.

Carrow, E. *Carrow Elicited Language Inventory*. Austin, Tex.: Learning Concepts, 1974.

Carrow, E. *Carrow Test for Auditory Comprehension of Language*. Austin, Tex.: Learning Concepts, 1973.

Chomsky, N. *Aspects of a theory of syntax*. Cambridge, Mass.: MIT Press, 1965.

Crabtree, M. *Houston Test of Language*. Houston: Houston Press, 1958.

Dayan, M., Harper, B., Molloy, J.S., & Witt, B.T. *Communication for the severely and profoundly handicapped*. Denver: Love Publishing, 1977.

Duffy, L. An innovative approach to the development of communication skills for severely speech handicapped cerebral palsied children. Unpublished masters thesis, University of Nevada, Las Vegas, 1977.

Dunn, L.M. *Peabody Picture Vocabulary Test*. Circle Pines, Minn.: American Guidance Service, 1965.

Garcia, E., & DeHaven, E. Use of operant techniques in the establishment and generalization of language: A review and analysis. *American Journal of Mental Deficiency*, 1974, *79*, 169-178.

Goldstein, K. *Language and language disturbances*. New York: Grune and Stratton, 1948.

Gray, B., & Ryan, B. *A language program for the nonlanguage child*. Champaign, Ill.: Research Press, 1973.

Harris-Vanderheiden, D., & Vanderheiden, G.C. Basic considerations in the development of communicative and interactive skills for non-vocal severely handicapped children. In E. Sontag, J. Smith, & N. Certo (Eds), *Educational programming for the severely and profoundly handicapped*. Reston, Va. The Council for Exceptional Children, 1977.

Hart, V. *Beginning with the handicapped*. Springfield, Ill.: Charles C. Thomas, 1974.

Hollis, J., Carrier, J., & Spradlin, J. An approach to remediation of communication and learning deficiencies. In L. Lloyd (Ed.), *Communication assessment and intervention strategies*. Baltimore: University Park Press, 1976.

Johnson, D., & Myklebust, H. *Learning disabilities: Educational principles and practices*. New York: Grune and Stratton, 1967.

Karnes, M. *Goal: Language development*. East Longmeadow, Mass.: Milton Bradley, 1972.

Kent, L.R. *Language acquisition for the retarded or multiply impaired*. Champaign, Ill.: Research Press, 1977.

Kirk, S., McCarthy, J., & Kirk, W. *Illinois Test of Psycholinguistic Abilities*. Urbana: University of Illinois Press, 1968.

Lee, L. *Northwestern Syntax Screening Test*. Evanston, Ill.: Northwestern University Press, 1969.

Lee, L. A screening test for syntax development. *Journal of Speech and Hearing Disabilities*, 1970, *35*, 103-112.

Lenneberg, E. *Biological foundations of language*. New York: Wiley, 1967.

McCarthy, D. Language development in children. In L. Carmichael (Ed.), *Manual of child psychology* (2nd ed). New York: Wiley, 1954.

Mecham, M.J., Jex, J.L., & Jones, J.D. *Utah Test of Language Development*. Salt Lake City: Communication Research Associates, 1967.

Myklebust, H. *Auditory disorders in children*. New York: Grune and Stratton, 1957.

Skinner, B.F. *Verbal behavior*. New York: Appleton-Century-Crofts, 1957.

Smith, R.M., Neisworth, J.T., & Greer, J. G. Classification and individuality. In J.T. Neisworth & R.M. Smith (Eds.), *Retardation: Issues, assessment, and intervention*. New York: McGraw-Hill, 1978.

Snyder, L., Lovitt, T., & Smith, J. Language training with the severely retarded: Five years of applied behavior analysis research. *Exceptional children*, 1975, *42*, 8-15.

Stremel-Campbell, K., Cantrell, D., & Halle, J. Manual signing as a language system and as a speech initiator for the non-verbal severely handicapped student. In E. Sontag, J. Smith, & N. Certo (Eds.), *Educational programming for the severely and profoundly handicapped*. Reston, Va.: The Council for Exceptional Children, 1977.

Tawney, J.W., & Hipsher, L.W. *Systematic language instruction*. Danville, Ill.: Interstate Printers, 1972.

Terman, L., & Merrill, M. *Stanford-Binet Intelligence Scale 1972 norms edition*. Boston: Houghton Mifflin, 1973.

Topper, S.T. Gesture language for a nonverbal severely retarded male. *Mental Retardation*, 1975, *13*, 30-31.

Vanderheiden, G.C., & Grilley, K. *Non-vocal communication techniques and aids for the severely physically handicapped*. Baltimore: University Park Press, 1975.

Vicker, B. The communication process using a normal means. In B. Vicker (Ed.), *Non-vocal communication system project*. Iowa City: University Hospital School, The University of Iowa, 1974.

VonBruns-Connolly, S., & Shane, H.C. Communication boards: Help for the child unable to talk. *The Exceptional Parent*, 1978, *8*, 19-22.

Wallace, G., & McLaughlin, J.A. *Learning disabilities: Concepts and characteristics*. Columbus, Ohio: Charles E. Merrill, 1975.

Wechsler, D. *Wechsler Intelligence Scale for Children–Revised*. New York: Psychological Corporation, 1974.

Wehman, P. *Curriculum design for the severely and profoundly handicapped*. New York: Human Sciences Press, 1979.

Chapter 6

Self-Help Skills Training

Their inability to care for their own bodily needs may be the single largest deterrent to full integration of the severely mentally retarded into the mainstream of school and society. The self-help skills in this chapter will include a discussion of the teaching skills involved in toileting, eating, and dressing. It should be noted that many severely retarded students will require physical assistance to complete the self-help skills. This assistance should be built into the instructional sequence and gradually faded out as the learner becomes more proficient at performing the skill sequence.

BASIC SKILL AREAS FOR SELF-HELP TRAINING

The discussion here limits self-help skills to the areas of toileting, eating, and dressing. Grooming and hygiene skills have been assigned to the chapter on social skills since, at their highest levels, they include skill sequences that are more social in nature. Note that the list of basic skills shown in Table 6-1 can be utilized in a number of ways in the instructional process:

1. to identify a learner's areas of strength and weakness
2. to develop instructional content and techniques focusing upon the individual's need areas
3. to evaluate learner progress in attaining basic skills.

The list suggests important self-help skills; however, readers are urged to rearrange the skills, insert additional skills or change the list in any manner that meets the instructional needs of the severely handicapped. Furthermore, since all learners will not be able to achieve competency in all areas, careful program monitoring and setting goal priorities is important.

Table 6-1 Basic Skill Areas for Self-Help Training

Skill Area: Toileting	Definition
1. General gross motor abilities	demonstrates the ability to: a. maintain balance b. move to toilet area c. sit supported d. sit unsupported
2. Approaches bathroom area	demonstrates the ability to enter bathroom area in an appropriate manner
3. Eliminates when placed on toilet	remains dry and/or unsoiled if staff takes learner to toilet/will eliminate when taken
4. Self-initiation	requires no assistance from teacher in toileting and will remain dry and/or unsoiled
5. Accompanying toileting skills	demonstrates ability to flush toilet and wash and dry hands
6. Nighttime toilet training	demonstrates ability to remain dry and/or unsoiled through the entire night

Skill Area: Eating	Definition
1. General motor skills	demonstrates ability to a. hold head erect and steady b. hold food in mouth c. swallow d. chew solid food e. bring hand to mouth
2. Finger feeding	demonstrates ability to bring bite-size pieces of food to mouth, chew them, and swallow
3. Drinking from cup	demonstrates ability to bring cup to mouth and drink with little or no spilling
4. Uses utensils	demonstrates the ability to grasp and properly use a. a spoon b. a fork c. a knife

Table 6-1 continued

5. Uses napkin	demonstrates proper use of napkin in wiping hand and mouth
6. Pours liquids	demonstrates ability to pour liquid from a pitcher or container into a glass without spilling
7. Serves food	ability to properly transfer a portion of food from a bowl or plate to one's own plate without spilling
8. Group eating	the ability to eat properly at the same table with other people
9. Passes food	upon request or on signal, the learner will pass a table item (bowl, salt shaker and so on) properly

Skill Area: Dressing	Definition
1. Undressing	ability to remove clothes properly a. shoes b. socks c. trousers d. underwear e. shirt f. sweater or jacket
2. Unbuttoning	ability to unbutton any size button without assistance
3. Zipping and unzipping	ability to zip and unzip any size zipper once the zipper is engaged
4. Dressing	ability to put on clothes properly including: a. socks b. underwear c. trousers d. shirt e. sweater or jacket f. shoes
5. Buttoning	ability to button any size button without assistance

Table 6-1 continued

6. Zipper engaging	ability to engage both parts of the zipper without assistance
7. Unbuckling and buckling	the ability to properly engage and disengage a belt without assistance
8. Lacing shoes	the ability to properly lace a shoe engaging all eyelets
9. Tying shoes	appropriate cross-lacing that results in a shoelace being tied independently

TOILET TRAINING THE SEVERELY RETARDED LEARNER

Of all the social behaviors, independent toileting as a self-help skill is among the most important to be taught to the severely retarded learner. As the young child passes into adulthood, incontinence repels the attempts for interaction by even the most dedicated of workers. Incontinence also causes the child or adult to be a social outcast, a problem to deal with in school, and a disruptive factor in the home.

Independent toileting can also be one of the more difficult self-care skills to teach because the elimination of body waste is learner controlled. Because of this factor, the section on toilet training will be the most detailed section of the chapter. While briefer, the other sections could be modified and modeled on this section.

Bowel and Bladder Control and Readiness for Instruction

It is totally useless to attempt to teach the young severely retarded learners any toileting skill unless they have reached a certain level of growth and maturity. While there appears to be great variability in the rate of acquisition of developmental milestones, the majority of youngsters achieve control of the sphincter between fifteen and eighteen months.

Other skills also play an important role in determining readiness for toilet training. The learners, whether child or adult, must have sufficient motor control including balance and the ability to walk and sit. Additionally, it will certainly help if the learners have enough auditory receptive language to understand simple commands. Deficits in auditory acuity could be overcome, however, since gestural prompts could be used (see chapters on motor skills and language).

Prior to any toilet training, learners should have a thorough physical examination including a urogenital examination and a test of kidney function. Certain problems such as a prolapsed rectum could make it impossible for a learner to control bowel function. Neurological damage can also cause a person to be incontinent as control of the sphincter is dependent upon the ability of the central nervous system to exert control. If a learner is severely disabled, at least partial control may be taught. For some learners whose deficits are gross and generalized, including severe crippling disorders, independent toileting may be beyond their capabilities.

There are some other physiological and psychological signs that indicate a young learner is ready for instruction in toileting. Physiological readiness includes an awareness of being wet or soiled, including showing you wet pants, removing them, and pulling or tugging at pants just prior to wetting. The psychological readiness factors include independent and imitative behaviors as well as a desire to please adults or parents. Some older severely retarded learners may not exhibit these signs as they have already learned that incontinence is a good way to get attention. So, in the absence of any medical problems and the presence of the other skills, the instructor is ready to begin instruction.

Pretraining Period

Before beginning to do any toilet training, it is a good idea to chart the learner's elimination behavior for about seven days or until a fairly consistent pattern is witnessed. This baseline will assist the instructor in discovering "expected" times for elimination. Exhibit 6-1 shows a chart that could be used, putting a U for urination and BM for bowel movement.

Exhibit 6-1 Baseline for Urination/Bowel Movement

A.M.	MON.	TUES.	WED.	THURS.	FRI.
8:00					
8:15					
8:30					
8:45					
9:00					
9:15					
9:30					
9:45					
10:00					
←					

Now, once the instructor has charted for this period of time and has a fairly good idea of the time(s) where success is likely, she must remove the diaper from the learner and replace it with training pants or regular underwear. Training pants or underwear are used because they are easier to get down and much more uncomfortable to wear if they are wet or soiled.

Training Period

Too often toileting becomes a battleground where professionals or parents stake their authority, and the children attempt to exert their control. All instruction in toileting should be done matter-of-factly and approached no differently from instruction in dressing or eating, despite the fact that it is the least attractive and the most unpredictable of the self-care skills.

Following is a general procedure for teaching toileting. For some students the instructor may have to shape each step; others may generalize well and move ahead without reinforcement. Note that further task analysis may be required for certain tasks or certain children. Once training begins, the sessions should be held daily. One final hint, even when working with a young child and a potty chair, all instruction should take place in the bathroom. This will prevent the instructor from having to reteach and the students from having to relearn or unlearn a behavior later on.

The following procedure is recommended for teaching toileting:

1. Take the learner into the bathroom. Some students, especially those who have engaged in the "great toileting war" before, may scream and throw a tantrum when the instructor attempts to get them in the bathroom. In this case, reward the learner for appropriate behavior as you approach the bathroom and continue to shape until he enters the bathroom.
2. Approach the toilet or potty chair. In some cases the instructor may have to shape the learner's approach to the toilet.
3. The instructor takes the learner's hands and helps him push his underwear or training pants down to his ankles, or asks the learner to do this if he can understand and complete the task.
4. The instructor seats the learner on the toilet or potty chair for ten minutes, or asks the learner to do this if he is able. Appropriate sitting behavior may have to be shaped, including rewarding the learner for sitting on the toilet with his clothes on for gradually longer time periods.

At first, ten minutes is a long enough period of time. If the learner does not eliminate, he should be removed from the toilet and returned again after five minutes has elapsed. Remember, the learner is being placed on the toilet at the times the chart indicates a high probability of success, give or take a few minutes.

5. If the student urinates or has a bowel movement he should be rewarded immediately. (Rewards can take many forms—see Chapter 3 for a discussion of reinforcement.)

The instructor should remain with the student the entire time he is sitting on the toilet so that the reward for success is *immediate,* and the learner can determine why he is being rewarded. Interaction with the student during this time should be minimal in order for the learner to concentrate on the task at hand.

6. Following a bowel movement (or urination for females), place his/her hand on the toilet paper, unroll a sufficient amount, tear it, and fold it. The instructor's hand should guide the student's hand and have him wipe carefully, and then dispose of the paper properly. Hart (1974) indicated that females present particular problems when being taught to wipe themselves. Since germs spread from the anus to the vagina can cause vaginal, kidney, or bladder infections, females *must* be taught to wipe from front to back (vagina to anus), never back to front. If the female urinates, a blotting action is sufficient (Hart, 1974).

The task of wiping with toilet paper can be a complex one for severely motorically involved students. It involves skills such as grasp and release, finger dexterity, motor control, and movement. Some of these skills may need to be taught before a student can master wiping (see Chapter 4 on motor skills).

7. After urination or bowel movement is completed and the learner has wiped himself, he should be removed or remove himself from the toilet seat, turn around, and flush the toilet.

The instructor may have to help the learner through this procedure, particularly guiding his hand to flush the toilet. For many students, the flushing sound and running water are highly rewarding, so only flush the toilet if the student eliminates.

8. The instructor then guides the student's hands to pull the training pants or underwear all the way up, or asks the student to do this himself if he has learned this as part of his dressing skills.
9. The instructor next takes the student to the sink, turns on the water, and has him wash and dry his hands. Hand washing will be discussed in detail in Chapter 7.

By the way, accidents are quite likely to occur throughout the training process. When accidents happen, ignore them. Any anger, frustration, or scolding on your part is likely to have the opposite effect, that is, become reinforcing to the student. Simply clean up the mess and the learner without comment. If the learner is older (beyond six to eight years old) he should be required to do the clean-up himself. If accidents persist, you may wish to review your training procedure and check for any instances of inadvertent rewarding of inappropriate behavior.

Teaching Self-Initiation

Independent toileting is not achieved until students will interrupt what they are doing and go to the toilet themselves. When this is achieved, a real milestone in training has been reached, as the learners will be assuming greater responsibility for their actions and demonstrating more independence. Any attempt on the part of the learner to self-initiate, i.e., tugging or pulling at the instructor, pointing toward the bathroom, or moving toward the bathroom himself, must be promptly rewarded. Foxx and Azrin (1973) noted that a single self-initiation is evidence that learners understand that they should toilet themselves and will be rewarded for doing so.

Later on the instructor can extinguish the learners' need to signal that they are ready to toilet. True self-initiation requires that the learners move to the bathroom area independently without calling attention to themselves.

In public school settings, teachers will often establish a toileting schedule for each child in the class and make sure that the child is placed on the toilet at the correct time. If the teacher does not allow for maximal flexibility, then self-initiation may present a problem. Problems will also occur if the bathroom is not near the classroom or if the child's physical problems necessitate assistance in toileting. All of these problems may be overcome, however, if the teacher is alert to any signals the learners give and is prompt to reward attempts at self-initiation.

As the learners become consistent in their self-initiating behavior, all prompts should be gradually reduced and reinforcement faded out. The motivation to remain dry should become part of the learners' general behavioral repertoires and should require no further presentation of rewards.

During this and prior attempts at toilet training, the involvement of the student's parents is important. However, some parents may resist, especially if their previous attempts at toilet training were met with screaming resistance or an inability to lift and/or handle a heavy, older student. Usually if toilet training has been successful in the school setting, parents will find reason for optimism and show an eagerness to become involved in all subsequent aspects of the training process.

Nighttime Toilet Training

Toilet training to prevent accidents at night is usually not part of a public school teacher's duties. However, since this text may be used by personnel working in institutions for the retarded, a discussion of nighttime training is in order. Enuresis, or bed wetting, is a common problem among even populations of nonretarded youngsters. In fact, nearly 10 percent of the nonretarded population have accidents at night. Bed wetting among nonretarded populations in the absence of physical or psychological problems can persist until early adolescence.

Bed wetting is quite prevalent among the severely and profoundly mentally retarded with approximately 75 percent of institutionalized severely retarded people incontinent at night (Foxx & Azrin, 1973). Foxx and Azrin (1973) discuss the problem of nighttime incontinence, listing the following contributing factors: lower learning capacity, physical and sensory disabilities, relative insensitivity to staff disapproval, and failure of staff to provide disapproval. Additionally, the individual is definitely less alert and attentive at night, and interrupting sleep to toilet is a greater inconvenience than interrupting daytime activities.

The elimination of bed wetting should not be attempted until daytime incontinence is eliminated. Thus, work on independent daytime toileting first, then train the person to be dry at night.

The following sequence is recommended for nighttime toilet training:

1. The trainer should place a bed wetting detection unit or system on the student's bed. This unit usually is a pad or pads placed under the bottom bed sheet. These pads are sensitive to moisture and immediately sound an alarm when the student begins to urinate. The sound of the alarm can be raised on the better units to a level that will arouse the learner and alert the trainer.
2. Every hour throughout the night the student should be aroused and made to feel her dry sheet. The trainer should promptly reward her and praise her for this.
3. After the second step is completed, the trainer takes the learner to the toilet and seats her for ten minutes. If she urinates, the trainer rewards her immediately.
4. The trainer then initiates sequence of flushing, hand washing, etc., and returns her to her bed.
5. If the learner did not urinate in Step three, the trainer simply returns her to her bed.
6. Any successful attempts at self-initiation should immediately be rewarded. If necessary, the trainer assists the learner to return to her bed.

Naturally there will be accidents in the nighttime toilet training sequence. Accidents should be ignored. Learners should not be scolded or shouted at. The trainer will simply (1) have the learner remove the wet sheet and place it in the proper receptacle, (2) remove alarm apparatus and have the student wipe off the mattress, (3) replace the alarm apparatus and cover it with the bottom sheet, making sure the student does not handle it, and (4) take the student to the bathroom area, have her remove her wet garments, wash her genitals, and put on a pair of dry pajamas or other nighttime apparel. Any conversation with the learner should be conducted in a neutral, businesslike tone.

As the learner assumes responsibility for remaining dry at night, her motivation should be greater and rewards will not be required. The wet bed alarm can be removed. Any future accidents should be treated routinely.

One final note, teaching toileting skills to other handicapped or multihandicapped individuals was not specifically addressed here. As indicated earlier, self-initiation requires ambulation, sight, and at least motor control of one arm and hand. For an individual who does not have these skills or for whom the skills cannot be taught, unassisted or independent toileting is not a realistic goal. For the nonambulatory learner, transportation will need to be provided to the toilet area. Depending upon the severity of involvement, bladder and/or bowel control may not be possible, so training should only be conducted for whatever function the learner is capable of controlling.

TEACHING INDEPENDENT EATING SKILLS

Learners will have to be able to hold their heads erect, hold food in their mouths, swallow, and chew solid food before they can learn independent eating skills. If learners do not possess these skills, the instructor may have to incorporate them in the instructional sequence (see the chapter on motor skills for teaching skills in holding one's head erect).

Remember, especially when working with younger severely retarded children, there is a certain developmental sequence a nonretarded child follows in acquiring eating skills. The nonretarded child is reasonably adept at eating independently at approximately three years of age. There is a similar sequence for the severely retarded learner, but the skills will develop at a later age.

Swallowing

Some severely retarded individuals may exhibit a great deal of difficulty swallowing even liquids. For these individuals, instruction will begin by teaching them to swallow liquids. Using a liquid the student enjoys (fruit juices are good and nutritious as well), the instructor fills a cup to the top and puts it in the mouth behind the teeth and on top of the tongue. Once the liquid is in the mouth, the learner's lips must remain closed so no liquid escapes. If the student is incapable of keeping his lips closed, the instructor uses her fingers to hold the lips together. The instructor then massages the throat muscles with her other hand to encourage the learner to swallow the liquid. The instructor must make absolutely certain that when she brings any liquid to the learner's lips, his head is tilted slightly downward. If the liquid "runs" down the learner's throat, he isn't learning to swallow it.

Students may resist these procedures. The instructor should not force the learner to take more than one mouthful at a time, making sure he swallows all the liquid before she attempts to have him drink some more. Additionally, some students will exhibit reflexive gagging. To eliminate this reflexive gagging, the instructor can desensitize the inside of the mouth by brushing it with a toothbrush.

Holding Food in the Mouth

In order for the student to hold food in his mouth, he must have control of his tongue and lips. The ability to control one's tongue and lips is essential for learning to eat, but is also important for developing speech. To assist the learner in keeping his lips closed, the instructor may:

- stimulate the lips by brushing them and rubbing them with fruit juice or other tasty liquid.
- when providing the learner with either food or drink, hold the student's lips together after removing the spoon or cup, and use a verbal cue such as "Keep your lips closed."
- place something like a "razor thin" orange slice or apple slice between the learner's lips, and encourage him to keep his lips closed around the slice.
- dip the flattened end of a plastic straw in honey and place it between the student's lips for a period of five seconds, gradually increasing the time the learner is required to hold the straw.
- always use a verbal cue as in item two to remind the learner to keep his lips closed. Also, a gentle touch of the instructor's fingers to his lips will serve as a physical prompt and reminder.

The ability to control the tongue is also important to keeping food in the mouth. Various tongue exercises were discussed in the chapter on language development. One area not covered in that chapter is the in-and-out or tongue thrust movement that many severely retarded youngsters exhibit. Since this thrusting will cause the learner to actually push food out or knock it off the spoon, it will be necessary to teach her to allow food and utensils to touch her tongue without it reflexively thrusting out. This may be accomplished by the following techniques:

1. The instructor will insert the spoon horizontally in the learner's mouth, carefully avoiding touching the tongue tip (most sensitive part) and placing the food in the side of the mouth.

2. When the learner routinely accepts food in this fashion, the instructor will begin to place consistent food like mashed potatoes or applesauce in the middle of the tongue while encouraging the learner to keep her tongue in her mouth.

3. The instructor will teach the student to move her tongue down or to the side to accept food into her mouth. (Chapter 5 noted that this is best accomplished by placing a sticky substance like peanut butter or a sucker in the learner's mouth where the instructor wants the learner to place her tongue.)

Chewing

Some students' diets will have consisted mainly of liquids. If so, they will have to learn to chew solid foods. A diet consisting solely of liquified foods is neither as nutritious nor as normal as it should be.

Chewing skills should be taught starting with semisolid foods that do not require a great deal of chewing. Foods of this type include: applesauce, mashed potatoes, cottage cheese, or slightly mashed vegetables (can be done with a fork). The following sequence of activities is recommended. The instructor should:

1. place the food in the student's mouth.
2. grasp the student's chin with her fingers just below the lower lip.
3. gently move the jaws in an up and down movement, verbally cueing the student, "Chew this food."
4. use soft chewing gum to provide the participant with practice in chewing.
5. gradually shape the learner's chewing to a rotary movement. This involves having the learner's tongue lift the food, put it on the surface of teeth, and chew it in a "rotary-circular" fashion.
6. treat any resistance or spitting-out of food routinely. The instructor should not scold the student or show anger, but simply wait and place another spoonful of food in the learner's mouth with the verbal cue, "Chew the . . . ."

When teaching students to chew solid food, liquified foods must be discontinued, as well as any between-meal snacks in order to force the learner to chew in order to eat.

Independent Feeding

Once the learner is capable of holding his head erect, keeping food in his mouth, chewing, and swallowing, the instructor should determine if he can bring his hand to his mouth. If he can't make this movement, he will have to learn this skill. The learner can be encouraged to bring his hands to his mouth if his fingers are coated with honey or jelly or some other sticky substance the learner enjoys eating. The instructor should move the fingers to his mouth and let him lick the substance off. Eventually the learner will get the idea, and may begin learning finger feeding.

Finger Feeding

Finger feeding should begin with relatively soft, but not likely to crumble, foods. Included among this group would be block cheese, cookies, toast, and granola. For teaching finger feeding the instructor would:

1. place the learner in a high chair or at a chair in front of a table. To ensure comfort, the table top should hit the learner just below midchest. If the student does not maintain good sitting balance, use pillows to prop her up (also see Chapter 4 on motor skills for the teaching sequence for sitting).
2. then place the bite-size chunks of food on the tray or table one at a time, and verbally cue the student: "Pick up the_____ and put it in your mouth." The learner should be assisted as much as necessary, but help should gradually fade as the learner becomes proficient at this skill. The learner should receive more food only after she chews and swallows the preceding piece.
3. offer bite-size bits of food that are more difficult to chew, i.e., celery, carrots, meat, once the learner seems capable of this movement and chews well.
4. next use smaller pieces of food like raisins or cereal. This activity can be used in conjunction with the development of a pincer grasp if the student has not acquired this skill.
5. progress to larger foods that require the student to take a bite and hold the rest until she chews and swallows the one mouthful. Bananas are an excellent practice food for this activity until the learner masters this skill. Then peanut butter and jelly sandwiches and other fruit can be tried.

Drinking from a Cup

Teaching the student to drink from a cup is an extension of the hand-to-mouth movement. The instructor will use a plastic (or some other unbreakable material) glass or cup to avoid accidents that could result from broken glass. The student should already have mastered holding a liquid in his mouth and swallowing from a glass held by the instructor before he learns to drink from a glass independently. As will be the case with the remainder of the independent eating skill activities, the learner must be in a sitting position (supported if necessary) at a table in a comfortable position. In light of this, the fact the student will be seated is assumed and will not be repeated. The instructor will:

1. begin by filling the cup or glass half full of the learner's favorite liquid and placing it on his tray or table.
2. place both of the student's hands around the glass and cue him to "Pick up the glass." The instructor will give as much assistance as the student needs to complete the task, gradually fading this help as the student demonstrates the skill to do it independently.
3. when Step two is mastered, have the learner grasp the cup or glass in his dominant hand and complete the movement.
4. provide sufficient practice until the student is able to complete the sequence of grasping the glass in one hand, raising it to his mouth, tilting the glass to take in the liquid, swallowing the liquid, and returning the glass to the table without spilling.

Eating with a Spoon

Once the participant has mastered eating finger foods and drinking from a glass, she is ready to learn to use a spoon. Eating with a spoon is a continuation of the hand-to-mouth movement. The instructor will:

1. place the handle of the spoon in the learner's palm and wrap her fingers around it. If the person cannot grip the handle, the instructor can place a wooden or plastic cylinder over the handle to make the grip larger.

Some severely retarded individuals may not be able to grip even the spoon with a modified handle. For these individuals, a device called the Gripper (sold by Childcraft Corporation) may be used. The Gripper is a glovelike wrap that is used to secure peoples' hands around an object they are attempting to hold. The Gripper comes in a set with both a left hand and a right hand wrap. One further modification in the spoon may be required. Some severely retarded learners may have a severe biting reflex. This reflex causes them to bite down hard anytime the front of the mouth or the teeth are touched. For the student with a severe biting reflex, a spoon covered with vinyl or the commercially available latex spoon should be used to reduce damage to gums and teeth.

2. put his hands over hers and guide the spoon into the bowl. A bowl with a suction cup under it will prevent the bowl from slipping around. Fill the spoon halfway with food. Use a food that will stick to the spoon such as mashed potatoes, pudding, or ice cream.

3. help the student bring the spoon up to and into her mouth. When nonretarded individuals learn to eat with a spoon, they are apt to turn the spoon in their mouths and spill considerable amounts of food. The instructor should be prepared for this as practice will gradually cause the turning of the spoon to cease and the spilling of food to decrease.

4. gradually fade his assistance as the student gains confidence and proficiency in filling the spoon and bringing it to her mouth without any spilling.

5. then teach the student to hold the spoon with her thumb, index, and middle fingers. This skill should only be taught to persons with a strong enough grasp and the ability to use a spoon without the special handle. The instructor will place the spoon so that the handle rests on the middle finger and is supported on top by the index finger and thumb, and if necessary, place his hand over the student's and hold the spoon in this position in her hand. Again, repeat the earlier sequence until the learner is capable of doing this independently.

Eating with a Fork

Teaching the individual to eat with a fork follows the same general sequence as teaching her to eat with a spoon. It is probably a good idea to teach eating with a spoon first, making certain that the student has completely mastered this skill sequence. For safety purposes, the tines of the fork should be dulled so that the individual does not cut her mouth. In the initial stages of training with a fork, the learner will use it like a spoon, that is, she will employ a scooping motion. If the student has mastered holding the fork with her thumb and fingers, she is ready to learn to spear her food. The spearing movement will take some time to teach as the learner's natural tendency will be to stab at the pieces of food. Bite-size pieces of relatively soft foods are best for teaching the spearing movement since the piercing will be easier. Cubes of cooked potatoes, carrots, or broccoli make good practice foods. When beginning instruction, the instructor will put his hand over the learner's even if she has mastered the hand-to-mouth movement with a spoon. The instructor will guide the learner's hand into the dish to spear a carrot cube, and bring the fork up and into the mouth, continuing to assist the learner as long as necessary. Assistance in bringing the fork up and into the mouth will probably be faded first, as this was already mastered in spoon feeding. Assistance here was largely for safety's sake. Teaching the actual spearing action will probably take longer; but with practice and shaping, it can be mastered.

Using a Napkin

Teaching the student to use a napkin is a natural part of the skill sequence of independent eating. As such, it should be taught simultaneously with finger feeding and with continued prompting, rewarding, and encouraging its use, appropriate napkin usage will be firmly established in the learner's behavioral repertoire.

In the initial instruction for napkin usage, the instructor should use moist towelettes. These are most efficient for removing large amounts of food, especially dried food, and they are completely disposable. The teaching sequence for napkin usage follows. The instructor should:

1. open a towelette, grasp one of the participant's hands, and wipe the excess food from it.
2. take a clean towelette, open it, and place it in the clean hand. Then put his hand over the hand with the towelette, grasp the learner's other hand and clean off the excess food, using a verbal cue like, "See how we clean our hands with a napkin."
3. place his hand over the learner's and bring the towelette up to wipe off the learner's mouth, using a verbal cue like, "We also wipe our mouth with a napkin." If both wiping the hands and wiping the mouth are taught at the same time as part of the same complete act, the student will not have to learn them as separate and possibly confusing acts.
4. continue assisting as long as it is necessary, gradually fading the hand prompt until the learner can complete the act independently and appropriately.
5. switch to cloth Handi Wipes for napkin usage when the student becomes more skilled with spilling and messes are sharply reduced. When used dry, these Handi Wipes can remove food easily and absorb liquids because of their rough surface. Additionally, they can be laundered and used again.
6. switch to a paper napkin after the learner has gained proficiency in using the napkin or Handi Wipe. Paper napkins are the most practical since they are cheaper in the long run and can be disposed of easily.
7. teach the student when to use the napkin, using physical or verbal prompts. The instructor can shape napkin using behavior by immediately rewarding the student for using the napkin properly without any prompting. All prompts and rewards can be gradually faded as the student demonstrates appropriate use of the napkin.
8. train the student to place the napkin on his lap after using it and disposing of it or leaving it on his tray or table at the completion of the meal. The instructor can teach this final part of the skill sequence by placing the napkin on the learner's lap after he uses it and rewarding him for leaving it there. The

instructor can gradually shape the learner's behavior in placing the napkin on his lap or disposing of it. Actually, Steps 7 and 8 are taught simultaneously so that knowing when to use the napkin is learned at the same time as where to place the napkin after the learner uses it or when he completes the meal.

Cutting with a Knife

Teaching the severely retarded student to use a knife is a skill that comes long after she learns to use a spoon and fork. The student will learn to use the knife for spreading first, and later acquire the ability to use a knife for cutting food.

The following sequence should be used to teach the use of a knife for spreading and cutting. For spreading, the instructor should:

1. present the student with a nonserrated knife and a slice of bread with a mound of whipped butter in the middle.
2. place the knife in the learner's preferred hand with the instructor's hand over hers. With her other hand, demonstrate how to hold the slice of bread.
3. demonstrate the spreading motion from the center out to the edges.
4. gradually reduce his physical prompting and guiding until the learner is capable of doing this independently.

For cutting, the instructor should:

1. provide the learner with a knife with a serrated edge. The preferred knife would be one with the small, closely spaced teeth to reduce the likelihood of accidents. The instructor then places the knife in one hand with the learner's forefinger over the top of it and the fork with the tines down in the other.
2. show or guide the student in placing her fork tines down into the food to be cut.
3. demonstrate or use his hand over hers and gently saw the food to be cut, using a slow, steady back and forth motion.
4. have the student bring the fork to her mouth (tines down) and remove the food.
5. make certain the student is taught to place her knife next to or across the plate when it is not being used.

The method of cutting with a knife described here would probably not meet the approval of any etiquette guides. However, trying to teach the severely retarded individual to cut the food, place her knife down, change hands with the fork, and finally use the fork (tines up) would be far too confusing and awkward.

As would be the case with any skill sequences, there will be individuals who, for one reason or other, will never learn the sequence. The teachers should use their knowledge about their students and their good judgment to determine which sequences are appropriate for which learners.

Pouring Liquids

If the severely retarded individual is to learn to be an independent person, he will need to be able to pour his own liquid at mealtime. Obviously not all students will be capable of learning this skill, but it should be taught to all those who are able. The instructor should:

1. begin by presenting the learner with a small, empty pitcher (a creamer is a good training device as it resembles a small pitcher), and ask him or show him how to grasp the handle and hold it independently.
2. fill the small pitcher half full of water, and present the student with a large, empty plastic bowl. The instructor should guide the student's hand or on command, have him pour the contents of the pitcher into the bowl, and reward him for his efforts.
3. repeat Step 2 using a larger (standard) pitcher in place of the bowl. The learner should practice (with as little assistance as possible) pouring liquid from the creamer into the pitcher.
4. fill the large pitcher half full of water, and have the student practice pouring its contents into the large bowl. It is all right if the student uses both hands on the large pitcher.
5. fill the pitcher full of the learner's favorite liquid and have him pour it into a large mouth glass. He can drink from the glass as a reward.
6. have the student pour liquid from a full pitcher into a standard drinking glass. Again, he can drink from the glass as a reward.

Depending upon the learner's ability level, additional steps may be needed in this teaching sequence. For example, the glass may need to be secured by a suction cup until the student learns to steady the pitcher in one hand and hold the glass in the other.

Serving Food

When the teachers' goal is to have each student achieve his maximal level of independence, they must attempt to teach each student all those behaviors that make integration into the mainstream of society realistic. To prepare a severely retarded person to eat independently at home, in school, or in a restaurant, the teacher must show the retarded person how to serve himself foods that are on the table. This skill will also facilitate group eating behaviors that will be discussed later in the chapter. The instructor should:

1. present the student with her lunch or dinner already on her plate except for one food item. It will probably facilitate instruction if that one item is a favorite food, for example, mashed potatoes.
2. place the bowl of potatoes with a spoon in it in front of the student, and encourage her or guide her with his hand if necessary to take one spoonful of potatoes to her plate and turn the spoon until the potatoes slide onto her dish. The instructor should then remove the bowl of potatoes.
3. continue this procedure of placing bowls of different types of foods in front of the learner until she is capable of serving herself one scoop independently.
4. increase by one food at a time the number and variety of foods the student is required to serve herself. The eventual goal is for the student to serve herself all the foods that are on the table.

Group Eating

Many times the severely retarded person eats only with other severely retarded individuals or alone because of poor eating habits. Hopefully, use of these teaching skill sequences will allow the student to become an independent eater capable of total participation in a group eating activity.

The Wabash Center Guide (1977) provided a number of suggestions for use in the group eating experience:

1. If the student resists new foods or skills, put him through the experience by gently insisting on performance.
2. If the student likes a great deal of attention or praise, ignore undesirable behavior and praise only when he does what you expect.
3. If the learner consistently seeks your approval and copies you, eat with him and explain at his language level what is expected.
4. Tell parents and others your goal and training methods. Have parents observe the group so they can follow the same procedure at home.
5. To increase motivation to learn new skills and habits, present the eating experience at a time when the student is likely to be hungry. Be sure he likes the food that is being served.
6. If the learner is highly distractible, you may want to begin instruction in group eating by having him eat in a room or area with no visual distractions, possibly behind a screen. Also be sure the room is slightly cool. As he becomes able to tolerate distractions, include him in a group of one or two others.

7. If the learner likes food but does not want to join the group, sit him at a table, give him the food. If the learner leaves the table, take the food away. *No food* unless he joins the group. Ask the parents or workers not to feed him before the sessions. Gradually increase the number of other participants in the group eating situation until the learner is comfortable eating with groups.

Passing Food

The final skill in the sequence of independent eating skills involves teaching the learner to pass food to others upon request. This skill can often be taught near the completion of the sequence on serving food to oneself. When the student demonstrates adequate skill in serving himself, the instructor should request that he pass each bowl to her as he finishes serving himself. At first, the student may not easily release the bowl and the instructor will have to encourage and reward him for doing so. There may be a few accidents, such as dropped bowls and spills. The instructor must be patient, encouraging, and reward successful approximations until the behavior is firmly established.

TEACHING INDEPENDENT DRESSING SKILLS

From a developmental standpoint, nonretarded children learn to undress before they learn to dress themselves largely because undressing is easier. Furthermore, nonretarded individuals do not acquire complete independence in dressing (excluding selection of garments) until about five to six years of age. Thus it will take many hours of practice for a severely retarded person to acquire the skills and proficiency necessary for independent dressing.

For this particular teaching sequence, a backward or reverse chaining procedure is used. The reverse chaining procedure means that the last step in the task is taught first. For example, when teaching the learner to put on a pair of socks, the instructor begins by putting on the sock for him and pulling it up except for the last two or three inches. The learner then pulls the sock up the final few inches himself. When the learner is successful at this step, the instructor would put the sock on all the way to the ankle, then above the heel, below the heel, midfoot, and the toe. At this point the instructor stops helping the learner, and he is required to pull it on completely unassisted. The learner receives reinforcement when the sock is pulled up completely with the sequence continuing with the instructor gradually reducing assistance at each step and finally stopping at a point just prior to the first step of the task.

During the initial instructional attempts the students may not exhibit sufficient motor control to master some of the dressing sequences. In this event the use of oversize clothes can facilitate manipulation of the clothing. The complete sequence can be taught with oversize clothes until total mastery is achieved. Then the instructor can gradually reduce the size of the clothing until the learner's appropriate size is reached. Oversize buttons, zippers, and snaps in actual clothing may also be used to teach these skills. Once again, the instructor should gradually reduce button, zipper, and snap size until "normal" or average sizes are reached. Finally, we strongly discourage the use of buttoning boards and dressing frames to teach these skills; too many students have difficulty transferring the skills from the board or frame to their body, and the confusion that results can slow down the teaching process.

All the steps in each reverse chain will be presented despite the apparent redundancy, so that the instructor may convert each of the steps in the sequence into an instructional objective suitable for utilization in an Individual Educational Plan (IEP) or daily lesson plan.

Removing Socks

1. Put a sock on the learner's foot, barely covering his toes. Place his thumbs on either side of the band and have him pull the sock off.
2. Put the sock on the learner's foot midway between the toes and heel. The sock should be removed with the thumbs grasping the band.
3. The sock is now placed just below the heel and removed in the same fashion as Steps 1 and 2.
4. Put the sock on the learner's foot just above the ankle. Have him remove it by using his thumbs to grasp the band at either side.
5. In the final step, the sock is placed on the learner's foot completely. Have the student remove it using the same thumb grasp procedure.

Removing Underwear and Trousers

Teaching an individual to remove underwear and trousers involves exactly the same reverse chain of tasks. Teach the student to remove his underwear first, following this instruction by substituting trousers for underwear.

1. Put the learner's underwear on one leg at the ankle. Have him grasp the bottom of the underwear and remove them.
2. Put the learner's underwear on both legs at the ankles. Have the learner remove the underwear one leg at a time by grasping them at the bottom. If the student does not have the ability to balance on one foot, have him remove the underwear while sitting down.
3. The underwear are now placed at the knees. The learner can pull them down by placing a thumb in either side of the waistband and rolling the underwear down and off.

4. With the underwear on the student's thighs, have him remove them using his thumbs as described in Step three above.
5. In the final step, the learner removes underwear that are on completely.

Removing T-shirts and Pullover Shirts or Dresses

1. Place the shirt, T-shirt, or dress on the learner's head with the opening at the hairline. Have him place his hands on either side of the neckband and pull the shirt off.
2. Put the shirt on the learner's head with the opening between the nose and mouth. Using the grasping technique cited in Step one above, have him remove the shirt.
3. The shirt should now be placed with the opening around the neck with the learner removing it as described previously.
4. In this step, the shirt should be placed around the neck with one arm completely on and one arm half on. The learner must be taught to pull the shirt off as indicated in Step three while straightening out his arms one at a time to get the shirt off completely.
5. Place the shirt on with both arms in but rolled up to the chest. Have the learner remove it.
6. Finally, the shirt is put on completely, and the student must roll it up under his arms and remove it as in the previous steps.

Removing Jackets and Sweaters

1. Place the jacket or sweater on one of the learner's arms at the elbow. Have her grasp the sleeve and pull the jacket off.
2. Place the jacket on one of the learner's shoulders and have her remove it by grasping the sleeve and pulling it off.
3. The jacket should be placed on one arm completely and at the elbow on the other arm. Have the learner grasp the sleeve of one arm behind her back and pull the jacket off. Then with the unclothed arm have her grasp the sleeve and pull the jacket off the other arm.
4. The jacket should be completely on. The learner removes it during this step in the chain.

Removing Shoes

During the initial training the instructor will teach the learner to remove shoes without ties or shoes with the laces already loosened. Sometime later in the training when the learner has learned the many facets and skills involved in dressing and undressing, the instructor will also teach him to untie laces and remove his shoes.

1. Place a slip-on shoe or shoes with the laces untied halfway on the learner's foot. Have her grasp the toe of the shoe and have her remove it.
2. Place the shoe on the learner's foot just below the heel. Have her remove it.
3. The shoe should then be placed on the learner's foot with the heel halfway out. Have her grasp the shoe and remove it.
4. With the shoe on all the way and the laces untied, the learner should be able to completely remove the shoe.

Unbuttoning

1. Place a garment on the learner with all buttons unbuttoned except for one that should have the top half of the button still in the buttonhole. Have the student use her thumb to push it the rest of the way out.
2. The button should have one small part of the button inserted in the hole. Using her thumb, the student should push the button through the hole.
3. In this step the learner is presented with a button that is buttoned completely. Have her place her thumbs and index fingers on the edge of the shirt and the button. Tip the button into the hole and through the hole.
4. Increase the number of buttons to be unbuttoned one at a time until the student can unbutton a coat or shirt.

Zipping and Unzipping

1. Place a garment on the individual zipped almost all the way to the top. Have him place his thumb and index finger on the tab and pull it up to his neck.
2. Have the garment three-fourths of the way zipped and have the student complete the task.
3. In this step the zipper should be zipped halfway. Once again have the learner grasp the tab and complete the zipping.
4. Insert the tab into the slot, and have the learner grasp the engaged zipper in one hand and complete the zipping.

To teach unzipping the instructor simply reverses the procedure above *starting* with the tab inserted into the slot. (A later section of this chapter presents the reverse chain sequence for teaching an individual to engage a zipper.)

DRESSING

In the dressing skill sequence, the steps are presented for the reverse chains for putting on socks, underwear, trousers, shirts, dresses, shoes, coats, buttoning, engaging a zipper, buckling, lacing, and tying shoe laces.

Putting on Socks

1. Place a sock on the learner's foot with the band above the ankle. Have her hook her thumbs on either side of the sock, place her index fingers on the outside, and pull the socks all the way up.
2. Place the sock on the foot with the band on the ankle. The learner then pulls the sock up.
3. Place the sock on the heel and have the participant pull it all the way up.
4. Place the sock just below the heel. This step may require a little extra practice as it is a bit more difficult to pull the sock up from this position.
5. Place the sock on at midfoot with the learner pulling it the rest of the way.
6. Place the sock on just over the learner's toes. Have her put it on all the way.
7. Hand the learner a sock that is rolled (band to toe), and have her put it on over her toes, roll it to her ankle, secure the heel properly, and pull it all the way up.
8. Have the learner roll the sock herself and repeat the sequence in Step 7.

Putting on Underwear and Trousers

Teaching the student to put on underwear and trousers involves exactly the same reverse chain of tasks. Teach the learner to put on his underwear first, following this instruction by substituting trousers for underwear. Initially use trousers with an elastic waistband and later move to those with snaps, buttons, or zippers as the student gains more confidence and becomes proficient at this skill. Some students may not progress beyond trousers with elastic waistbands.

For the learner with poor balance or poor motor control, instruction in putting on underwear and trousers should occur with the student sitting on the floor or on a small chair.

1. Place the underwear (or trousers) on the learner with the waistband resting on the pubic arch. Have him hook his thumbs in the waistband and pull them all the way up.
2. Place the underwear on the learner with the waistband at the thighs. Again have the learner employ the hooked thumb grasp to pull the underwear up to his waist.
3. With the underwear at the learner's knees, have him complete the task of pulling them up to his waist.
4. In this step the underwear should be placed over the ankles.
5. Now place the underwear on one ankle only. This step will require that the learner grasp the waistband, insert his leg through the hole, and pull the underwear all the way up.

6. In the final step the learner is required to put on his own underwear unassisted. Again if balance or motor control is a problem, have the learner complete this step sitting down.

Putting on T-shirts, Pullover Shirts, and Pullover Dresses

1. Put a T-shirt on the learner with both arms through the sleeves and rolled up to the chest. Have the student grip the shirt on either side and pull it the rest of the way down.
2. Put the T-shirt on the student with one arm completely through the sleeve and one arm halfway through the other sleeve. Have him complete the movement necessary to pull the shirt on all the way.
3. With the shirt on one arm only, the student must be taught to put his arm through the other sleeve and complete the movement sequence.
4. In this step the shirt should be at the neckline without either arm in the sleeves. At this point some fairly difficult or awkward motor movements must be executed. It may take a great deal of practice before the learner is capable of progressing beyond this step in the sequence. The learner must be taught to put one arm through the sleeves at a time and then pull the shirt down.
5. Now the shirt should be placed with the opening between the learner's nose and mouth. Have him pull the shirt down over his head and complete the sequence in Step 4.
6. In this step the neckline of the shirt should be at the student's hairline. Then the learner completes the movement.
7. Finally, the learner is handed a shirt and he must complete the movement independently.

Putting on Shoes

1. Put a slip-on shoe on the learner's foot with the heel halfway in. Tell or demonstrate to the learner the pushing movement required to put the shoe on all the way.
2. In this step of the chain, the student is required to put the shoe on when her heel is out all the way. At this point it is wise to teach the learner to use a shoe horn. Many children and mentally retarded individuals will force their feet into shoes, thus bending and gradually "breaking" the back of the shoe. The use of the horn will prevent this from occurring. Also if it is taught as a part of the sequence, it will not have to be introduced later as a new skill. So, place the horn in the learner's hand, have her insert it against the back of the shoe, and slide her heel down the horn into the shoe while she slides the horn up and out. Don't become frustrated even though this step will probably take a great deal of practice and time to teach.

3. Place the shoe at the learner's midfoot. Again use the horn and have the learner slide her foot into the shoe.
4. Place the shoe on the learner's foot with the toes all the way in. The learner should be able to slide her foot nearly all the way before she places the shoe horn in and completes the movement.
5. Now present the learner with the shoe on the floor in front of the appropriate foot (if using a tie shoe, hold the tongue back) and have the student put the shoe on correctly.
6. The learner must be taught which shoe goes on which foot. It may be necessary to use a few stimulus clues to teach right and left such as taping a piece of red tape to the toe of the right foot and inside the right shoe. Continue using this prompt until the learner is fully able to put her shoes on and gradually remove the prompt when the learner is able to do this independently.
7. Simply present the learner with a pair of shoes. She will be required to put the shoes on the correct feet (without tying), appropriately using the shoe horn.

Putting on a Coat or Sweater

1. Put a coat on the learner with one arm completely in the jacket sleeve and the other in up to the elbow. Have the learner straighten out his arm and slide it through the sleeve.
2. Put the coat on the student with one arm through the sleeve and the other arm at the shoulder. Have the learner complete the movement necessary to put his arm through the sleeve.
3. Put the coat on the learner with one arm through the sleeve. Teach him to reach around behind his back, locate the sleeve opening, and slide his arm through the sleeve.
4. In this step the coat should be placed on the learner's one arm up to the elbow. He should grasp the coat in his opposite hand, pull it up to the shoulder, and then follow the sequence acquired in Step three above.
5. Present the learner with the coat. He should grasp the collar of the coat with his left hand and slip his right arm into the sleeve and pull the coat up to the shoulder. The rest of the sequence already acquired may be followed to complete putting on a coat independently.

Hart (1974) noted that children often put a coat on backwards or upside down. This problem can be overcome by standing behind the child, placing the coat front up, bottom facing you on the table. Take the child's left hand in your left hand as he faces the coat. Grasp the right side of the coat at shoulder level with his left hand and place his right arm into the right sleeve. Now take the right hand and grasp the left side of the coat, placing the left arm in the left sleeve. The coat may now be adjusted at the shoulder by having the learner pull on it at the shoulders.

Of course, the instructor should then proceed to teach the learner the independent method of putting on the coat.

Buttoning

1. Place a garment on the student with all the buttons buttoned except for the top one which should have half of the button (on the vertical plane) through the hole. (Oversize buttons may be used and gradually reduced in size down to the "normal" size for coats or shirts.) With the thumb underneath and the index finger on top the learner should push the button through the hole. The button is then pulled through with the thumb and index finger of the opposite hand.
2. The button is placed with the tip touching the buttonhole. Using the finger placement procedure described in Step 1, the student should complete buttoning the button.
3. The learner now must independently button the top button of the garment.
4. Increase the number of buttons to be buttoned one at a time until the student can button all the buttons on a coat or shirt.

Engaging a Zipper

The section of this chapter that described the reverse chain sequence for zipping and unzipping did not discuss the actual engaging of the zipper as this is a higher level and more complex motor task. When students reach the level where they have mastered all of the sequences previously described, they are probably ready to learn how to engage a zipper.

1. With the slide engaged into the tab, the student holds the bottom of the jacket and slides the zipper up with her other hand.
2. The student has a jacket on with the slide engaged in the tab halfway. She holds the bottom of the jacket and slides the zipper up.
3. In this step the slide is not engaged in the tab, but both parts are lined up closely by the teacher. The learner must grasp the slide in one hand and the tab in the other, insert the slide into the tab (making sure the bottoms are even), grasp the tab and the bottom of the coat, and slide the tab up.
4. In the final step, the learner should put the garment on (learned earlier in the sequence) and engage the zipper independently by sliding the slide into the tab and pulling it to the top.

Unbuckling and Buckling a Belt

The reverse chain for buckling a belt is presented here. When teaching the student to unbuckle, simply reverse the sequence presented here.

1. The learner has a belt on with the end halfway through the loop. Have him grasp the end of the belt with his fingers and pull the belt all the way through the loop.
2. Next, the belt should be in the peg but just at the beginning of the loop. The learner must slide the belt end under the loop and pull it through all the way.
3. The belt should now be placed with the peg halfway through the belt. The learner must push the peg the rest of the way through the belt and continue with the sequence described in Step 2.
4. In this step, the learner must insert the peg into the belt by himself and then complete the sequence.
5. At this stage the belt end is partially inserted in the buckle. The student must grasp the buckle and slide the belt end into and through the buckle completing the sequence as described.
6. With the buckle in one hand and the end of the belt in the other, the learner must engage the buckle and the belt and complete the sequence described earlier.

Lacing Shoes

When teaching the student to lace shoes, Hart (1974) recommends tying two laces of different colors together to make a long lace so that the learner can really see the alternate use of the laces.

1. The learner's shoe should be laced almost to the top with the ends of the two-colored laces halfway through the last eyelet. The learner should grasp the ends of the laces in each hand and pull them tight.
2. In this step, only the plastic tip of the lace end should be engaged in the last eyelet. The learner must grasp the plastic tip and pull the lace ends until they are taut.
3. All the eyelets should be filled except the top right one. The learner should grasp the end of the lace and push the plastic tip through the eyelet, making sure it is pulled completely through the opening.
4. In this step, both top eyelets should be empty. The learner must fill one eyelet first and then cross the lace and fill the final eyelet.
5. Repeat the sequence described above, dropping down one row of eyelets at a time, alternating the holes. The learner must understand and should be able to determine visually that the laces must be crossed as the holes are filled.

6. When you reach the bottom pair of eyelets, teach the learner to lace them from the inside out so that subsequent lacing will be from the outside in all the way to the top. Additionally, teach her to pull the laces completely through the bottom holes so that the two lengths are even.

Tying Shoe Laces

Hart (1974) indicated that learners must have good hand and finger control before they will be capable of tying their shoes. Thus it is not wise to try to teach the last dressing task usually learned until the learner can use his fingers well enough to learn the task.

1. The learner is presented with his shoes on his feet and both loops of laces engaged. The learner simply has to grasp the ends of the loops and pull them taut.
2. The learner releases the grasp on the left loop, grasps the new loop that has been pushed through the hole and pulls the loops taut.
3. The learner now pushes the right lace through and under the left lace loop with his right index finger, grasps the loops, and pulls them taut.
4. In this step the learner brings the right lace all the way around the left loop, pushes under the left loop with his right finger, grasps the loops, and pulls them taut.
5. The learner brings the lace end to the middle of the lace forming the left loop, brings the right lace all the way around the left loop, pushes under the left loop with the right finger, grasps, and pulls them taut.
6. The student crosses the right lace over the left lace, tucking the top under the bottom lace, and pulls it taut to form a knot. Then he brings the lace end to the middle of the lace forming the left loop, brings the right lace around the left loop, pushes it under with the right finger, grasps and pulls them taut. (This sequence was adapted directly from Fredericks, Riggs, Furey, Grove, Moore, McDonnell, Jordan, Hanson, Baldwin, & Wadlow, 1976, p. 42.)

SUMMARY

The ability to care for one's own needs in the self-care area is certainly fundamental in achieving self-sufficiency and independence. In this chapter, the authors have presented detailed task analyses of the skills involved in toileting, dressing, and feeding. These task analyses not only serve as examples of the technique, but can also be used as a framework for preparing detailed instructional objectives for I.E.P.'s and lesson plans.

The areas presented in this chapter are directly related to success in school or sheltered settings. If severely retarded persons are to become better assimilated into society, then they must demonstrate better self-help skills. It may be necessary to spend more time on these skills than any others, but the potential payoff is great if the possibility of successful integration into society is increased.

REFERENCES

Foxx, R.M., & Azrin, N.H. *Toilet training the retarded*. Champaign, Illionis: Research Press, 1973.

Fredericks, H.D., Riggs, C., Furey, T., Grove, D., Moore, W., McDonnell, J., Jordan, E., Hanson, W., Baldwin, V., & Wadlow, M. *The teaching research curriculum for moderately and severely handicapped*. Springfield, Illinois: Charles C. Thomas, 1976.

Hart, V. *Beginning with the handicapped*. Springfield, Illinois: Charles C. Thomas, 1974.

Wabash guide to early developmental training. Boston: Allyn & Bacon, 1977.

Chapter 7

Social Skills Training

Inadequate social skills are among the factors preventing full integration of the severely mentally retarded into the mainstream of school and society.

In dealing with social skills, emphasis will be placed upon using amenities and displaying good manners as well as appropriate sexual behavior. A distinction (arbitrary and perhaps one in which disagreement could be raised) is made between social development and personality development; these need to be separated because certain social skill items relate closely, and more appropriately, to self-help items. Personality development, including self-concept, appropriate play, and the development of good interpersonal relationships will be discussed in Chapter 8.

BASIC SKILL AREAS FOR SOCIAL SKILLS TRAINING

Professionals may vary in their opinion as to the list of possible basic skills one must possess to be considered to have adequate social skills. Regardless, most nonretarded learners acquire this repertoire of basic social skills in the course of normal childhood development or through early preschool or school experiences. Because of severely limited intellectual abilities, the mentally retarded fail to acquire these basic social skills in the same manner as their nonretarded peers. Beleaguered parents often throw up their hands in frustration when they cannot teach their severely retarded child these skills. This frustration leads to having the parent do the act for the child, thus fostering further dependency and social inadequacy.

The learner's level of functioning in this important area can be assessed by employing selected sections of the adaptive behavior instruments described in Chapter 2 or other measures designed to determine behavior in these areas. The following list of basic social skills needed by severely retarded persons to function more adequately in societal situations could also be used to assess the learner's functional level. This list (Table 7-1) presents and defines basic skills and concepts in social skills areas including:

- hygiene/grooming
- manners
- physical appearance and care of belongings
- sex education

Table 7-1 Basic Skill Areas for Social Skills Training

Skill Area: Grooming/Hygiene	Definition
1. Washing hands	ability to independently wash and dry hands including: a. turn on water b. wet hands c. lather hands d. rinse hands e. dry hands
2. Brushing teeth	ability to independently brush teeth including: a. put paste on brush b. brush teeth up and down and back and forth c. rinse mouth
3. Washing face	ability to wash face independently including: a. wetting b. lathering c. rinsing d. drying
4. Nasal hygiene	demonstrates ability to keep nose clean and free of mucous including: a. use of tissue b. blowing properly c. disposing of tissue
5. Bathing and showering	demonstrates ability to shower or bathe independently including: a. wetting b. lathering c. rinsing d. drying e. applying deodorant
6. Shampooing hair	ability to independently wash hair including: a. wetting b. lathering c. rinsing d. repeating b and c e. drying
7. Combing the hair	ability to use a comb (or brush) to independently comb the hair into place

Table 7-1 continued

Skill Area: Grooming/Hygiene	Definition
8. Shaving	ability to use an electric razor independently including: a. lubricating face (armpit, leg) b. applying electric razor c. cleaning razor
9. Feminine hygiene	ability to use a feminine napkin or tampon properly and independently

Skill Area: Manners	Definition
1. Amenities	learner properly uses (signs or vocalizes) amenities in a variety of situations including: a. please b. thank you c. excuse me d. I'm sorry e. may I f. hello g. goodbye

Skill Area: Physical Appearance/ Care of Belongings	Definition
1. General appearance	the way an individual presents himself to others by dressing appropriately for an occasion, weather conditions and so on
2. Care of belongings	the learner demonstrates the ability to fold clothes and hand clothing on hangers
3. Posture	the learner can stand erectly and walk with a normal gait

Skill Area: Sex Education	Definition
1. Biological aspects	the learner knows the differences between males and females
2. Social aspects	overt sexual behaviors do not occur in public places
3. Health aspects	the learner demonstrates appropriate hygiene practices regarding the genitals

TEACHING GROOMING AND HYGIENE

Proper grooming and hygiene are essential skill areas for the severely retarded learner to master. Because of difficulties in other skill areas such as toileting or eating, the severely retarded person tends to be messy from spilled food or have body odor from the smell of dirty diapers. Thus, teaching the individual to independently maintain his person will not only aid in successful integration, but will also allow teachers and/or child care workers to concentrate their interaction on teaching other skill areas.

Washing Hands

Begin by teaching the individual to wash his hands. It is often recommended that this skill be taught as an extension of toileting so that the participant learns to toilet, wipe, flush the toilet, and wash and dry his hands. Thus toileting becomes a complete act.

The instructor's knowledge of the student will determine where in the sequence of skills to begin. If the learner will enter the bathroom area and approach the sink readily, the instructor may begin by teaching him to turn on the water. If the student will not approach the bathroom, the instructor will have to shape his behavior. (See section on toilet training.)

1. Have the student put his hand on the cold water handle (the L-shaped lever is the ideal faucet handle for initial training) and turn it on about one-quarter of the way.
2. Now the student should turn the hot water faucet on approximately one-quarter of the way. The temperature of the water should be "tested" to insure that it is warm but not hot.
3. In this step the student should place both hands under the water and get them wet.
4. Have the student take a bar of soap in one hand and rub it back and forth in his hands until he has raised sufficient lather. The soap should be replaced in the soap tray.
5. The student should rub his hands together making sure he washes both the palms and the back of the hands.
6. Introduce the use of the fingernail brush at this step in the sequence. Demonstrate to the learner the proper method of using the brush: the hands should be palms up with the fingers bent; the nails should be facing up; with the brush in the other hand, the learner should scrub under the nails with a back and forth motion. Replace brush on tray or sink top.
7. Both hands should be placed under the tap and rinsed. Be sure the learner rinses the backs and palms, under his nails, and between his fingers.

8. Once the rinsing is completed, the water is turned off. The learner should reach for a towel or paper towel and wipe his hands in a back and forth motion. If the learner is using a paper towel, proper disposal should be taught during this step in the sequence. If a cloth towel is used, it should be folded over a towel bar so that it will dry thoroughly.

Incidentally, the learner should be taught to tidy up the bathroom sink area after he uses it. This should include wiping spilled water from the sink top so that the sink area is left in the same good condition as when you began the instruction.

Brushing Teeth

1. Begin by having the learner twist the cap off the toothpaste tube and putting it where it will not be lost.
2. The learner should pick up the brush in her preferred hand, turn on the cold water, and wet the bristles of the brush.
3. With the brush in the preferred hand the learner should pick up the paste and squeeze (from the bottom) enough paste out to cover the bristles.
4. The brush should be inserted in the mouth and the learner should begin with her molars. The sides of the teeth and the top surface should be brushed in an up and down and back and forth motion, making certain that the crevices between the teeth are brushed. The movement should be continued until all tooth surfaces have been brushed.
5. The learner should expectorate the toothpaste into the basin, reach for a paper cup, fill it with cold water, and rinse her mouth completely.
6. The learner should rinse her brush off and return it to the brush holder, wipe her mouth, dispose of the cup, and turn off the water.
7. The student should get the cap and return it to the tube properly. The sink area should be cleaned off thoroughly.

Of course, it will probably be necessary to break the above sequence down into a number of small steps to teach it to a severely retarded learner. In fact it is likely that a task analysis of this skill would yield up to thirty small steps to be mastered before a learner can be expected to brush her teeth independently.

Washing the Face

1. Begin by having the learner turn on the water and regulate the temperature as described in the hand washing sequence.
2. The learner should take a washcloth and wet it with water.
3. With the washcloth in one hand, the learner should take a bar of soap, wet it, lather the cloth, and return the bar to the soap dish.

4. With the cloth open and across both hands, the student should lower his face towards the basin and begin to scrub the facial area in the following order: forehead, cheeks, chin, next to and across nose, behind ears, and under the neck.
5. The student should rinse the soap from the washcloth and with it still wet, rinse his face in the order listed above making sure all soap is removed.
6. The learner should turn off the water, pick up a towel, and wipe his face and hands thoroughly.
7. The student should hang the towel and wash cloth on a towel bar so that they dry properly.
8. The sink area should be cleaned thoroughly.

Nose Care

Many severely retarded individuals will constantly have "runny noses" due to upper respiratory problems and infections. Proper nose care is essential to having the severely retarded person become more acceptable to others.

1. Have the learner open a facial tissue.
2. Place the tissue over the nose in a tentlike fashion bringing the index and middle fingers of each hand over the tissue and the sides of the nose. The learner should not squeeze the nostrils tightly or cleaning will be difficult.
3. First teach the student to wipe the nose gently.
4. In the next step, the learner should be taught to blow her nose by breathing through the nostrils in an exaggerated fashion. Make sure the learner does not blow too hard or close her nostrils too much as this can force mucus into the eustachian tube and cause an infection of the inner ear. The wiping motion learned in Step 3 above should be applied simultaneously as the learner blows her nose.
5. The student should be taught immediate and proper disposal of used tissue.
6. It is also a good idea to teach the learner to cover her mouth and nose with a facial tissue when she coughs or sneezes.

Bathing and Showering

1. The learner should be taught to first turn on the water from a position outside the tub area and adjust the water temperature.
2. The learner should undress or remove a bathrobe, step into the tub carefully using either a hand rail or the side of the tub for support. It may also be a good idea to put nonskid decals on the bottom of the tub to prevent slipping accidents.

3. If the learner is bathing, he should sit and wet his entire body; if he is showering, he should stand and turn around until his body is wet.

4. The student should take the washcloth, open it, and wet it as he did for face washing. After securing the bar of soap, the learner should fully lather the cloth and return the bar to the soap holder.

5. The learner should begin by washing his face and neck area, rinsing the soap off the wash cloth, wetting the cloth, and rinsing his face and neck. Repeat Step 4.

6. The learner should wash his arms, arm pits, and upper torso. The rinsing sequence taught in Step 5 should be repeated. Repeat Step 4.

7. In this step, the learner should wash his legs, groin, genitals, anus, and feet. The learner should repeat the rinsing sequence described in Step 5.

8. If the learner is showering, the water should be turned off (either hot first or both faucets simultaneously) and the wash cloth rinsed, rung out, and hung over the towel bar. If the student is bathing, he should release the water from the tub, allowing it to drain while he dries off.

9. The student should step out of the tub onto a bath mat, take his bath towel, unfold it, and begin to dry his body in the following order:
    a. face and neck area
    b. arms, arm pits, and upper torso
    c. legs, groin, genitals, anus, and feet.

10. The towel and bath mat should be folded and hung over the towel bar to dry.

11. The student should be taught to rinse out the tub after the water has drained so that the bathroom area is left in an orderly condition.

12. It is highly recommended that the use of underarm deodorant (body talcum, foot powder, and lotions, would be optional and up to the teacher, parent, or child care worker) be taught as part of the bathing sequence. In this way it is part of the complete act, and the use of deodorant will become a daily routine. Depending upon preference, sticks, roll-ons, or sprays may be used. Make sure the learner uses it appropriately and covers the entire area.

Washing the Hair

Teaching the student to wash her hair can be taught as a follow-up skill sequence to showering once showering has been completely mastered. This sequence involves teaching the learner to carry her unbreakable bottle of shampoo to the tub area when she needs to wash her hair.

1. After the student has completed Step 7 of the showering/bathing sequence, have her bend over and thoroughly wet her hair.

2. The learner should remove the cap from the shampoo and pour a small quantity into her palm. The bottle of shampoo should be returned to the bathtub shelf or ledge.
3. The shampoo should be worked into the hair and scalp until a good lather is raised. Teach the student to use her fingertips to work the lather in thoroughly. The movement sequence should be the front of the hair, the crown, the back, and finally, the sides.
4. After completing Step 3, the student should rinse all the soap lather from her hair, face, and neck.
5. Repeat Step 2 only have the learner put the cap back on the bottle.
6. Repeat Step 3.
7. Repeat Step 4.
8. Have the learner initiate the sequence beginning with Step 9 of bathing/showering. The learner should dry her hair by rubbing it briskly with the bath towel.

Combing the Hair

Combing the hair can be taught earlier as a self-care skill or it may be taught once the learner masters washing his hair independently. If it is taught after washing, make sure the student's hair is almost dry.

1. The learner should stand in front of a mirror. With the comb in his preferred hand, the learner should comb his hair forward with a number of strokes.
2. If the learner wears a part, this should be marked with the comb.
3. The comb should be placed in the part and the learner should comb down, away from the part.
4. With the comb back in the part the learner should comb toward the other side of the part.
5. The learner should comb the back of his hair down.
6. The other side (opposite from the part) should be combed down.
7. Finally, the learner should comb the front of his hair to the side (usually it is away from the part).

Shaving

While you may wish to teach the student to use a safety razor to shave, we recommend the use of an electric razor for both males and females. There are a number of reasons for this, but the major one is safety. The electric razor eliminates the nicks and cuts an individual is likely to get from a safety razor, and it eliminates the need to handle used and new razor blades.

1. Begin by having the learner apply a good commercial pre-razor solution to lubricate the face (armpit or leg) and soften the beard.
2. The learner should plug the razor in, turn it on, and place it under his sideburn. Using an up and down motion, the learner should continue until the hair has been removed and the skin is smooth.
3. The action taught in Step 2 should be continued on the other cheek and the neck. Particular care is needed under the nose and around the chin as the contours of the face may make getting a clean shave a problem.
4. Once the learner has completed shaving, the razor should be turned off and unplugged. Depending on the brand of electric razor chosen, some maintenance will be required. Teach the student to clean the hair from the razor head employing the manufacturer's recommendations.
5. The razor should be put away before the student rinses his face. This will insure that no accidents will occur involving electrical shock. Once the razor has been stored away, the learner should rinse his face employing the sequence learned earlier.
6. The application of after shave lotion may be taught as part of the shaving sequence. In this way it becomes part of the action, and the use of shaving lotion completes the act.

Feminine Hygiene

Preparation for feminine hygiene ideally begins prior to the young girl's first menstruation. This preparation should be done by the child's mother; but for those children who are institutionalized, it will be necessary for a teacher or the nurse to do the instruction. The sequence of activities to teach the female learner about menstruation is adapted from Bender and Valletutti (1976, pp. 200-202).

1. For the female student who has not yet begun to menstruate, prepare her for its eventuality by showing her a film on menstruation, showing her pictures, reading about, or demonstrating with a mannikin or science model. Communicate to the learner that when menstruation begins, it is something to feel good about because it means that she is growing up and becoming a woman. Assure her that there is nothing to be afraid of and that it happens to all women.
2. Communicate to the student that the menstrual flow is blood that is meant to be lost and is not like bleeding after being cut or injured.
3. Write to companies that sell feminine hygiene products, and ask them for any brochures, films, or educational materials on menstruation (e.g., Kimberly-Clark Corporation). Show these materials to and use with the learner.

4. Show the student various types of sanitary napkins.

5. Demonstrate the purpose of the sanitary napkin or pad. Show her that the sanitary napkin or pad can be used to absorb the blood from a woman's vagina. Show her how it absorbs the blood so that it will not stain the woman's underwear or clothing.

6. Practice putting on a sanitary napkin. Use the kind of sanitary napkin that sticks to the panties since it is the easiest to handle and requires no belt. Show her how to determine which is the sticky side by feeling both sides with her fingers, and assist her in sticking the sticky side to her panties. Show the student how to wrap up the used sanitary napkin and dispose of it.

7. Show the girl a sanitary belt and explain its use. Demonstrate how the tabs of ordinary napkins fit through the plastic or metal fasteners on the sanitary belt. Be sure the longer fastener is in the back of the body and the shorter fastener is in front.

8. Have the student practice using a sanitary napkin and belt and a self-sticking napkin.

9. Assist the student in identifying signs that menstruation is beginning. Help her put on a napkin.

10. Show the learner a tampon. Take the directions provided by the manufacturer and develop a sequence to teach the student how to insert, remove, and dispose of the tampon. The parent, nurse, teacher, and, when possible, the student herself should choose the method most appropriate to the needs and abilities of the student. Whether the student uses a napkin, a belt or a tampon should depend on menstrual flow and the individual's ability to use each device.

11. Tell the student she should tell an appropriate person (mother, teacher, or responsible adult) when she has begun to menstruate. Praise the student if she tells you she is beginning to menstruate and has taken appropriate precautions.

12. Put the student on a napkin or tampon changing schedule, perhaps every other time she goes to the bathroom to void. In the early stages, check to see if this is being done.

13. Tell the student she should dispose of used sanitary napkins or tampons by rolling up the soiled napkin (soiled side inside) or tampon and wrapping it in toilet paper, a paper towel, or a small paper bag, and discarding it in the proper receptacle. When the student is having her period, check to see that she is disposing of sanitary napkins or tampons properly. Remind the student not to flush them down the toilet.

14. Communicate to the student the need to be prepared by keeping a napkin or tampon with her at all times. Check at regular intervals to see that the student has one in her handbag.

15. Tell the student that she should not announce her period or discuss it with everyone. Help her to select someone with whom she should discuss it in case she needs help and for record keeping purposes.
16. Stress the importance of cleanliness during menstruation. The student should wash, bathe, or shower daily because of the added glandular activity.
17. Tell the student who menstruates to notify her parents, guardians, or other responsible adult if she has not had her period during the time she expected it.

Once the student masters the skill sequences in the grooming area and can perform the actions independently, it is essential that instruction focus on the "when" of bathing or shaving. For the learner to be completely independent, he must be taught that it is necessary to bathe daily or brush his teeth in the morning, after meals, and before bedtime. A procedure that routinizes these skills so that they are virtually programmed into the student's daily activities is recommended. Also, while a learner may bathe in the morning, further activities that day that would lead him to perspire or become dirty would necessitate another shower or bath. If possible, this should be taught to the learner. Many individuals may not be capable of benefiting from this instruction, so the instructors' knowledge of the learners will determine how much of the "when" they teach the learners.

OTHER SOCIAL SKILL DEVELOPMENT

The development of the other social skills begins at a very early age and continues throughout life. This training area for the severely retarded will include manners, sex education, physical appearance, and care of personal belongings.

Social development training should not be considered as a separate curricular area. It should be woven into the general instruction of self-help, communication, physical education, and leisure-time skills. The time for teaching social skills is quite flexible; however, the most appropriate points can be determined by examining the instructional objectives for each child. As students reach various levels of maturity, new social skills can be introduced. Manners are a skill area that can be taught at an early age once the physical skills of eating have been mastered. Included are the general courtesies of greeting, sharing, and awaiting one's turn. Physical appearance training is also important and should include selecting appropriate dress or understanding what to wear in various situations, an awareness of body cleanliness and proper facial expressions, and care of personal belongings.

Sex education is generally not covered with normal children in the public school curriculum. For the severely retarded, sex education is an important instructional area. The severely retarded must be taught to understand their own bodily functions, feelings, and how to deal with them. Sex education can be treated as a separate area with a special time period set aside for its instruction, or it can be integrated with dressing, hygiene, and self-help skills training.

Manners

Many interpersonal skills would be highly desirable for the severely retarded yet their intellectual and verbal limitations restrict items others take for granted. Despite their obvious shortcomings, the overall goal for this area should be for the person to function at the highest level possible relative to social and interpersonal situations. It seems that the more appropriate a student's interactions and behaviors are, the more acceptable that person will be. Due to this human behavioral trait, the student who can interact at even a minimal level will be happier and feel a part of the group.

Fundamental Amenities

please	may I
thank you	hello
excuse me	goodbye
I'm sorry	

Activities

1. The social amenities vocabulary can be taught to verbal or nonverbal students. The instructor should model the correct response such as "thank you" or "please" during all conversations and situations where appropriate. When the student hands the instructor an object, the response should be a pleasant "thank you."
2. Role playing and creating situations that demand amenities help the student understand appropriate usage. Whenever someone enters the room, select students should be assigned as greeters. Total class time should be taken to act out the appropriate response such as "hello" and a hand shake. Create in-class situations whereby the teacher and child exchange objects saying "thank you." Set up a simple obstacle course and design situations where students say "excuse me," "I'm sorry," and "thank you," and await their turn.
3. Field trips offer the best exposure to proper usage of amenities. Elevators, shopping centers, and entering and exiting public transportation offer excellent training situations for "excuse me" and "thank you."

PHYSICAL APPEARANCE AND PERSONAL CARE OF BELONGINGS

Physical appearance is extremely critical to an individual's social interaction and acceptance. The student should be taught to dress appropriately and take care of his physical appearance and personal belongings once the mechanical actions of dressing and grooming are mastered. The following activities provide instructional situations for teaching understanding and knowledge in this area.

General Appearance

1. After dressing a mannikin, tell the student how good it looks. Talk about each clothing item. Next point out other students in the class who are dressed properly. Finally, discuss what the student is wearing.
2. Dress a mannikin according to the weather outside telling the student that this is "what you wear when it's ——— outside."
3. Show students what they should wear out of doors. Have students choose from several items what they would wear to go outside, swimming, or to bed. Encourage students to make a choice between two obviously opposing garments and reinforce the correct choice with edibles and secondary reinforcers. Build up the decision-making skill by expanding the selection to more than two garments, requiring finer discriminations.
4. Have students match garments with the part of the body on which they are worn. Require students to point to their body parts as you show the garment and say its name. Put the garment on the student and continually verbalize its name and where it is worn. Begin with these items and progress as each is accomplished:

   a. coat   f. socks
   b. dress   g. shorts (underwear)
   c. pants   h. panties
   d. shirt   i. pajamas
   e. shoes   j. skirt

5. Have students identify garments as you name them. Begin with the actual clothing and progress to pictures as the task is mastered.
6. Match clothing items such as shoes and socks, undershirt and shorts, coat and hat, pajamas and slippers. Teach their association by reinforcing the student's choice of matching pairs.
7. Matching garment size and color can be taught through reinforcement techniques. First, teach the student to match colors and sizes, then progress to matching socks by color and secondly, by size.

Facial Appearance and Posture

So often a handicapped individual calls undue attention to herself because of an unusual facial expression, posture, or gait. Students can learn to ameliorate their cosmetic problems through these activities:

1. Using a mirror, show the student the correct appearance, or point out the problem to her such as drool on the face or a dirty nose. Reward wiping the nose or mouth with primary reinforcers (edibles, patting on the back or praise). Reinforce holding the mouth closed and work on keeping the tongue in the mouth. Be careful that the attention you give to these concerns does not reinforce the undesirable behavior. Reinforcement must be given only for the desired behavior.
2. Have students imitate your facial expressions and build up the amount of time the student maintains the act using an intermittent reinforcement schedule.
3. Apply gelatin about the nose and lips and instruct the student to wipe it off. Apply the gelatin substance with enough force that the student can feel its presence. Using a mirror, have the child touch the substance and then remove it.
4. Warm melted wax can be applied to the facial areas and allowed to dry. Show students what it looks like in the mirror and assist them in wiping it off. Eliminate the mirror and practice locating the wax using only the skin receptors.
5. Stepping correctly is a skill some students must be taught. To eliminate a shuffle gait, students can be forced to lift their feet by walking through snap rings or prone ladders. Contingencies should be used to eliminate hunched shoulders and drooping heads. Full body mirrors allow the student to see himself as the instructor positions the body parts.

Care of Personal Belongings

Students can be taught to fold, hang clothes, and place their shoes next to the bed or in the closet. For a select few, shoe shining is also a teachable skill. Following are the sequential teaching instructions for handling clothing. Of course, instruction in dressing and undressing and hooking a coat hanger on a closet rail are prerequisites.

Placing Pants on a Hanger

There are several ways that pants can be manipulated when putting them on a hanger. This is only one method.

1. If the pants are on the floor, the individual begins by picking them up with one or both hands. He should bring them to his lap (if in a wheelchair) or lay them on a couch, bed, or table.
2. The pants are then moved to a position so that the seat and back of the pant legs are laying across the front of the individual (in the same position as laying a child on his side across your knees for a spanking).
3. Next, the bottom leg is arranged to lay flat without any twists.
4. Proceed to straightening the top leg, removing all twists.
5. Align the pant legs until they are flush at the edges with the inseams touching.
6. Pick up the coat hanger with one hand, holding it near its neck.
7. Grasp both pant cuffs at the front of the leg and squeeze them together lightly.
8. Next, lift the pant cuffs, which are being squeezed together, slightly (3-4 inches is ample).
9. Align the opening on the coat hanger with the pant cuffs.
10. Slide the opening of the coat hanger over the pant cuffs until it stops against the other hand and wrist holding the pant cuffs.
11. Holding the coat hanger firmly at the neck, release the pant cuffs with the other hand.
12. Slide the coat hanger to the center of the pants.
13. Lift the pants with one or both hands.

Shining Shoes

This rather extensive task analysis of shining shoes is presented, not because this is the most crucial social skill, but rather to show that even this skill requires many steps for mastery by the student.

Prerequisites to shining shoes include spreading newspaper, holding a shoe, wiping objects with a cloth, opening shoe polish containers, applying a substance to a rag or brush, and applying that substance to another object. The materials needed for instruction are a newspaper, polish, applicator, and brush. The following is the sequence for polishing shoes:

1. The student spreads several pieces of newspaper on the table or floor in front of herself.
2. Both shoes are placed on the newspaper.
3. The shoe polish container is opened and placed on the newspaper.
4. The polish applicator brush is picked up with the right hand (if right handed).
5. The polish container is held securely against the floor with the remaining hand.

6. Polish is applied to the brush.
7. The polish container is released and the same hand is slid into one of the shoes.
8. Holding the shoe against the newspaper, the student applies polish to the shoe on all sides.
9. The student places the shoe at the top of the newspaper at a point farthest away from her and removes her hand.
10. The polish container is again held securely as more polish is applied.
11. The container is released, and the same hand is slid into the remaining shoe.
12. Holding the shoe against the newspaper, the student applies polish to the shoe on all sides.
13. The hand is slid from the inside of the shoe.
14. The student slips her free hand inside the shoe first completed (at the top of the newspaper) holding it to the newspaper.
15. The applicator brush is placed on the newspaper.
16. The free hand picks up the buffing rag or brush.
17. The shoe is brushed.
18. The hand is removed from the shoe and placed inside the remaining one.
19. Holding the shoe securely to the newspaper, the student brushes it as in Step 17.
20. The hand is removed from the shoe.
21. The buffing rag or brush is placed in the shoe shine kit.
22. The polish applicator is placed in the shoe shine kit.
23. The polish container is closed and placed into the kit.
24. The shoes are placed to one side of the newspaper.
25. The newspaper is wadded or folded and placed in the trash can.
26. The shoe shine kit is put in its storage place.

A number of clothing care sequences can be taught to the severely retarded. Several examples have been provided to illustrate the requisite skills required prior to teaching each task and the extremely involved nature of the tasks that people take for granted.

Sex Education

Sex education is a critical instructional area for mentally retarded persons. However, because sex education is a particularly controversial subject, parents and school officials should meet prior to any instruction to come to agreement on what content, if any, in sex education will be taught in the public school. There are many reasons why the retarded need sex education, and the reasons may be used to persuade parents to agree to and cooperate in sex education instruction.

Bass (1972) presents a rationale for providing sex education to the mentally retarded. Her reasons for sex education instruction include:

- As a group, the mentally retarded are more confused about their identities, self-images, and sexual roles.
- Ignorance of acceptable social behavior and lack of social skills causes problems in relating to others.
- Lack of judgment and inner control often lead to impulsive sexual behavior.
- Because the severely retarded have few outlets and interests, they are likely to be confused about impulses and feelings they do not understand.
- The mentally retarded are quite prone to expressing their affection for others through physical contact because of a lack of verbal abilities.

In addition, the following reasons should be considered:

1. The retarded tend to lack the ability to discriminate between activities best conducted in public and those that must be done in private.
2. Overt sexual behaviors of retarded adults make integration into school and society difficult because the behaviors raise the fears of parents and community members regarding rape, molestation of children, and so on.
3. "Normalcy" requires certain heterosexual relationships to be conducted in a proper manner. Instruction in this area is necessary for most retarded people.

The scope of a sex education program for severely retarded persons would include instruction in three major areas:

1. *Biological*—the names of the sex organs, the anatomical differences between males and females, and the act of sexual intercourse. Intercourse should be discussed only when parents consent to it and the intellectual, social, and emotional level of the student would make this instruction necessary.
2. *Social*—basic instruction in the elimination of overt sexual behaviors including fondling, kissing, hugging, and exhibitionism; the need to conduct sexual practices like masturbation in private; the practice of socially acceptable public behaviors with members of both sexes; and avoiding sexual exploitation.
3. *Health*—instruction in menstruation, the use of condoms to prevent venereal diseases, the use of birth control devices, cleanliness and hygiene of the genital organs, and the elimination of self-abusive behaviors.

The nature of the following recommended skill sequences may be shocking to the timid. However, the presentation is straightforward because we sincerely believe in the critical need for this information to be imparted to the severely retarded person. Remember, parental or guardian consent must be obtained prior to any instruction in this area.

Biological Aspects of Sex Education

A number of areas in this broad category and some suggested activities to teach the topics will be presented.

1. The names of the sex organs can be taught during the time the student bathes or during shower time in aquatic therapy. As the learner washes the various parts, you should provide him with the correct anatomical name. Some severely retarded learners may use street slang terms to describe the sexual organs. Do not respond negatively to any of his responses, simply substitute the correct name.
2. Introduce the student to the dolls or plastic models that display all body parts including genitals. Label the names of the organs and briefly discuss function.
3. Basic differences between males and females can be taught, again using nude dolls or models. Students should understand which model is a male or female and why it is male or female. The instructor can also have the students dress the dolls or models in clothing appropriate for the sex. Later pictures of clothed males and females can be introduced with the students identifying the male and female according to dress, hair style and make-up.
4. Sexual intercourse should be approached from the standpoint of appropriateness regarding time and place. Any public attempts at sexual intercourse should be stopped, and only under appropriate circumstances is it allowed. Additional instruction may overlap regarding prevention of pregnancy and venereal diseases.

Social Aspects of Sex Education

1. Any overt sexual behaviors such as fondling the genitals, kissing, hugging or exhibitionism should be eliminated using the extinction techniques described in Chapter 3.
2. Students who masturbate in public should be stopped and the behavior eliminated using extinction techniques. Masturbation in private (more appropriate places) should be selectively ignored.
3. Appropriate interactions with peers of both sexes should be reinforced. Modeling, role playing, and field trips to places where adults are engaging in socially acceptable behaviors should be used to facilitate proper social exchanges. Physical education and leisure skills training provide excellent opportunities for students to practice social skills.

4. Role playing and other simulated demonstrations can be used to show students how to avoid situations where sexual exploitation is likely to occur. In this context, sexual exploitation would include: being fondled, hugged, or kissed by strangers or peers when it is undesirable; having sexual intercourse or performing sexual acts when the student does not want to; or undressing because someone tells him to do it.

 The student may be taught to report any incidents of sexual exploitation to teachers, child care workers, and/or parents.

Health Aspects of Sex Education

1. Instructional techniques regarding menstruation were described in the section on hygiene.
2. While it is unlikely that the severely retarded learner would understand the nature and cause of venereal diseases, it is still important to teach him (or her) the means to prevent venereal diseases. The simplest way to do this is to teach male students to use condoms and female students to make sure that their partners wear them. Only students who have a high enough functional level should receive instruction in this area.

 Since it is also unlikely that a male student can be taught to put a condom on properly using indirect techniques, a male teacher should teach the skill using the task analysis technique described in Chapter 3. There are many examples of this technique in this chapter.
3. The use of birth control devices and the birth control pill can be taught using a film or pictures of the devices. Since these devices require a physician's prescription, and in some instances, require that a physician insert them, this instruction should be conducted by a school nurse or doctor.
4. Cleanliness and hygiene of the genital organs can be taught as part of the instructional procedure for bathing. Uncircumcised males should be taught to keep the head of the penis clean. Female students should be taught about feminine hygiene, especially during menstruation. Again, instruction in this area can be done using the task analysis procedure.
5. Any self-abusive sexual behaviors such as inserting objects into the vagina or the insertion of the penis into objects should be stopped and eliminated using the extinction techniques described in Chapter 3.

SUMMARY

 This rather extensive chapter has presented detailed task analyses of the skills involved in socialization. Since these areas are especially crucial for successful integration of the severely retarded, the treatment of grooming/hygiene, manners, appropriate dress, personal care of belongings, and sex education has been highly detailed and extensive.

The task analyses presented in this chapter serve not only as examples of the technique, but also as a framework for preparing detailed instructional objectives for I.E.P.'s and daily lesson plans.

REFERENCES

Bass, M.S. *Developing community acceptance of sex education for the mentally retarded.* New York: SIECUS, 1972.

Bender, M., & Valletutti, P.J. *Teaching the moderately and severely handicapped (Vol. 2).* Baltimore: University Park Press, 1976.

Chapter 8

Personality Skills Training

What is known about the personality of mentally retarded persons? Unfortunately, the answer is very little; little attention has been paid to the personality characteristics of the mentally retarded for a number of reasons—

- Most of the research conducted in the area of retardation has concentrated on cognitive characteristics or biological-physiological aspects of the various syndromes.
- Few states require that a personality test be used to certify retardation.
- The most commonly used instruments for personality assessment are not useful for the mentally retarded because they require considerable verbal skills.

Additionally, much of what is known about the personality of the mentally retarded is suspect since a great deal of the existing research contains serious methodological flaws (MacMillan, 1977). In fact as Heber (1964) noted:

> The extreme paucity of experimental data bearing on the relationship between personality variables and behavioral efficiency of the retarded person is indeed remarkable in view of the generally acknowledged importance of personality factors in problem solving. Textbooks are replete with statements describing the retarded as passive, impulsive, rigid, suggestible, lacking in persistence, immature, and withdrawn, and as having a low frustration tolerance and an unrealistic self-concept and level of aspiration. Yet, not one of these purported attributes can be either substantiated or refuted on the basis of available research data.
>
> It is apparent that the mentally retarded and particularly those who are institutionalized, have a substantially higher prevalence of psychotic and psychoneurotic disorders than the general population. . . . The few

183

striking and consistent findings from the meager investment in "personality research" with the retarded converge in highlighting the importance of motivational variables. Even severely retarded persons appear to be responsive to variations in incentive conditions; social reinforcement in the form of verbal praise and encouragement or just simple attention appears to be at least as effective as with normal persons. There is a strong suggestion that the performance of retardates may be depressed as a function of generalized expectations of failure and that proportionately more retarded than normals may respond to the threat of failure with decreased rather than increased effort (p. 169).

In spite of these acknowledged problems, personality skills training should still be included as a curricular component for the severely retarded. As Hutt and Gibby (1976) noted, the retarded person faces some unique problems and special stresses. For instance, life in the United States is geared largely for the average person. Retarded persons who are developing more slowly can be expected to encounter more stress in the simple process of living so that they are likely to be degraded more often and rewarded less frequently. Other aspects of retardation, such as physical features, gross motor incoordination, or sensory deficits may cause further hardship in the personality development and adjustment of the retarded persons.

This chapter will present an overview of personality factors in the mentally retarded and discuss two primary areas that are critical to improving the qualities of an individual's personality. These major areas include: (1) developing the self-concept and relating to others and (2) teaching play behaviors. Each area will be examined relative to its importance or need, characteristics, and suggestions for instruction.

OVERVIEW OF PERSONALITY FACTORS IN THE MENTALLY RETARDED

Many definitions of personality have been proposed like Cromwell (1967, p. 67) who defined personality as a term that "refers to the recurring, long-term aspects of behavior that characterize individual differences among people." MacMillan (1977) cautioned that the emphasis in this definition is on behaviors that are persistent over time as opposed to behaviors that are occasional or transient and not characteristic of the individual. A similar definition proposed by Allport (1961) described personality as a dynamic organization that determines the person's characteristic behavior and thought. Again, the stress is placed on characteristic behaviors, ones that are relatively persistent and stable.

In order to utilize such definitions, educators must search the environment and the individual for the factors that influence behavior. The characteristic ways in which an individual behaves are developed during the first few years of life, even though later experiences often modify these behaviors.

Webster (1970) described his attempt to locate a child who was "simply retarded" for purposes of comparison with clients with various emotional problems. After reviewing a series of 159 cases, he was unable to identify one child whose emotional development was truly comparable to a nonretarded child of the same mental age. Robinson and Robinson (1976) cautioned, however, that the social demands placed upon an individual are chronological age relative so that retarded persons are exposed to situations and taught rules to which younger nonretarded children are not exposed. Thus it is important to look not only at mental age, but also the effects of previous experiences. Retarded individuals may exhibit serious deficits in later development due to the impact of resentment, deprecation, overprotection, rejection, comparison to siblings and peers, and the unsuccessful competition that they experience first in their home situations and later in school and society.

In spite of the cautions that have already been elaborated about research into personality characteristics of the mentally retarded, some aspects of personality in retarded persons will be discussed here.

Anxiety

Anxiety is a difficult concept to define although it is generally considered to be "a state of arousal in which the individual senses a vague danger signal, but does not identify it with a specific stimulus . . ." (Robinson & Robinson, 1976). While anxious people may not know what specific stimulus arouses that set of feelings, they nonetheless feel tension.

Heber (1964) noted clinical evidence that as a group, the mentally retarded are more anxious than nonretarded individuals. Robinson and Robinson (1976) cited research that supported Heber's contention and noted that mentally retarded children, adolescents, and young adults consistently manifested higher levels of anxiety than nonretarded individuals of the same age or younger. Given the previous description of the problems faced by retarded individuals, this result is not unsuspected.

If people experience extremely high levels of anxiety, they can become so incapacitated that they are incapable of acting or functioning. On the other hand, a certain level of anxiety can even facilitate performance. Robinson and Robinson (1976) suggested that the retarded not be totally shielded from anxiety producing situations; instead their experiences should be regulated so they learn to cope without freezing into inaction. In fact, providing a retarded person with coping skills and the feeling of competence that will come with repeated success at solving or performing complex tasks will probably be more effective at reducing anxiety than overprotection (Robinson & Robinson, 1976).

Positive and Negative Reaction Tendencies

Zigler (1962) conducted research on social deprivation in institutional settings and developed a theoretical construct regarding the behavioral reactions of institutionalized retardates toward adults. He noted that many retarded individuals exhibited an increased desire to interact with adults, a trait he ascribed to early social deprivation. This particular trait Zigler labeled positive reaction tendency. On the other hand, Zigler noted that certain retarded children hesitated to interact with adults, a trait he suggested was due to previous negative experiences with certain adults. Zigler labeled this trait as negative reaction tendency. Whichever of the tendencies is stronger will determine the trait pattern the individual child will exhibit, although both tendencies may exist in the same child.

Again, the task becomes to provide a warm socially accepting and reinforcing environment to reduce the negative reaction tendency and strengthen the positive one. Robinson and Robinson (1976) summarized the results of research studies where there was a comparison of voluntary persistence on two different parts of a boring two-part task. During the first part of the task, the experimenter maintained a warm, socially reinforcing attitude for some subjects and a neutral attitude for others. The child approaching the task with both a positive and negative reaction tendency tended to persist longer at the second part of the task when the first part of the task was conducted under the reinforcing condition.

Frustration and Aggression

Frustration and aggression are often characteristic of institutionalized retarded populations. Often crowding, lack of privacy, a reduction of normal outlets, and a lack of ability to communicate needs create a frustration level that often results in aggression. Unfortunately, few studies have been conducted on frustration or its effects. Then too, we often become entangled in a chicken and egg question—the aggression may have existed before a retarded person was placed in an institution, with aggression being the cause more than the result of the institutionalization.

One form of aggression in institutionalized retarded populations is territoriality. Paluck and Esser (as reported by MacMillan, 1977) conducted two investigations of territoriality. In the first, they discovered that institutionalized retarded clients tended to establish spatial territories in their wards, which they protect. Groups will dominate certain areas, for example, toys and furniture. When someone from outside the group threatened the territory, aggressive behavior was observed. In the follow-up study, the experimenters described fights and other aggressive incidents in which control of some areas of the experimental room was challenged.

Expectancy of Failure

Life in the United States is geared for the average person. Because of rather severe deficits in intellectual, and often physical capabilities, the severely retarded experience far more failure than success. When failure becomes a constant expectation, individuals may adopt behavioral responses that do little to insure either future success or even the willingness to attempt a new task. This behavioral response pattern has been termed expectancy of failure.

Robinson and Robinson (1976) noted that mentally retarded persons may adopt a number of responses to deal with expectancy of failure:

1. They may learn to expect failure and react impassively when it happens.
2. They may resort to stereotypical responses reflecting a lack of effort and involvement.
3. They may simply avoid situations threatening failure.
4. They may employ excuses and defenses to explain their inability to succeed.
5. They may come to accept extremely low rates of success that other non-retarded individuals would not accept.

Perhaps the severely retarded person would not be capable of perceiving constant failure, thus not developing an expectancy for it; but there are implications for the teacher presenting new learning tasks to a person who has failed extensively. It is an excellent technique to begin new instruction with old, familiar tasks of a similar nature so the learner can first experience success. In fact, the teacher can often facilitate success by arranging the environment for the learners to experience large amounts of success to counteract their view of themselves as not capable of doing anything correct (Robinson & Robinson, 1976).

Self-Concept

While the self-concept is thought to be an important distinguishing quality, there has been relatively little research conducted in this area. Of course, the present instrumentation in self-concept assessment requires verbal skills often beyond the capability of verbally limited retarded individuals.

The research that has been conducted on the self-concept of retarded persons is inconclusive. Bialer (1970) suggested that the available evidence indicates that no single pattern exists vis-à-vis the self-concept of the retarded. That is, some mentally retarded individuals view themselves in a positive light; others see themselves quite negatively. It is also noted that the intelligence quotient and self-perceptions are highly correlated; the higher the IQ, the more likely it is that the person will see himself favorably. One fact Bialer (1970) also noted was that when retarded subjects were asked to indicate how they would do on a task, they were likely to predict far greater success than they were likely to achieve.

DEVELOPING THE SELF-CONCEPT AND RELATING TO OTHERS

This chapter deviates from the pattern presented in the other "methods" chapters. Instead of discussing personality skills development entirely from the standpoint of assessing entering behavior, developing objectives and so on, this chapter will present some suggestions for modifying the classroom or residential unit to stimulate the development of a positive self-concept. To some extent this chapter provides a systematic approach for teaching play behaviors (including objectives, checklists, and so on) but it should be viewed more from the viewpoint that the environment in which programming occurs can be directly and indirectly beneficial to the development of important skills. This approach has been adopted because the ideas presented here are integral to the teaching of skills that will occur in the other areas and may not be specifically identifiable as a content area capable of standing on its own.

The time or point in an individual's life that a mental impairment occurs has a significant effect on personality development. Those who are mentally retarded from birth or early childhood will exhibit feelings and attitudes that are conveyed to them by their parents and siblings. Depending on the nature of these attitudes, the child will react accordingly. Individuals who become severely impaired at a later point in their life may have a completely different personality structure due to normal parental and sibling interaction during the early years.

All human beings require certain kinds of psychological experiences to aid in their personality development. Three primary experiences or needs, according to Baroff (1974), contribute to a healthy view of one's environment.

- *Structure*—Individuals have a basic need for order, which is also manifested in people's need to be able to predict events and to possess a sense of familiarity with their lives.
- *Self-esteem*—This need is synonymous with self-concept and is people's sense of usefulness or adequacy about themselves. Three subneeds are viewed as making up people's self-concept, and it is the sum of their contribution that encompasses its total development.
  - *Intimacy*—the need to be loved and to give love to others. Individuals must experience positive interactions with people they look up to and respect.
  - *Success*—each person must feel some degree of accomplishment and possess a sense of competence.
  - *Autonomy*—everyone needs to feel they have some control over their lives and the events which occur daily.
- *Self-expression*—All people have a need to pursue activities that they enjoy. They possess a drive to seek out activities from which they derive pleasure and self-satisfaction.

Despite the functional level of the severely retarded, the three primary psychological needs must still be met. Of course, while their level of sophistication by "normal" standards will be markedly depressed, they still remain critical.

Structure can be developed through interactions with parents, siblings, and teachers that are systematic and consistent from day to day. Students must be able to feel an order to their experiences. When specific actions occur, a consistent reaction can be expected to follow. Familiar faces, household furnishings, animals, rooms, voices, and toys all provide feelings of an ordered life.

Self-esteem or self-concept is present in all retardates to some degree. Family acceptance is one of the strongest determinants of how they will eventually feel about themselves. In cases where an individual has been showered with affection and love, a personality eventually emerges that is open and trusting. By comparison, a child that is shunned, mistreated, or ignored will usually exhibit a very withdrawn and avoidance-laden character.

The development of a healthy self-concept requires many successful experiences in performing simple tasks and through interactions with other people (Kolstoe, 1976). Table 8-1 lists behaviors and concept areas that help students understand who they are and how they feel about themselves.

Table 8-1 Behaviors and Concept Areas to Promote the Development of Self-Concept

1. Make the students feel that you care. Touch, speak in soothing tones, and take care of their personal needs in a pleasant manner.
2. Encourage them to do things (self-help skills, manipulative activities, etc.) and offer praise for the smallest of accomplishments.
3. Say their names, and talk to them about their size, color of hair, favorite foods, and all things that apply to them.
4. Talk about their age and relate their age to yours and others.
5. Talk about objects that belong to them. Discuss their characteristics and how they are theirs and only theirs.
6. Work on body identification, naming body parts and their functions. Touch each part and have the students move, or perform a simple action with that part.
7. Identify and discuss objects that belong to others.
8. Teach the children to recognize other family members by name and by picture. Show students where they fit into the family structure.
9. Teach the children how to greet another person when spoken to. The students' response may be a handshake, verbal response, or facial expression.
10. Teach children to take care of a pet, plant, and personal belongings.
11. Teach students to recognize their own picture.
12. Teach the children to move their own bodies even with the limitations they have. Show praise and appreciation for what they can do.
13. Teach the children how they can use their senses, smell, taste, touch, etc.; and praise their ability to discriminate as it occurs.
14. Teach as many self-help skills and manipulative tasks as possible.

There are many variables that are woven in mazelike fashion to form the human personality. Cognitive processes and skills, self-motivation, environmental stimulation, and biological factors all interact forming the total personality. Depressed intelligence and physical limitations restrict an individual's natural avenues for personality development; however, through attention, recognition, acceptance, and love, all human beings can begin to improve their inner feeling about themselves and the world they live in.

TEACHING PLAY BEHAVIORS

Play versus Work

The measure of an individual's personality is how he interacts and reacts to elements and situations in the environment. One of the first forms of spontaneous interaction for children is play. For normal children, it is a time of discovery, enjoyment, and creativity.

Play brings to children new and different experiences from which they can gain information concerning themselves and their relationship to the world. For children, play is their work, whether it is reciting a nursery rhyme or opening the front door to let the dog out. In scientific terms, work and play can be discussed as different concepts by the way they are measured. Work can be measured quantitatively by the amount of effort or power required to do something. Play, on the other hand, must be measured on a value scale according to the amount of enjoyment or pleasure that is attained. Therefore, by this definition, play could be measured as work and vice versa depending on how it is measured and the individual's attitude.

The Need for Play

Normal children spontaneously seek out play activities, which change as the child grows. Jean Piaget (1962) divided play into three developmental categories. The first type, sensorimotor play, begins in infancy and continues through age two. At this point children begin to acquire control over their motor movements, coordinating their actions with their perception of their effects. Touch, smell, sight, sound, and the kinesthetic sense are used to explore their growing world. They find continual pleasure in making things recur and enjoy the attention of others as new discoveries are made.

The second stage, symbolic or representational play, occurs between the ages of two and six years. This is the time when children begin to play using symbols to represent objects or events. Images of how events occurred can be replayed again and again using other objects as the characters. For example, children at this stage may string a row of blocks together to represent a freight train, and pull them along complete with sound effects.

Games with rules exemplifies the third stage of play. Children now incorporate a rule structure to their games. Most games require an understanding of the social concepts of cooperation, taking turns, and competition with oneself or others.

Children do not separate play from learning, but experience both through their own enjoyable exploratory process. They begin to master their own neuromuscular system along with entering into a symbolic world. The world of fantasy and imagining are compared to real events and characters. Children are able to manipulate all types of objects and materials, studying their interaction and relationships with them, society, and each other.

The need for play experiences is obvious. It is not only pleasurable, but it amends the individual's social, mental, and physical development. Thus, play for the mentally retarded is just as important to their development as it is for the nonhandicapped.

Characteristics of Play

Garvey (1977) provided a number of descriptive characteristics of play cited as critical to its definition:

1. Play is both pleasurable and enjoyable. Therefore, even when the individual does not exhibit signs of glee, it is still positively valued by the player.
2. Play does not have any extrinsic goals. Its motivations are intrinsic and serve no other objectives. In fact, it is more of an enjoyment of the means, rather than an effort to meet some particular end. In utilitarian terms, it is inherently unproductive.
3. Play is both spontaneous and voluntary. Play is not obligatory, but is freely chosen by the player.
4. Play involves some active involvement on the part of the player.
5. Play has certain systematic relations to what is not play.

Garvey (1977, p. 5) noted that the scientific study of play is important since play has been linked to "creativity, problem solving, language learning, the development of social roles, and a number of other cognitive and social phenomena."

Goals for Play for the Severely Retarded

Note that the severely retarded will not play spontaneously—they must be taught to play. Anyone who has visited or worked in the wards of institutions for the retarded is all too familiar with the scene of retarded individuals sitting, doing nothing, because they have never been trained to play. Yet any professional who has seen a retarded person learn to play knows that play helps retarded children and adults become happier, better adjusted, less dependent, and more socially acceptable.

Carlson and Ginglend (1961) described goals for play in five different areas.

1. *Mental Health*—This area has been described as the most important. Play can help create a happier, more accepting atmosphere in both the home and the school. Play can be one area where the severely retarded person nearly always succeeds, and thus develops self-confidence, a feeling of belonging, and a feeling of security.

   Carlson and Ginglend (1961) noted that growth in mental health can be measured if the child or young adult becomes happier, easier to manage, exhibits self-control, accepts direction, and exhibits a positive attitude toward school.

2. *Social Development*—Professionals often assume that this area is the only goal for play activities. Actually social development through play has two aspects: (a) adjustment of the learner to the group and the instructor and (b) the development of the ability to care for oneself.

   When teaching learners to adjust to the group, the instructor teaches them to share and play with other individuals, to follow directions and accept discipline, and to demonstrate future willingness to join in group activities. These objectives can facilitate the learners' integration, not only into school (with the teacher as group leader) but also into the family where the parent may function as leader.

   Social development through play will also focus upon growth in the self-help skills—eating, dressing, and hygiene. The learners will be expected to develop a greater attention span, develop the ability to deal with increasing amounts of stimulation, develop new interests, and learn how to play constructively when they are alone (Carlson & Ginglend, 1961).

3. *Physical Development*—Physical development is an extremely crucial area for all severely retarded learners. Most severely retarded individuals will have coordination difficulties with accompanying large muscle hypotonia or underdevelopment. Additionally, the learners will exhibit fine motor difficulties that prohibit manipulation of small objects.

   Play activities involving movement and the use of large and small muscles must be designed to assist the learners to improve motor and muscular coordination. These activities would include walking, running, jumping, carrying, pulling, pushing, bending, stretching, rolling, lifting, grasping, and stacking (Carlson & Ginglend, 1961).

4. *Language Development*—The importance of communication for the severely retarded can not be overstressed. Play activities can provide multiple opportunities for the participants to learn how to listen and to learn to associate sounds with directions, body parts, and objects. Additionally, play can help the learners to understand important concepts like size, location, and emotion.

Of course, play can also stimulate the development of preverbal language skills like blowing, tongue movement, and lip placement. These difficult and often boring activities can be greatly enhanced if coupled with play or gamelike activities.

5. *Intellectual Development*—The learners' IQs will not be increased through play, but the instructor can assist them to become more observant of things in their environment and to hear sounds and to remember. Carson and Ginglend (1961) noted the first ability might be described as visual discrimination and memory. Activities in this area would include puzzles, matching, sorting, missing objects, colors, and reproducing patterns.

The second ability is usually referred to as auditory discrimination and memory. The student learns to follow spoken directions, identify sounds, rhythms, and tunes, and identify animal sounds (Carlson & Ginglend, 1961).

Designing Play-Learning Areas

Bowers (1975) noted that play, development, and learning form a continuous and integrated process. As such, "the outdoor play environment should be related to and be an extension of the education goals of the classroom" (Bowers, 1975, p. 8).

The instructor involved in designing a play area for severely retarded learners must consider their motor developmental needs, their safety, and their need for the opportunity to engage in creative play. Additionally, as Gerson (1975) has noted, equipment utilized for the play area must be appropriate for the learners' physical stature and for the individuals' mental age. When working with severely retarded teenagers or adults, the equipment must not appear childlike, but will need to be large, sturdy, and colorful.

While Bowers' (1975) play area equipment and outside play area were utilized for preschool children, they could also be employed with school-aged students for whom the play objectives were consistent or similar. The outside equipment described by Bowers (1975) consisted of interconnected, multilevel, brightly colored, carpeted table tops. The play area provided for many under-over, up and down, around and through activities. On one end of the play center, the designers placed a transparent four- by eight-foot, one-half-inch thick Plexiglas sliding surface. Thus, the participants could slide down or walk up the slope. Additionally, the play center had movable vinyl-covered 12-inch polyurethane foam jumping areas attached to it for a variety of jumping and rolling activities.

Bowers (1975) noted that the needs of children for physical development include involvement in physical activity in which the learners experience vigorous contraction of muscles in moving the body up, over, down, under, and through a variety of environmental challenges. Basic movements such as crawling, climbing, running, jumping, swinging, and sliding are engaged in by students when the environment permits and is conducive to safe play.

When developing outside play areas, the teacher assumes responsibility for the students' safety. Bowers' (1975, pp. 76-80) checklist (see Table 8-2) is reproduced to assist responsible adults in the examination and evaluation of the environment in which play takes place.

The Structured Playroom

Gerson (1975) described the composition of the structured playroom at the Rainier School as a program where students are taught the satisfaction of interacting with toys, objects, and their peers. This learning process is achieved through the systematic teaching of play skills broken down into simple workable steps. The structured playroom emphasizes three major areas: structure, socialization, and success.

"Structure" employs the teaching system of routine and repetitive activities called patterning in a room designed to accommodate ten stations. Groups of students participate in the activity room; however, individual skill objectives are maintained for each student at his success level within each station on a daily basis. Students are further introduced to a structured environment by: (1) following the same play activities in the same order daily, and (2) using the same oral and sign vocabulary for each activity.

Socialization

The structure of the play activities is held within an atmosphere conducive to socialization. Students are not identified as performing at a lower level nor are high activities given special considerations. Group support and enthusiasm are promoted by the teacher as those students who are resting or waiting are active spectators, clapping hands and shouting words of encouragement. Activities are also designed to create parallel and cooperative play situations, which foster taking turns and sharing.

Table 8-2 Evaluation Checklist for Playgrounds

ENVIRONMENT

Quiet play areas allow children to sometimes tune out the rest of the world. Privacy is needed for children since the playground may offer the only opportunity for some children to be alone. A "kid-sized" place, a low wall around a sand box, an enclosed tree house or fort, a simple roof to provide a shaded place, or wind break can be the nook or cranny where the child can be away from the commotion for awhile. Trees and other plantings can also provide shade and privacy.

A sand and water area gives a new dimension to playgrounds. An avoidable aspect of modern living—littering by cats, dogs, and people—must be considered when planning this area.

INSTALLATION

Efficient use of space and materials in the play environment will significantly affect the amount of enjoyment children will experience. Alternatives for play can be maximized by pieces of equipment that are rearrangeable and at the same time built of durable materials that have strength and stability when put together.

MAINTENANCE

Playgrounds should not be built for the convenience of custodians, yet the question of permanency is usually paramount. Concrete and steel are easy to hose down, yet such materials are not necessarily easy on the soft bodies of children. Whatever equipment is available, as deterioration occurs due to weather and the normal usage by children, equipment should be repaired, improved, or be removed from the playground.

EQUIPMENT

Needs Supervision—On-site leadership is part of the human component of a playground. Experienced play leaders offer guidance, leadership, and direction to children. They make an environment potentially more healthy and safe, in as much as children are not always the masters of their own fate in many playground situations.

Performance of Another Child—Mutual trust can be developed; however when the situation is turned into competition, invisible dangers may be created in which losing may be deadly.

Does Not Cause Dizziness or Disorientation—Inertial effects of rotary motion on a piece of equipment do not necessarily add to the inventiveness and judgment-making abilities of children.

Has Appropriate Step Height—Step height should be controlled to an appropriate size for the range of children expected to use them. A child should not be required to step above his knee height to reach the next highest step.

Provides Appropriate Bar Spacing—The spacing of bars on climbing apparatus

Table 8-2 continued

should not exceed 14 inches for children under six years old. For children over six years old, an acceptable space is from 14 to 18 inches apart.

Provides Appropriate Rail or Rung Size—Climbing apparatus rungs, and ladder and platform protective rails, should be cylindrical in all cases. The diameter should permit a firm grip without allowing the encircling fingertips to touch the palm of the hand. Pipe size should be from 1″ to 1¼″, inside diameter.

Has No Sharp Edges or Corners—Sharp edges and corners present a constant hazard to children and should therefore be eliminated. The difference between a sharp or rounded corner can be a deep gash or a bruise.

Has Splinter-Free Surfaces—Structures which are sanded during construction often become increasingly smooth from the constant polishing by kids' contact. One answer to splinters is to let children play.

Provides Non-Slip Surfaces—Standing surfaces should be large enough for free movement. Good traction is essential and should provide sure footing without being sticky.

Has Soft Moving Parts—A "soft" environment automatically adds to safety and positive movement experiences. Where practical limitations do not allow soft parts upon which to move, safety and practical considerations do not have to be incompatible. Chances for injury can be minimized using alternative products such as vinyl-coated materials, soft plastics, and energy absorbing foams.

Is Built at Appropriate Height—It seems reasonable to expect the height from which a child falls will influence his injuries. The problem here is the preschool child usually exceeds the design limits of an eight foot piece of equipment and the danger of an injury producing fall is not apparent until too late. Equipment does not have to be eight feet tall to be exciting and interesting.

Has Wide Sliding Surface—The low wide slide is the alternative for children which allows for many children going up and down in many different ways while not exceeding the design limits of the slide.

Has Protective Rails or Sides—Standing surfaces should have continuous protective rails within comfortable reach of both hands at each side. There should also be a secondary bar beneath the handrail to prevent slipping underneath and falling to the ground. On sliding surfaces the siderails or sides should prevent a child from toppling over the side from a seated position.

Placement Considerations—Components of an active play area should be arranged so that children doing one thing will not run into some part of the structure or interfere with children doing something else.

Has No Radical Angle for Climbing—The angle of inclination on ladders or other climbing devices should allow children to stand vertically on one level without the legs contacting the next upper level with the lower leg.

Has Protected Pinch Points—Pinch and crush points should be designed so that fingers and hands cannot get caught under normal use or abuse.

Has Adequate Openings for Crawl Spaces—Openings must be large enough so as not to inhibit the child or the usefulness of the equipment unless the nature of the crawling activity is inherently unsafe.

Table 8-2 continued

IMPACT SURFACES UNDER EQUIPMENT
When a child falls on a surface the energy of the impact is often dissipated by displacing or fracturing the bones. The need is for the surface to deform slowly or in other words absorb the impact. Playground surfaces can range from soils, through concrete or asphalt surfaces, to fabricated rubber or plastic foam combinations. It is essential to have a high energy absorbing material under an active play structure.

ACCESSIBLE TO HANDICAPPED CHILDREN
Simply stated, those with mental, physical, or emotional disabilities must be able to go easily to play areas and be able to use the equipment free of barriers. If handicapped children can use the equipment, any child will be able to participate on the playground.

Source: L. Bowers. *Play learning centers for preschool handicapped children,* pp. 76-80, ©1975. Reprinted by permission of the author.

Success

The nature of the structured play stations promotes success as students have the opportunity to perform the same tasks daily (until they are learned and used in cooperative and spontaneous play) with the same vocabulary and contingencies. Students become familiar with the program activities and teacher expectancies, which in turn provide them with feelings of security, independence, and an opportunity for improved skill development.

The goal for the participant becomes one of helping the individual feel as if he is a total person learning specific skills and the care of equipment.

Playroom Equipment and Stations

The equipment used in the structured playroom is neither elaborate or expensive. Much of it is handmade as few toys are constructed for the adult-size students in this program. Large, colorful, and sturdy toys are designed for durability and a nonchildish appearance, yet for a young mental age. Illustrations of the equipment can be viewed in Appendix A.

The ten play activity stations are arranged much like a standard obstacle course. As illustrated in Figure 8-1, students enter the structured playroom and take a seat on the bench before moving through the nine remaining stations.

Figure 8-1 Structured Playroom

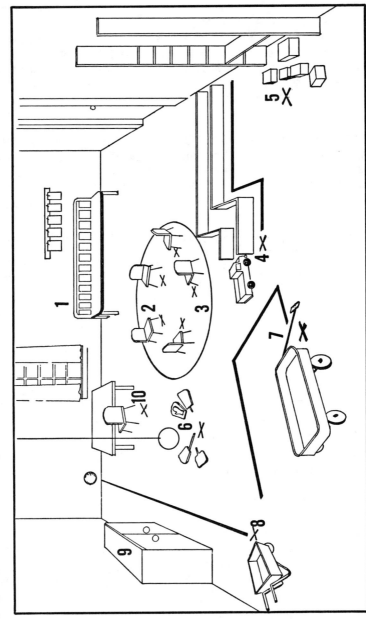

Source: From Be big somewhere: The structured playroom for the severely and profoundly retarded, *by D. Gerson, pp. 7-10,*
© 1975. Reprinted by permission of the author.

Station 1. The Beginning Bench: students assemble on the bench upon entering the activity room. This station is important for establishing the
tone of the activity area, teaching proper sitting posture, and
socialization skills of sitting close to another person without bother-
ing them.

Station 2. The "X"cellent X: Vinyl plastic tape Xs are placed on the floor to
designate an area where control and perceptual motor exercises
such as musical chairs are conducted. Xs are also placed at each
remaining station to designate their starting point.

Station 3. You too can be a bouncer . . . It's a Kick: Ball activities to teach the
skills of bouncing, receiving, kicking, passing, rolling, striking,
etc., are conducted in the circle of Xs area. Balls of varying size and
composition are used.

Station 4. Please be Pushy: A durable wooden truck weighing approximately
6 pounds, 12 inches long and 8 inches high is pushed along a
wooden track. The track is 14 feet long and 16 inches wide with 5
inch high wooden sideboards to restrict the direction of movement.
A red line is taped alongside the track and each student is encouraged to crawl along its path as the truck is pushed.

Station 5. Don't knock that Block: Finger dexterity, palmer and pincher
grasp, motor coordination, and sorting skills can be improved
through block stacking. A "retainer" that is 6 feet high and 14
inches wide is used as a framework. This structure has 25 slots for
removable shelves and is securely fastened to the wall. Students
utilize the framework to practice stacking and sorting blocks of
different size and color.

Station 6. How to be a Hit: Eye-hand coordination and visual tracking skills
can be improved by striking a hanging whiffle ball. This skill
progresses from hitting the ball directly with the hand to using a
badminton racket. Proponents of the structured playroom suggest
this teaching sequence for striking:
a. hit the ball with the hand.
b. hit the ball with mitten-racket, a custom built plywood racket
head, 11 inches long, 8 inches wide (at widest point) with a
mitten stapled on it.
c. hit the ball with mini-mini racket, 11 inches long, 8 inches wide
and 4 inch handle.
d. hit the ball with mini-racket, 11 inches long, 8 inches wide, 9
inch handle.
e. hit the ball with standard badminton racket.

Station 7. Wagon Ho: The pulling skill is taught using a toy wagon which the
student guides along a route designated by 2 inch vinyl tape on the

floor. The student is encouraged to use his imagination and project himself into the activity.

Station 8. Wheelbarrow Along: Pushing a wheelbarrow along a tape line requires gross motor coordination, strength, and eye-hand coordination. The student is encouraged to follow the line pushing the wheelbarrow where upon reaching the end it strikes a squeeky squeeze ball or noise-maker taped to the wall. The squeeze ball not only reinforces the activity, but provides the cue to pull the wheelbarrow back along the line to the starting position. As the student becomes skilled, carrying and dumping objects with the wheelbarrow can be introduced.

Station 9. Toys and Language Master: Once the student has completed the previous activities, he is encouraged to pick a toy from the toy shelf or cabinet. This activity requires the student to make a choice and also utilize the individual time available to him. The language master can be introduced as an enjoyable activity which promotes fine motor coordination for its operation coupled with language activities.

Station 10. Play Space: A table and chairs supply the area for a child's independent play activities. The toy or language master selected at Station 9 is taken to this area for independent play. Upon completion of the free-play time period, the student puts the toy away in the storage cabinet.

Charting Performance

The method or tool for measuring student progress in the structured playroom consists of daily records using individual data sheets (Exhibit 8-1). Daily records are kept for each student. Each sheet has a key at the top of the page that indicates the type of cueing needed to perform the task. Once the task is completed, the instructor circles the level of cueing (number) that corresponds with the performance observed. The daily data sheet accommodates six objectives that are taken from the quarterly assessment sheet. Each daily objective sheet allows space for ten days of recording. Once a daily data sheet is completed, times can be drawn between the "cueing level" numbers and a performance graph available. At this point, student performance can be evaluated and further decisions can be made concerning the modification of objectives and/or instructional techniques. Following each 10-day period, a new daily objective sheet is started. Hopefully, this device will be used in conjunction with another behavioral assessment device (i.e., Behavioral Observation Assessment—Table 8-3). Students in the structured playroom are evaluated four times a year using the assessment sheet illustrated in Table 8-4. The assessment sheet written in objective form is used with corresponding criterion reference tests (see Exhibit 8-2 for example format).

Exhibit 8-1 Daily Data Sheet

NAME   John

TEACHER   Bill   AREA   Structured Play

1. Spontaneous Independence

2. Independence on Command

3. Verbal Cueing

4. Minimal Physical Cueing

5. Aware of Command but No Response—Complete Shaping

6. No Response—Complete Shaping

OBJECTIVE   to sit on designated spot

ASSESSMENT # OR PROGRAM   42

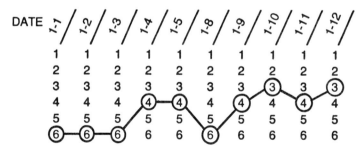

COMMENTS:

Exhibit 8-1 continued

OBJECTIVE   to stack blocks

ASSESSMENT # OR PROGRAM   24

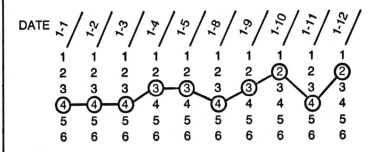

COMMENTS:

OBJECTIVE   to grasp handles

ASSESSMENT # OR PROGRAM   35

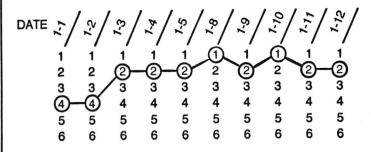

COMMENTS:

Exhibit 8-1 continued

OBJECTIVE   to turn toy around

ASSESSMENT # OR PROGRAM   34

DATE   1-1 / 1-2 / 1-3 / 1-4 / 1-5 / 1-8 / 1-9 / 1-10 / 1-11 / 1-12 /

1	1	1	1	1	1	1	1	1	1
2	2	2	2	2	2	2	2	2	2
3	3	3	3	3	3	3	3	3	3
④	④	④	④	④	④	④	④	④	④
5	5	5	5	5	5	5	5	5	5
6	6	6	6	6	6	6	6	6	6

COMMENTS:

OBJECTIVE   to hit ball with racket

ASSESSMENT # OR PROGRAM   21

DATE   1-1 / 1-2 / 1-3 / 1-4 / 1-5 / 1-8 / 1-9 / 1-10 / 1-11 / 1-12 /

1	1	1	1	1	1	1	1	1	1
2	2	2	2	2	2	2	2	2	2
3	3	3	3	3	3	3	3	3	3
4	4	4	4	④	④	④	④	④	④
5	5	5	5	5	5	5	5	5	5
⑥	⑥	⑥	⑥	6	6	6	6	6	6

COMMENTS:

Exhibit 8-1 continued

OBJECTIVE   to push wheelbarrow

ASSESSMENT # OR PROGRAM   36

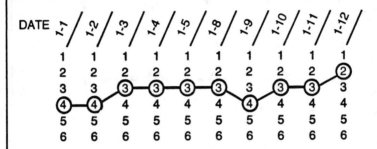

DATE

COMMENTS:

Source: From *Be big somewhere: The structured playroom for the severely and pro-foundly retarded,* by D. Gerson, p. 86, © 1975. Reprinted by permission of author.

Table 8-3 Behavior Observation Sheet

SKILL SCALE NUMBERS

1. Does the student demonstrate small movements (eyes, fingers, etc.)? Note which body parts are involved.
2. Does the student demonstrate large movements (head, arm, legs)?
3. Does the student help himself in eating?
4. Does the student help himself in dressing?
5. Does the student help himself in toileting?
6. Does the student attend to the teacher?
7. Does the student work or play alone?
8. Does the student work or play with the teacher?
9. Does the student's work stop immediately if the teacher's full attention is withdrawn?
10. Does the student play at the side of but not with other students?
11. Does the student play with one other student?
12. Does the student play with a group (2 or more students)?
13. Does the student choose a toy by himself?

ANECDOTAL COMMENTS

14. Note the exact kind of instruction a student can understand and respond to by appropriate action. Give examples.
15. Note the exact words, sounds, sentences used in student's classroom behavior.
16. Note the readiness with which the student cooperates with the teacher.
17. Note the student's ability to make contact with the teacher, with the students in the group, with other students, and with adults.
18. Does the student exhibit any leadership qualities while participating within a group?
19. When given a free choice, what does the student play with?
20. How long does the student concentrate on an activity when assigned to that specific activity?
21. How long does the student concentrate on an activity when given the opportunity to choose what activity? What is the activity?
22. Note the behavior when the student is expected to work or attend for short periods in small groups.
23. Note displays of initiative, curiosity, aggression, withdrawal, lack of interest, length of enthusiasm, lack of energy, and special interests.
24. Note the slightest change in a student's behavior.
25. Note drawings and spontaneous creative efforts.

Table 8-3 continued

NAME: HALL:

DATE OF BIRTH: TIME OF RECORDING:

DATE OF RECORDING: RECORDER:

ACTIVITIES OBSERVED:

SKILLS SCALE

NUMBERS	NEVER	SELDOM	SOMETIMES	ALWAYS

ANECDOTAL COMMENTS

CONCLUSION

TIME OF RECORDING: DATE OF RECORDING:

RECORDER: ACTIVITIES:

SKILLS SCALE

NUMBERS	NEVER	SELDOM	SOMETIMES	ALWAYS

ANECDOTAL COMMENTS

Source: From Be big somewhere: The structured playroom for the severely and profoundly retarded, by D. Gerson, ©1975. Reprinted by permission of the author.

Table 8-4 Assessment Sheet

Student ————————— Teacher ————————— Class ——

**RAINIER SCHOOL STUDENT SUMMARY EVALUATION FORM —
SCHOOL YEAR**

KEY:
Y = Yes
N = No
O = Not Applicable

Selected Objectives	Initial (Sept.)	Midyear	Year-end (June)	Summer
INTERACTS WITH TOY				
1. Looks at toy				
2. Picks up toy spontaneously				
3. Picks up toy on T direction				
4. Returns toy to appropriate place				
5. Plays with toy spontaneously for 1 (one) minute				
6. Squeezes and/or manipulates toy				
7. Assembles toy with three parts				
8. Disassembles toy with three parts				
BALL				
9. Rolls ball				
10. Rolls ball to T				
11. Rolls ball to designated person				
12. Retrieves ball				
13. Kicks the ball				
14. Imitates throwing ball overhand				
15. Imitates throwing ball underhand				
16. Throws ball to designated person				
17. Catches ball				
18. Plays catch				
19. Plays 3-corner catch				
20. Holds badminton racket				
21. Hits suspended ball with badminton racket				
22. Imitates dribbling				
BLOCKS				
23. Grasps block				
24. Stacks one block on another 3″ × 3″ × 1″				
25. Stacks one block on another/1″				
26. Stacks three blocks				
27. Imitates stacking of three blocks				
28. Places blocks in row on horizontal surface				
29. Imitates placing blocks in row on horizontal surface				

Source: From Be big somewhere: The structured playroom for the severely and profoundly retarded, by D. Gerson, © 1975. Reprinted by permission of the author.

Table 8-4 continued

PUSHING TOYS
30. Pushes toy automobile to and fro
31. Rolls toy automobile
32. Rolls toy automobile to designated person
33. Returns toy automobile
34. Turns toy automobile around to forward position

WHEELBARROW
35. Grasps handles of wheelbarrow
36. Pushes wheelbarrow to designated person

STANDING IN SPECIFIED AREA
37. Sits in chair on command
38. Sits in chair for 5 (five) minutes
39. Sits on chair upon command when in a group of 3
40. Sits on chair upon command when in a group of 6
41. Sits on designated spot when placed
42. Sits on designated spot on command
43. Sits on designated spot for 5 (five) minutes
44. Sits on designated spot upon command when in a group of 3
45. Sits on designated spot upon command when in a group of 6
46. Stands on designated spot when placed
47. Stands on designated spot on command
48. Stands on designated spot for 5 (five) minutes
49. Stands on designated spot upon command when in a group of 3
50. Stands on designated spot upon command when in a group of 6

AWARENESS OF SELF/PEERS
51. Identifies self by pointing
52. Identifies self by pointing to picture of self
53. Identifies self by pointing to picture of self using 2 distractors
54. Identifies self by pointing to image of self in group picture
55. Looks at designated person on command
56. Says first and last name in response to question
57. Looks at designated person on command in a group
58. Identfies peer within a group by pointing
59. Identifies peer by pointing to picture of peer using 2 distractors
60. Identifies peer by pointing to image of peer in group picture
61. Says first name in response to question
62. Says last name in response to question
63. Identifies peer by saying first name in response to question
64. Identifies peer by saying last name
65. Identifies peer by saying first and last name
66. Points to adult on command
67. Points to adult on command within a group
68. Identifies Teacher by pointing
69. Identifies Teacher by saying last name

Exhibit 8-2 Criterion-Referenced Test Example

SUBJECT: _____ Socialization-Structured Play _____

SKILL: _____ To hit suspended ball with racket _____

I. Skill Description:
   Hits suspended ball with racket

II. Criterion Test:
   A. Equipment and Materials
      1. Whiffle ball suspended 4″ lower than S chest level
      2. Badminton racket
   B. Test Procedure:
      1. S stands within racket's reach of suspended ball
      2. T gives racket to S
      3. T says, "Hit the ball with the racket"
      4. T may give direction two times within 10 seconds
   C. Criteria for YES:
      S: Hits ball with racket head 10 seconds after
         first T direction
   D. Criteria for NO:
      S: 1. Does not respond
         2. Fails to hit ball with racket head within 10
            seconds after first T direction
         3. Fails to hit ball with racket
   E. Scoring Instructions:
      1. Mark Y or N on Student Evaluation Form

Play Table Activities

Often play is thought of as an activity involving the large muscles used in running, jumping, and crawling. Play should also involve some quiet activities with the play table as the central focus. The play table can be a round or rectangular table set off in the classroom with enough room for four students. The play table provides an excellent place for nonambulatory learners to participate in individual or group play. When initiating the play table concept, the instructor will want to develop a number of activities that initially require supervision and direction. By carefully supervising the learner's activities, the instructor can provide activities that insure success and the student's continued interest in play table activities.

Many of the skills the learner develops during play table time will enhance the skills necessary for occupational competency. The actual teaching procedures will be described in Chapter 10. The following activities are recommended for the play table (Carlson & Ginglend, 1961):

1. *Pegboards*

   Aside from being fun, pegboard work can develop fine motor movements and finger dexterity as well as eye-hand coordination. Pegboards can also be used to increase attention span, teach color, position in space, and improve visual memory for patterns (copying and reproducing patterns).

2. *Sorting and Matching*

   At this stage the learner does not have to know the colors—it is enough for him to match objects of the same color. Start with two colors of great contrast (i.e., red and white) so that the visual discrimination is simplified. To reduce confusion, add colors one at a time. Sorting and matching different shapes and sizes can also be utilized for skill development.

3. *Stringing beads*

   Have the learner string, count, and match color/shape of round and square beads. Students can also make necklaces and belts to wear and enjoy.

4. *Grouping*

   Students can participate in play table activities that require them to group objects by their one common element: color, size, shape, etc.

5. *Crayons*

   Large, primary size crayons can be used for learners to learn to scribble and color. Initially, you may wish to cut forms out of posterboard and oaktag, place them on newspaper and have the learner scribble-color over them. Eventually, and as the student exhibits good finger and motor control, you can have him color within the lines of large pictures or drawings.

6. *Clay*

   Many students enjoy playing with clay because of the sensory stimulation (touch and smell) it provides. However, clay work must be supervised and should begin with simple rolling, squeezing, and patting activities. Learners may be encouraged to make "snakes," "pizzas," "hamburgers," "hot dogs," "ropes," etc. Shapes can be cut out of clay using an inexpensive set of cookie cutters or plastic molds. As the student learns to handle clay fairly well, various handcraft projects may be introduced.

7. *Puzzles*

   Puzzles are fun and even the severely retarded student can learn to complete fairly difficult puzzles of five to nine pieces. However, begin instruction using puzzles of one or two pieces. Preferably the puzzles should be the wood-inlay type, bounded by a frame and backing. Aside from the enjoyment involved, puzzles can be used to develop skills in finger dexterity, eye-hand coordination, following directions, language, etc.

Handicrafts

Arts and crafts for the mentally retarded do not enjoy a "good reputation" among professionals in special education. Unfortunately, handicraft activities are often abused by the classroom teacher, particularly when they are used as busywork or time wasters. When used properly, however, handicrafts can help the retarded learners feel some accomplishment because they will have a tangible finished product, enhance social development, and assist in the development of physical and sensory skills. Additionally, handicraft work is fun.

The following activities are suggestions for handicraft work with severely retarded students (Carlson & Ginglend, 1961).

1. *Decorative Printing*
   Students can be taught to decorate paper using a wide variety of materials. For example, sponges can be cut into cubes and used to apply various colors to paper. Objects such as blocks, spools, and dowels can be employed to make interesting and rather intricate designs on wrapping paper or greeting cards for holidays.

2. *Finger Painting*
   Finger painting is usually an exciting expression medium for the severely retarded student. It provides sensory stimulation unlike almost any other activity. Allow the students to "do their thing" initially, but remember even this will become boring unless they do something with it. The students can make figures, shapes, do color blending, handprints, footprints, bodyprints, and finger-paint prints.

3. *Pasting*
   The instructor will need to teach the learner two types of pasting: (1) covering rather large areas completely with paste and sticking them to something else and (2) pasting small objects in place on a larger object. It is best to begin with the former and proceed to the latter once the learner demonstrates sufficient competency. Later activities can involve having students make paper hats, medallions, belts, wall decorations, greeting cards, and the like.

4. *Cutting*
   Many severely retarded students will exhibit great difficulty in learning to cut with a scissors. Usually learners can make one cut, but lack the control to open the scissors and cut again. A number of adaptations may be employed such as the double-handled scissors in which both the student's and teacher's fingers are put in the holes and the initial cutting pressure is applied by the teacher. These adaptations can be used until the learners demonstrate sufficient control to use the scissors independently. Using the blunt end scissors,

learners should begin by cutting strips of half-inch construction paper. In this way, only one snip is necessary. Later students can progress to: (1) cutting pieces of paper; (2) cutting along a straight line; (3) cutting strips; (4) cutting along a curved line; (5) cutting more complex shapes staying on the lines (use squares, triangles, rectangles, etc.); and (6) cutting circles holding the paper with hand not used for holding the scissors.

When students master cutting and pasting, they are ready to attempt more complex craft activities like making construction paper bracelets, hats, oriental lanterns, bird cages, and baskets.

5. *Tearing and Folding*
The severely retarded learner does not always require instructions in tearing paper. The term *tearing* used here refers to the tearing of strips and bits of paper suitable for use in papier-mâché. Tearing also helps develop the grasp and fine muscles in the hands. Then, too, it is a socially acceptable form of destruction.

Folding can be taught by first having students fold a piece of paper in half using a guide like a ruler or piece of balsa wood. Next, they can fold in half without the guide, and eventually progress to folding in more complex patterns. These skills will come in handy when the students make papier-mâché bowls, tunnels, puppets, and doilies. Folding can be practiced when the learner makes a soldier hat.

6. *Weaving and Sewing*
Carlson and Ginglend (1961) noted that weaving and sewing employ a common basic skill that requires an understanding of the terms over and under, or up and down, or from the top and from the bottom. Once learners understand these concepts and can push a needle up or down as necessary, they are ready to do these crafts. The instructor can purchase or copy simple patterns for weaving place mats, baskets, etc. Sewing skills can be developed through simple embroidery and sewing cards.

Music Activities

Music is an excellent means to develop positive personality characteristics. Through group music activities, the severely retarded learner can experience happiness, satisfaction, security, and a real sense of belonging. Singing is a way for people to express emotion appropriately since songs may be happy, sad, serious, or silly.

When choosing songs for music activities, try to select those which are primarily "action" songs. Group singing does not need to be childlike; in fact, the popularity of group sings for nonretarded adults can be substantiated by the former popular television show "The Mitch Miller Show."

SUMMARY

This chapter provided an overview of personality development in severely retarded individuals. While there is a dearth of research in this area, an attempt was made to synthesize the information that is currently available.

The development of personality skills was discussed from the standpoint of activities to improve the learner's self-concept. The need, characteristics, and suggestions for using play as a therapeutic and educational medium were presented.

Play-learning centers and their safety considerations were discussed along with the structured playroom concept used at the Rainier School in Buckley, Washington. Data collection techniques, goals, objectives, and criterion-referenced tests were included for exemplary purposes.

As a final instructional component, table games and suggested "quiet" activities, which can be conducted in the classroom or residential setting, were outlined.

REFERENCES

Allport, G.W. *Pattern and growth in personality.* New York: Holt, Rinehart and Winston, 1961.

Baroff, C.S. *Mental retardation: Nature, cause and management.* New York: Wiley, 1974.

Bialer, I. Relationship of mental retardation to emotional disturbance and physical disability. In H.C. Haywood (Ed.), *Social-cultural aspects of mental retardation.* New York: Appleton-Century-Crofts, 1970.

Bowers, L. *Play learning centers for preschool handicapped children.* Research and Demonstration Project Report. Tampa, Florida: University of South Florida, College of Education, Professional Physical Education Program, August, 1975.

Carlson, B.W., & Ginglend, D.R. *Play activities for the retarded child.* New York: Abingdon, 1961.

Cromwell, R.L. Personality evaluation. In A. A. Baumeister (Ed.), *Mental retardation: Appraisal, education, and rehabilitation.* Chicago: Aldine, 1967.

Garvey, C. *Play.* Cambridge, Massachusetts: Harvard University Press, 1977.

Gerson, D. *Be big somewhere: The structured playroom for the severely and profoundly retarded.* Unpublished manuscript, Rainier School, Buckley, Washington, 1975.

Heber, R.F. Personality. In H.A. Stevens & R. Heber (Eds.), *Mental retardation: A review of research.* Chicago: University of Chicago Press, 1964.

Hutt, M.L., & Gibby, R.G. *The mentally retarded child* (3rd ed.). Boston: Allyn and Bacon, 1976.

Kolstoe, O.P. *Teaching educable mentally retarded children.* New York: Holt, Rinehart and Winston, 1976.

MacMillan, D.L. *Mental retardation in school and society.* Boston: Little, Brown, 1977.

Piaget, J. *Play, dreams, and imitation in childhood.* New York: W.W. Norton, 1962.

Robinson, N.M., & Robinson, H.B. *The mentally retarded child.* New York: McGraw-Hill, 1976.

Webster, T.G. Unique aspects of emotional development in mentally retarded children. In F.J. Menolascino (Ed.), *Psychiatric approaches to mental retardation.* New York: Basic Books, 1970.

Zigler, E. Rigidity in the feeble-minded. In E.P. Trapp & P. Himelstein (Eds.), *Readings on the exceptional child.* New York: Appleton-Century-Crofts, 1962.

Chapter 9

Mobility Skills Training

A basic skill required for citizens within our society is the ability to travel independently within the community. In order to fulfill basic needs and to strive toward self-actualization, citizens in this complex society move about and interact with their environment. People travel daily to go to work, to shop, to socialize, and to engage in leisure-time activities (Laus, 1977, p. ix).

The idea that severely mentally retarded individuals can be taught independent travel skills is rarely proposed, even by professionals in the field. In fact, the President's Committee on Mental Retardation's 1972 publication on *Transportation and the Mentally Retarded* suggested that there was a dearth of specific programs designed to provide instruction in independent travel to mentally retarded individuals. Perhaps the two major reasons for this lack of programming are a lack of qualified instructors and extremely low expectations for the capability of severely retarded individuals for independent travel.

As with all instruction for the severely retarded, professionals must not only raise their expectations but prepare the type of appropriate program to facilitate the instruction of independent travel skills.

EARLY PROGRAMS OF TRAVEL INSTRUCTION FOR THE MENTALLY RETARDED

One of the earliest programs of independent travel training for moderately and severely retarded persons was described by Tobias (1963). In this program potential clients of a sheltered workshop in New York City were made aware that one of the program prerequisites was independent travel to work each day.

215

Tobias (1963) followed a specific procedure to train clients in independent travel skills:

1. A member of the facility staff was assigned as a personal tutor to accompany the client from and to his home by the most appropriate means of public transportation.
2. The staff person was responsible for the safety of the client.
3. The parents received assurances that self-travel would only be permitted when mastery of the route was established.

Further experience in this training program led Tobias (1963) to suggest general practices for all clients receiving travel instruction:

1. Close client supervision by staff is employed to reduce parental anxiety.
2. Professionals and parents share the client's successful achievements to reinforce even reluctant approval.
3. The trainee's anxiety is reduced by verbal assurances and direct assistance as long as it is required. Partial successes are always rewarded with praise. When the client completes the program successfully, he receives a diploma in a public ceremony to the applause of parents and peers.
4. The training process must be designed to allow for the slow acquisition of cues that have relevance for the client. Appropriate landmarks such as stores or newspaper stands must be substituted for printed street signs. The most limited literacy is utilized even if it involves initial letters or a few digits.
5. Special difficulties such as pushing turnstiles, inattentiveness, or lack of ability to identify coins must be overcome by a special tutoring program.

One significant finding of the Tobias (1963) effort was that while there was a relationship between intelligence quotients and the ability to benefit from travel training, the level of intelligence required has been generally overestimated. Tobias (1963) noted that travel instruction was proven feasible with clients whose IQs were under 30.

Cortazzo and Sansone (1969) described a program in which nearly two hundred profoundly to moderately mentally retarded clients at eight activity centers throughout the United States were taught independent travel skills. The IQ range of the group that learned independent travel was 12 to 55 with a mean IQ of 33. Cortazzo and Sansone (1969) listed seven major phases of their travel training program:

1. selection of trainees
2. teaching identification fact-skills
3. teaching pedestrian skills

4 teaching the travel route

5. teaching the handling of money

6. teaching conveyance identification

7. counseling parents

One of the early selection criteria for this program was an IQ of at least 30; however, the authors immediately realized that the IQ was an unimportant criteria in the trainee selection process. There is no evidence of any relationship between the IQ and the ability to learn independent travel, nor is the IQ a valid predictor of a person's success or lack of success as an independent travel trainee (Tobias, 1963; Kubat, 1973; Laus, 1974).

One interesting area of the Cortazzo and Sansone (1969) travel training program involved teaching clients basic facts about themselves, their homes, and the activity center; identification of stationary and moving objects; traffic, street, and safety signs; community helpers; and warning signals including flashing and red lights, whistles, and sirens. The following items were included in the list of basic facts:

Self	taxi	local
name	push-pull	entrance
home address	press	exit
phone number	push to open	change
age	move to rear	information
parents' names	men	tickets
	ladies	telephone
Center	women	deposit money
name of center	restroom	fare
address	danger	in-out
phone number	high voltage	up-down
director/instructor's	keep out	stairs
name	shelter	caution
	no smoking	escalator
Signs	emergency door	tokens
stop-red	take cover	safety zone
go-green	men working	crossing
walk-green	explosives	
don't walk-red	detour	
cross	use other door	
bus stop	use other exit	*Warning Signals*
train station	closed	sirens
downtown	police	whistles
uptown	conductor	flashing lights

Colors	Numbers	Time
red	1 through 25	morning
green		noon
amber	Police Signals	afternoon
	to cross	evening
	to stop	night
Money	right-left	hour
penny 1¢	middle	half-hour
nickel 5¢		
dime 10¢	Weather (Radio & TV)	
quarter 25¢	threatening	
half dollar 50¢	rain, snow, fog	
dollar $1.00	temperatures	

When teaching these fact skills, it was recommended that the trainee be taken into the community to identify actual signs, signals, and objects along with classroom instruction (Cortazzo & Sansone, 1969). Laus (1977) pointed out that while the list was a useful guide of facts that an independent traveler might need to know, there was no indication of a sequence for teaching these facts, whether they were a requirement for independent travel, and whether they need to be included in an ongoing curriculum beginning at an early age.

Kubat (1973) reported on another travel training program for the retarded at the Columbus Community Center in Salt Lake City, Utah. Thirteen clients with mental ages from six to twelve and IQs in the mild to moderate range were taught to travel independently to and from the Center.

The program reported by Kubat (1973) had four different instructional phases:

1. instruction of appropriate bus riding behaviors
2. route familiarization
3. simulation of the bus ride
4. riding the bus

In 1974, Laus reported on a program in the Pittsburgh Public School System. In the first year of this program, thirty-five pupils learned to travel independently using public transportation between home and school (Laus, 1974).

THE LAUS ORIENTATION AND MOBILITY PROGRAM FOR SIGHTED MENTALLY RETARDED INDIVIDUALS

The rest of this chapter will be devoted to a description of an orientation and mobility program designed by Dr. Michael D. Laus while he was an orientation and mobility specialist for the Pittsburgh Public Schools, Pittsburgh, Pennsylvania. During this time Mori (the senior author of this book) was a doctoral student at the University of Pittsburgh, but also a former employee of the Pittsburgh Public Schools and personal friend of Dr. Laus. The fact that Mori was in Pittsburgh during the time that this unique and remarkable program was in successful operation is the major reason why it is being presented as the orientation and mobility program for this text. While there may be other programs available, first-hand experience with this program led us to strongly urge use of the specific (with modifications, of course, where necessary) attributes of the Laus program. Readers who are interested in a personal description of the trials and tribulations Dr. Laus (1977) encountered in establishing this program are encouraged to secure a copy of his textbook.

Candidate Selection

Laus (1977) described the candidates for orientation and mobility instruction as students of a center for the trainable mentally retarded whose IQ range was 25 to 50. One of the immediate actions Laus initiated was to change the name of the program from travel training to orientation and mobility training. The orientation and mobility comes from independent travel training programs for the blind. Laus chose this terminology because the process is a dynamic one. Mobility involves not only the physical movement from one location to another, but also the ability to establish and maintain contact with the realities of the surroundings (orientation). Candidates for the Laus program had to:

1. demonstrate social emotional readiness;
2. be able to learn basic routines;
3. be able to distinguish a particular bus from a set of others; and
4. be able to make action decisions and to initiate movement (Laus, 1977, p. 35).

Each of the prerequisite skills is described in some detail by the author and will be explored in this chapter.

Social emotional readiness requires that an individual be capable of dealing and interacting appropriately with unfamiliar people and situations. The process of independent travel is fraught with possible disturbances or disruptions to normal routine, which would affect an individual's ability to make judgments and decisions. For this reason it is important to select candidates who have a high stress tolerance (Laus, 1977).

The second criterion described by Laus (1977) involves the ability of the trainee to respond consistently to designated stimuli and thereby learn basic routines. In the Laus program travel routes are broken down into a chain of behaviors composed of stimulus-response units. In order to maintain orientation, the trainee must be able to respond correctly and consistently to a designated stimulus or risk becoming disoriented.

The third criterion involved the selection of the appropriate bus from all other buses. To do this, the trainee had to be able to discriminate the specific numbers (i.e., 81) from all other numbers. Laus (1977, p. 37) noted that this did not require the learner "to identify numerals, know the value of numerals, perceive them in any order; the only requirement is that a candidate be capable of knowing the difference between numerals that identify his bus and numerals that do not."

Finally, all candidates had to demonstrate the ability to self-initiate the routines and skills that they have learned (Laus, 1977). Because reliance on others was not encouraged, learners had to be able to initiate movement and action independently. Severely retarded individuals are highly dependent upon adults for direction. Independent travel calls for the person to recognize stimuli (such as a bus number) and then quickly initiate movement towards that bus. Hesitation can result in the person missing his bus and immediately becoming disoriented, thus, Laus's (1977) recommendation that candidates be able to make direct and purposeful movements and actions.

To determine whether an individual possesses or can be taught the four requisite skills, input must be gathered from a team of professionals and later, the student's parents. Included as sources of information are: (1) classroom teachers, (2) school psychologist, (3) speech therapists, (4) school nurse, (5) other school specialists, and (6) the parents.

Laus (1977) employed two specific forms to gather information from professionals and parents. Exhibit 9-1, which was completed by teachers and therapists, is included for your information.

Gaining Parental Cooperation

Once candidates are identified, it becomes necessary to secure parental permission for them to become involved in the orientation and mobility program. Parents may offer strong resistance to the notion that their "child" can be taught to travel independently for a number of reasons. Cortazzo and Sansone (1969) discussed the anxieties expressed by parents whose children were candidates for traveling training and these included:

- sexual molestation
- kidnapping
- injuries or accidents
- getting lost
- ridicule by others
- failure to learn because of retardation
- helplessness in emergencies

Exhibit 9-1

Form 1

ORIENTATION AND MOBILITY INFORMATION SURVEY

Name _____Age _____
Address _____
Room No._____IQ_____No. of Siblings_____
Hearing Impairments _____Vision Impairments_____
Speech Impairments _____
Other Physical Impairments_____
Medical Impairments _____
   1. Does pupil get along with his peers? _____
   2. Does pupil get along with familiar adults?_____
   3. Does pupil get along with unfamiliar adults?_____
   4. Does pupil deal appropriately with new and unexpected situations?_____
   5. Does pupil exhibit any bizarre behaviorisms?_____
   6. How long of a time period can pupil attend to a task in a group setting?_____
   7. How long can the pupil attend to a task in a one-to-one situation?_____
   8. Does pupil follow directions? _____
   9. Can you rely on pupil to complete a task once it is begun? _____
  10. Is pupil able to identify and distinguish green, yellow and red? _____
  11. Is pupil able to identify and distinguish green, yellow and red signals of a traffic light? _____
  12. Is pupil able to count objects?_____
  13. Can pupil recognize numerals?_____
  14. Is pupil able to identify money?_____
  15. Is pupil able to exchange money accurately?_____
  16. Can pupil read basic street signs? _____
  17. Is pupil able to speak coherently?_____
  18. Is pupil able to communicate orally his or her home address and phone number?
  _____
  19. Is pupil able to use a public pay phone independently?_____
  20. Does pupil initiate conversation, or does he only respond once he is addressed?_
  _____
  21. Does pupil initiate movement within classroom or building or does he wait for direction? _____
  22. Does pupil have to be told to do everything? _____
Remarks_____
_____
_____
_____
_____
_____

Source: From *Travel instruction for the handicapped,* by M.D. Laus, pp. 38-39. © 1977. Reprinted by permission of Charles C. Thomas, publisher, Springfield, Illinois.

- physical stress on the health of the retarded
- dangers in traveling in inclement weather
- failure to recognize impending dangers or hazardous situations
- detriment to parents' already precarious health because of worry

Of course, many of these concerns relate to the parents' unawareness of the capability of the mentally retarded for independent travel. The task of the teacher or professional then becomes one of intervention in which the parents receive sufficient counseling and/or other supportive services to accept their child's needs for a more normalized living routine.

The relative inability of any retarded person to cope with the natural and social demands of his environment may be exaggerated by parents' tendency to overprotect. Sharlin and Polansky (1971) noted that overprotection tends to perpetuate this child's dependence on his parents and prevents his acquiring adaptive skills of which he is capable.

Saenger (1957) conducted a survey in which he attempted to evaluate the extent of overprotection in families of adults who had attended classes for the mentally retarded (IQ below 50) in New York City. While the estimates of the interviewees are acknowledged to be subjective, they did suggest overprotection in about four out of every ten families in this group. Approximately three out of ten families made an attempt to actively encourage independent behavior by their child. Certain variables were found to be related to overprotection and included: physical handicaps, Down's syndrome stigmata, and a vacant expression. Saenger (1957) concluded that overprotection might serve to compensate for real or expected rejection based upon the retarded person's appearance.

Robinson and Robinson (1976) noted that while overprotection is difficult to assess, certain factors that may be present are suggestive of it. The factors suggestive of overprotection include: (1) adaptive behavioral ratings much lower than mental age would suggest (in the absence of crippling physical or sensory defects), (2) children who continually ask for assistance, (3) children who demonstrate poor large-muscle coordination in the absence of physical impairment, and (4) children who have difficulty separating from their mothers.

What can the teacher or counselor do to eliminate overprotection and foster a climate of receptiveness to training in orientation and mobility? Linde and Kopp (1973) describe a number of ways teachers/counselors can help parents face reality issues, the day to day management problems of having a severely retarded person in the family. First, the professionals can serve as sounding boards and allies. When they function in this capacity, they serve to communicate to parents a respect for the capabilities of the mentally retarded person, something which the parents may have lost sight of during difficult times. Additionally, the professional can serve to reestablish the expectations of the parents for the child's becoming a worthy and contributing member of the family.

Secondly, a teacher/counselor can serve as a role model, communicating a respect for the rights of the mentally retarded to experience ordinary risk taking. In this capacity the teacher/counselor is called upon to help parents realize that "overprotection endangers the client's human dignity, and tends to keep him from experiencing the risk taking of ordinary life which is necessary for normal human growth and development" (Perske, 1972, p. 195). This role modeling may include allowing parents to observe their child interacting with the teacher/counselor or other adults in the school or sheltered workshop, especially when this interaction is characterized by adult to adult relationships.

Thirdly, teacher/counselors can strongly urge parents to communicate with or join parent groups. If reluctant parents are given an opportunity to meet other parents whose children have engaged in "risky" instruction, it often facilitates cooperation and commitment. In other words, some parents will listen and respond to other parents far better than they will to professionals.

Laus (1977) advocates a counseling approach to secure parental cooperation that includes: (1) the provision of valid and useful information about the ability of the retarded to engage in independent travel and the safe instructional process which would lead to this goal; (2) the free choice of parents to decide whether their child will or will not receive orientation and mobility instruction; and (3) internal commitment that is built into the program by having parents share in the travel route planning and other program details.

This framework has been provided so that teacher/counselors may become involved in the process of securing parental cooperation for mobility training. Remember, parents are people with genuine concerns for the safety of their child. Teachers will need to become involved in the process of assisting parents to recognize the benefits of orientation and mobility instruction.

Teaching Orientation and Mobility Skills

Laus (1977) described the teaching of orientation and mobility skills as having five distinct phases:

1. analyzing the skill
2. assessing entering behavior
3. arranging for training in the component units
4. describing and demonstrating the skill
5. providing for the three basic learning conditions

The skills involved in independent use of a bus were analyzed in terms of stimulus-response units (S-R). The S-R units involved in riding a public bus from the center to home are the following (Laus, 1977, p. 62):

S   Identify bus-stop sign

R   Stand by the bus-stop sign

•

S   Identify bus

R   Enter bus

•

S   Face driver

R   Pay fare

•

S   Identify unoccupied seat

R   Sit down

•

S   Identify landmarks for alighting

R   Ring buzzer

•

S   Door opens

R   Alight from bus

•

S   Faced with familiar neighborhood

R   Walk home

The next step, assessing entering behavior or the individual's level of present functioning, is conducted by an analysis of the *Orientation and Mobility Information Survey* and a parent interview. Once parents are involved in the counseling sessions to gain their cooperation, they become an important source of information. Laus (1977) employed a specific questionnaire (see Exhibit 9-2) *Parent Interview Form*, to gather data on the candidate's entering behavior.

Training in component areas is provided by teachers, parents, or the orientation and mobility instructor. Often the skills will need to be further task-analyzed into small sequential steps and practiced and reinforced until the student masters the sequence of skills. For example, the student may require instruction in paying the fare. This skill may be further broken down into:

Exhibit 9-2

Form 2

PARENT INTERVIEW FORM

Name _____

Parent of _____

Address _____

1. Does your child play unsupervised in your neighborhood? _____
2. How far is your child permitted to play away from home? _____
3. Does your child travel independently to a friend's or relative's home? _____
4. Does your child travel independently and make purchases at a local business? _

_____

5. Is your child able to handle money responsibly? _____
6. Does your family routinely use public transportation? _____
7. Has your child used a public transit bus in your company? _____
   How often? _____
8. Where has your child traveled by public transit while accompanied by others? __

_____

   How often? _____
9. Does your child regularly use a public bus? _____
   For what purpose? _____
Comments _____

_____
_____
_____
_____
_____

Source: From *Travel instruction for the handicapped* by M.D. Laus, pp. 65-66, ©
1977. Reprinted by permission of Charles C. Thomas, publisher, Springfield, Illinois.

---

1. remove wallet from trousers/purse
2. display his pass to driver
        or
   remove appropriate coin(s)
3. deposit a ten-cent ticket in fare box
        or
   deposit correct change in box
4. indicate to driver that he wishes a transfer receipt
5. hold the transfer receipt in his hand
6. close wallet
7. return wallet to pocket/purse
   (Laus, 1977, p. 67)

Each component skill is practiced using simulation activities and verbal instructions.

The fourth area, describing and demonstrating the skill, involves the actual instruction of the student on an individualized travel route between school and home (Laus, 1977). In this instance the recommended teaching method is to employ regularly scheduled public conveyances.

During the instructional process, the learner uses the normal means of transportation. Beginning at the center or school a round trip between home and center is completed. Laus (1977) recommended that only one basic travel route be taught in order for the student to learn the skills and become comfortable with the route. Once this occurs to the satisfaction of the instructor, alternate routes and different destinations may be attempted.

Finally, the basic learning conditions of contiguity, practice, and feedback are combined into the teaching situation (Laus, 1977). Contiguity, or the almost simultaneous occurrence of stimulus and response occurred when a backward chaining sequence was used for instruction. The final component of the sequence is taught first with further instruction proceeding in a backward fashion. Practice or repetition is a key element for teaching independent travel. Once instruction began, Laus (1977) noted that it continued until the learner was able to perform the complete task. It was noted that it took between four days and four weeks of daily instruction (average 2.5 weeks) per pupil (Laus, 1977). Feedback, the final element, was provided verbally to each participant. Laus (1977) selectively reinforced appropriate behaviors to shape the learners' behavior to have them respond appropriately to each unit of the component chain.

The program for teaching orientation and mobility to severely retarded individuals is admittedly one-sided. In other chapters, a greater variety of techniques was presented with substantial flexibility and latitude for instructors to modify and present their own instructional strategies. This is not the case with the instructional strategy for independent travel. A *single* methodology has been completely endorsed here for a number of reasons.

1. the method has documented evidence of its success;
2. it is specifically delineated and described by the author; and
3. instruction in independent travel (orientation and mobility) is rarely included in traditional teacher-training programs, thus the need to employ a tested program presented in a "cookbook" fashion.

SUMMARY

This chapter described early programs of independent travel instruction for the mentally retarded. The Laus Orientation and Mobility Program for Sighted Mentally Retarded Individuals was described and discussed in detail.

Certain factors involving independent travel for the severely retarded must be noted:

1. research indicates that individuals with IQs under 30 can be taught independent travel skills;
2. there is no evidence establishing a relationship between IQ and the ability to learn to travel independently;
3. IQ is not a valid predictor of a person's success or lack of success as a candidate for travel training;
4. factors including social readiness, the ability to follow routines, and the ability to make decisions and initiate movement are most critical to learning independent travel skills.

REFERENCES

Cortazzo, A.C., & Sansone, R. Travel training. *Teaching Exceptional Children*, 1969, *3*, 67-82.

Kubat, A. A unique experiment in independent travel. *Journal of Rehabilitation*, 1973, *2*, 36-39.

Laus, M.D. Orientation and mobility instruction for the sighted trainable mentally retarded. *Education and Training of the Mentally Retarded*, 1974, *9*, 70-72.

Laus, M.D. *Travel instruction for the handicapped.* Springfield, Illinois: Charles C. Thomas, 1977.

Linde, T.F., & Kopp, T. *Training retarded babies and pre-schoolers.* Springfield, Illinois: Charles C. Thomas, 1973.

Perske, R. The dignity of risk. In W. Wolfensberger (Ed.), *The principle of normalization in human services.* Toronto: National Institute on Mental Retardation, 1972.

President's Committee on Mental Retardation. *Transportation and the mentally retarded.* Washington, D.C.: National Center for Educational Research and Development (DHEW/OE), 1972.

Robinson, N.M., & Robinson, H.B. *The mentally retarded child* (2nd ed.). New York: McGraw-Hill, 1976.

Saenger, G. The adjustment of severely retarded adults in the community. Albany: Interdepartmental Health Resources Board, 1957.

Sharlin, S.A., & Polansky, N.A. The process of infantilization. *American Journal of Orthopsychiatry*, 1971, *42*, 92-102.

Tobias, J. *Training for independent living.* New York: Association for Help of Retarded Children, 1963.

Chapter 10

Occupational Skills Training

Currently in the United States there is a period of national commitment to the development and enhancement of all handicapped persons regardless of the severity of their condition. To achieve this goal, it is necessary to provide training in occupational skill development. Many professionals lose sight of the fact that a severely retarded child grows up to be a severely retarded adult. Unlike the mildly retarded individual, the severely retarded person will never be easily assimilated into the societal mainstream. Unfortunately, few alternatives are available for severely retarded adults, the majority of whom will languish in institutions after they reach the maximum age for school attendance.

In 1962, the President's Panel on Mental Retardation recommended decentralization of institutional services and a range of community-based services for the total range of moderately retarded individuals from preschool through adult life. A variety of services were proposed by the panel including: sheltered environments, adult activity centers, and community-based group homes.

Burton (1976) noted that although vocational programs for the moderately retarded adult are defended on the basis of consistency with the normalization principle, there are problems in developing the work potential of the moderately retarded person—all the problems identified as relevant to vocational preparation of the moderately retarded exist in greater magnitude for the severely retarded adult. As Blue (1964) noted, preparation for sheltered employment requires early and extensive training in the following areas:

1. gross and fine motor skills
2. perseverance
3. sustained performance
4. response to motivation and rewards

When educators fail to initiate these experiences early on in the severely retarded person's schooling, they may be predetermining that student's failure in sheltered settings.

This chapter will discuss skill development in occupational education as a continuum of training that is interwoven throughout the severely retarded individual's educational experience. Occupational education begins in preschool and continues throughout the person's life.

The areas of discussion in this chapter will include the basic skill areas for occupational education and teaching techniques for the basic skill areas.

Finally, the tone is set for this chapter by citing Wolfensberger's (1967) vocational creed for the retarded. He suggested that this creed was consistent with the cultural values of United States society and contributed to the habilitation of the retarded:

1. A working retardate is generally a happier person. Work gives self-esteem and a feeling of accomplishment and worth.
2. Work lends adult status to a retardate, and thus adds to his dignity in the sight of others.
3. In our work-oriented society, positive attitudes will generally be expressed toward the worker, and negative ones toward the drone. Thus, the retardate's adjustment will be enhanced by the community attitudes he encounters.
4. The family of the working retardate is, generally, a better adjusted family. Since work tends to make the retardate more acceptable, it engenders positive attitudes in the family benefiting the retardate indirectly.
5. A retardate capable of working will be less likely to become an economic burden to his family or society.
6. A working retardate contributes to the economic welfare of society.
7. He earns an income that is likely to give him more of the material benefits enjoyed by the majority of our citizens.
8. Idleness can lead to nonadaptive or maladaptive behavior (p. 233).

BASIC SKILL AREAS FOR OCCUPATIONAL EDUCATION

We can certainly identify basic skills and knowledge one must possess in order to perform any task or job successfully. For most nonretarded learners these basic skills are learned in the course of normal development or through school experiences. On the other hand, the severely retarded learner often fails to gain an adequate grasp of these basic skills and, therefore, fails to function competently in occupationally relevant situations.

A list of basic skills needed by severely retarded individuals to function in occupational roles is presented in Table 10-1. This table adapts a portion of the Basic Skill/ Concept Index (Phelps & Lutz, 1977) and incorporates competency and behavior lists developed for this book by Mori and Masters. This list presents and defines basic skills and concepts relevant to occupational education in seven major skill areas:

1. communication
2. social/self-help
3. mobility
4. recreation
5. perceptual/fine motor
6. gross motor/physical
7. work adjustment

It should be noted that the list of basic skills can be used in a number of ways in the instructional process:

1. to identify the learner's areas of strength and weakness
2. to develop instructional content and techniques focusing upon the individual's need areas
3. to evaluate learner progress in attaining basic skills

The list is neither exhaustive nor complete, but rather a reference. Users should rearrange the skills by category, insert additional skills, or modify the skill list in any way necessary for it to meet the instructional needs of their students. Additionally, not all students will be able to achieve competency in all areas. The instructors' knowledge of the unique pattern of the learner's abilities and deficits will determine which skills they choose to teach and those that they realize the learner is not capable of achieving. Finally, occupational skill development should not be an appendage to the school program. Rather, it is a basic thread to be woven into the educational structure from preschool through adulthood. Many of the basic skills can be developed early in the severely retarded person's life and further developed and refined through occupationally related instructional experiences in the activity center or sheltered workshop.

Table 10-1 Basic Skill Areas for Occupational Education

Skill Area: Communication	Definition
1. Sound localization	determines the source or location of sounds
2. Listening	listens attentively for sound patterns from the environment and words spoken by others
3. Discrimination (Auditory)	a. figure-ground—focuses on a word or sound without having the background or setting interfere b. distinguishes differences between sounds and words c. retains a sequence of sounds within words and words within sentences d. reacts to voice tone and inflection and recognizes emotions and feelings
4. Identification of objects	comprehends words as symbols for objects and eventually as concepts
5. Nonverbal reception	reacts and recognizes the meaning of gestures
6. Responds to instruction	comprehends new task with physical prompt, modeling, or verbal description
7. Follows directions	retains information in proper sequence for immediate action or recall a. initially one step b. two to four steps c. more than four steps
8. Expressive communication	expresses needs, actions, objects, feelings, and concepts through: a. gesture b. sign language c. communication board d. voice

Skill Area: Social/Self-help	Definition
1. Independent toileting and maintenance of personal hygiene	takes care of toileting needs and practices appropriate washing and bathing habits
2. Cooperativeness	exhibits a willingness to carry out tasks or activities that are taught and interacts appropriately with teachers and peers
3. Attentiveness	listens to directions, follows instructions, and attends to task as required
4. On-task behavior	maintains performance until the task is completed
5. Appropriate behavior	does not exhibit unappropriate gestures, verbalizations, actions, and mannerisms
6. Absence of supervision	maintains a consistent work rate when unsupervised; works well without direct continuous supervision

Table 10-1 continued

Skill Area: Mobility	Definition
1. General mobility skills	demonstrates social-emotional readiness; is able to learn basic routines; has the ability to distinguish public conveyances; and is able to make action decisions and initiate movement
2. Movement	walks or moves to various locations with little or no problem: a. workshop (activity center) b. general vicinity of workshop c. around the home
3. Independent travel	assistance to travel to various destinations a. home to workshop (round trip) b. within neighborhood c. community

Skill Area: Recreation	Definition
1. Recreation in the activity center	appropriate participation in scheduled recreational activities
2. Recreation in the community	appropriate participation in public recreational programs

Skill Area: Perceptual/ Fine motor	Definition
1. General perceptual/fine motor abilities	demonstrates ability to move and control head, eyes, fingers, and mouth; is able to reach and grasp with: a. palmar grasp b. pincher grasp
2. Form perception	can recognize the qualities of size, shape, and texture
3. Form discrimination	can distinguish differences in forms using qualities of size, shape, and texture
4. Color discrimination	can recognize and distinguish colors and shades
5. Haptic discrimination	can recognize differences in texture, weight, size, shape, and composition through touch and movement
6. Finger dexterity	can efficiently use the fingers to complete tasks and manipulate small objects and hand tools
7. Speed and accuracy	can combine skill areas to complete tasks quickly and correctly within physical and intellectual limitations

Table 10-1 continued

Skill Area: Gross motor/ physical	Definition
1. General gross motor abilities	demonstrates ability to: a. control head b. sit c. crawl, kneel, climb d. bring hands to midline e. walk or move
2. General physical health	has stamina, endurance, and relative resistance to fatigue
3. Physical strength	can lift, carry, push, and pull objects within certain limits ranging from seat work (moves less than 10 pounds) to very heavy work (moves over 100 pounds)
4. Eye-hand coordination	uses eyes and hands (fingers) together to perform a variety of tasks
5. Eye-hand-foot co-ordination	uses eyes, hands (fingers) and feet together to perform a variety of tasks
6. Bi-manual coordination	uses both hands together to perform a variety of tasks
7. Manual dexterity	can use hands efficiently to complete a number of movements such as turning, twisting, pulling, pushing, etc.; can use hand tools and operate machinery

Skill Area: Work adjustment	Definition
1. Punctuality	appears at job station on time: a. in the morning b. after breaks c. after lunch
2. Correction	completes task correctly after a specific number of corrections a. 10+ b. 5 to 10 c. 3 to 5 d. less than 3
3. Responsibility	does not leave job station inappropriately
4. Sociability	does not display disruptive behaviors or interfere with others
5. Initiative	works consistently with varying degrees of supervision: a. 10+ contacts by supervisor b. 5 to 10 contacts c. 3 to 5 contacts d. less than 3 contacts

Table 10-1 continued

6. Absence of attention seeking	does not initiate inappropriate contact with supervisor
7. Independence	works independently under the following conditions:
	a. alone at a table
	b. alone, with others at the table
	c. assembly line work
8. Perseverance	works on a job continuously from start to finish
9. Safety	avoids hazardous actions, movements, and conditions in the workshop setting

Source: From *Career exploration and preparation for the special needs learner* by L.A. Phelps and R.J. Lutz, pp. 235-242. © 1977. Reprinted by permission of Allyn and Bacon, Inc. Boston, Mass.

Many procedures and techniques for teaching the basic skill areas of communication, social self-help, mobility, recreation, perceptual-fine motor, gross motor-physical, and work adjustment have been covered in previous chapters of this text. A few specific subskills within several of the broad basic skill areas have yet to receive attention; therefore, it is essential that these training components be discussed.

Communication: Subskill/Training Cue Words

A fundamental vocabulary of words, signs, or gestures that corresponds to actions, objects, and equipment is critical to the teaching process. Without a method of communication, new skills are more difficult to teach, and work can be hazardous because warnings cannot be given. The following Table 10-2 lists the fundamentals of communication cues appropriate for the activity center and the sheltered workshop:

Table 10-2 Communication Cues

Action Words	Commands
Push Pull Carry	Stop Start No
Lift up Hold Turn on/off	Stand up Sit down
Put down	

Communication: Subskill—Action Words

Students should receive exposure to the actions of push, pull, carry, and turn in all training areas; however, due to intellectual limitations, these concepts will seldom carry over (generalization) to other tasks in the activity area or sheltered workshop.

In most work settings the economic usefulness of an individual will depend on his ability to operate simple tools, machines, and/or perform manual skills. Often opposing actions such as lift up and put down can be best taught in conjunction.

Nearly all instruction that involves teaching new skills requires two components. First, a reinforcer must follow the manual action; and second, the word(s) must be spoken or a sign presented prior to and during the manual action. It is also recommended that actual tools and machinery be used instead of simulated equipment that serves no actual function. The following are suggestions for teaching:

- *Pushing in a Stationary Position*
  With the student standing or sitting at a table, contract the arms with palms facing an empty box. The instructor moves the box to the student's hands until its corners are touching the hands. As the instructor says "push" the student is assisted in straightening the arms until the box moves the arms' length.
- *Pushing and Moving*
  For students who are ambulatory, the act of pushing should also be taught using a laundry cart, shopping cart, and dolly. Initial training should be done by pushing the cart through sturdy guides and along a brightly colored tape path on the floor. Guide rails should be of heavy pipe or smooth wooden construction and used only in preliminary training sessions.
- *Pull and Push*
  Pulling the handle of a drill press down and pushing it back up serves as an excellent training task. Of course, a drill bit is not used, and the machine is turned off until the individual is ready for its operation.
- *Lift/Carry/Put Down*
  Lift up, carry, and put down can be taught together using flour sacks, light boxes, and wooden logs. Students must be physically handled by the instructor so that they assume a safe lifting posture. The following skill sequence may be used:

  1. student stands in front of item to be lifted
  2. instructor positions herself directly behind student
  3. instructor tells student to "lift up" the object
  4. instructor's hands are placed on student's hips
  5. instructor's knees are positioned behind student's

6. instructor holds student at the hips and pushes against the back of the knees, forcing student to a squat position
7. student is directed to "lift up" the object
8. student is assisted by instructor to a standing position
9. student is instructed to "carry" object to a given point (at least 5 steps)
10. instructor stands behind student with hands on the student's hips
11. student is again forced to squatting position and told to "put down" object

- *Turning*
  The verbal cue and visual symbol of turn are used in teaching students to use hand tools. Instruction should begin with large arm movements using a "homemade" wrench device or a large ratchet handle attached to a fixed bolt. Turning clockwise or counterclockwise can be taught by pairing the cue of turn on or off with manual assistance in the appropriate direction. Reinforcement should follow appropriate movements.
- *Stop/Start*
  Instruction for stop and start begins in early motor programs, yet students may not respond to such commands in the work area without training. Students should be taught the meaning of stop in a variety of task situations by physically restricting further motor actions while giving the verbal or visual cue.
- *Stand up/Sit down*
  The two fundamental actions of standing and sitting on command are necessary to teach if a student is to change positions for different job tasks. The training procedure remains the same—force the individual to perform the act while pairing the cue. Reinforcement is given once the response is completed successfully.

Social/Self-Help: Subskill—On-Task Behavior and Supervision

Training techniques for toileting, bathing, and shaving were provided in previous chapters; however, the areas of initiating and keeping a student on task with and without supervision remain.

Direct supervision is often a problem due to student/teacher ratios. For this reason several monitoring systems are suggested that require few personnel and a limited amount of direct contact once the task is learned. The key to developing on-task behavior lies in three parts: (1) breaking the task into small achievable steps that lead to the terminal behavior; (2) the reinforcer and its schedules; and (3) verbal and gestural cues associated with the task. According to Crosson (1969) successful training requires the administration of immediate and continuous reinforcement after the correct completion of each step that approximates or leads to the terminal behavior. Once the steps of the task have been mastered successfully, the schedule of reinforcement can be altered gradually until the payoff comes at the completion of an entire sequence or even several sequences. When performance becomes reliable and consistent, reinforcers can be changed, eventually becoming the "higher order" type.

A problem common to many teachers is that their student's production or maintainence of on-task behavior drops severely when they leave the student's immediate vicinity. Much of this behavior is unknowingly brought on by the teacher. Teachers want students to succeed so they "hover" over them, making sure that everything goes smoothly. Pampering and consoling often contribute to the student's conditioned need for support and attention.

Social/Self-Help: Subskill—Production Monitoring

Direct teacher contact must be gradually phased out and replaced by individual monitoring systems. One method works on the same principle as biofeedback; however, it is partially controlled by a production supervisor.

Each work station is equipped with a green light or quiet sounding buzzer. A floor supervisor is stationed in a room where the activities of each worker can be viewed continually. Each work station light and buzzer is connected to a monitoring panel that the floor supervisor controls. Workers are taught that rewards will be dispensed only when the green light is turned on or the buzzer is not sounding. The floor supervisor controls the light, leaving it on when the worker is producing and turning it off when he is not. For blind individuals, the buzzer is sounded when production stops or slows down. Rewards are given out according to each worker's reinforcement schedule and are dispensed in several ways: (1) through direct administration by a production assistant or (2) a mechanical electronically controlled device. Traditionally, it has been difficult for one person to observe a large number of workers and dispense rewards appropriately. With a light or buzzer system, continuous monitoring can be achieved with only two supervisors who have little or no direct interaction with the learners.

Perceptual Fine Motor: Subskill—Perceptual Information

Teaching students to perceive forms by various attributes, color, shape, size, or texture and make discriminations requires a number of instructional tasks. Hopefully, students will reach a point where they can perform these functional skills across tasks, materials, people, verbal language cues, and settings that they frequently encounter (Williams, Coyne, Johnson, Scheuerman, Swetlik, & York, 1977). According to a study by Gold and Barclay (1973) moderately and severely retarded adults with measured intelligence quotients ranging from 20 to 57 can be taught to make visual discriminations of bolts varying in length by one-eighth inch.

This study suggests that severely retarded individuals can be expected to make the same visual discriminations performed by "normal" individuals. Based on this finding an inference can be drawn that intelligence may be related to the length of time it takes to identify what the problem is and not discriminatory ability itself.

It is recommended that the instruction of perceptual information begin with teaching perception of form, form discrimination, then color recognition and discrimination. During initial instruction periods, it is also helpful to teach the task area (i.e., form perception) with the same teacher using the same verbal cues and in the same setting. Changes can be introduced, thus promoting learning and accommodation to varying situations.

Perceptual Fine Motor: Subskill—Form Perception

The recognition of shape, size, and texture are qualities that will be extremely useful in performing work tasks.

Shape

The introduction of perceptions involving shape begins by teaching the learner to perceive roundness. Instruction is initiated by introducing objects that are round, i.e., tables, tops of coffee cups, or balls of various sizes. The students must put their hands around the object in order to receive information haptically as well as verbally and visually. Additional experiences include: (1) having students feel objects in the room and work setting that are round; (2) crawling on mats following a brightly colored taped circle; (3) sitting in a circle holding hands; (4) making circular motions with the hands and drawing circles on the blackboard; and (5) forming a circle with elastic rope using a group of people.

Whenever students are exploring an object, the teacher should verbally describe the shape, saying the name over and over. The following shapes are important: (1) round, (2) circle, (3) rectangle, (4) square, (5) triangle, and (6) cube.

The learners' recognition of various shapes can also be evaluated by placing objects in front of them and asking the learners to point to the "round" object. Students may also demonstrate their understanding by reaching into a bag of mixed shapes and removing the one that corresponds to the verbal cue.

The instructional sequence for teaching shapes should begin with one specific form (i.e., roundness) before progressing on to others.

Size

"Big" and "little" are two concepts that should be taught. This teaching can be accomplished in much the same way as in teaching form perception. Touching, holding, crawling over, lifting, and carrying "big" objects serve as learning experiences. The instructor should guide the students' fingers and arms around the outside of the object as its size is described. As a number of "big" objects are explored, the instructor can begin pairing word "big" with shapes previously learned.

Once the concept of "big" has been established, learners are ready for the opposing size of "little." Instruction relative to this should again include hands-on experiences with much verbalization by the instructor. As mentioned in Chapter 12, motor activities for teaching size include putting the student through movements to make them "big" or "little" are excellent training experiences.

Texture

Four basic textures to be taught are rough, smooth, hard, and soft. As with all concepts, the opposites should not be taught until their counterparts are firmly established.

Rough textures allow maximal stimulation; therefore, they should be introduced first. Students should feel coarse sandpaper, bristle brushes, prickly mats, and other rough materials with their face, feet, hands, back, tongue, and stomach. Objects and articles within the room that are rough, including the student's clothing, should be pointed out. These tactile objects should be introduced one at a time with the instructor's description of their qualities.

The concepts of smooth, hard, and soft are also taught in a tactual, feeling manner. Objects can first be explored through all appropriate sense avenues, and later understanding of each concept can be evaluated by the instructor through student identification of objects that are rough, smooth, hard, and soft. The final test of form perception will determine if the student can understand object constancy—that an object maintains the same name or meaning regardless of its position, the direction it is pointing, or with minor changes (Lerner, 1976).

Perceptual Fine Motor: Subskill—Form Discrimination

The ability to recognize and distinguish the fine differences that exist within the qualities of shape, size, and texture is called form discrimination. This ability requires the individual to make perceptual judgments through the accurate manipulation of the hands, fingers, eyes, and body. Once accurate perceptions of forms have been perceived, differences between objects and events can be taught using, at first, gross comparisons between learned forms.

The following discriminations should be presented to the severely retarded:

Shapes: Round-Circle/Square
          Square/Rectangle
          Circle/Cube
          Square/Rectangle/Triangle

Size: Big/Little
         Large/Small
Textures: Rough/Smooth
         Hard/Soft

Perceptual Fine Motor: Subskill—Color Matching (Sorting)

Students generally learn to match colors before they understand differences between colors. In teaching the color matching skill, sorting boxes and 6″ x 6″ colored cards are used. The following instructional sequence is provided:

Step 1. Student is given two red cards and one sorting box that is marked with a red card. The student is instructed to place the red cards one at a time in the sorting box.

Step 2. One blue box is added. The red cards are removed from the red box and placed in a stack with the blue card. The student is taught to place the cards in the appropriately colored boxes.

Step 3. All cards are removed and one more blue card is added to the stack. Student places cards in appropriate boxes.

Step 4. One green box is added. Cards are removed and placed in a stack. One green card is added. The student places cards in appropriate boxes.

Step 5. All cards are removed and one more green card is added to the stack. Student places cards in appropriate boxes.

Step 6. One yellow box is added. Cards are removed and placed in a stack. One yellow card is added. The student places cards in appropriate boxes.

Step 7. All cards are removed and one more yellow card is added to the stack. The student places cards in appropriate boxes.

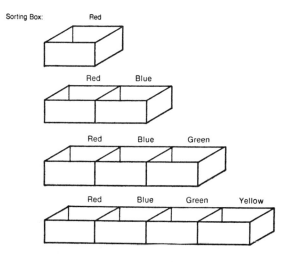

The matching skill may take hours and even days of practice; therefore, lessons should be conducted daily in the same format, using identical directions. Once Step 7 is reached, additional colors may be introduced using the same procedure. Some students may need to work on Steps 1 and 2 for a long period of time before moving on to additional colors. The student's success at mastery of this task will influence success in achieving color discrimination.

Perceptual Fine Motor: Subskill—Color Discrimination

Color discrimination or the ability to recognize fine differences between colors requires more than the simplistic skill of matching colors. In matching, students are taught that colors are the same; however, in discrimination, differences must be learned.

Once matching is mastered, the concept that colors are different can be introduced. There are many methods of teaching this concept, and the following is only one suggestion:

Step 1. Instructor places two red 6'' x 6'' cards and one blue 6'' x 6'' card in front of the student. Instructor places the two red cards together and says that they are the same. The two red cards are placed in front of the student in a pile. The blue card is first placed next to the red pile and the instructor says, "this card is different" as it is placed to the right. The piles are then taken away, and the same procedure is used again with the student placing the cards in appropriate positions and the instructor verbalizing "same and different."

Step 2. Instructor places two blue cards and one red card in front of the student. The same procedure as described in Step one is again followed with this set of cards. Additional sets of cards are introduced that have two matching colors and one unmatched color.

Teaching Color Labels

It may be useful in some situations for students to know their colors; however, in most work situations, the skill is not needed and only requires endless training hours and eventual failure. In some cases students will learn their colors after hours of practice only to forget them after a week's absence.

The teacher must think realistically when teaching academic skills and determine if the time spent is really worth the effort, especially if the skill will not be used in the work setting. Of course, teaching the names of colors does not require the learner to verbalize the color names. Instead, students can demonstrate their recognition of colors (if nonverbal) by gestures or pointing as the instructor says their names. The following activity can be used to teach the nonverbal learner the names of colors:

Place one red 6'' x 6'' card and one blue 6'' x 6'' card in front of the student. Tell the student which one is red ("this is red") and which is blue ("this is blue"). Next, direct the student to point to the red card and then the blue. Cards of different colors may be mixed with the colors previously learned in order to make sure the student understands which card is red, blue, etc.

Perceptual Fine Motor: Subskill—Speed and Accuracy

After a manipulative skill is learned, another teaching phase must take place— that of improved speed and accuracy. For the severely retarded, the absence of willingness or motivation to improve their performance is often coupled with poor finger and general muscular coordination. Due to this situation, training must include methods to stimulate motivation as well as techniques to improve finger dexterity and eye-hand coordination.

Motivation

Reinforcement is the major device used to increase motivation, which holds true for any person whether it is a bonus at the end of the month or a superior grade earned following completion of an assignment. Severely retarded learners may be taught to respond to peer pressure and attention; therefore, races, quotas, or contracts may be effective. Competition in its simplest form may be understood as students work to beat the clock, the teacher, or a fellow student. Egg timers or an hour glass may help the student gain some feeling for performing at an increased pace. Working to music, a metronome, or hand-produced rhythm may also produce positive results.

Although improved speed has its benefits, the teacher must also make sure that accuracy or quality is not sacrificed.

Finger Dexterity and Small Muscle Coordination

Research indicates that a near perfect correlation exists between measures evaluating a child's awareness of his fingers and the ability to manipulate the fingers in small motor movements (Benton, 1959; Ghent, 1961; and Ayres, 1964). Therefore, as Cratty (1967) suggests, fine motor programs must be designed to improve the student's perceptual awareness of the fingers and hands.

Creating perceptual awareness of the hands and of objects through the hands can be enhanced through manipulative activities such as finger painting, modeling and squeezing clay, wadding paper, molding Silly Putty, and feeling objects in a box. In these tasks, the emphasis is not on the final product, but on the manipulative act of moving and feeling.

The ability to manipulate objects with the fingers and move them from place to place also depends on two attributes: (1) the ability to feel objects in the fingers (sensitivity), and (2) eye-hand integration as objects are lifted, moved, and released (Cratty, 1967). These two qualities can be improved through manipulative practice using objects to be picked up, sorted, or assembled. Of course, training should begin with large objects and progress to smaller ones. In moving objects from one place to another, the size of the receptacle may be decreased as skill is improved.

Three additional qualities important to finger dexterity are aim, steadiness, and eye-hand tracking. Improvements in arm and steadiness can be enhanced through peg board activities (progressing from large to small), placing dots within a circle on a piece of paper using a paint-tipped finger or pencil, and placing objects in slots or receptacles.

Eye-hand tracking is a skill commonly associated with handwriting or drawing. Even though it is rather remote that handwriting will be used in the work setting for the severely retarded, acts such as taping, sealing, cutting, labeling, and folding all require the ability to make continuous hand movements using the guidance provided by the eyes.

Instruction in eye-hand tracking can begin with making vertical and horizontal hand movements, first without anything in the hands as the eyes lead. Next, motor tasks involving the movement of objects along a specific path can be used. In these activities a tracking wire or similar device (Figure 10-1) can serve as an intermediate step to unrestricted eye-hand movements. The tracking wire can be simply constructed of a two-inch by four-inch board, common washers, and a heavy electrical wire. The student moves the washers from point "A" to point "B" one at a time in a left to right direction. As tracking skill improves, more difficult tracking wire configurations can be taught as illustrated in Sample 2, Figure 10-1.

Figure 10-1 Tracking Wire

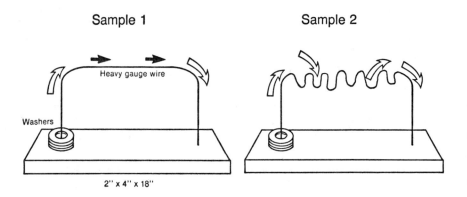

Sample 1   Sample 2

Control of eye-hand movements may also be taught using channel drawing. "Channel" or parallel lines are drawn on paper in various forms as shown in Figure 10-2. The student then draws between the border lines. At first, lines should be placed one to two inches apart. As skill improves, the distance between the guidelines can be reduced. A helpful training technique is to first cover the bordering guidelines with Elmer's glue. After it has hardened, the child will be provided a tactile cue each time the pencil or marker touches the sides. According to Cratty (1967), drawing lines or making movements in a transverse direction (upper right to lower left or upper left to lower right) are more difficult than horizontal or vertical strokes. As a final step, curved and compound shapes may be taught.

Work Adjustment: Subskill—Punctuality

Punctuality is one skill area that should be taught as part of the severely retarded learner's early school experience. The student needs to know that certain activities begin or end at a definite time. The teacher can assist in developing punctuality by associating certain times of the day, or when the student is capable, a certain time (i.e., 12:00 noon), with a definite activity. For example, if lunch is always at 12:00 noon, students can be taught that when the clock is at 12:00, all students must be present in the cafeteria. The schoolroom clock can be used as a teaching material by placing brightly colored triangles at the various times when activities are to begin. Thus class always begins at 9:00, break is at 10:00, lunch at 12:00, and

Figure 10-2 Channel Drawing

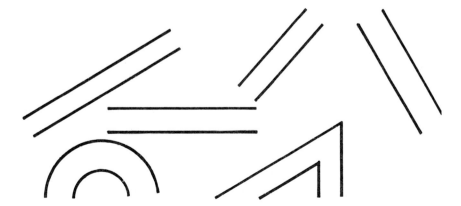

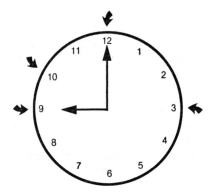

school is over when the bus comes at 3:00. In this fashion, students learn to associate time with activities they should be doing or places they should be.

In an activity center or workshop setting, two brightly colored light bulbs may be displayed in a prominent place for all clients to see (the lights may be paired with a buzzer or bell for blind clients). Thus when the green bulb is on, all clients should be at their work station. A red or other colored bulb may be used to signify break time or lunch time. Reinforcement should be used for clients who appear at their work station on time or as the green light comes on.

Work Adjustment: Subskill—Correction

With this skill, clients or students will learn to complete a task correctly after they have received a specified number of corrections. The instructor should attempt to reduce the number of corrections a student requires to successfully complete a task. When students continually do a task incorrectly, one of two conditions can be said to exist. First, it is possible that a task has not been broken down into small enough steps in order to ensure mastery. The instructor may have to further task-analyze the routine into smaller steps to facilitate learning and build these steps into the instructional sequence. Second, it is also possible that the students are reinforced by the instructor's corrections and can really do the task correctly. In this case the instructor must withdraw the learners from the task and teach them the sequence all over using edibles or some other primary reinforcement system. Put the learner back on the task and do not give any direct assistance. Primary reinforcers may have to be used continuously until the learner can be moved to an intermittent schedule and still maintain acceptable accuracy and productivity.

Work Adjustment: Subskill—Responsibility

This skill area can be taught using the light system described for teaching on-task behavior. When students leave their job station inappropriately, the light goes off and they are not rewarded. The student can be reinforced for requesting to leave the job station or leaving the station independently for appropriate reasons including: using the restroom, getting materials or supplies, requesting assistance, or going on break. The idea here is to teach students the conditions under which leaving the job station is appropriate. They should be reinforced only for these actions. Any time learners leave the job station inappropriately, they are not rewarded and can, in fact, be reprimanded.

Work Adjustment: Subskill—Initiative/Absence of Attention Seeking

The problem of excess supervision that professionals tend to apply to severely retarded individuals can unknowingly create students and subsequently workers who rely on external cues before initiating action. The instructor's role is to instill in students a relatively high degree of initiative (defined as consistent work behavior with minimal supervision) and an absence of attention-seeking behavior.

Classroom teachers can develop these skills by gradually reducing their direct supervision of students as they become proficient at performing various tasks. One way of doing this might be to provide continuous reinforcement for students who work consistently without supervision. Reinforcement systems and strategies already described may be utilized. When a high number of supervisory contacts are required, reinforcement should be reduced or eliminated completely.

Eventually, working without supervision is put on an intermittent schedule of reinforcement. This behavior can be maintained with the appropriate reinforcement schedule. Once the learner can delay gratification of reward for a sufficient period of time or when the work itself becomes gratifying, supervisory contacts become minimal.

A related behavior, absence of inappropriate contact, can be easily developed by having the instructor or supervisor ignore inappropriate student contacts. If ignoring the inappropriate contact does not extinguish the behavior, some other aversive technique may need to be applied.

Work Adjustment: Subskill—Independence

This skill area requires that students learn to work independently alone and relatively isolated, alone with others sitting nearby, and with a group in a cooperative fashion. Teaching learners to work independently alone can be facilitated by using a study carrel set off in the classroom. The student should be reinforced for independent work done in the carrel.

Once students are working independently in the carrel under an intermittent reinforcement schedule, they should be moved from the carrel to a large table where other students are working on different tasks. Reinforcement should be given when (and only when) the student works appropriately and independently. The student must be able not only to ignore the distraction of others, but also to be as nondistracting as possible.

Eventually, as students demonstrate the ability to work alone with others around them, they should be introduced to group tasks requiring a degree of sharing and cooperation. Often cooperation and sharing can be taught best in gamelike or recreational pursuits with transfer to other situations. In any case, the idea is for the student to learn to work cooperatively with others. Again, cooperative work should be reinforced continually at first, with intermittent reinforcement given as the students demonstrate the correct behavior.

Work Adjustment: Subskill—Perseverance

Perseverance, seeing a job through to completion, is another skill area that can be taught in early school experiences. The teacher should present tasks the students can complete in a relatively short period of time (it is a good idea if it is a task students have already learned). The students should be reinforced only when they complete the task. Since reinforcement is presented only upon task completion, the time for task completion should be gradually increased. For example, if the instructor begins with a task learners can complete in ten seconds, the instructor should increase task completion time in ten-second intervals until the learners' tolerance limits are reached.

Eventually the time spent on task completion should increase until the learners can complete a task from start to finish for a predetermined amount of output. The goal is to teach the student to maintain a steady, accurate job completion rate within a set of limiting criteria, i.e., fatigue, job difficulty, and physical disabilities. However, note that 90 minutes is considered a normal work interval. It will take considerable practice and reinforcement to reach this goal.

Work Adjustment: Subskill—Safety

The focus in this area is on teaching the student to avoid hazardous actions, movements, and conditions in the workshop setting. Included in this subskill would be instruction on: handling sharp objects and hand tools, handling dangerous substances, wearing safety clothing and/or protective equipment, using electrical equipment, and reacting to emergency warnings (lights, sirens, and buzzers).

1. Handling sharp objects and hand tools

The instructor should demonstrate the correct use and storage of sharp objects and hand tools, praise students for appropriate usage of such objects, and correct them about unsafe use of sharp and pointed objects.

2. *Using electrical equipment*

Students must first be taught the location of the on-off switch. The instructor should demonstrate turning equipment on and off and the safe use of the equipment. Reward the students as they use equipment safely. Distractions during the operation of electrical equipment are one of the leading causes of accidents, so stress that students should not talk while working on the equipment.

3. *Handling dangerous substances*

The students are likely to handle many "dangerous" substances in the sheltered workshop setting, i.e., glues, ammonia, paint, and paint thinners. Demonstrate the safe way of opening, using, and storing these materials. Allow the learners to practice opening cans or jars filled with water until they are able to do this safely. Safe use of these materials often involves wearing protective equipment and clothing.

4. *Wearing safety clothing and/or protective equipment*

Show the students various types of protective equipment: gloves, goggles, and hard-toe shoes. Have the students put on the equipment (provide assistance as necessary) and use it appropriately for a variety of tasks. Praise students who use the equipment appropriately. Do not allow any students to work on a task such as painting or sanding unless they locate and use the appropriate safety clothing and protective equipment.

5. *Reacting to emergency warnings*

Included among emergency warning devices would be buzzers, bells, sirens, and flashing lights. The appropriate reaction to each device may be taught step by step. For example, when the siren goes off or the buzzer sounds, the students should be able to initiate a series of movements in a predetermined sequence that will remove them quickly and safely from the danger area. Fire drills can be used to practice the skills developed in this area.

THE ACTIVITY CENTER

For the severely retarded individuals who possess some work skills but lack those skills requisite to competitive employment, the sheltered workshop is the key postschool program. However, many severely retarded individuals may lack or never possess the repertoire of skills necessary for placement in a sheltered workshop. An alternative for this group is a continuation of training and prevocational experiences in an adult activities program.

Cortazzo (1967) defined activity programs as:

> organized rehabilitation services providing severely retarded individuals beyond school age with training in daily living activities to enable them to live with less dependence upon others. The training starts at the level of performance related to the simplest of adult living skills and progresses to the point where these persons are able to assume increasing adult responsibilities (p. 31).

Cortazzo (1967) described the five major objectives of the adult activity program as follows:

1. To provide the mentally retarded with a socially acceptable pattern for daily living. . . The appropriate behavior for most adults is to leave home some time during the day, engage in some purposeful and acceptable activity, and then return home later.
2. To help the mentally retarded make the important transition into adult living through training in the adult living skills and adjustments such as proper and appropriate grooming, homemaking, traveling, work habits and skills, etc.
3. To work closely with parents and help them understand, accept, and develop the new role of the severely retarded adult in the family. By the very nature of this condition the parents must be involved in the program.
4. To provide an alternative to institutional living. Parents who had to place their retarded sons or daughters in an institution due to lack of community services would be given an opportunity to withdraw them and place them in an activity program.
5. To prepare the mentally retarded who have the potential in the necessary skills and adjustment for advanced programs, such as workshops and other vocational centers (p. 248).

Program content varies, but the major function of the activity center remains the provision of meaningful activity that is a source of satisfaction and a means of increasing personal, social, and vocational skills (Baroff, 1974). Generally, program content in the activity center consists of eight major areas (Baroff, 1974, p. 337):

1. work
2. self-help skills
3. social skills
4. household skills

5. community skills
6. academics
7. recreation
8. communication

Each of these content areas will be described in detail in the following section of this chapter.

Work

The deficiencies in work adjustment of the majority of activity center clients are in attention and perseverance. The activity center usually employs simple subcontract work, often drawn from typical sheltered workshop contracts, to train clients to attend to task and persist for the normal work interval of 90 minutes. Simple sorting, one-step assembly, stacking, or folding contracts are used in conjunction with systematic reinforcement to increase the time the client will persist at work related tasks.

Cortazzo's (1968) research suggested that nearly 42 percent of the clients discharged from 52 activity center programs were subsequently employed in a sheltered workshop. Thus it does not matter whether it is a lack of personal/social or work adjustment skills that preclude placement in a sheltered workshop setting; there is ample evidence to suggest that even profoundly retarded individuals can acquire the requisite skills for adequate adjustment in the sheltered workshop. Cortazzo (1968) suggested, however, that his findings could not support the conclusion that individuals who eventually are placed in a sheltered workshop achieved this placement because of the training provided them in activity centers. The need for further research was documented.

Self-Help Skills

This area of training in the activity center most often involves grooming and hygiene. Some severely retarded clients will also require training in toileting, dressing, and feeding although school or institutional programs should have prepared the client in all self-help areas.

Baroff (1974) provided a detailed list of the grooming skills taught to adults in activity programs:

1. body appearance and cleanliness
   a. washing
   b. bathing
   c. showering
2. brushing teeth

3. washing and combing hair
4. shaving (at least with an electric razor)
5. use of cosmetics and deodorants
6. care of nails

The authors have provided detailed activities for teaching all these skills in previous chapters.

Social Skills

Baroff (1974, p. 338) defined the objectives of social skill training as pertaining to the development of "more mature (age appropriate) ways of expressing feelings, managing impulses, and relating to others." Unfortunately, the majority of severely retarded individuals display behaviors that are childlike, in fact, behaviors that are more consistent with their mental ages. Cortazzo (1963) provided numerous examples of these behaviors. The behaviors could be grouped according to inappropriate activities, inappropriate behavior, and attention seeking.

1. Inappropriate activities include playing with dolls, toys, guns, or children's coloring books.
2. Inappropriate behaviors, in this context, refer to the reactions to being denied their own way. Often severely retarded adults will cry, sulk, become moody, or throw a temper tantrum.
3. Attention seeking is pursued to seek self-assurance or intimacy. The adult retarded individuals can often be found interrupting adult conversations or injecting their own irrelevant conversation. Additionally, they will try to shake hands with members of the staff frequently and inappropriately.

Fortunately, these inappropriate behaviors can be extinguished through the use of behavior modification techniques or through the modeling effects of more mature clients and employees. However, the real root or cause of the problem is the reinforcement of these behaviors that occurs in public school settings. Laus (1976) reported on a number of incidents in a large, northeastern center for moderately retarded school-aged individuals. Included among the behaviors that were inappropriately reinforced by the teaching staff were:

- teaching and calling seventeen- and eighteen-year-old students the juvenile form of names, i.e., Joey or Sammy
- allowing sixteen- to nineteen-year-old students to carry lunch boxes with cartoon characters on them

- encouraging handshaking, hugging, and kissing when these actions are totally inappropriate most of the time in the school setting
- allowing students to walk holding hands with one another as they alight from the bus

The professional teaching staff of schools providing educational programs for severely retarded youngsters are in a position of significant influence over pupils. Teachers constitute a significant part of the school environment and through their behavior convey important messages that influence the perceptions and attitudes of pupils (Laus, 1976).

Laus's (1976, p. 49) analysis of teacher-pupil interaction in a trainable center leads him to conclude:

1. Teachers behaved toward students in a manner not appropriate to their chronological age level.
2. (There were) incidents where teachers . . . reinforced deviant behavior of students.
3. (There were) incidents where students were unable to make decisions and initiate actions or normal socialization activities.

Thus, it is imperative for public school personnel to provide an educational framework within which each severely retarded student can learn social behaviors that are age/situation appropriate.

Household Skills

The majority of activity centers provide training in an array of common household skills. In addition to the feeling of satisfaction the clients derive from making a positive contribution and being more independent, training in this area also reduces the clients' dependence upon others in the setting where they live. To meet this objective, clients were taught to dust, run a vacuum sweeper, sweep and mop a floor, wash windows, clean a bathtub and toilet, and put things away. In addition, clients are also taught to make a bed (includes changing the sheets), hang their clothes, wash and iron clothes, sew, use small appliances, answer the telephone, mail letters, and various outdoor chores.

Cooking or meal preparation provides another training area for clients. Activity center clients are taught to prepare simple meals, including the operation of a stove and other kitchen appliances, setting the table, clearing the table, washing and drying dishes, putting dishes and utensils away after meals, and general kitchen clean-up. In this phase as in all self-help activities, parental or institutional staff should be involved so that the training received in the center is reinforced in the home or the institution (Baroff, 1974).

Community Skills

This area of training is also referred to as travel training or orientation and mobility training. The key elements here are: (1) to first train clients to travel independently to and from their homes to the activity center and (2) within the clients' abilities, to travel independently to places of interest in the community (parks, movie theatres, etc.). Mobility instruction is critical, since the ability to travel independently is the key prerequisite to acceptance in a sheltered workshop program. In spite of the importance of independent travel, Cortazzo (1968) found that only eight of the 68 (12 percent) activity centers he surveyed provided travel training instruction.

Independent travel is essential, and research cited earlier (Tobias, 1963; Laus, 1974) certainly substantiates the fact that a severely retarded individual can be taught to use public transportation. Baroff (1974) recommended that any individuals who could not be taught to accomplish the trip from home to center independently could at least be taught to travel to a central pick-up point so that a portion of the travel burden on others is reduced.

Academics

Cortazzo (1968) found that academics were taught in a majority of activity center programs despite the severe intellectual limitations of the clients. Included in instruction were such skills as: counting, identifying coins, making change, identifying numbers, telling time, writing signatures, identifying functional words (e.g., men, women, danger, exit), filling out applications, recognizing signs, recognizing symbols, cooking, and using measurements. While the essence of academics at this level is considered functional (Baroff, 1974), training occurs despite Mithoug and Haring's (1977) finding that workshop supervisors rated many of these skills as not essential to successful functioning in a sheltered setting. In fact, as Laus (1976) noted, most of the pressure for academic instruction comes from parents who feel much more comfortable with academic training and acceptance than they do with training and competence in other areas designed to make the severely retarded more independent.

Recreation

Recreation was a common activity in nearly 60 percent of the activity centers surveyed by Cortazzo (1968). Included among the typical recreational pursuits were dancing, parties, basketball, swimming, bowling, trips, spectator sports, hiking, day camping, physical education, and overnight camping.

While there is some educational value in the recreation activities, much of it occurs to bring pleasure to the clients. Chapter 12 provides an extensive discussion of adapted physical education and recreation.

Communication

Cortazzo (1968) reported that some form of communication skills training occurred in nearly 50 percent of the activity centers surveyed. Often this training takes the form of group discussions, telephone usage, language development, and even speech therapy. As noted in the section on language training, it is critical to assist students in developing some form of communication skills. Safety factors necessitate that clients working around machinery are able to understand verbal or gestural messages conveying dangerous conditions. In addition, if clients can identify objects, respond to instruction, and follow directions, learning new job-related skills is greatly facilitated.

Prevocational Training in the Public School

Activity centers and sheltered workshops are constantly faced with a dilemma—that of meeting scheduled production contracts and improving worker training and/or rehabilitative skills. In the case of the sheltered workshop, if time is spent training and teaching basic preskills, production time is minimal and contracts are lost.

The solution to this problem is obvious—young children must be provided with prevocational training of a diverse nature in the public schools that will lead to future economic usefulness. This means that some time must be set aside daily to teach occupationally related tasks beginning with classroom activities for eight-year-olds and continuing with a public school activity center or prevocational training program.

A number of high priority skill areas and subabilities should be recognized by trainers as critical to the work potential of the severely retarded. A list of skill areas and subabilities is provided in Table 10-3; however, it should not be considered exhaustive or complete. If students receive early and continuous training within these areas, they will have an opportunity to master higher ability level jobs in the future.

The subabilities contained in Table 10-3 are listed along a continuum. Skills commonly taught as requisites in the classroom are placed under or near Phase I. Those generally taught in a prevocational program or activity center are listed between Phase I and Phase II. Skills listed directly under Phase II should be taught in an activity center but are more traditionally found in the sheltered workshop.

Table 10-3 Prevocational Skill Areas and Subabilities.

	Phase I		Phase II
Skill Areas:	School Program	Prevocational	Activity Center Sheltered Workshop
PUSH/PULL	walker scooter board buggy large ball hand toys	push cart shopping cart tricycle (peddling) wagon hand press lever chair	dolly wheelbarrow rolling bundle hand truck factory 4-wheel cart foot press lever
LIFT/CARRY	wooden blocks small boxes paper bags balls	large boxes large paper shopping bags open containers of liquid buckets closed paint cans logs	cement blocks open containers of liquids gunny sacks
OBJECT MANIPULATION	clay Legos pegs and peg boards stacking ring zippers buttons wadding paper sanding tinker toys blocks wire tracking	remove masking tape from roll safety pins stringing beads sewing cards stringing a chain through a hole in a keychain putting on rubber bands remove bottle cap needle and thread	fastening a clasp on keychain tying simple knots tying string around package cleaning ear phones needle and thread rubber stamps

SORT/COLLATING

cleaning metal parts with
  cloth
  pipe cleaners
  coloring

Sorting objects by shape, size, color, and weight

blocks	cardboard sheets	clothes
	screws	tiny metal chips
	nuts/bolts/washers	
	pages by size	

PICKING UP OBJECTS
(fingers)

blocks	heavy cardboard	washers
toys	marbles	nuts/bolts
balls	plastic pickup sticks	plastic and metal chips
cup		(fingers and tweezers)
drinking glass		

DISCRIMINATION

Taste/Smell/Size/Shape/Sounds

bitter	blocks	bell
sweet	paper	buzzer
		animals

Colors
red
blue
green
yellow

finding holes in clothing

Color/Objects-size-function

white	clothes
black	nuts and bolts
purple	machine parts
pink	
brown	

WRIST ROTATION

jar lids	screw drivers	crescent wrench
large nut and bolt	box and wrench	ratchet and socket
bolt boards	open end wrench	hand can opener
stringing a spool	ball point pen parts	
door knobs	baby bottle tops	
keys and locks	bottle cap (twist on)	
	putting in a light bulb	

Table 10-3 continued

Phase I Skill Areas:	School Program	Prevocational	Activity Center Sheltered Workshop	Phase II
BOXING/WRAPPING	closing top of box open and close shoe box open and close envelopes fold page of paper in half filling box with stuffing	securing package with string fold page of paper into thirds stuff envelopes making prefolded boxes	fold small piece of cardboard (perforated) wrapping packages (mailing) wrapping packages (gifts)	
SEALING/TAPING	tapes two edges together (masking tape) seals envelope (licking)	applies glue to paper edges and cements them together applies rubber cement to edges (cements together) seals envelopes with damp sponge	seals container with string tape for mailing operates bundling machine	
ASSEMBLY SKILLS	pop beads and blocks snap rings cap on Flair pen or similar pen belt buckle plastic snap-on caps for drink bottles works on own but with supervision	bubble pipe stem and bowl writing pen parts bolt/washer/nuts (large size) bolt board split key (cotter pin) chain bracelet (clasp) key chains jewelry box (bracelet) bicycle brake works next to others on an assembly line	bolt/washer/nut (small size) lamp (wiring & parts) ricco badge (security and radiation badges) circuit boards	

HAND TOOL OPERATION

mallet	hammer	seam ripper	sewing machine
paint brush	scissors	rug hook	drill press
scissors	paint brush	tweezers	crescent wrench
eraser	box end wrench	open end wrench	heat sealer
template	screw drivers	foot press	laminator
crayon	simple levers	hand press	staple gun
	stapler (hand)		air hose
	hole punch		soldering gun

WEIGHING AND MEASURING

matching objects of same weight	balance scale	standard scale with pointer
	use of measuring stick	

The Activity Center in the Public School

Very little has been written regarding the establishment of the activity center in the public school setting. Kolstoe and Frey (1965) described programs in which public schools established and operated their own sheltered workshops, so the obvious downward extension into the activity center is logical.

If possible, the center should be located in the school building or in a nearby structure. There must be adequate facilities for storing and shipping the finished products and for receiving raw materials. Generally, sheltered workshops have a minimum of one hundred square feet per client; but in the case of activity centers where the subcontracts are likely to be light assembly or reclamation, space requirements would not be as great.

The school administration should provide the basic equipment including typical office furnishings, work tables and benches, hand tools, and some power tools (most likely a drill press, a table saw, electric sander, and a sewing machine).

In the activity center it is not necessary to have as large a staff as in a sheltered workshop. In fact, a director who establishes policy and procures contracts and a supervisor who helps meet production schedules and oversees quality control would be the essential staff.

The school activity center would be used to train older severely retarded students in work-related skills while special education classroom personnel provided training in all other essential areas. The main purposes of the school activity center are as follows:

1. to evaluate the student-client's level of personal, social, and vocational skill development
2. to help teachers to provide classroom instructional programs to maximize and maintain the student's level of development and remove serious deficits in identified areas
3. to provide training in work related skills under realistic conditions
4. to teach the student-client to do jobs that have immediate transfer to community activity centers or sheltered workshops
5. to assist the student-client in making a smooth transition to some postschool program

As Linde (1963) noted in his description of an activity center program:

> These people take great pride in their work products (work, success, and self-esteem). They are frequently given the chance to help run off interoffice memos on a Mimeograph machine kept right in the room. Activities of this kind (are) reinforcement for work well done. . . (p. 26).

Obviously, the benefits to be accrued by the student-client are immense while the cost and effort are modest. Certainly, the school operated activity center is a major step forward in the preparation of severely retarded students to become members of the community.

Training within the Activity or Prevocational Center

Instructional training in vocational related tasks requires the systematic application of verbal cues and reinforcers to a sequence of small behavioral steps. For example, preskills within the areas of sorting, folding, assembly, and taping are task-analyzed as follows:

Sorting

Instruction in sorting can be carried out using a number of objects and a variety of placement containers. Pie tins, muffin pans, cartons, wooden trays with compartments, or boxes can serve as holding containers. Pins, marbles, parquetry blocks, wooden chips, clothes, dishes, washers, bolts, and nuts are only a few examples of items that can be used to enhance manual dexterity and discrimination abilities.

Sorting is an essential preskill for most sheltered workshops as it is often a component of many contracts. To improve worker potential, training in sorting should be planned sequentially and recorded continually. Care must be taken to insure that each student receives exposure to a variety of sorting tasks involving discrimination by size, shape, texture, weight, and color. The skill of sorting using a wooden sorting box is task-analyzed:

Task Analysis/Sorting Parquetry Blocks by Shape:

1. With his right hand, the instructor places one square block in front of student.
2. Instructor assists student in putting square block in first container marked with square block. (Reward student).

Task Analysis/Folding Small Cardboard Sheets:

Folding is an equally important preskill to teach the severely retarded as it is used in numerous vocationally oriented tasks. Various types of folding should be taught to students before reaching adolescence and by all means before entering the sheltered workshop. The following folding sequences provide respectively the requisite training for (1) lining a jewelry bracelet box and (2) stuffing an envelope:

1. The student picks up white cardboard insert with either hand.
2. Student positions cardboard sheet so that the inscription or emblem is right side up and in a horizontal position.
3. Student holds cardboard sheet between thumb and forefinger by the top right-hand corner.
4. Student folds top right-hand edge downward at perforation.
5. Student slides thumbs and forefingers to the left approximately 1 to 2 inches.
6. Student folds top edge downward.
7. Student slides thumbs and fingers again 1 to 2 inches and continues in this manner until the entire top edge is folded downward.
8. Student rotates cardboard sheet to the left until it is standing on end.
9. Student places thumb and forefingers at top right and progresses across, folding downward as in previous folding phase until reaching the end.
10. Student rotates cardboard sheet to the left until the long unfolded edge is on top.
11. Student places thumbs and forefingers at top right and progresses across, folding downward as before, until the end is reached.
12. Student rotates cardboard sheet to the left until the unfolded remaining edge is at the top.
13. Student places thumbs and forefingers at the top left corner and folds downward on perforation.
14. Student proceeds across top as before until reaching the end.
15. Student turns cardboard sheet over and places on table so that bent edges are facing upward.
16. Student presses downward with the left hand to hold cardboard securely.
17. Student runs fingers along raised edge and presses it downward to form a smooth, even crease.

Task Analysis/Folding Standard Size Business Paper

Requisites: 1. Use of one or both hands
2. Can pick up a sheet of paper from a pile

In teaching this skill, several instructional techniques and devices can be used. In some cases a jig can be built that will keep the piece of paper square to the student and provide a visual and/or tactile cue for the position of the folds. It is recommended that such devices be constructed only when all training efforts without the jigs have been exhausted.

1. The student (if right-handed) secures the bottom middle of the sheet between thumb and forefinger of right hand.

2. The student folds bottom of paper toward the top of page with right hand and stops when bottom of page aligns with top third of page.
3. The student aligns folded portion to square edges of paper using the right hand.
4. The student, with right hand resting lightly against the table, holds bottom edge in aligned position.
5. The student spreads fingers of left hand and moves to position just under the right hand.
6. The student moves left hand toward the bottom of the page pushing downward to make crease.
7. The student moves left hand to right bottom corner of crease.
8. The student spreads fingers of left hand and draws them across the crease from right to left, stopping at the left corner.
9. The student secures top middle of page between thumb and forefinger of right hand.
10. The student brings top of page toward crease and stops at second mark (if jig is used) or point marked with right hand.
11. The student brings top edge of page toward bottom crease stopping at the second folding mark (on table top or jig) with right hand.
12. The student aligns edges of the page by moving the paper with the right hand.
13. The student pushes downward against paper and holds securely with right hand.
14. The student spreads fingers and positions them above the right hand.
15. The student slides left hand upward to form crease.
16. The student moves left hand to right top corner of crease.
17. The student slides left hand from right to left pushing downward to secure crease.

Task Analysis/Sorting Parquetry Blocks by Shape

Requisites and Procedures:

A long multicompartment sorting box with shapes attached to corresponding compartments is placed in front of the student. Six square blocks and six circular blocks are introduced first. (See Figure 10-3.)

Figure 10-3 Sorting Box

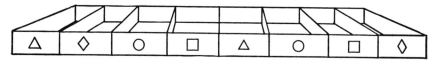

1. The student picks up one square block with assistance when told to pick up the square block.
2. The student places square in corresponding compartment with assistance.
3. The student picks up second square block with assistance when told to pick up the square block.
4. The student places square in corresponding container when told to put square block here. (Instructor points to container.)
5. The student picks up square block on command.
6. The student places square block in container on command.
7. The student picks up remaining square blocks and places in container one at a time.
8. The student picks up circular block on command with assistance.
9. The student places circular block in corresponding compartment with assistance.
10. The student picks up second circular block on command with assistance.
11. The student places circular block in compartment on command without assistance.
12. The student picks up and places remaining circular blocks in compartment without assistance.
13. The student, given two squares and two circular blocks, places them in their corresponding compartments.

The same training sequence is used as other shapes are added one at a time until the student can sort at least ten blocks of each shape.

Task Analysis/Nut and Bolt Assembly

Requisites: 1. Use of both hands if jig is not used.
           2. Pincher grasp
Materials and Procedure: A large plastic bolt and nut are introduced first because they are lightweight and easier to control. Both are placed in front of the student.

1. The student picks up bolt using pincher grip with threaded end protruding from the thumb end of the hand.
2. The student points threaded end of bolt toward the face and holds securely.
3. The student picks up nut by its casing using pincher grip.
4. The student moves nut to bolt centering the hole.
5. The student turns nut clockwise.
6. The student screws nut to end of threads.

In some cases a spike or thin extension is glued or soldered to the end of the bolt to aid in the alignment step (see Figure 10-4). However, this should be phased out rapidly once the student begins to experience success.

Figure 10-4 Bolt with Spike Extension

Task Analysis/Taping the Tops of Boxes

Requisites: 1. Use of two hands (one hand can be used, but not with this
sequence)
2. Cutting tape with scissors or on tape dispenser
Materials and Procedure: A wooden retainer bracket, roll dispenser, or a roll of
one-inch tape and scissors can be used in taping to top flaps of a cardboard box of
approximately 18 by 14 inches in size. The student is seated at a table with the
materials placed in front of him.

1. The student closes the flaps on the top of the box.
2. The student places bracket (which is adjusted to box size) over the top
   center of the box to secure flaps (see Figure 10-5) for bracket).
3. The student removes approximately 12 inches of tape from a dispenser or
   roll.
4. The student cuts tape with dispenser or scissors.
5. The student aligns tape to cover the length of the top flaps beginning at the
   center retaining bracket and extending over the end of the box about 2
   inches.
6. The student smooths tape to box surface.

Figure 10-5 Wooden Retainer Bracket

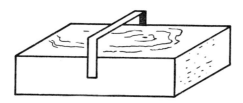

7. The student removes approximately 12 inches of tape from dispenser or roll.
8. The student cuts tape with dispenser or scissors.
9. The student aligns tape to cover the length of the top flaps beginning at the opposite side of the center retaining bracket and extending over the end of the box about 2 inches.
10. The student smooths tape to box surface.

In this task, additional strips of tape may be added across the width or length of the box top for support. These steps can be sequenced in the manner just described.

SUMMARY

This chapter provided a rationale for occupational training for the severely retarded. Various basic skill areas were presented, along with suggested teaching activities designed to assist students to achieve the skills. The activity center was also described as a possible training site for acquiring these skills.

A systematic plan for determining a severely retarded person's basic skill and ability level in seven areas crucial to success in a sheltered employment setting was developed. Once a person's skill level is determined, training can begin in the areas including:

- communication
- social/self-help
- mobility
- recreation
- perceptual/fine motor
- gross motor/physical
- work adjustment

Evidence was cited that documents the fact that even severely retarded people can learn complex assembly tasks like those required of an employee in a sheltered workshop.

REFERENCES

Ayres, A.J. Perceptual-motor dysfunction in children. Monograph from the Greater Cincinnati District Ohio Occupational Therapy Association Conference, 1964.

Baroff, C.S. *Mental retardation: Nature, cause, and management*. Washington, D.C.: Hemisphere, 1974.

Benton, A.L. *Right-left discrimination and finger localization*. New York: Hocker-Harper, 1959.

Blue. C.M. Trainable mentally retarded in sheltered workshops. *Mental Retardation,* 1964, *2,* 97-104.

Burton, T.A. *The trainable mentally retarded.* Columbus: Charles E. Merrill, 1976.

Cortazzo, A.D. *A guide to establishing an activity program for mentally retarded adults.* New York: National Association for Retarded Children, 1963.

———— A guide to establishing an activity program for mentally retarded adults. In E.L. Meyen (Ed.), *Planning community services for the mentally retarded.* Scranton, Pennsylvania: International Textbook, 1967.

———— An analysis of activity programs for mentally retarded adults. *Mental Retardation,* 1968, *6,* 31-34.

Cratty, B.J. *Developmental sequences of perceptual-motor tasks: Movement activities for neurologically handicapped and retarded children and youth.* Palo Alto, California: Peek, 1967.

Crosson, J.E. A technique for programming sheltered workshop environments for training severely retarded workers. *American Journal of Mental Deficiency,* 1969, *73,* 814-818.

Ghent, L. Developmental changes in tactual thresholds on dominant and non-dominant sides. *Journal of Comparative and Physiological Psychology,* 1961, *54,* 670-673.

Gold, M.W., & Barclay, C.R. The learning of difficult visual discrimination by the moderately and severely retarded. *Mental Retardation,* 1973, *11,* 9-11.

Kolstoe, O.P., & Frey, R.M. *A high school work-study program for mentally subnormal students.* Carbondale: Southern Illinois University Press, 1965.

Laus, M.D. A rationale and procedures for the development of instructional strategies for teaching trainable mentally retarded adolescents utilizing the normalization principle. Unpublished doctoral dissertation, University of Pittsburgh, 1976.

Laus, M.D. Orientation and mobility instruction for the sighted trainable mentally retarded. *Education and Training of the Mentally Retarded,* 1974, *9,* 70-72.

Lerner, J.W. *Children with learning disabilities* (2nd ed.). Boston: Houghton Mifflin, 1976.

Linde, T. Social development for trainable retardates. *Rehabilitation Record,* 1963, *4,* 24-27.

Mithoug, D.E. & Haring, N.G. Community vocational and workshop placement. In N.G. Haring & L.J. Brown (Eds.), *Teaching the severely handicapped* (Vol. 2). New York: Grune and Stratton, 1977.

Phelps, L.A., & Lutz, R.J. *Career exploration and preparation for the special needs learner.* Boston: Allyn and Bacon, 1977.

President's Panel on Mental Retardation. *A proposed program for national action to combat mental retardation.* Washington, D.C.: U.S. Government Printing Office, 1962.

Tobias, J. *Training for independent living.* New York: Association for Help of Retarded Children, 1963.

Williams, W., Coyne, P., Johnson, F., Scheuerman, N., Swetlik, B., & York, R. Skill sequences and curriculum development: Application of a rudimentary developmental math skill sequence in the instruction and evaluation of severely handicapped students. In N.B. Haring & L.J. Brown (Eds.), *Teaching the severely handicapped* (Vol. 2). New York: Grune and Stratton, Inc., 1977.

Wolfensberger, W. Vocational preparation and occupation. In A.A. Baumiester (Ed.), *Mental retardation appraisal education rehabilitation.* Chicago: Aldine, 1967.

Chapter 11

The Sheltered Workshop for Severely Retarded Learners

The concept of sheltered employment is a relatively simple one—to provide a means for certain employees to work productively under highly controlled conditions. As Gearheart and Litton (1975, p. 120) noted, "sheltered employment may be the only feasible means whereby the (mentally retarded) individual can become a contributing member of society."

Sheltered employment may be provided in a number of ways, but most commonly it is provided through a sheltered workshop. The sheltered workshop as a means of providing sheltered employment for the moderately retarded is a relatively new concept, originating in the early 1950s (Burton, 1976). Only recently have professionals proposed sheltered settings for the severely retarded. Gold (1973a) described research in which mentally retarded subjects were taught to increase productivity both quantitatively and qualitatively. In other research (Gold & Barclay, 1973; Gold, 1972; Levy, Pomerantz, & Gold, 1977) ample evidence was presented that severely retarded individuals can be taught complex visual discrimination and assembly tasks, the foundation of many sheltered workshop contracts. This data prove that the need exists to provide a vehicle for planning and implementing sheltered workshop programs for severely retarded individuals.

HISTORY OF SHELTERED WORKSHOPS

Workshops began in Europe some four hundred years ago. Influenced mainly by the writings of the Spanish humanist, Juan Luis Vives, local communities established workhouses for impoverished indigents with little or no skills. Among this population were some handicapped individuals.

The first actual workshop for the handicapped was started by Valentin Huay in 1784. He felt that blind individuals could be taught to be self-supporting, productive workers. While his workshop concept ultimately failed in preparing the blind

269

for competitive employment, it served as a stimulus for the development of workshops for the blind in Europe and the United States (Gearheart & Litton, 1975).

Gearheart and Litton (1975) noted that the first United States workshop for the blind was started in 1837 at the Perkins Institute for the Blind. This workshop produced items that were sold commercially including brooms, brushes, and mattresses. Eventually, other workshops opened, mainly in connection with schools for the blind; but while they were successful in providing training to blind clients, they all operated at a substantial loss.

Around 1950, parent groups became vocal and financial sponsors of workshops. The National Association for Retarded Children was an avid supporter of sheltered workshops for retarded individuals, and the period of 1953 to 1957 witnessed a growth from 6 to 108 sheltered workshops for the mentally retarded in the United States (Gearheart & Litton, 1975).

WORKSHOPS FOR THE MENTALLY RETARDED

While sheltered workshops for the retarded have been in existence for less than thirty years, they still follow the same pattern as workshops established for other handicapped individuals. Burton (1976) noted that the type of work done in workshops for the mentally retarded can be divided into three categories:

1. Production of new products: This particular category involves small profit items of an arts and crafts nature manufactured by the clients.
2. Repair or salvage: A second type of workshop work involves the solicitation of items from the community (such as old clothing or furniture) that are repaired or refinished and then sold.
3. Subcontract with business or industry: The third type of work category is usually the most lucrative since it involves contracts with industry for assembly, packaging, sorting, or other types of production work on a piecework basis.

Since the nature of severe mental retardation is diverse in its effects upon the individual, different types of sheltered workshops with various goals are essential. Gold (1973b) described three alternative types of sheltered workshops designed to meet the diverse needs of the population of severely retarded adults:

1. Traditional sheltered employment: The focus of this alternative is habilitation/rehabilitation with the ultimate goal of client placement in competitive employment.

2. Long-term sheltered employment: In this alternative the focus is terminal employment in a sheltered setting for the population of retarded individuals who will never be able to function in the competitive labor market.
3 Multidisability sheltered employment: A sheltered workshop of this type is usually comprehensive enough to provide services for a wide range of handicapping conditions. Additionally, it is flexible enough to provide both transitional and terminal placements.

PROGRAM PLANNING AND OCCUPATIONAL TRAINING IN THE SHELTERED WORKSHOP

Mithoug and Haring (1977) advocated a vocational training and placement program that utilizes general behavior analysis procedures. Behaviors are targeted and precisely specified prior to any treatment and evaluation. Target behaviors include both skill and work adjustment requisites with client assessments focused on job relevant behaviors. In this fashion, all training objectives are appropriate and lead to the terminal goal for the individual client.

This particular approach may be outlined as follows (Mithoug & Haring, 1977):

1. Analyze the skills required to complete the job task; pinpoint the behaviors expected by the supervisor as necessary adjuncts to performing those skills; and specify the motivational system employed on that job to maintain performance, encourage conformity to rules, and discourage deviant behavior.
2. Assess the client's levels of skill development relevant to the job, supporting work patterns, and motivational control needs.
3. Specify behavioral objectives for each of the deficiencies identified in 2 above.
4. Develop and implement a training program to achieve each of these objectives by employing behavioral principles that specify appropriate procedures for cueing and reinforcing the target behaviors.
5. Continuously evaluate "through direct measurement" progress towards behavior aims. These measures may include, for example, the number of cues required to elicit the response during acquisition, the elapsed time following a cue before the response is emitted, the time interval between correct responses, the number of correct or incorrect responses per unit of time, the duration of a response, and the percent of correct or incorrect responses per response period.
6. Place the client on the job for a trial period with maximum follow-up support, while continuing to monitor and evaluate his behavior on all relevant dimensions specified during training.

7. Increase on-the-job training if performance maintains.
8. Gradually decrease follow-up support (pp. 267-268).

Many of the job skills that are requisite to success in a sheltered setting can be taught during the school program as part of the prevocational experience or in an activity center. One way to determine which job skills or tasks are important is to analyze the types of contracts commonly secured by workshops. Mithoug and Haring (1977) reported on a survey conducted by the vocational training program for the severely handicapped at the Experimental Education Unit of the University of Washington. Workshop supervisors were asked to respond to a form ranking the subtask skills in decreasing order of frequency for their workshop. The results of this survey for all workshops combined is presented in Table 11-1.

It might be noted that all of the high frequency subtasks are common to most sheltered workshops, while the medium and low frequency subtasks will vary widely depending upon the subcontracts involved.

In order to teach clients to perform these subtasks, it is often necessary to employ instructional procedures that will shape the worker's response repertoire toward successive approximations of the desired final response. One method of doing this is to completely task-analyze a skill area into a number of small sequential steps leading to a final terminal response. As an example, Crosson (1969) task-analyzed the sequence of steps necessary for successful operation of a drill press. Initial responses involved body placement and movement while the

---

Table 11-1 Subtask Skill Rankings for Sheltered Workshops by Task Frequency

High Frequency	Medium Frequency	Low Frequency
Sealing	Sorting	Bending
Assembly	Machine use	Rubber banding
Boxing	Folding	Stamping
Placing	Counting	Wire striping
Bagging	Cleaning	Unpacking
Cutting	Collating	Sizing
Labeling	Wrapping	Capping
Taping	Drilling	Wire crimping
Weighing	Punching holes	Wire wrapping
Measuring	Painting	Use of hand tools
Box assembly	Stuffing	Rolling
Stapling	Filling	Dipping
Stacking	Blueing	Use of hand truck
		Picking from stack
		Use of air hose
		Uncapping
		Writing numbers

final response involved the rotation of the drill press forearm downward, returning it to the original position, and releasing the handle.

In the next section of this chapter, the authors will present task analyses of six separate subtask operations common to sheltered workshop contracts. The subtasks themselves are ranked from easiest (hand assembly) to most difficult (machine use). The first (Exhibit 11-1) is a hand assembly folding task for placing liners in a jewelry box. It should be noted that this is a job-specific analysis to a jewelry box liner, but the steps involved in folding and assembly could be generalized to any folding/assembly contract.

The second task analysis, Exhibit 11-2, presents the sequence of steps required in the task of bagging buttons. This task requires the worker to be able to weigh and bag.

Exhibit 11-3 presents the task analysis for using a hand press to make buttons while Exhibit 11-4 depicts the sequence for button cutting with hand tools. Even though the sequence for making buttons (Exhibit 11-3) involves machine use, button cutting by hand (Exhibit 11-4) is a slightly more difficult task.

The next task analysis presented, Exhibit 11-5, is Crosson's (1969) sequence for drill press operation.

Finally in Exhibit 11-6, the operation of a laminator is analyzed into its component steps.

Exhibit 11-1 Hand Assembly/Liners for Bracelet Jewelry Box

Requisite skills: 1. folding the edges of small cardboard sheets along prestamped perforations
2. color discrimination (black and white)
3. recognition of the top or "right side up" for a piece of paper that has an inscription or emblem

Steps: The worker:

1. picks up white cardboard insert with one hand
2. folds the four edges downward on the prestamped perforations
3. inserts white liner into lid of jewelry box
4. picks up black cardboard insert
5. folds the four edges of black liner downward
6. inserts black liner into bottom of jewelry box
7. closes jewelry box and places in finished container

Exhibit 11-2 Hand Manipulation/Button Bagger

Steps: The worker:
1. locates completed buttons
2. pours completed buttons onto weighing side of ratio scale
3. places one button in balance cup
4. adds or removes buttons on weighing side of scale until the arrows on meter line up
5. takes all buttons from the scale and the balance cup and pours them into the rolled plastic
6. makes sure heat sealer is plugged in
7. places open end of rolled plastic beneath sealing lever
8. presses down sealer and holds for three seconds
9. lifts sealer
10. pulls sealed end of plastic and enclosed buttons to other side of sealer
11. presses down sealing lever to seal bottom end
12. cuts plastic beyond bottom seal
13. places finished bags in appropriate box

Exhibit 11-3 Hand and Machine Assembly/Novelty Buttons Using a Hand Press

In this activity a hand or foot press may be used. If a foot press is used, all the steps are identical except for numbers 10 and 13. Replace these steps by the words "depress foot pedal."

Steps: The worker:
1. locates cuttings
2. locates correct size pinbacks
3. locates correct size shells
4. locates board for placing 25 completed buttons
5. attaches assigned number of paper clips to board for client identification
6. places shell in left machine die
7. straightens printing by rubbing against table edge
8. aligns printing on top of shell in left die
9. pushes left die beneath press
10. pulls handle down firmly
11. places pinback (sharp edge up) in right machine die
12. pushes right die beneath press
13. pulls handle down firmly
14. pushes left die beneath press again
15. removes completed button from right die

Exhibit 11-4 Hand Tool Operation/Button Cutter

Steps: The worker:
1. lays carpet on cutting table
2. places cutting block on the carpet
3. locates mallet
4. locates appropriate size cutting die
5. locates box in which to place cuttings
6. locates hand counter
7. takes unit out of pigeon holes
8. places unit on cutting block
9. lines up cutting die with printing
10. strikes cutting die with mallet
11. places cut-out printing in box
12. records completed unit on hand counter
13. cleans up work table

Exhibit 11-5 Drill Press Operation/Holes for Pencil Holders

According to Crosson (1969, p. 815) the sequence of behaviors for the operation of an industrial drill press involves the following 16 steps:

Steps: The worker:
1. assumes position facing drill press
2. adjusts position, moving right shoulder in line with drill
3. extends left hand to stack of precut blanks
4. removes blank from stack
5. transfers blank to drilling jig
6. aligns and positions blank in alignment block well
7. removes left hand—closes 2nd, 3rd, and 4th fingers against palm
8. with palm down, places exposed surface of 2nd finger against lower edge of blank
9. places thumb against near edge, index finger against far edge of blank—grasps firmly
10. extends right hand to drill press lever
11. opens and lifts hand, palm facing lever
12. extends thumb, forming V with index finger
13. brings palm in contact with tip of lever with shaft intersecting V
14. slowly rotates forearm downward (minimal interval 5 seconds) allowing shaft to rotate through V
15. extends forearm directly toward rear of machine, allowing lever to rest at base of thumb as soon as lever reaches the point where it ceases to rotate
16. releases and allows lever to return to initial position

Exhibit 11-6 Machine Operation/Laminator

Steps: The worker:

1. turns machine on
2. watches for red light on machine to go out (this indicates that machine is ready for use)
3. turns handle on left side of machine to lower roller onto plastic
4. takes appropriate printed sheets from pigeon holes
5. counts number of prints on each sheet to determine how many sheets will be needed to make a unit (72 prints)
6. turns on motor switch
7. lines up printed sheet evenly with plastic on laminating machine
8. feeds printed sheet into the machine
9. counts each sheet until the number necessary to complete a unit have been laminated
10. leaves extra space of plastic between completed unit and new unit when feeding
11. records on hand counter the number of units as completed
12. turns handle on left side of machine to lift roller off plastic
13. turns off motor
14. turns off machine

JOB SKILLS IN THE SHELTERED WORKSHOP

For students fortunate enough to receive good preskill training in an activity center or public school prevocational program, the employment picture is extremely favorable.

Sheltered workshops are in the business of filling contracts for money, and therefore, they can seldom afford the time, money, and staff involved to teach basic work habits and fundamental skills. Once a student reaches the workshop, only minimal training should be needed to teach the skills required to complete new jobs such as the ones presented here.

In teaching new job skills, it is sometimes necessary to instruct the student how to assume a particular body position, such as holding a hand in a particular manner. When this situation occurs, Crosson (1969) suggests that "artificial cues" be used to provide additional understanding or increased awareness. Examples of this include painting an outline of a hand on a drill jig to offer a visual cue or reminder of the appropriate hand position, or telling a student to make his hand like a gun (if such a position were desired).

The preceding are simply samples of task analyses that workshop staff could use to teach the skills necessary to complete various subcontracts. The actual process of task analysis was presented in Chapter 3.

SHELTERED WORKSHOP LAYOUT

The sheltered workshop can vary widely in design and construction. Brolin (1976) noted that many factors account for the uniqueness of each workshop facility, i.e., the attitude of the board of directors, the community where the shop is located, type of client served, the number of clients served, amount of money available, the staff, and the agency philosophy. Allen (cited in Brolin, 1976) noted that several definite guidelines could be established:

1. All rooms should be at ground level. Steps should be avoided, halls should be at least eight to twelve feet wide, exits not more than 100 feet from any room, and some windows should be able to serve as exits (45 percent opening).

2. Percentage of building space available for several operations should be as follows: staff offices, 10 percent; client workshop area, 40 percent; receiving and storage, 25 percent; multipurpose room(s), e.g., recreation, instruction, lunch, 20 percent; and the rest rooms, 5 percent. The rule-of-thumb is 100 square feet per client and the basic building should not be less than 8,000 square feet.

3. The building should be constructed of block and bricks. Advantages of this kind of construction are long life and low maintenance, fire insurance rating, safety of client, better financial investment, and compliance with federal and state regulations (however, this is expensive).

4. Taking into account the size of the building and program, allow for ample acreage for parking, delivery service for products, outdoor recreation, future expansion, and esthetic purposes.

5. Plant layout should consider that the rehabilitation facility has two products—the rehabilitation of the person and the economics of the work performed.

6. Locate in a new industrial park, if possible (pp. 217-218).

Brolin (1976, p. 219) presented a diagram of a suggested physical layout for a sheltered workshop. That diagram is reproduced in Figure 11-1.

Figure 11-1 Suggested Physical Layout for Sheltered Workshop

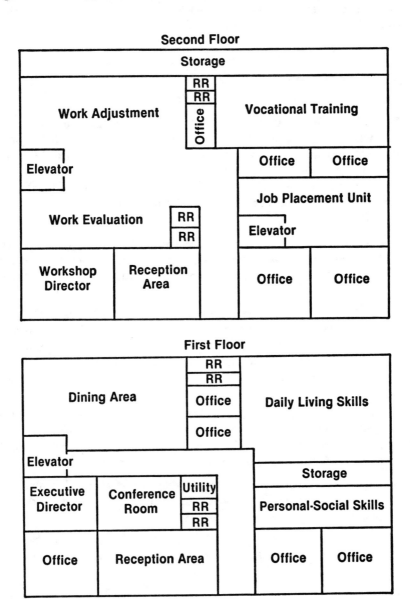

Source: From *Vocational preparation of retarded citizens*, D.E. Brolin, p. 219. © 1976.
Reprinted by permission of Charles E. Merrill Publishing Co., Columbus, Ohio.

SHELTERED WORKSHOP STAFF

The number of staff required by a sheltered workshop will vary according to facility size. For example, a small shop (20 to 25 clients) would require only a director, a work foreman, work supervisors, and a secretary-bookkeeper. As the facility becomes larger, it is necessary to add a contract procurement manager, or a work evaluator to the staff.

Staff composition and ratios for conducting a vocational program in small, intermediate, and large facilities are presented in Table 11-2.

Table 11-2 Suggested Guidelines for Staffing a Sheltered Workshop

Type of Staff	Ratio
Small Facility (to 30 clients daily)	
Director	1
Work Foreman (often combined) Work Evaluator	1 to 2 supervisors
Work Supervisors	1 to 15 clients
Secretary/Bookkeeper	1 to 30 clients
Intermediate Facility (to 100 clients daily)	
Director	1
Production Manager or Assistant Dir.	1 to 100 clients
Contract Procurement Manager	1 to 100 clients
Work Evaluator	1 to 100 clients
Workshop Foreman	1 to 5 supervisors
Work Supervisors	1 to 15-20 clients
Secretary	1 to 50 clients
Bookkeeper	1 to 100 clients
Support Staff (as needed)	
Psychologist	
Rehabilitation Counselor	
Special Education Teacher	
Engineer	
Physician	
Attorney	
Physical Therapist	
Occupational Therapist	
Social Worker	
Large Facility (over 100 clients daily)	
Director	1
Assistant Director	1
Production Manager	1
Business Manager (accountant)	1
Contract Procurement Manager	1 to 100 clients

Table 11-2 continued

Type of Staff	Ratio
Work Evaluator	1 to 100 clients
Work Foreman	1 to 5 supervisors
Work Supervisor	1 to 15-20 clients
Job Placement Counselor	1 to 100 clients
Driver	1 to 50 clients
Secretary	1 to 50 clients
Bookkeeper	1 to 100 clients
Support Staff (as needed)	
Psychologist	
Rehabilitation Counselor	
Special Education Teacher	
Engineer	
Physician	
Attorney	
Physical Therapist	
Occupational Therapist	
Social Worker	

Presented next is a brief outline of staff functions and training so that a sheltered workshop can carry out a majority of the functions to achieve the major program objectives.

The Workshop Director

It is suggested that the director have at least a B.A. degree in psychology, special education, or a related field of study, although larger facilities often employ a master's level person or an individual with an earned doctorate (Gearheart & Litton, 1975).

The director is responsible for the total program of the workshop and has direct authority over all workshop personnel. It is his responsibility to implement policy established by the board of directors. He has the authority (with the advice of board members) to hire and fire all personnel and to see that existing personnel are used to the ultimate advantage of all clients. Another important responsibility of the director involves public relations and the maintenance of good working relationships with related community, business, and professional agencies. Certainly, the director must understand (and often perform) many of the business aspects of operating a sheltered workshop. Of course, it is critical that the director understand mental retardation and the principles and practices of rehabilitation, education, and the world of work so that he is able to review all individual clients' programs for adequacy and effectiveness. He must be able to work with (and supervise) workshop staff to maintain effective intra-agency communication and act as a liaison to the board of directors regarding staff personnel matters such as wages, policies, and work conditions. Finally, the director must be aware of existing government standards (federal, state, and local) to insure compliance with health and safety regulations.

The Production Manager or Assistant Director

From an organizational standpoint, the production manager or assistant director is the "second-in-command" in line authority in the workshop. She has the responsibility to plan, develop, and direct all contract work programs in the workshop. A key element of this person's function is the advancement of the skills and capabilities of the employees consistent with the scope of the contracts. In addition, the production manager must supervise personnel assigned to the production area (contract procurement manager, work evaluator, and foremen). While the key factor in the background of the person filling this job is supervisory experience in industry, the job is likely to go to a college graduate.

Contract Procurement Manager

The contract procurement manager is a key person in an intermediate or large facility, while the job is often combined with another role in small workshops. While a college degree is not usually a requirement for this position, many contract procurement managers have some college or junior college training. The major functions of this person are to negotiate with industry for subcontract work and to develop consumer marketing resources when appropriate. The key element to negotiating contracts is complete knowledge of the workshop's productive resources including: (1) program objectives, (2) the contract's potential contribution for client training, (3) how the contract can be task-analyzed into component parts, and (4) the profitability to the workshop. Gearheart and Litton (1975, p. 126) noted that contract procurement also involves an "analysis of the job skills involved in each production phase of any given contract, the space and training time required, safety aspects, relationship to other contractual possibilities . . . and a host of other factors."

Work Evaluator

The work evaluator's duties involve the assessment of the potential work capability of each client. On-going comprehensive evaluation is critical for staff members interested in the client's vocational growth and potential. Essentially, evaluation is conducted in the following areas:

1. Work adjustment—includes factors such as punctuality, perseverance, reaction to supervision, etc.

2. Work performance—includes qualitative and quantitative measures of productive ability in workshop contract tasks based on shop norms or industrial norms.
3. Motor and physical abilities—include the client's general health, stamina, tolerance to fatigue, and dexterity.
4. Social self-help—includes the factors important to social acceptance—grooming, hygiene, as well as attentiveness and cooperativeness.

Some workshops do not employ highly systematic evaluation procedures, preferring instead to purchase evaluation services from private or public agencies. In addition to the functions already listed, the work evaluator often serves as a job placement counselor, securing competitive employment placements for the most competent clients.

Work Foreman

The foreman is responsible for directing the activities of the work supervisors and raising the clients' total program to the highest possible level. She assists supportive staff in planning and organizing client training activities, supervises the housekeeping functions of the workshop, instructs clients in the performance of selected jobs and the use of tools and equipment, and maintains communication and coordination with the floor supervisors.

The staff described to this point are often referred to as basic workshop staff; and while the titles and exact functions may differ, the essential duties and responsibilities described must be carried out for the workshop to function smoothly and meet its objectives. In addition to the staff already described, many sheltered workshops employ the services of professionals in many other disciplines including: (1) psychologist, (2) rehabilitation counselor, (3) special education teacher, (4) engineer, (5) physician, (6) attorney, (7) physical therapist, (8) occupational therapist, and (9) social worker. The administrative table of organization for an intermediate size sheltered workshop is presented in Figure 11-2.

THE INDUSTRIAL SHELTERED WORKSHOP

In this text a rather clear distinction has been made between the organization and purposes of an activity center and the organization and purposes of a sheltered workshop. The description of the sheltered workshop presented the traditional workshop as it operates today. In actuality, this description differs from the conception of the ideal sheltered workshop—the industrialized workshop. Unfortunately, the majority of workshops today mix the purposes and activities of the activity center with those of the sheltered workshop. The staff of the sheltered

Figure 11-2 Example of a Table of Organization for an Intermediate Sheltered Workshop

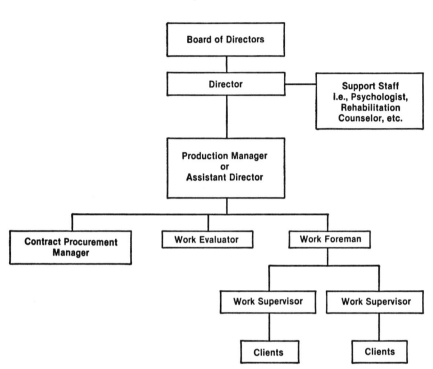

workshop provide training in recreation, mobility, and self-help skills—the type of training that should and must occur both in school prevocational programs and the activity center. In fact, clients should only enter the industrialized workshop after they have mastered all the basic skills with the workshop providing training in the actual job skills required to complete a contract and minimal training in work-related areas.

The school experience, including the in-school activity center or workshop as well as postschool activity center training, should prepare clients to enter the workshop ready to become, with proper training, workers. If necessary, the workshop can have a separate activity center area where training in self-help skills and social skills can occur; but the two areas should remain as distinct as possible.

It is critical to raise the expectations of professionals regarding the ability of the severely retarded to do complex tasks in sheltered settings. As Levy et al. (1977, p. 234) noted, the studies employing 14- and 24-piece bicycle coaster brake and electronic circuit board assemblies "represent considerably more difficult tasks than are usually associated with the severely handicapped and are, therefore, useful for demonstrating the large discrepancy between the current level of functioning and unknown potential of retarded persons.'' So, if the school prevocational program and the activity center can focus their training upon the basic skill areas (Table 10-1, Table 10-3), then the severely retarded can be productive workers in the industrialized workshop.

The rest of this section will include a description of an actual industrialized sheltered workshop, which operates in a large northeastern city.

The Northside Industrial Workshop has been designed after a small industrial shop with medium industrial equipment and an assembly line operation. The work experience offered to the employees is relatively new and unfamiliar, yet demanding and challenging. Emphasis is placed mainly on work output, good work habits, and learning of new skills.

The contract work performed at this workshop is the fabrication of fibre-board boxes used in local brewing companies. This contract offers a variety of work tasks ranging from simple labor jobs to the skilled operation of wire stapling machines. Work tasks are ranged in a hierarchy so that a sequential advancement through these tasks facilitates the mastery of each one. The total contract operation includes six job assignments. These are: (1) Stitching ends—operating a stapling machine, which requires a high level of eye, hand, and foot coordination; (2) Breaking—folding the box bodies on six prescored lines. Four or five bodies are folded at a time requiring a high degree of physical strength and stamina; (3) Stitching flaps and ends—requires eye, hand, and foot coordination; (4) Inserting partitions—involves the use of hand tools such as wire cutters and steel hand cutters. Collapsed partitions must be opened and placed in the bottom of each box. Requires some speed and coordination; (5) Closing lids—requires pushing flaps of two sectioned lid into a slot for tight closure. Requires some concentration, dexterity, and stamina; and (6) Loading and unloading—carrying three or four boxes onto a truck and stacking from floor to ceiling. Requires balance, coordination and judgment.

The industrial training program begins with an orientation followed by on-the-job training at this workshop. The graduation of steps is one designed to closely guard against failure. All basic knowledge is gained in the instructional period and is followed by actual work adjustment training in a structured work environment. The final step is a move into community employment for those clients capable of functioning in competitive employment.

Intake Procedure

Trainees are selected through a staff team approach. All potential clients are interviewed and evaluated by a vocational rehabilitation counselor, production manager, and social worker.

Initially, the individuals will enter the workshop for a one-day evaluation to determine their eligibility to enter the program on a more permanent basis. The purpose of this evaluation is to give the prospective employees an opportunity to see exactly what type of work they will be expected to do, and also to determine whether or not they will be suitable for future training. Staff will evaluate the individual in the following areas:

1. *Physical functioning:* Determine whether or not individual is physically capable of performing the various jobs at a normal expectancy; determine if balance, coordination, dexterity, and strength are within normal limits, and adequate for industrial requirements. Also, efforts will be made to determine if the prospective employee has obtained any special skills in the industrial area prior to entrance into the program.
2. *Intellectual functioning:* Determine individual's ability to follow instructions effectively; determine how frequently instructions must be repeated before individual can perform the job assignments independently and accurately; determine whether or not and to what extent an individual can recall and retain an industrial schedule. Also, reading and writing aptitudes will be assessed during this one-day evaluation. Life management skills such as operating a telephone, telling time, using the bus system, and ability to exchange money will be assessed.
3. *Affective functioning:* Individual's ability to work with peers in a team effort; ability to adjust and cope with a variety of job changes; ability to accept criticism without resistance or hostility; and ability to accept supervisory authority.

After completion of this one-day evaluation, staff will meet to determine whether or not the individual has the potential to benefit from this program. If the client is not accepted, the referring agency will be notified by phone, followed by a written report, explaining the reasons for this decision. This report will include recommendations to improve the individual's acceptability. The individual can be reconsidered for this program at a later time, when the referring agency feels sufficient progress has been achieved in eliminating deficits or improving function.

If the employee is accepted, all involved agencies will be notified, and if possible, a starting date will be given. If there is no immediate opening in the program, the individual's name will be placed on a waiting list and the individual will be offered placement when an opening becomes available.

Training Program

The training program consists of a three-phase sequence designed to progressively increase the complexity of tasks and gradually shift from simulation to actual work.

Phase I—Evaluation-Orientation

When individuals enter the program, they will receive three weeks of diagnostic evaluation and exposure to training in efficient methods of performing industrial work. The evaluation will involve:

1. A work sampling whereby these individuals will have the opportunity to perform all tasks in the workshop: i.e., stitching, closing boxes, loading and unloading boxes, breaking, inserting partitions.
2. Social and community skills necessary to be successful in a competitive employment environment. Under this, world of work attitudes will be instilled through a progressive program designed to determine what is required on a job; i.e., employee attitudes, employee interaction with peers, punctuality, using break time appropriately, and other job-related responsibilities.

If requirements for advanced training are not met upon completion of the evaluation period, the individual will be terminated from the program after consultation with the referring agency.

Phase II—Training

Those individuals who show promise after the initial three weeks will then enter the training program. This phase will last from six months to not more than one and one-half years. In this period the employee will experience the actual pressures and responsibilities needed to function effectively for eventual competitive placement. During this time, training will be confined to the following areas:

1. *Work adjustment training*—The workshop is designed to conform to a prototype industrial plant. Employees are required to follow the rules and regulations of the workshop at all times. These rules and regulations are reasonable and within the employees' ability to follow them.
2. *Skill training*—Employees are trained in a variety of skills. Once one skill has been mastered, the employees are then trained in a new and more demanding task.
3. *Safety training*—Employees are continually reminded of the hazards of their assigned jobs. Only accepted methods of job performances are permitted and employees must adhere to these methods. Safety training also includes accident reporting and monthly fire drills.
4. *Personal maintenance*—Includes activities that are designed to make individuals aware of appropriate modes of grooming, personal hygiene and clothing, both in the work setting and the community itself.

Phase III—Placement and Follow-up

The employee will begin interviewing for competitive employment. Once an individual is placed, the rehabilitation and job placement counselor will maintain frequent contact with the employer and employee to evaluate the individual's progress.

It should be emphasized that the Northside Industrial Training Program is designed to (1) teach light industrial work and (2) develop appropriate work attitudes and behaviors. It is not designed to alter inappropriate or deviant behaviors. These should be dealt with prior to referral.

THE SHELTERED WORKSHOP IN THE PUBLIC SCHOOL

While public schools have traditionally employed a variety of ways of providing work experiences for mildly retarded youngsters, few have attempted to provide work experience for moderately retarded pupils. Attempts at providing in-school work experience for the severely retarded are unknown at this time.

However, Kolstoe and Frey (1965) described a public school program that established its own sheltered workshop. A similar model could be employed by many public school systems to provide work experience for the severely retarded. In the program described by Kolstoe and Frey (1965) students spent one-half day in the workshop and the other half day in the school program. The tasks performed in the workshop included simple assembly, reclamation of furniture, and a subcontract as a primary manufacturing unit.

The school sheltered workshop should serve the following purposes:

1. to evaluate vocational potential
2. to evaluate work-related skills
3. to assist the student in developing the skills, attitudes, and behaviors related to work adjustment under realistic conditions
4. to assist the student to do jobs that have immediate transfer to community activity centers or sheltered workshops
5. to serve as a permanent (for as long as the law allows the school system to provide services) placement for less able students
6. to serve as a transitional (to bridge the gap) program to facilitate the student's eventual placement into a postschool program such as an activity center or a sheltered workshop

The type of facilities necessary to provide for an adequate workshop have already been described. Given the design of most school buildings, it is likely that a school system would have to secure a building away from the school environment, which is probably beneficial to students, as it would create a distinction between school-related and work-related experiences. Naturally, any site selected would have to comply with federal, state, and local regulations regarding health and safety.

Space requirements vary widely according to the type of contract work done; however, it is generally accepted that an operation of subcontract, reclamation, and light manufacturing have a minimum of one hundred square feet per student (Kolstoe & Frey, 1965). In order for a facility to serve 40 students, for example, and to include locker, washroom, and lunchroom areas as well as office reception room, storage, shipping and receiving, and finally work space, a minimum of 4,000 square feet would be essential.

Kolstoe and Frey (1965, p. 120) suggested that certain equipment was basic including:

1. office equipment such as desks, chairs, file cabinets, typewriters, adding machines, Mimeograph machine, reception and lounge area furniture, and a tape recorder
2. shop area (equipment such as) work tables of sit-down and stand-up height must be provided along with adjustable chairs. An assortment of hand tools and miscellaneous items such as fire extinguishers, dollies, hand truck, time clock with card rack, fans, and scales . . . beginning power tools would probably

include a drill press, a jigsaw, table saw, electric handsaw, belt sander, and at least two sewing machines.
3. means of transportation (such as) a heavy-duty stationwagon or carry-all or light truck.

The personnel described in the section on sheltered workshops would have to be duplicated in a school sheltered workshop, even as far as the student-client to staff ratios presented.

If the school workshop is to function as an evaluation-training center, it will be necessary for it to provide experiences that allow student-clients to move through a hierarchical series of work tasks from simple labor to more skilled operations. Minimal standards should be established for each job task, and the student-clients should not be allowed to move to the next stage until they have mastered the standards of the preceding level. However, the main focus must be on the development of work adjustment areas, and not on the development of specific job skills. If the work adjustment skills are mastered during the school years, advanced job skills can be easily taught in the postschool sheltered setting. Of course, it is that much better if the student-clients have mastered both work adjustment and some work skills prior to workshop entry.

It will be absolutely essential for student-clients to receive pay for their work. The most common arrangement would be pay based on piece-rate basis at a level commensurate to what workers in industry would receive for a similar job. Thus student-clients have some incentive for improving productivity; although as Gold (1973a) has noted, the successful completion of the task itself has strong reinforcing properties for student-clients. Gold's (1973a) findings would obviously raise some questions about the assumptions currently held that pay, in some form, and praise are the only reinforcers available for work.

The type of subcontract work secured by a school workshop would vary although it could certainly be similar to the contract work in community workshops. These contracts could include the following:

- assembly
- packaging
- collating and preparing mailing for the school district
- repair of school furniture
- reclamation
- contracts unique to the economy of a region. As an example of this, a community workshop in Las Vegas, Nevada, sewed scarves for the late Elvis Presley, who distributed these scarves to admiring female fans. Since Presley's death, the workshop has actually increased this contract because it supplies many of the "Elvis impersonators."
- manufacturing simple items

This or any workshop will probably never be self-supporting. Either the school district must subsidize its operation or secure donations or gifts from local private sources such as businesses, professional groups (e.g., medical associations, dental associations), and other organizations (e.g., Rotary, Kiwanis, Lions, Elks).

Finally, any school operated sheltered workshop would need to maintain contact with the school district's pupil services department as well as establish liaison and coordinative contacts with local and state agencies. The contacts must be established to secure vital services and to plan and coordinate efforts to secure placements for students after they leave the public school setting. Included among the agencies to be contacted are:

- Bureau of Vocational Rehabilitation
- Association for Retarded Citizens
- Mental Health/Mental Retardation Offices
- Department of Public Welfare or Public Assistance
- State Schools and Hospitals
- Community Group Homes

In conclusion Gearheart and Litton (1975) noted:

> Though many factors have combined to encourage the establishment of additional workshops, to improve the operations of existing ones, and to suggest that sheltered work outside of an organized workshop may be of real value, there remains a shortage of well-organized, efficiently managed facilities. Federal funding has provided a major impetus, but as federal funding varies, the states are not always willing to assume a greater share of financial responsibility. American society has taken a much more positive stand toward its responsibility for the handicapped in recent years, but is is difficult to successfully use the same type appeal on behalf of adults as is sometimes used regarding handicapped children. The force of court decisions that dictate the manner in which the public agencies must provide for the under-21 TMR [Trainable Mentally Retarded] may not successfully carry the principle into the adult years. The movement of the retarded from large institutions back to the community is underway, but adequate provision at the community level has not yet been accomplished. This critical area of need may require a great deal of effort and emphasis on behalf of advocates for the retarded if sheltered employment for all mentally retarded who can benefit from such opportunity is to become a reality (p. 138).

SUMMARY

This chapter traced the history of the sheltered workshop. The work done in sheltered workshops was described along with the three types of sheltered workshops available for severely retarded clients. The program planning, occupational training, job skills, physical layout, and staffing patterns of a sheltered workshop were presented. A great deal of emphasis was placed upon providing the training to the severely retarded so that they could function in an industrialized sheltered setting. The industrialized sheltered setting was described in great detail. The chapter concluded with a description of the sheltered workshop in the public school setting.

REFERENCES

Brolin, D.E. *Vocational preparation of retarded citizens.* Columbus, Ohio: Charles E. Merrill, 1976.

Burton, T.A. *The trainable mentally retarded.* Columbus: Charles E. Merrill, 1976.

Crosson, J.E. A technique for programming sheltered workshop environments for training severely retarded workers. *American Journal of Mental Deficiency,* 1969, *73,* 814-818.

Gearheart, B.R., & Litton, F.W. *The trainable retarded.* St. Louis: C.V. Mosby, 1975.

Gold, M.W. Stimulus factors in skill training of retarded adolescents on a complex assembly task: Acquisition, transfer, and retention. *American Journal of Mental Deficiency,* 1972, *76,* 517-526.

———Factors affecting production by the retarded: Base rate. *Mental Retardation,* 1973a, *11,* 41-45.

———Research on the vocational habilitation of the retarded: The present and future. In N.R. Ellis (Ed.), *International review of research in mental retardation.* New York: Academic Press, 1973b.

Gold. M.W., & Barclay, C.R. The learning of difficult visual discrimination by the moderately and severely retarded. *Mental Retardation,* 1973, *11,* 9-11.

Kolstoe, O.P., & Frey, R.M. *A high school work-study program for mentally subnormal students.* Carbondale: Southern Illinois University Press, 1965.

Levy, S.M., Pomerantz, D.J., & Gold, M.W. Work skill development. In N.G. Haring & L.J. Brown (Eds.), *Teaching the severely handicapped* (Vol. 2). New York: Grune and Stratton, 1977.

Mithoug, D.E., & Haring, N.G. Community vocational and workshop placement. In N.G. Haring & L.J. Brown (Eds.), *Teaching the severely handicapped* (Vol. 2). New York: Grune and Stratton, 1977.

Chapter 12

Adapted Physical Education and Recreation Skills Training

Physical education for the severely retarded is generally referred to as adapted physical education or special physical education. The concept of adapted physical education as it exists today has as its central theme the basic premise that all individuals, regardless of their limitations, can benefit from physical activities, sports, games, and rhythms suited to their interests and capacities. More specifically, adapted physical education as defined by the Center for Physical Education and Recreation for the Handicapped is:

> . . . a diversified program of developmental activities, games, sports, and rhythms suited to the interests, capacities, and limitations of students with disabilities who may not safely or successfully engage in unrestricted participation in the vigorous activities of the general physical education program (I.R.U.C., 1976, p. 17).

Another definition describes adapted physical education as:

> . . . (a) science of identifying problems within the psychomotor domain and developing instructional strategies for remediating these problems and preserving ego strength (Sherrill, 1976, preface, xviii).

COMPONENTS OF ADAPTED PHYSICAL EDUCATION

Adapted physical education for the severely retarded is based on the same principles as those identified for higher functioning individuals. According to *Adapted Physical Education Guidelines* (1976), adapted physical education includes physical activities:

293

- planned for individuals with learning problems resulting from motor, mental, or emotional disabilities or dysfunctions;
- planned for purposes of habilitation, rehabilitation, remediation, or physical development;
- designed for modifying movement capabilities;
- planned to promote maximum/optimum motor development;
- conducted in a school setting or within a clinic, hospital, residential facility, day care center, or other environment where the primary intent is to influence learning and/or movement potential through motor activity; and
- conducted in either regular physical education or special adapted physical education classes depending upon functional abilities, needs, and individualized program of a student (1976, p. 19).

THE NEED

Physical education for the severely impaired is an essential component of the daily training curriculum. Many individuals in this dependent group not only possess disabling conditions that foster inadequate motor development, but spend much of their waking hours in sitting or prone positions. Unfortunately for the majority of this time, they are not engaged in meaningful or purposeful activity.

Physical education programs are frequently viewed by the lay person as "those gym classes" where instruction involves: (1) calisthenics for fitness and flexibility; (2) games; and (3) dual and individual sports. Physical education programming for this population can involve these activities, but is more specifically concerned with: (1) sensory awareness; (2) following directions; (3) gross and fine motor skills including the basic locomotor movement patterns; (4) social interaction and development; (5) balance and posture; (6) aquatics; (7) rhythms; and (8) perceptual motor development. All activities of either a corrective or remedial nature are presented at the student's instructional level.

SETTING UP THE PROGRAM—A TEAM APPROACH

Planning the physical education program requires the cooperation and expertise of individuals familiar with and interested in the individual's total development. Members of this group should include the following:

- a physician who is cognizant of the individual's capabilities and limitations
- a physical therapist if physical limitations are of significance*
- an occupational therapist*

- a speech and language therapist*
- parent or guardian
- regular teacher or staff person
- adapted physical educator*
- recreation specialist/therapist*
- nurse*

(*Depending upon availability and appropriateness)

In some metropolitan settings, all of these team members may be available within one school, center, or institution. If this situation exists, the student has the benefit of specialized training in addition to the opportunity for programming where instructional areas can be reinforced and built upon in a variety of ways.

TEAM MEMBERS

For the physician, ongoing information concerning the student's developmental history, physical limitations, and medications is essential. Specific assessment and remedial prescriptions may be required for those exhibiting serious physical limitations that require special handling techniques or corrective exercises. The activities of daily living, speech, and language can be greatly enhanced if all the educational personnel understand the goals and objectives identified by occupational, speech, and recreational therapists, and the adapted physical educator. If physical education services are to be performed by a specialist, it is essential that staff and instructional personnel work closely with this individual in order to reinforce the skills taught by each.

An extremely important member and often the most influential is the parent(s) or guardian. For those individuals who live at home, the parent is instrumental in helping such students reach their maximum potential. In this setting exercises and activities may be carried out on a regular basis. Similarly, convalescent centers and residential training facilities may be receptive to a simple schedule, if encouragement and communication exist. Of course for many programs certified therapists, adapted physical education, and recreation professionals do not exist. Oftentimes the existing staff possess limited or no training in special physical education and have little access to the services performed by trained specialists. In the remaining pages of this chapter a full spectrum of physical education activities and techniques will be presented. This discussion will provide a fundamental understanding that will be useful to potential teachers, direct care staff, education specialists, volunteers, and parents.

ASSESSMENT

Requisite to any physical education program is the understanding of what the individuals can do (strengths) and what they cannot do (weaknesses). This procedure begins with a medical examination performed by a licensed physician. Next, each student's medical file and cumulative record should be examined. During this phase the teacher should note not only physical limitations, but medications, previous programming, behaviors, recency and type of testing, and levels of skill development. As a final step, norm-referenced and criterion-referenced tests, checklists, and informal techniques are administered. The Basic Movement Performance Profile shown in Exhibit 12-1 is just one example of an assessment instrument that can be helpful in planning an adapted physical education program for the low functioning retardate. (For a more thorough coverage of assessment instruments, consult Chapters 2 and 4 of this text.) Upon completion of the assessment process, instructional strategies, materials, and equipment can be selected.

INSTRUCTIONAL LEVELS

Sensorimotor

In normal child development the time between birth and two years is labeled by Piaget as the sensorimotor period (Flavell, 1963). This stage is characterized by the activities of moving, hitting, biting, mouthing, and all other forms of physical manipulation. The child learns about the properties of space, time, permanence, location, and causality through the sense avenues. The senses available for exploring the environment are: (1) kinesthetics (movement of muscle and joints); (2) tactile; (3) audition (hearing); (4) smell; (5) vision; (6) taste; (7) vestibular (balance); (8) temperature; (9) pain; and (10) common chemical sense (Sherrill, 1976).

It is theorized that learning is built upon a foundation of movement and manipulative experiences (Kephart, 1960; Barsch, 1965; and Cratty, 1967). The individual interacts with his environment gathering and storing information which is used to establish further relationships that will be called upon in the future. Therefore, it is, according to some theorists, one's early motoric experiences that mold the perceptions and provide the fundamental data for concept formation.

The severely retarded are typically operating at a sensorimotor level of development and require physical education instruction within four basic areas: (1) awareness, (2) movement, (3) manipulation of the environment, and (4) posture and locomotor skills (Sherrill, 1976).

Exhibit 12-1 Basic Movement Performance Profile Score Sheet: Perfect Score Is 80.

Name: _____   Sex: _____   School: _____   Date: _____

Age: _____   Total Score: _____

Mental Retardation Classification: _____

Circle appropriate basic movement response.

1. Walking
   0—Makes no attempt at walking
   1—walks while being pulled
   2—walks with toe-heel placement
   3—walks with shuffle
   4—walks with heel-toe placement and opposite arm-foot swing

2. Pushing (wheelchair)
   0—makes no attempt to push wheelchair
   1—makes some attempt to push wheelchair
   2—pushes wheelchair once with arms only
   3—pushes wheelchair with continuous motion for 10 ft.
   4—pushes wheelchair carrying adult occupant continuously for 10 ft.

3. Ascending Stairs (up 4 stair steps)
   0—makes no attempt to walk up stairs
   1—steps up one step with assistance
   2—walks up four steps with assistance
   3—walks up 4 steps, two feet on each step
   4—walks up 4 steps, alternating one foot on each step

4. Descending Stairs (down 4 stair steps)
   0—makes no attempt to walk down stairs
   1—steps down one step with assistance
   2—walks down 4 steps with assistance
   3—walks down 4 steps, two feet on each step
   4—walks down 4 steps, alternating one foot on each step

5. Climbing (4 rungs; 1st choice, ladder of slide; 2nd choice, step ladder)
   0—makes no attempt to climb ladder
   1—climbs at least one rung with assistance
   2—climbs 4 rungs with assistance
   3—climbs 4 rungs, two feet on each rung
   4—climbs 4 rungs, alternating one foot on each rung

Exhibit 12-1 continued

6. Carrying (folded folding chair)
   0—makes no attempt to lift chair from floor
   1—attempts but not able to lift chair from floor
   2—lifts chair from floor
   3—carries chair by dragging on the floor
   4—carries chair 10 ft.

7. Pulling (wheelchair)
   0—makes no attempt to pull wheelchair
   1—makes some attempt to pull wheelchair
   2—pulls wheelchair once with arms only
   3—pulls wheelchair with continuous motion for 10 ft.
   4—pulls wheelchair carrying adult occupant continuously for 10 ft.

8. Running
   0—makes no attempt to run
   1—takes long walking steps while being pulled
   2—takes running steps while being pulled
   3—jogs (using toe or flat of foot)

   2—steps down from chair
   3—jumps off chair with two foot take-off and landing with assistance
   4—jumps off chair with two foot take-off and landing while maintaining balance

12. Throwing (overhand softball, 3 attempts)
    0—makes no attempt to throw
    1—grasps ball and releases in attempt to throw
    2—throws or tosses ball a few feet in any direction
    3—throws ball at least 15 ft. in air in intended direction
    4—throws ball at least 30 ft. in the air in intended direction

13. Hitting (volleyball with plastic bat)
    0—makes no attempt to hit ball
    1—hits stationary ball fewer than 3 of 5 attempts
    2—hits stationary ball at least 3 of 5 attempts
    3—hits ball rolled from 15 ft. away fewer than 3 of 5 attempts
    4—hits ball rolled from 15 ft. away at least 3 of 5 attempts

4—runs for 25 yds., with both feet off the ground when body weight shifts from the rear to front foot

9. Catching (bean bag tossed from 5 ft. away)
0—makes no attempt to catch bean bag
1—holds both arms out to catch bean bag
2—catches bean bag fewer than 5 of 10 attempts
3—catches bean bag at least 5 of 10 attempts
4—catches bean bag at least 8 of 10 attempts

10. Creeping
0—makes no attempt to creep
1—will assume hands and knees position
2—creeps with a shuffle
3—creeps alternating hands and knees
4—creeps in a cross-lateral pattern with head up

11. Jumping Down (two foot take-off and landing from 18 in. folding chair)
0—makes no attempt
1—steps down from chair with assistance

14. Forward Roll
0—makes no attempt to do forward roll
1—puts hands and head on mat
2—puts hands and head on mat and pushes with feet and/or knees in an attempt to do roll
3—performs roll but tucks shoulder and rolls to side
4—performs forward roll

15. Kicking (soccer ball)
0—makes no attempt to kick stationary ball
1—pushes stationary ball with foot in attempt to kick it
2—kicks stationary ball several feet in any direction
3—kicks stationary ball several feet in intended direction
4—kicks ball rolled from 15 ft. away in direction of roller

16. Dynamic Balance (4 in. beam with shoes on)
0—makes no attempt to stand on beam
1—stands on beam with assistance
2—walks at least 5 steps with assistance
3—walks at least 5 ft. without stepping off beam
4—walks at least 10 ft. without stepping off beam

Exhibit 12-1 continued

17. Hanging (2 hands on horizontal bar)
   0—makes no attempt to grasp bar
   1—makes some attempt to hang from bar
   2—hangs from bar with assistance
   3—hangs from bar for at least 5 seconds
   4—hangs from bar for at least 10 seconds

18. Dodging (a large cage ball rolled from 15 ft. away)
   0—makes no attempt to dodge ball
   1—holds up hand or foot to stop ball
   2—turns body to avoid ball
   3—dodges ball at least 5 of 10 attempts
   4—dodges ball at least 8 of 10 attempts

19. Static Balance (standing on one foot with shoes on)
   0—makes no attempt to stand on one foot
   1—makes some attempt to stand on one foot
   2—stands on one foot with assistance
   3—stands on one foot for at least 5 seconds
   4—stands on one foot for at least 5 seconds with 5 lbs. weight in the same hand as elevated foot

20. Jumping (standing long jump, 3 attempts)
   0—makes no attempt to jump
   1—jumps with a one-foot stepping motion
   2—jumps from crouch with two foot take-off and landing at least 1 ft.
   3—jumps from crouch with two foot take-off and landing at least 2 ft.
   4—jumps from crouch with two foot take-off and landing at least 3 ft.

Source: From *Special physical education,* by H.F. Fait, pp. 208-209. © 1972. Reprinted by permission of W.B. Saunders, Philadelphia, Pa.

Of course, the adapted physical educator is not the only one who will be teaching through sensorimotor activities. Speech, physical, and occupational therapists and instructional personnel will also teach at this particular level. The major instructional difference between the physical educator and other staff teaching through the motoric medium will be in the type of sensorimotor activities, equipment, facilities, and in some cases instructional materials.

Despite instructional differences that exist between curricular areas, all educational interventions are designed to meet the goals and short-term objectives selected by an interdisciplinary team of concerned professionals. Table 12-1 is a partial listing of activities commonly used by the physical education, motor, or recreation specialists and incorporates those suggested by Webb (1969).

Table 12-1 Sensorimotor Experiences in the Adapted Physical Education Setting

Behavior	Therapy Activity	Equipment
Improving awareness	1. Rolling-crawling-scooting	1. Textured mats or rugs constructed of differing materials, airflow mattress, water bed
	2. Moving and touching body parts in front of mirror	2. Full-length mirrors
	3. Instructor moves student's limbs through a range of motion	3. Mats or airbag—attach bells or rattles to student's arms or legs
	4. Student following moving objects with the eyes and moves the head to locate sounds	4. Flashlight tracking, hanging ball or brightly colored block rattles, bell or telephone ring rolling ball with beeper or bell inside
	5. Reflexive reactions to movement, sound, pressure and light	5. Large ball to test protective reaction whistle squeezing-cuddle-hugging moving in water-falling-righting reaction

Table 12-1 continued

Behavior	Therapy Activity	Equipment
Improving movement	1. Bouncing, rolling, rocking, lifting, start and stop actions, swaying, and swinging	1. Bouncing on airbag and trampoline Therapy pool Mat with rough, smooth, hard, and soft surfaces Rocking horses Swings and suspended seats Water bed Hammocks Scooter board Rhythm instruments Tip board
Improving manipulation of the environment	1. Touch and reach	1. Touch swinging objects Feel various textured and sized balls Manipulate toys and objects in sand, dirt, and water Clapping, Orff activities
	2. Striking	2. Large beach ball Splashing water Kicking in water Moving legs or arms in a striking action
	3. Holding and grasping	3-4. Rhythm instruments Sponges, nerf balls, bean bags, rope, wadding paper, towel pull.
	4. Throwing	
	5. Building trust in one therapist	5. Therapist
	6. Push-pull-lift	6. Push scooter board or large ball away from body Pull cord to ring bell or retrieve objects such as pull toy or scooter Universal gym Lift hands, feet, head on command Lift weights, bean bags, small objects

Table 12-1 continued

Behavior	Therapy Activity	Equipment
Improving posture and locomotion	1. Head control	1. Lift head using chest support
	2. Rolling	2. Mat, water, or air mat
	3. Crawl	3. Crawler, mat, scooter board
	4. Sit	4. Water, airflow mat, supporting chair, water bed
	5. Stand	5. Standing table, assistance from therapist and aquatic therapy
	6. Walking	6. Assistance from therapist Walker Parallel bars Water with support from therapist Pushing weighted cart Snap rings
	7. Riding three-wheeled bicycle	7. Tricycle with feet straps—modified seat for support and safety
	8. Climbing	8. Blocks with supportive hand rail or practice stairs Ladder in water or activity room

Sensorimotor/Awareness

It is difficult to identify activities and techniques at this level that are dramatically different from those staff members in other curricular areas will employ. The adapted physical educator's techniques may vary to a limited degree because of space available for instruction or access to a swimming or therapy pool. Another difference may be in the equipment—larger mats, trampolines, water beds, airflow mattresses, and parachutes.

Using the advantages that space, equipment, and special facilities offer, the physical educator can create unique experiences to stimulate the central nervous system and improve muscle tone. Reflexive actions can be elicited or inhibited using various positioning techniques and movements. Noisemakers inside moving objects, rattles, and balloons or cards attached to the spokes of wheelchairs may stimulate the auditory modality. Tactile sensory awareness can be increased by introducing the participant to water, sound, and varying textures of specially designed mats. Greater visual awareness can occur as the children respond to objects, their own movements, and facial expressions in front of a full-view mirror.

Sensorimotor/Movement

The adapted physical education setting provides endless opportunities to expose the participant to varying degrees and types of movement. Initially, the specialist provides the movement actions through passive manipulation of various body parts. The student's limbs can be moved through the range of motion or the total body can be rocked, bounced, rolled or swayed using apparatus such as airflow mats, trampolines, swings, and scooters. As movements become self-initiated, mats, swings, and an aquatic environment can provide the tools to strengthen the muscles, increase confidence, and develop balance to a point where sitting, standing, and locomotor skills can become attainable. The movement level teaches the participant what it looks and feels like to move and what objects look like when they move.

Sensorimotor/Manipulation of the Environment

In the physical education setting the participant is provided with experiences that promote discovery and manipulation of objects. Students are taught to touch, grasp, reach, strike, and throw, thus improving their ability to understand and control objects within the immediate environment. Fundamental communication skills are beginning to surface and an attachment relationship with one or more instructors may begin to occur. The physical educator may be able to elicit basic movement actions (i.e., push, pull, reach) upon simple commands. Elementary games that incorporate rhythm, clapping, grasping, and responding to verbal labels (Orff-Schulwerk method that will be discussed later in this chapter) and simple action games are encouraged.

Sensorimotor/Posture and Locomotion

Posture can be improved through balance activities using mats, airflow mattresses, corrective strength exercises, and aquatic therapy to name just a few.

Locomotor movement patterns can be taught as the specialist repeatedly moves the student's limbs through the desired range until the pattern is remembered and the student can reproduce it independently. Mirrors and verbal cues should be used with all movement instruction to provide additional avenues for learning.

Patterning techniques, aquatic therapy and Orff-Schulwerk activities can play an important role in the acquisition of basic motor skills. Vast amounts of equipment are also available to the physical educator, and full consideration should be given to the merits of modified scooter boards, parallel bars, snap rings, climbing apparatus, supportive devices, and balance boards.

Perceptual/Motor Skills Level

Sensorimotor skills require a combination of incoming sensory information and a motor response. Perceptual-motor activities are viewed as either synonymous with or as an elaboration of sensorimotor skills. If interpreted as the latter, perception becomes a refinement of sensory information whereby stimuli are recognized and provide meaning to the individual based on previous experiences.

An individual operating at a perceptual level according to Kephart (1971) is beginning to understand that the relationships that exist between concrete objects can also take on new relationships by manipulating their elements. Kephart (1971) provides this example:

> The squareness of a square form does not itself exist as a quality of any perception. It emerges from the manipulation in an orderly fashion of the elements (sides and angles) against each other within the perceptual structure. Once having emerged, it becomes an element itself, and it is this emergent element, not the concrete elements, upon which we depend for recognition and meaningfulness (p. 30).

Using this particular theoretical view, the primary difference between sensorimotor and perceptual-motor skills is not the activity itself as much as how the individual performs the skill mentally. As perceptual information is gathered and stored, it must be matched to motor information. The two basic avenues for monitoring all movements are tactile and kinesthetic, which in turn will hopefully correspond accurately to the individual's perceptions. Once the perceptual-motor match is made, perceptual information and motor information will have the same meaning. Table 12-2 provides a number of activities that are often viewed as perceptual-motor in nature. Note their similarity to the sensorimotor activities in Table 12-1.

Table 12-2 Perceptual-Motor Techniques and Activities in the Adapted Physical Education Setting

Skill Area	Activity	Equipment
Balance and Posture Static	Sitting, standing or balancing on the side; Balance on one foot (eyes open or closed)	Rope to hold onto Balance Beam Lines on floor Airflow mattress Balance board Standing table Swimming pool
Dynamic	Walking on varied surfaces, lines, balance beams, or ladder. Moving in the water to walk, roll, float, etc. Walk on knees, bunny hop	Painted or taped line Balance beam Water bed Tires Snap ring Ladder Swimming pool Mats
Body Image	Identify body parts using "Simon Says," touching parts to the surroundings, parachute games while requiring specific actions. Performing movements such as angels-in-the-snow	Mirrors Parachute
Positions in Space	Movements of the body to make oneself small, large, long, thin, etc. Moving to the nearest, furthest wall and return. Moving fast. Moving in crawler, walker, or wheelchair, up, over, under, beside, and between obstacles, swimming over, under, and through objects Jumping, leaping, hopping (with or without assistance) turning toward named objects in the room	Activity area Obstacle course (poles, cardboard boxes, rope, cones, etc.) Cord, Hoola Hoops and floats Turn toward the door, mats, teacher, etc.
	Instruct student to roll sideways, walk forward, backward, and on tip-toes	Mats

Table 12-2 continued

Skill Area	Activity	Equipment
	Step to rhythm or clap hand to legs to a beat	Orff activities
Imitations of Movements	Imitating movements made by instructor (arms, legs, and locomotor actions)	Swimming pool Orff activities
	Imitate actions performed by teacher in shaking, holding up high and down low, etc., with parachute	Parachute
Auditory Discrimination Memory and Sequencing with Motoric Actions	Clap as I do! Stamp as I do! Moving (walking and crawling) until the drum or music stops; fielding a beeper ball; rolling from different directions; move to the beat set by the instructor's instrument	Orff activities Record player Drum Beeper ball Triangle Shaker or rattle
Visual Tracking and Eye-hand Manipulation	Fielding rolling objects; visually follow an object attached to a cord and moving to the student	Balls of various sizes and weights Cord or clothesline with object attached
Eye-hand, Eye-foot, Eye-head manipulation	Striking balls or objects with hands, head, or feet; kicking, catching, hitting, paddling, splashing, striking activities; Bouncing balls, tossing objects at a target; walking or crawling on a pattern, design or color; and pulling or pushing	Balloons Balls Hanging objects, i.e., plastic milk carton Swimming pool Ring toss Bean bags Obstacle course Bally-ho Foot print patterns on the floor Tether ball Wagon Universal gym Push cart

Balance and Posture

Two types of body balance exist—static and dynamic. Static balance is the ability to maintain equilibrium in a stationary position such as in sitting or standing. Dynamic balance is the ability to maintain postural control when the body is in motion as in walking, running, jumping, or turning.

Body Image

Labeling, naming, and understanding the function of body parts can be enhanced through movement activities involving specific limbs or parts. Body image is a theoretical construct individuals seem to acquire once perceptions of their own bodies have been internalized. Hopefully, the participants develop accurate images of what their bodies can do and what they look like.

Positions in Space

The adapted physical education teacher can provide activities that require an individual to view the world from different body positions. Actions of this type build the students' perceptions of what their bodies can do and present conceptual data relative to size, shape, and direction. A common term associated with this area is spatial relations. It refers specifically to one's perception of the position of an object in space, the body to another object, or of one object to another.

Imitation of Movements

Imitative movements require the participant to recognize the action to be made and carry it out with a minimal amount of overflow to other limbs. Training in this area is not for muscle development, but to enhance the participant's awareness of the body's movement.

Auditory Discrimination, Memory, and Sequencing with Motoric Actions

Auditory discrimination is defined by Chalfant and Scheffelin (1969) as the ability to distinguish whether two acoustic stimuli are the same or different. Rhythmic activities such as clapping or striking a drum to a pattern or beat require the participant to process the auditory stimuli. First the information is received through the eyes and ears, then retained in memory and finally reproduced in the correct sequence. Walking, marching, rhythmic splashing, and paddling while swimming all require a sequencing of actions within a temporal framework. Discrimination, learning, memory practice and concepts related to sound qualities can be taught by pairing movements to an auditory beat.

Eye-hand, Eye-foot, and Eye-head Manipulation

The ability to locate an object with the eyes and move the hand to where the object is located is called eye-hand coordination. Striking objects with the feet or even lifting the foot to the support peg on a wheelchair requires eye-foot coordination. Physical education activities that improve this type of coordination are extremely important to the severely retarded. The idea of teaching eye-head coordination may at first sound absurd; however, few things can match its importance when it comes to communicating with a head pointer or locating where a sound came from.

ORGANIZING INSTRUCTION

Regardless of the techniques used in the teaching of physical education and recreation skills, an organizational plan for activity implementation is essential. The choice of an instructional procedure with this special population requires consideration of the following basic factors:

1. attention span is extremely short
2. aggressive or abusive behavior may be predominant
3. one-to-one or one-to-two instruction is generally the rule
4. verbal directions must be in short, clear statements
5. students cannot usually convey feelings of sickness, pain, or fatigue, therefore, extra caution must be taken
6. safety must be taught and never taken for granted
7. fatigue will usually occur rapidly

Circuit Training

With adequate instructional personnel, several different activities can be performed simultaneously in separate designated areas for a specified time period. In circuit training small groups are stationed about the activity area and rotated after a predetermined amount of time has elapsed. Each station should be organized to accommodate the number of participants, their attention span, disability, and type of activity.

Some instructional problems can be avoided by assigning students to ability groups, as any homogeneity within this heterogeneous group is helpful. Even within each ability group the instructor will find it necessary to make additional adjustments and modifications to instructional techniques, amount or types of assistance, and levels of performance. Station operation should be conducted under an explicit set of directions with its instructor establishing a routine that can be followed easily. It is also recommended that the participants repeat the same circuit several times so that they have an opportunity to become comfortable and competent at each activity. The number and type of circuits to be used are limitless as they can be set up in a gym, hallway, pool activity area, or out-of-doors. Stations can be color coded, numbered, or labeled in a manner to expedite movement from activity to activity. In summary, the restrictions that hamper circuit training instruction lie within the minds of the instructors.

Figure 12-1 illustrates a color-coded circuit used to teach gross motor skills. Participants move at five-minute intervals through five stations, making two or three complete circuits in an instructional period.

Continuous versus Interval Training

Continuous training or exercising for long periods of time without stopping is not recommended with the severely retarded. Respiratory conditions, heart problems, and low fitness are only a few of the reasons for avoiding continuous training.

Interval training is far more effective as an instructional technique. Short exercise or activity sessions with break periods between are recommended as they allow the participant to recover physically before the body is again engaged in activity. The length of work and rest intervals depends on each participant's stamina and required recovery time.

INSTRUCTIONAL TECHNIQUES

Patterning

A method of teaching fundamental motor skills employed by several facilities including the Rainier School, Buckley, Washington, is called patterning. This method was found to be highly successful with severely and profoundly retarded students that had not previously experienced structured physical education instruction.

Patterning according to Rudolph (1977) is defined as the systematic instruction of fundamental locomotor and behavioral skills taught by routine and repetition. The term routine refers to the daily use of teaching methods and skills in the same continuous structure and at the same level of expectancy.

Patterning has been used as a treatment method with brain damaged individuals for years. It is based on the theory that if daily motor patterns are artificially imposed on the brain, the undamaged parts of the brain will gradually take over the damaged parts, making new and independent movements possible. Proponents of the patterning technique believe that low functioning students lack the ability to participate successfully in games of low organization and recreational activities because they lack the necessary *fundamental* motor skills.

Figure 12-1 Activity Room with Color-Coded Circuits for Locomotor Skills Training

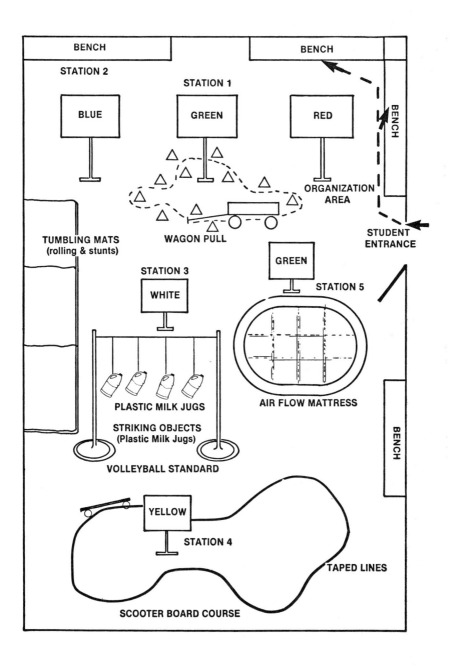

The Rainier gross motor patterning program begins by teaching crawling for two reasons: (1) it is a basic movement skill that can usually be performed successfully (sometimes with supportive aids) and (2) it strengthens the muscles of the shoulder girdle that will be used in lifting, pushing, and pulling. The locomotor treatment program progresses to skills of walking, balance, and climbing as illustrated in Figure 12-2. In the patterning program students are instructed what to do from the moment they enter the activity room until the time they leave. Once a skill is learned it is practiced each day with new fundamental skills added periodically. Rudolph (1977) offers the following suggestions to insure maximum success in a patterning program:

Figure 12-2 Physical Skills Gross Motor Learning Model

EQUIPMENT: Mat-Snap Rings-Stairs-Walking Board

PROCEDURE: Student will begin at crawling mat and proceed through all stages of learning model. Reversal of sequence is recommended.

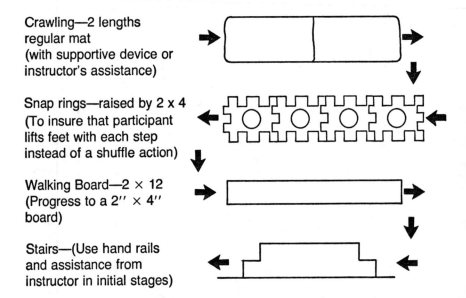

Crawling—2 lengths
regular mat
(with supportive device or
instructor's assistance)

Snap rings—raised by 2 x 4
(To insure that participant
lifts feet with each step
instead of a shuffle action)

Walking Board—2 × 12
(Progress to a 2″ × 4″
board)

Stairs—(Use hand rails
and assistance from
instructor in initial stages)

Source: From *Physical skills for the severely and profoundly handicapped* by L. Rudolph. Unpublished manuscript, 1977. Reprinted by permission of the author.

- edible reinforcers should be used in the initial training stages;
- simple verbal commands are used in all phases of instruction;
- as skill is acquired, social reinforcers replace edible reinforcers;
- treatment procedures for deviations in motor performance should be continually revised and recorded as all the treatment techniques are in the experimental stage.

A complete description of locomotor skills training can be obtained in *Physical Skills for the Severely and Profoundly Handicapped* (Rudolph, 1977).

RECREATION TRAINING

Chapter 8 of this text provides the basic fundamentals for teaching play skills. Training of this nature is a prerequisite to teaching recreational and leisure time skills. Recreation occurs during leisure or free time in many ways. It can be organized in the form of a planned afternoon activity period, or unstructured, such as free play or recess. Although games or activities may have strict rules, they are considered recreational as long as the participant finds them relaxing, enjoyable, or amusing.

The term *recreation* implies free choice; therefore, if a person does not wish to participate in an activity, it cannot be mandated, which could present a problem for severely retarded individuals because, historically, recreational activities and opportunities to learn fundamental skills and to make choices have not been available. To complicate matters, the nature of the mental handicaps and the individual's emotional state may limit participatory behavior.

Some professionals in the recreation field feel strongly that students should not be forced to participate in so called "recreational activities." In teaching the retarded, this is an immediate decision which must be faced. According to Nugent (1971) students should never be abusively forced to participate; however, they can be "nudged" into taking part.

If it were not for strong encouragement or "nudging," many severely retarded individuals would not learn how to play or experience activities designed for personal enjoyment and satisfaction. Far too many severely retarded individuals possess behaviors including apprehension, lethargy, and fear that simply add to a conditioned nonparticipation attitude.

It is necessary to view recreation and leisure time skills training somewhat differently for the severely retarded. For this group, recreation may always appear to be a form of work or structured part of the day because it is an activity that "must be done."

From a recreational specialist's point of view, recreational activities prevent idleness so common to the retarded and improve: (1) physical development, (2) social interaction, (3) group adjustment, (4) vocational aptitude, and (5) personal independence.

In summary, recreation and leisure skills training may at first be neither voluntary nor fun. Basic skills must be taught in a highly structured atmosphere before the limitations and intense supervision can be gradually reduced to a point where simple decisions or choices can be made by the participant.

Therapeutic Recreation

Therapeutic recreation is a term used to denote recreational services and activities for individuals with mental, physical, emotional, and/or social problems. Personnel certified in this field are called therapeutic recreation specialists and are employed in facilities such as child centers, day care centers, recreation centers, nursing homes, residential homes, camps, YMCAs and YWCAs, homes for the aged, public recreation and parks departments, and hospitals. Therapeutic recreation specialists are not always available in all care and educational facilities for the severely retarded. Therefore, when these conditions exist, direct care personnel or specialists within related disciplines must be called upon to facilitate recreation and leisure skills programs.

In settings where recreation specialists are employed, it is common for them to participate as members of an interdisciplinary team. Recreation specialists along with adapted physical education, physical therapy, occupational therapy, music therapy, and dance therapy staff may all function as one professional unit, working collectively to prescribe activity programs for participants.

Adapted Physical Educator versus the Recreation Specialist

It is often difficult to observe distinct boundaries of responsibility between the adapted physical educator and the recreation specialist. Historically, adapted physical educators have been employed in the public schools as teachers and therapeutic recreation personnel in health care or institutional settings. At this point in time, each can be found in all types of settings if certification requirements are satisfied.

The role of the therapeutic recreation specialist is expanding rapidly from one of working primarily in hospitals or institutions to that of providing recreational services in community-based living facilities, parks and recreational programs at city and county levels, and public school programs.

If a distinction is to be made between these specialists, it can begin with their professional training (college coursework and practicum experiences) and the type of program they are qualified to administer. The adapted physical educator's primary responsibility is for physical education instruction that improves the participants' understanding and appreciation of their bodies' capabilities. The therapeutic recreation specialist is responsible for a number of enrichment areas that lead to the appropriate use of leisure time. A listing of the general objectives of the therapeutic recreation service reflects a broad spectrum, which can vary according to the needs of those being served (Kraus, 1978).

General Therapeutic Recreation Objectives

1. To provide constructive, enjoyable and creative leisure activities, seen as a general need for persons of all ages and backgrounds.
2. To improve morale and a sense of well-being and interest in life, as opposed to depression and disinterest or withdrawal.
3. To help individuals come to grips with their disabilities and to build positively on their existing strengths and capabilities.
4. To help individuals gain security in being with others and develop healthy, outgoing social relationships and a feeling of group acceptance.
5. To emphasize positive self-concepts and feelings of individual worth through successful participation in activity.
6. To help individuals gain both skills and attitudes that will assist them in using their leisure in positive and constructive, as opposed to negative and pathological ways.
7. To give experience in mastering simple tasks and reality situations that may be of pre-vocational value (p. 60).

Components of the Recreation Program

There are a number of elements which make up the recreational services for the severely retarded. Therefore, it is essential that all personnel working with the severely retarded understand the nature of the services provided and the roles of the recreational staff.

Assessment

A component of the individualized educational program mandated as a related service in Public Law 94-142 is some form of assessment in leisure functioning. For the severely retarded, many areas of leisure education need to be exposed at various points in the individual's development. Assessment becomes a process of selection for the staffing team as they collectively decide the type and number of experiences each student should receive.

Recreational intervention strategies must be based upon valid and reliable assessment measures. Once this is done, a competency-based model can be followed (Brannan, 1975).

Instructional Goals

The most important recreational goal for this population is to provide a variety of experiences in order for the individuals to be able to make choices of what they will do with their leisure time and be able to carry them out. This goal can be accomplished through experiences that provide physical contact and imitative play. Physical contact is necessary to develop the students' social awareness while imitative play enhances awareness of their body parts, physical coordination, observation skills, and the elementary components of a communication system.

Instructional Activities

Over twenty-five activity areas have been suggested for community-based recreation programs (Nesbitt, 1978). Of this group, the following skill areas are appropriate for this population on a simplified level:

Aquatics	Fitness
Arts-graphics	Games
Crafts	Music
Dance	Outdoor recreation/education
Drama	Sports—participant and spectator
Entertainment	Travel
(magic shows, movies, etc.)	

Recreators often assume that certain activities within the above categories will not be appropriate for the severely retarded. This assumption is totally unwarranted due to the fact that research is extremely limited relative to what can be accomplished with this group, and the research that does exist demonstrates far more can be achieved than was previously expected.

The skill areas listed indicate the importance of this comprehensive curricular service area. Its components spread across many areas of educational training and daily life skills. Exhibit 12-2 illustrates recreation's all-embracing content in an outdoor education/recreation program for the handicapped operated by the Portland Oregon Kiwanis Clubs in affiliation with Portland State University.

Exhibit 12-2 Portland State University Special Education Department Outdoor Education/Recreation

Portland State University
Special Education Department
Outdoor Education/Recreation
Experience/Skill Checklist
MT. HOOD KIWANIS CAMP PROGRAM

EVALUATION SYSTEM   Name of Camper _____

_____Not Observed or Employed with Camper

__1__Inappropriate for Camper   Date of Session:

__2__Performs with Verbal and/or   _____June 19-24   _____July 17-22
Physical Assistance   _____June 26-July 1   _____July 24-29

__3__Performs Independently   _____July 3-8   _____July 31-August 5
                _____July 10-15   _____August 7-12

1.0 PERSONAL

_____1.1 Communicates needs/ideas
_____1.2 Initiates communication
_____1.3 Follows directions/instructions
_____1.4 Initiates tasks
_____1.5 Completes tasks
_____1.6 Manages own time
_____1.7 Controls emotions
_____1.8 Accepts challenges
_____1.9 _____
_____1.10 _____
_____1.11 _____

2.0 SOCIAL

_____2.1 Cooperates with others
_____2.2 Socializes with others
_____2.3 Respects rights/property of others
_____2.4 Assists others
_____2.5 Develops friendships
_____2.6 Appreciates contributions of others
_____2.7 _____
_____2.8 _____
_____2.9 _____

3.0 SELF-HELP

_____3.1 Dresses/undresses self
_____3.2 Washes/showers self
_____3.3 Brushes teeth ·
_____3.4 Practices personal habits of cleanliness
_____3.5 Grooms self
_____3.6 Eats with utensil(s)
_____3.7 Practices acceptable eating/table habits
_____3.8 Cares for own belongings
_____3.9 _____
_____3.10 _____
_____3.11 _____

4.0 NATURE CRAFTS

_____4.1 Cuts with scissors
_____4.2 Tears and folds paper
_____4.3 Selects colors
_____4.4 Uses tools/materials correctly
_____4.5 Applies glue
_____4.6 Paints with materials/tools
_____4.7 Prints/colors with natural materials
_____4.8 Selects own project

Exhibit 12-2 continued

_____4.9 Demonstrates creativity
_____4.10 Follows one direction at a time
_____4.11 Follows more than one direction at a time
_____4.12 Completes project (follows sequence)
_____4.13 Works neatly
_____4.14 Helps with clean-up
_____4.15 _____
_____4.16 _____
_____4.17 _____

PROJECTS
_____4.18 Makes a name tag
_____4.19 Makes a sand candle
_____4.20 Dyes/batiks T-shirt
_____4.21 Makes fish print
_____4.22 Makes a nature project
_____4.23 _____
_____4.24 _____
_____4.25 _____

5.0 MUSIC/DRAMA
_____5.1 Listens to music/drama
_____5.2 Employs hand/body movements with music/drama
_____5.3 Pantomimes
_____5.4 Dances to music
_____5.5 Employs a steady beat
_____5.6 Sings familiar songs
_____5.7 Sings new songs
_____5.8 Sings on pitch
_____5.9 Constructs a musical instrument
_____5.10 Plays a rhythm instrument
_____5.11 Creates/contributes skit material
_____5.12 Participates in skit according to plans
_____5.13 Imitates during skit
_____5.14 Provides personal interpretation during skit
_____5.15 _____
_____5.16 _____
_____5.17 _____

6.0 NATURE
　　　Soil/Rock
_____6.1 Views/feels/smells soil
_____6.2 Views/feels/smells rock
_____6.3 Discovers unique characteristics of rock (i.e., weight, size, smoothness, roughness)
_____6.4 Discovers unique characteristics of soil (i.e., composition, smell, moistness, dryness)
_____6.5 Communicates proper subgroup names (i.e., clay, sand, pebbles, boulders)
_____6.6 Describes purpose in nature's web (ecosystem; i.e., water flow, erosion)
_____6.7 Describes man's responsibilities to environment (i.e., not littering or stripping areas of resources)
_____6.8 _____
_____6.9 _____

Water
_____6.10 Views/feels/smells water
_____6.11 Discovers unique characteristics of water (i.e., movement, temperature, smell, wetness)
_____6.12 Communicates proper subgroup names (i.e., Mirror Lake, lake, stream, pond)
_____6.13 Describes purpose in nature's web (ecosystem; i.e., plant growth, home for animals)
_____6.14 Describes man's responsibilities to environment (i.e., not polluting, water rationing)
_____6.15 _____
_____6.16 _____

Plants
_____6.17 Views/feels/smells plants
_____6.18 Discovers unique characteristics of plants (i.e., color, form, fragrance)

Exhibit 12-2 continued

_____6.19 Communicates proper/sub-group names (i.e., Rhododen-dron, shrub, flower, tree)

_____6.20 Describes purpose in nature's web (ecosystem; i.e., plants' relation to food chain, oxygen and air, soil)

_____6.21 Describes man's respon-sibilities to environment (i.e., preserve forests, care for own plants)

_____6.22 _____

_____6.23 _____

Animals

_____6.24 Views/feels/smells animals

_____6.25 Discovers unique characteristics of animals (i.e., color, smell, anatomy of fish)

_____6.26 Communicates proper/sub-group names (i.e., Rainbow Trout, fish, mouse, insect)

_____6.27 Describes purpose in nature's web (ecosystem; i.e., food)

_____6.28 Describes man's responsibil-ities to environment (i.e., preserve species, help main-tain balance, hunting seasons)

_____6.29 _____

_____6.30 _____

Atmosphere

_____6.31 Views/feels/smells atmos-phere

_____6.32 Discovers unique character-istics of atmosphere (i.e., warmth of sun, coolness of shade, wind, rain)

_____6.33 Communicates proper/sub-group names (i.e., Big Dip-per, star, wind, rain)

_____6.34 Describes purpose in nature's web (ecosystem; i.e., heat from sun, sunlight and water fcr plants/animals)

_____6.35 Describes man's responsibil-ities to environment (i.e., gas pollution, aerosols, burning trash)

_____6.36 _____

_____6.37 _____

7.0 CAMPING

Preparation

_____7.1 Rolls/unrolls sleeping bag

_____7.2 Lays out ground cloth

_____7.3 Pitches survival tent

_____7.4 Ties rope knots

_____7.5 Manages own gear

_____7.6 Packs a pack

_____7.7 _____

_____7.8 _____

Fire

_____7.9 Clears area for fire

_____7.10 Helps build rock fireplace

_____7.11 Gathers wood for fire

_____7.12 Breaks/chops wood

_____7.13 Builds fire

_____7.14 Maintains (feeds) fire

_____7.15 Stays appropriate distance from fire

_____7.16 _____

_____7.17 _____

Equipment

_____7.18 Operates a camp stove

_____7.19 Operates a camp lamp

_____7.20 Operates a flashlight

_____7.21 Operates a camera

_____7.22 Operates a compass

_____7.23 _____

_____7.24 _____

_____7.25 _____

Meals

_____7.26 Prepares own meal outdoors

_____7.27 Cooks own meal outdoors

_____7.28 Serves/eats own meal out-doors

_____7.29 Sets table

_____7.30 Clears table

_____7.31 _____

_____7.32 _____

8.0 PHYSICAL DEVELOPMENT

Mobility

_____8.1 Walks on various terrain (up/downhill)

Exhibit 12-2 continued

_____8.2 Climbs on various terrain (up/downhill)
_____8.3 Manipulates steps and inclines
_____8.4 Manipulates camp obstacle course
_____8.5 Manipulates paths and trails
_____8.6 _____
_____8.7 _____
_____8.8 _____

Strength/Endurance
_____8.9 Runs daily
_____8.10 Jogs daily
_____8.11 Completes calisthenics daily
_____8.12 Hikes to near destination
_____8.13 Hikes to far destination
_____8.14 Backpacks own gear
_____8.15 _____
_____8.16 _____

9.0 SPORTS
General
_____9.1 Throws/strikes ball
_____9.2 Catches ball
_____9.3 Plays volleyball
_____9.4 Plays horseshoes
_____9.5 Plays kickball
_____9.6 Shoots bow and arrow at target
_____9.7 _____
_____9.8 _____
_____9.9 _____

Fishing
_____9.10 Casts a line
_____9.11 Operates a fishing pole
_____9.12 Hooks a fish
_____9.13 Lands a fish
_____9.14 Cleans a fish
_____9.15 Prepares a fish
_____9.16 _____
_____9.17 _____
_____9.18 _____

Swimming
_____9.19 Enters pool safely
_____9.20 Sits/walks in water
_____9.21 Puts face in water
_____9.22 Blows bubbles
_____9.23 Holds breath under water
_____9.24 Plays in water
_____9.25 Jumps into water
_____9.26 Holds onto side of pool
_____9.27 Holds on and moves along side of pool
_____9.28 Floats/kicks with floating device
_____9.29 Face floats
_____9.30 Back floats
_____9.31 Prone glides/kicking
_____9.32 Back glides/kicking
_____9.33 Turns over
_____9.34 Swims (dog paddles, crawl)
_____9.35 Changes directions while swimming
_____9.36 _____
_____9.37 _____
_____9.38 _____

COMMENTS:

NAME OF DIRECTOR

COUNSELORS

Source: From Outdoor Education/Recreation Experience/Skill Checklist by S.A. Brannan. Reprinted by permission of the author and Portland State University.

Special Olympics/Physical Education and Recreation

A combined program of sports and games originated in the mid 1960s by the Joseph P. Kennedy, Jr. Foundation to provide physical education and recreational opportunities for the mentally retarded. The Special Olympics program under the leadership of Eunice Kennedy Shriver and Sargent Shriver began with a four-phase purpose:

1. to provide the mentally retarded with the opportunity to compete in various sports activities
2. to provide a means for altering community attitudes toward the retarded
3. to provide an avenue for the development and implementation of additional programs
4. to improve existing services for the retarded

Today's supporters and participants of the Special Olympics programs follow many of the traditional concepts set down years ago by founders of the original International Olympic Games. This tradition is emphasized by several qualities of the Special Olympics program as listed below:

1. A spirit of sportsmanship and love of participation for its own sake should be stressed during the games. Such qualities are reflected in the Special Olympics Oath, which should be recited by all athletes during the opening ceremonies of all Special Olympic Games.
2. A sense of pageantry and ritual should prevail throughout the games. Each Olympic games are to include colorful opening ceremonies, dignified award presentations to event winners, and formalized closing ceremonies.
3. The program will encompass a number of different sporting activities such as bowling, swimming, basketball, track and field, and soccer. Training programs begin at the local level, leading to area, state, and international games.
4. In keeping with the Greek "Olympic" ideal, the Special Olympic Games should include, in addition to the regular competitive events, clinics or demonstrations of other sports, skills, and activities in the arts such as dancing, rhythm, music, and painting.
5. During the Olympic games, an overnight stay is encouraged along with social activities such as dances, informal games, and/or sing-alongs.

Special Olympics in most communities now involves a year-round program with training sessions for volunteers, sports training for athletes, and Olympic Games by area, state, and national level. The International Olympics are held once every four years; and in 1977, the first Winter Special Olympics was held in Steamboat Springs, Colorado.

There are many facets of the Kennedy Foundation's programs. Not only do they include sports and games for retardates eight years and older, but an addition is the "Very Special Olympics" for preschool retarded children. In this program, sporting events and recreational activities are designed for its young participants. Another program designed to encourage the involvement of teachers, volunteers, and the families of retarded children in structured play activities is called Let's-Play-to-Grow. Its major purpose is to enhance the relationship among parents, siblings and special family members through shared activities.

An extension of the Special Olympics sports program for former Special Olympics participants is the recreation intern program. Mentally retarded individuals 18 years and older may apply for scholarships that pay approximately 50 percent of their wages during the first year if they are hired as recreation personnel. Recreation interns generally assist in offering recreational activities to other mentally retarded individuals in YMCA's, or city and county parks and recreation programs.

New horizons are always forthcoming in the Kennedy Foundation, and its latest effort is a metric education project funded through the Bureau of Education for the Handicapped. This project utilizes the vast Special Olympics network for the training and dissemination of metric education information to the Special Olympics volunteers and participants.

Sports and Games

All retarded, regardless of the functional level, can participate in the Special Olympics program. Some have questioned the benefit of competitive games; yet, because this is such a minor part in the total program, it remains insignificant. The following categories make up a growing list of official sports sanctioned by Special Olympics:

- basketball—run, dribble, and shoot
- soccer
- skiing
- swimming
- track and field
- Frisbee
- gymnastics
- bowling
- field hockey-floor hockey
- diving
- ice skating
- volleyball
- wheelchair events

The benefits of Special Olympics are numerous as it has provided training and education for the retarded as well as the general population; however, it should not be viewed as meeting the total physical education, recreation, and leisure-time needs for those with mental handicaps. Despite the limitations of Special Olympics, a blatant fact remains—until the Special Olympics program was organized, 45 percent of all mentally retarded children did not participate in any physical education. In addition, only 25 percent received as much as one hour a week *(A New Kind of Joy)*.

Orff-Schulwerk

A method of teaching developed in the early 1920s by a German composer named Carl Orff incorporates the areas of motor, music, and language. Orff believed that music should be a total experience involving feeling, movement, and speech. He reasoned that just as children learn to move and speak before they read and write, they should learn music on a physical level before proceeding to a cerebral level required for learning theory, chords, and reading notes. The term *Schulwerk* is a German word for school work that indicates the learning activities Orff has assembled for all participants. This unique educational work that incorporates rhythm instruments, hand clapping, foot stamping, and verse can be adapted to teaching a student of any intellectual level. As described by Bitcon (1976), Orff-Schulwerk can operate at the pre-intellectual level and can be totally nonverbal. Its success or failure depends totally upon the leader who must guide, interact, adjust, reinforce, and select appropriate materials.

Activity Sessions

Orff activities can be used in small groups, large gatherings, or in one-to-one situations. In most activities the teacher/leader should initiate a comfortable rhythm to correspond to a verbal chant, which is generally accomplished by patting the legs, hitting the floor, clapping hands, or shaking rattles. In order to facilitate active participation by those who possess blindness, cerebral palsy, and nonverbal speech development, assistance may be required from aides or volunteers.

One of the first activities generally used with a beginning group or when starting the session is a name game. The following activities selected from Bitcon's (1976) collection should be considered only as suggestions with endless possibilities for further modification.

Name Games

The instructor sets a simple rhythm by clapping her hands, then her knees; then she begins this verse:

Name Game
Name Game
Let's Play

A Name Game
I've got a name and
you do too!
My name's _____
Who are you?

In this game the participants may point to their name on a communication board, sign it, say it, or point to their picture. Here's another:

Hey gang, who's in town?
Everybody stop and look around.
Hey gang, who's in town?
Tell us your name, and then sit down.

In this activity the group is sitting up tall or standing. Participants each have a turn saying their name and then sit or lie down. Now try this one:

Names, Names
What's your name?
Names, Names
What's your name?

Again, students can sign, point to their communication boards, or speak in response to this activity. A final naming activity to be mentioned here involves all participants simultaneously:

Names, Names
We've all got names
Say your name,
We'll do the same.

Instruments

Instruments are also an important part of Orff-Schulwerk. These can be commercial, homemade, or just one's own body. As the instructor, you may want to ceremoniously introduce them, thus creating respect for their importance. Instruments commonly used are: tone bar, tambourines, xylophone, glockenspiel, banging gong, bells, wood blocks, triangle, gourd shaker, bamboo shaker and kazoo. In addition to these instruments, the following articles are easily adapted to rhythm sessions: washboard, bongos, ball, drinking glasses (with or without liquid), dish pan, trash can, wooden salad bowls, spoons, bottle caps nailed to sticks, sandpaper on blocks of wood, film cans with objects in them, and cigar metal containers with sand in them. Most objects can serve a dual purpose. First, students benefit from the movements involved through playing; and second, they are exposed to the many dimensions of sound. Several verses that can convey different qualities of sound are:

There are *loud* sounds
and there are soft sounds
Let me hear
your sounds! (or Can you make the same sounds?)

> Big sounds
> Little sounds
> Big sounds
> Little sounds
> Let me hear
> Your sounds

Bells are enjoyable, and the verses are very simple to do.

> I can clap
> I can sing
> Can you make
> This little bell ring?

> Swingin, flingin
> Who will make the bells
> Go ringin?

Modeling and Imitation

Qualities that can also stimulate learning are modeling and imitation. Orff-Schulwerk provides many "follow the leader" games. Examples include:

> Skittly, kittily
> Skittly, shi
> Do what I do
> After me

> Copy cat is
> The name of the game
> Anything you do
> We'll do the same

> Let's be copy cats
> And play a game
> Let's copy (name)
> And do the same!

In these activities the leader can make various body movements, strike instruments, or touch body parts depending on the functional level of each participant.

Sensori-Development

Orff-Schulwerk activities provide a natural facilitative device for sensorimotor training. Many resource materials are adaptable in this area such as the activities developed by Chaney and Kephart in *Motoric Aids to Perceptual Training* (1968). Valuable materials are also available by Cratty, 1966; Taylor, 1974; and Bradley, Konick and Leedy, 1968. Below are several examples of sensorimotor activities that employ the Orff technique;

> Soooooooooooooo Big
> __(name)__ is soooooooooooooo big.

This activity takes on real meaning for the participants if they are pulled up by the arms or shoulders as the verse is spoken.

Tickling is another technique which, if performed correctly, can be an enjoyable activity. With this verse, numerous objects can be introduced as tickling instruments (feather, brush, sponge):

> I'm a tickle, tickle
> tickle, tickle,
> tickle, bee!
> If I tickle you,
> Will you smile for me?

Scarves, hats, towels, and similar objects can become teaching tools for games typically played with very young children. This verse can be spoken as a towel is pulled over the face:

> Peek-a-boo,
> I see you!

Here's another using a hat:

> Who's that underneath that hat
> That hat
> Who's that underneath the hat?

Verses can also be used during washing, bathing, and role-playing situations using a shower cap and washcloth. These are excellent during aquatic therapy:

> Wash, wash,
> Washing me
> Wash this part you see!

In this exercise the teacher should emphasize sounds and selected body parts. If the participants are seated in a circle, the shower cap can be transferred from student to student as various body parts are washed. Here's another sensorimotor activity:

> Sighs, sighs
> and goodbyes
> Where, oh where
> Are your eyes
> (then on to "my eyes")

The list of sensorimotor activities is virtually endless as all types of objects such as body parts, mirrors, flashlights, bags of objects, and bean bags add new dimensions to each verse. The examples below illustrate only a few of the vast number of objects that can become teaching tools.

> Eenie, meanie
> Meinie, moe
> Where, oh where
> Are your toes? (my toes?)
>
> We have fingers,
> We have toes.
> Can you move
> All of those?
>
> Textures soft
> Textures smooth
> What are the textures
> That you choose?
>
> Reach deep into this mysterious bag
> Look with your hands—
> Not your eyes
> Your hands

Part I	My shoes are off
	My socks are showing
Part II	My socks are off
	Do you know how I'm going?
	Response—barefoot
Part III	How do you walk in your barefoot feet?
	How do you walk in your barefoot feet?

Here is a flashlight activity. Have the participants slap their legs when the light goes on or off while one person follows the light with the eyes.

> Light go off
> Light go on
> Off!
> On!
>
> Green light go
> Fast or slow
> Red light stop
> Right on the spot

Voice

Mouth and voice activities can be meaningful and enjoyable when performed through rounds and repetitive verse. The following verses direct the participant's attention toward the mouth and face:

> Chin chopper, chin chopper
> Chin, chin, chin
> Show us the place
> Where the food slips in
>
> There's something yucky
> In your mouth
> Spit it out!
> Spit it out!

With activities of this type, the teacher/leader should encourage the participants to find their mouths. The idea of mouth can be conveyed by squeezing it, rubbing it with ice, or actually placing food in it.

As stressed in Chapter 5, lip and tongue exercises are extremely important to developing speech communication. Here are several activities set to verse which promote this area. Don't forget to use props such as pinwheels, cotton balls, candles, flashlights, glitter, and feathers.

> Lick your lips
> Push your teeth
> Now make a sound
> With these

> Round and Round
> The pinwheel will go
> Let's see how hard
> You can blow!
>
> Shimmering, shimmering
> Light so bright
> Blow out the candles and
> Make it night

Food

Mealtime offers a natural teaching situation for Orff-Schulwerk and is the final instructional area to be discussed. The fact that food provides both a stimulus that can arouse the senses and a primary reinforcer, it can be used to facilitate many learning experiences. As explained by Bitcon (1976), activities scheduled during or near mealtime allow immediate experiences to be verbalized. Try these verse ideas during a physical education rest break.

> Munch, Oh munch, and
> Crunch, oh crunch
> What is __(name)__
> Having for lunch?

The next two verses may be performed independently or combined:

> My throat is dry,
> I want a drink,
> What kind of soda (or what kind of drink)
> Let me think!
>
> Soda pop bottles
> Pop! Pop! Pop!
> When the bottle's empty,
> Stop! Stop! Stop!

In this activity the participants and teacher/leader can pantomime the actions of drinking, making very dramatic gurgling sounds.

In addition to the content previously mentioned, Orff-Schulwerk activities are developed for many other areas. The authors have also modified the activities found in Bitcon's (1976) categories of holidays, colors, and art. Due to the brevity of this chapter and its topic, adaptive physical education and recreation, the reader is encouraged to consult the primary source material, *Alike and Different, the Clinical and Educational Use of Orff-Schulwerk* (Bitcon, 1976).

SUMMARY

The basic components of physical education and recreation programs for the severely retarded were presented in this chapter. Emphasis was given to the multidisciplinary team approach in planning and implementing instructional programs. Assessment was identified as critical for determining the individual's strengths as well as weaknesses, thus providing a foundation for instruction.

Sensorimotor activities were described that suggest a developmental approach to teaching. Activity examples and instructional procedures are to provide a springboard for additional ideas to augment the basic program.

The roles of adapted physical educators and therapeutic recreation specialists were described as overlapping in a number of areas. Despite the overlap, recreational program components were presented because differences in philosophical issues and content do exist.

A supplemental program, Special Olympics, was outlined; and its core components, Olympic style summer and winter sports and games, Let's-Play-to-Grow, recreation intern training, and metric education, were described.

A German instructional technique called Orff-Schulwerk was also presented. This teaching process utilizes activities that stimulate the participant's thinking, verbalization, imagination, and sense of rhythm through a combined motoric and musical medium.

The materials presented are to serve as fundamental instructional components for physical education and recreational programs.

REFERENCES

Adapted physical education guidelines, theory and practice for the seventies and eighties. Washington, D.C.: Physical Education and Recreation for the Handicapped: Information Research Utilization Center (IRUC), June 1976.

A new kind of joy, Washington, D.C., Special Olympics, Inc.

Barsch, R.H. *A movigenic curriculum.* Madison, Wisconsin: Bulletin No. 25, 1965.

Bitcon, C. *Alike and different, the clinical and educational use of Orff-Schulwerk.* Santa Ana, California: Rosha Press, 1976.

Bradley, W.T., Konick, G., & Leedy, C. *Daily sensorimotor training activities, A handbook for teachers and parents of pre-school children.* Palo Alto, California: Peek, 1968.

Brannan, S.A. Trends and issues in leisure education for the handicapped through community education. In E. Fauchild & L. Neil, (Eds.), *Common unity in the community.* Eugene, Oregon: The University of Oregon, 1975.

Chalfant, J.C., & Scheffelin, M.A. *Central processing dysfunctions in children: A review of research.* Washington, D.C.: U.S. Government Printing Office, 1969.

Chaney, C.M., & Kephart, N. *Motoric aids to perceptual training.* Columbus, Ohio: Charles E. Merrill, 1968.

Cratty, B.J. *Developmental sequences of perceptual-motor tasks: Movement activities for neurologically handicapped and retarded children and youth.* Palo Alto, California: Peek, 1966.

——— *Movement behavior and motor learning.* Philadelphia: Lea and Febler, 1967.

Fact sheet–teen program for the severely handicapped and retarded. San Francisco, California: Recreation Center for the Handicapped, 1972.

Fait, H.F. *Special physical education: Adapted, corrective, developmental.* Philadelphia: W.B. Saunders, 1972.

Flavell, J.H. *The developmental psychology of Jean Piaget.* Princeton, New Jersey: Van Nostrand, 1963.

Kephart, N.C. *The slow learner in the classroom.* Columbus, Ohio: Charles E. Merrill, 1960.

——— *The slow learner in the classroom.* Columbus, Ohio: Charles E. Merrill, 1971.

Kraus, R. *Therapeutic recreation service: Principles and practices.* Philadelphia: W.B. Saunders, 1978.

Nesbitt, J.A. *Educating the handicapped child for leisure fulfillment.* Iowa City, Iowa: The University of Iowa, Recreation Education Program, 1978.

Nugent, T. Recreation as a therapeutic tool in rehabilitation. In T.R. Collingwood (Ed.), *Therapeutic recreation and adapted physical education within rehabilitation.* Hot Springs, Arkansas: Arkansas Rehabilitation Research and Training Center, 1971.

Rudolph, L. *Physical skills for the severely and profoundly handicapped.* Unpublished manuscript, 1977.

Sherrill, C. *Adapted physical education and recreation.* Dubuque, Iowa: Wm. C. Brown, 1976.

Taylor, C. *Rhythm–A guide for creative movement.* Palo Alto, California: Peek, 1974.

Webb, R.C. Sensory motor training of the profoundly retarded. *American Journal of Mental Deficiency,* 1969, *74,* 284-289.

Contact sources include:

National Therapeutic Recreation Society
1601 North Lent Street
Arlington, Virginia 22202

Physical Education and Recreation Office
Division of Personnel Preparation
Bureau of Education for the Handicapped
7th and D Streets, S.W.
Washington, D.C.   20202

Chapter 13

Aquatic Therapy and Emergency Procedures

The natural buoyancy available to the human body in water makes this environment an extremely effective medium for movement activities. For many seriously physically impaired individuals, the therapy of a swimming pool makes the motor movements of sitting, standing, walking, twisting, and rolling possible for the first time. Its beneficial effects upon the body are paramount as it not only allows increased flexibility and muscle action, but is likely to improve the participant's total work output, perceptual awareness, self-concept, self-confidence, courage, and self-help skills (Sherrill, 1976; Fait, 1978).

Aquatic instruction can also be an extremely rewarding and satisfying experience for the aquatics teacher as well. The keys to successful experiences are:

1. appropriate teaching approaches
2. meaningful learner goals and objectives
3. adequate facilities and instructional equipment
4. knowledge of and compliance with health and safety considerations
5. understanding and use of appropriate handling and instructional procedures
6. knowledge of and ability to conduct appropriate activities and games

This chapter will focus upon the most common and practical planning and instructional considerations to follow in aquatic instruction.

After this brief introduction, readers have probably begun to mentally review their own swimming abilities. Although aquatic sessions can be taught by limited or nonswimmers, it certainly makes good sense that aquatics teachers possess adequate skills themselves.

Few people take the time to realize the responsibility they inherit as aquatic instructors. In most cases the instructor represents the most important and vital lifeline for the swimming participant. Due to this fact, any instructors who do not feel comfortable in the water and/or possess adequate swimming skills place themselves and others in unnecessary danger.

It is the recommendation of the American Red Cross that all aquatic instructors possess adequate swimming skills in addition to following and teaching recommended life saving practices. Superior, nearly cost free, swimming instruction is offered by the Red Cross in almost all geographic areas throughout the United States. Therefore, to assure the safety of others and themselves, aquatic instructors should not only know how to swim, but also hold a lifesaving certificate offered by the American Red Cross.

CONCEPTUALIZING INSTRUCTION

Several basic teaching procedures are employed by teachers when instructing physical education, including aquatic therapy. A traditional approach has been explanation-demonstration. This directive method has a degree of flexibility, depending on the teacher; however, it is essentially teacher-centered, quite rigid, and tightly structured. Another technique, which has more recent acceptance, is movement exploration. The guided discovery method, as it is called, generally requires the child to make decisions, solve problems, or exhibit creativity. Each approach, or a combination of approaches, has merit in specific cases. For the severely retarded, the explanation-demonstration model is generally found to be far more workable.

Explanation-Demonstration

In general when conducting physical activities using this approach, the teacher first explains a particular skill as it is demonstrated; next, the student performs; and as a final step, the teacher observes the student's performance comparing it to the preceding demonstration model. Deviations from this model are then evaluated as either acceptable or inferior. Implicit in this approach is structure. This principle is evident in that activities begin at specific times, follow a predetermined sequential order, and end when the skill is performed correctly. By its very directive nature, if a child is told to jump off the diving board and this activity is within his functional level, he *will* jump off the diving board. The "command" style of teaching, as it is often called, is generally found to be most successful with those who have a limited capacity to make rational decisions, think creatively, initiate purposeful actions, or understand verbal directions.

Movement Exploration

For severely retarded, a total movement exploration approach is not encouraged. Its major shortcoming lies in the questioning or decision-making process underlying each activity. In contrast to the explanation-demonstration approach, participants are given choices, asked questions, and expected to solve problems. Such an instructional situation requires the correct interpretation and understanding of verbal questions. Typically, the teacher will present a question or problem in this manner: "Show me how you can move from this side of the pool to that side of the pool." In this problem the student can select any locomotor method (crawl, walk, hop, swim). The major principle of this approach is that participants are told what to do, not how to do it. Although movement exploration is not appropriate with many severely handicapped, some can operate successfully through either a simplified problem-solving approach or a combination of both approaches. In actual practice, there are times when a combined approach is desirable because some students can benefit from the challenge of developing their own methods of performing motor skills. On the other hand, there are many situations that lend themselves better to an explanation-demonstration method where the teacher makes all the instructional choices.

ADMINISTRATIVE CONSIDERATIONS IN AQUATIC PROGRAMMING

The goals of an aquatic therapy program are an integral part of the student's total educational program. As the staff members, parents, specialists, and medical personnel work to meet the developmental needs and growth processes of each student, the aquatic therapy program can be extremely important. Depending on the needs of the student, program goals are often written to encompass the areas of improved fitness, movement, or level of activity. Program objectives are more specific and focus upon areas such as:

- range of motion
- spatial awareness
- body image
- independence and self-worth
- kinesthetic sense
- tactility
- enjoyment

- courage
- inner language concepts
- fitness
- muscle tone
- decreased spasticity
- time relationship

Implementation of the program topics such as those listed requires trained personnel, facilities, and equipment. Although many programs are forced to operate on limited funds, serious consideration should be given to several basic program components.

Facilities

The locker room and pool areas are both important training stations for motor development and activities of daily living. With this in mind, they should be equipped with the following:

1. floors with a nonslip surface (vinyl or rubber mats for hall runners and/or nonslip paint)
2. ramps for wheelchairs
3. walking rails near lockers and entries leading to the pool area
4. shower facilities equipped with outside water controls for the instructor or floor mounted on and off control buttons
5. doors wide enough to accommodate wheelchairs and halls wide enough to accommodate two wheelchairs
6. ramps entering the pool to accommodate a wheelchair
7. pool area ceiling materials that will not rot or absorb water vapor
8. toilet bowls and stalls designed to accommodate wheelchairs
9. ventilated cabinets large enough to store foam boards, swim fins, sponges, and other teaching apparatus
10. sunlamps or infrared lamps built into the ceiling to cut down the amount of water vapor
11. large ventilation fans in locker and office space near the pool and
12. wall hooks for hanging flotation equipment and inner tubes

In addition to this list, two major areas of concern for the locker room area should be cleanliness and temperature. Due to the fact that many handicapped individuals have poor body temperature control, no drafts should be apparent, and the room should remain at a constant temperature. Dressing floor areas should be covered by carpet or mats for students to lie on while being changed.

There are many adaptations within the pool area that should also receive consideration. The following suggestions involve small amounts of labor and capital:

1. warning lights in the deep water area
2. a radio or record playing at the shallow end of the pool
3. brightly colored floating buoys separating the deep areas from the shallow areas
4. the texture of the sides of the pool near the gutter can be changed with various depths. This can be accomplished with different tiles or texturized paint. Walls can also be color coded for different depths.

The Pool

Pool size and depth are important factors to consider when planning aquatic programs for the severely retarded. Large pools with varying depths may be advantageous when handling large groups, but they can be extremely costly to heat, require excessive maintenance, and present problems during instruction. Ideally, therapy pools should contain an adequate shallow portion for instruction at a depth between three and one-half to four feet. Total pool dimensions may vary; however, keep in mind that water temperatures should range in the low 90s in order to provide a relaxing effect on the muscles of spastic individuals. With increased pool capacity, higher water temperatures, and faster chlorine evaporation come increased maintenance problems and increased operating costs.

A relatively inexpensive aquatics program can be conducted using a portable pool. Porta-pools offer several advantages: (1) initial costs are small by comparison to conventional pools, generally ranging between $2,500 and $6,000 depending on size and depth; (2) they can be transported from location to location; and (3) following the instructional day, they can be covered and locked, improving safety and omitting added costs of fencing and supervision.

Health and Safety Aspects

Before any handicapped child enters an aquatic program, written approval from the family physician and parent should be on file. Although aquatic therapy has proven extremely beneficial to nearly all handicapping conditions, the following problems rule out swimming.

1. open cut or sores
2. infectious conditions such as ringworm, athlete's foot, and venereal disease
3. chronic middle ear disease and times when tubes are in the ears
4. severe heart and upper respiratory conditions
5. allergies to water and chlorine
6. severe inflammation of joints
7. uncontrollable seizures

Hydrocephalis and hemophilia present added concern especially if diving is a teaching component. In nearly all situations, including states of arrest, these participants should be protected from any further complications. Additional care must also be given to those with scalp and skin conditions due to the drying effects of chlorine. Moisturizing cream and hair conditioner should be applied to participants following the after-swim shower, expecially for Down's Syndrome or other persons with similar skin characteristics.

As an added note, teachers and parents have traditionally been extremely cautious as to the length of time swimming should occur after eating. Research reveals that swimming after eating presents no detrimental effects to swimming performance, cramps, or sickness (Karpovich & Sinning, 1971).

EMERGENCY PROCEDURES

Personal safety practices are everyone's responsibility in the aquatic environment. Often severely retarded individuals fail to comprehend the dangers that are possible when in the pool or pool area. The following are several general safety practices that should be taught and observed religiously:

1. Individuals should not be allowed in the water when overheated or tired.
2. Beware of overexposure to the sun.
3. Never allow individuals with inner tubes, arm cuffs, or other floatation devices to enter water over their heads unless directly supervised by a trained instructor.
4. Teach each participant how to signal for help if at all possible.
5. Don't allow anyone to swim unattended.
6. Have rescue equipment available and know how to use it.
7. Keep emergency numbers available.
8. Never allow running on the deck or in shower areas.

There are many safety practices that are not mentioned above; but with proper pool construction, equipment, filtration for sanitation, common sense, and plenty of trained instructors, most mishaps can be avoided.

Two safety practices not yet mentioned for the sole purpose of underscoring their importance are:

1. Always have an adequate first aid kit handy.
2. Be certain that at least one instructor in the group can competently administer artificial respiration and/or cardiopulmonary resuscitation (CPR).

General First Aid Practices

Swimming and aquatic therapy instruction can be conducted by individuals with varying degrees of swimming background and ability. However, for minimal safety at least one swimming instructor should possess emergency first aid skills. Although each public lifeguard trained by the American Red Cross has received instruction in this area, (a qualified lifeguard should be on duty during pool hours) it is comforting to know that fellow instructor(s) can spring into lifesaving action if the situation demands.

The contents of this section provide a general outline of the fundamental steps and rules for basic first aid.

Handling the Emergency

When a serious illness or injury occurs the instructor should be prepared to give immediate assistance for the following:

1. breathing difficulties
2. severe bleeding
3. shock
4. neck and spine injuries
5. heat stroke, heat cramps, and heat exhaustion
6. epilepsy

If any of these first aid emergencies should occur, the following steps are recommended:

1. Stay calm and don't panic. Provide reassurance to the victim that all will be fine (talk to the victim).
2. Don't move the victim from one place to another unless further danger is evident.
3. Place the victim in the body position that best suits the nature of the injury.
4. Protect the victim from overchilling by covering with blankets or clothing. If the ground is damp or cold, place blankets or clothing under the victim.
5. Determine the extent or cause of the injuries by finding out exactly what happened. Look for emergency medical identification on the victim.
6. Send someone for help either by calling the fire department, paramedics, physician, or ambulance service, or traveling for assistance.

The next emergency procedure is to check for injuries in a methodical manner.

1. Carefully loosen clothing.
2. Remove clothing to the point that an accurate check can be made for injuries.
3. Examine the victim's skin for abnormal coloration or temperature.
4. Check victim's pulse and state of consciousness.
5. If victim is unconscious, check for seizures, evidence of head injuries, and paralysis.
6. Examine the size of the victim's pupils and the expression in the eyes.
7. Check the body for open wounds and broken bones.

After the examination is made, the caregiver has a responsibility to:

1. Administer appropriate dressings, bandages, or splints.
2. Keep the victim in one location.
3. Stay with the victim and maintain a leadership role until qualified medical personnel arrive.

First Aid for Breathing Problems

Air passages can be obstructed or blocked anatomically or mechanically. Anatomical obstructions can have a number of causes, but generally result from:

- seizures with the tongue dropping back and closing the throat passage
- asthma attacks
- damage to the throat resulting from a sharp blow, swallowing corrosive poisons, or severe burns on the neck and face
- croup

Mechanical obstruction may be caused by a foreign object caught in the throat. Common examples are:

- dentures
- rocks or metal objects
- excessive mucus, saliva, or choking on one's vomit

Regardless of the type of obstruction, any victim that fails to regain control of the breathing process runs the risk of asphyxiation. Asphyxiation is a life-threatening condition that results from failing to breath or from breathing air that lacks appropriate amounts of oxygen or excessive amounts of toxic gases.

When insufficient amounts of oxygen are in the victim's bloodstream the symptoms of bluish colored tongue, lips, and fingernails appear. In addition, the pupils of the eyes become dilated, and the victim eventually loses consciousness.

Artificial respiration is one technique commonly used to restore the oxygen level within an individual who is having breathing difficulty. The mouth to mouth or mouth to nose techniques have been proven to provide far more effective ventilation than traditional manual methods (lifting the arms or chest).

Mouth to Mouth (Artificial Respiration)

The steps to giving mouth to mouth respiration are as follows:

1. Clear the mouth of all foreign matter (use the fingers to remove mucus, vomit, or objects).

2. Open the airway. (Place one of your hands under the victim's neck and the other on the forehead, arching the head back.)
3. While holding the victim's head in the arch position, grasp and pinch the nostrils closed with the hand that is on the forehead.
4. Open your mouth wide, take a deep breath, seal your mouth over the victim's, and in an even flow of air, blow into the victim. Your breathing should be at a high rate initially, then steady at a rate of one breath per 5 seconds for adults and one breath per 3 seconds for small children (note: with small children, you must expel smaller amounts of air (puffs) and with less pressure so as not to cause injury.)
5. Watch the victim's chest out of the corner of your eye as it rises as you blow.
6. Remove your mouth, turn your ear toward the victim's mouth and watch the victim's chest area. Listen for the victim to exhale as the chest falls.
7. Continue with the cycle of blowing into the victim and waiting for the chest to fall.

Mouth to Nose (Artificial Respiration)

1. Clear mouth and nose of all foreign matter.
2. Arch the victim's head backward as stated in the mouth to mouth method, and keep it arched with the hand on the forehead.
3. Use the other hand to push on the chin to close the mouth.
4. Taking a deep breath place your mouth over the victim's nose, make a seal, and blow into the nose.
5. Once you have blown into the victim, open the victim's mouth and allow the air to be exhaled.
6. Repeat the cycle until recovery medical assistance arrives, or the victim dies.

Clearing the Airway

In most cases the air passage (throat) will clear as the victim's head is arched back and the tongue is able to drop back (Step 2 of artificial respiration). If air does not exchange freely as you blow into the victim or allow the victim's lungs to exhale, there are several immediate actions:

1. Recheck the victim's arched head position. It should be arched fully.
2. If blockage continues, roll the victim onto the side and strike a firm blow between the shoulder blades with the edge or heel of your hand to free the material. A small child can be held upside down by the ankles or turned over one arm as several firm pats are struck between the shoulder blades.

If excess air has entered the stomach, it will bulge and possibly interfere with the victim's breathing, heart action, and/or cause vomiting. When the stomach bulges several procedures should follow:

1. Momentarily turn the victim on his stomach and turn the head to one side. Standing over the victim in a straddle position, bend forward sliding your hands underneath the victim's stomach.
2. Next lift upward to help empty the contents of the stomach.
3. Once the victim's stomach empties, return him to his back, clear the mouth of foreign matter, and resume artificial respiration.

Note: As an alternate method, the victim remains lying on his back as you press your hand(s) down on the stomach. Remember to turn the victim's head to one side.

As a final caution recognize the fact that some individuals may require artificial respiration even though they are breathing. In this case the victim may be breathing very shallowly or quite irregularly, thus needing assistance. If this situation occurs the rescuer should use artificial respiration (either mouth to mouth or mouth to nose), but time the lifesaving breaths by blowing into the victim as the victim's inhalation is made.

First Aid for Severe Bleeding

Anytime an instructor is working with severely mentally retarded, accidents may occur. Even though a physician or nurse may be close by, it may be the instructor's immediate action that saves a life.

If an injury results in spurting or gushing blood, first aid must be given immediately or death will result within several minutes.

There are several key actions to make when severe bleeding occurs:

- Apply direct pressure (hold a pad or bandage on the wound with pressure).
- Elevate the wound (raise the injured area higher than the heart).
- If direct pressure doesn't control bleeding, also apply pressure at the appropriate pressure point.
- If bleeding can't be controlled with any other means and the victim's life is seriously threatened, a tourniquet may be used.

Direct Pressure, Elevation, and Pressure Points

The first step to controlling bleeding is to place a gauze pad or clean cloth on the wound and apply pressure to the affected area. At the same time the direct pressure is applied, the injured area should be elevated to a level higher than the heart.

If the blood flow continues despite efforts through direct pressure and elevation, do not remove the protective pads or cloth, but add additional layers. If the bleeding continues, pressure must also be applied to the artery leading to the injury. There are several common pressure points on the body which when located and given firm pressure will limit blood flow through the artery (Figure 13-1).

If the wound were near the wrist, the appropriate pressure point would be located on the underside of the upper arm between the elbow and armpit. Pressure should be applied by first placing the fingers on the underside of the arm with the thumb opposite. The squeeze is made with the length of the fingers and not the fingertips.

If the injury occurred on the lower leg, the pressure point would be located on the center part of the crease in the groin area. By pushing the heel of the hand on this area, the femoral artery is forced against the pelvic bone limiting blood flow to the lower leg. Remember when the pressure point is used, it is done in combination with direct pressure and elevation.

Figure 13-1 Arterial Pressure Points

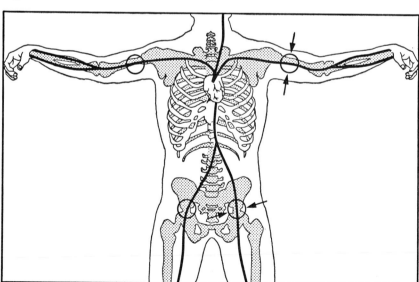

Applying pressure to the artery will limit blood flow to the injured area.

Use of the Tourniquet

If bleeding cannot be stopped by any other methods and life is severely threatened, the tourniquet can be used. According to the American Red Cross (1977), the tourniquet should be applied in the following manner:

1. Place the tourniquet just above the wound, but not touching the wound edges. If the wound is in a joint area or just below, place the tourniquet directly above the joint.
2. Wrap the tourniquet band tightly twice around the limb and tie a half knot.
3. Place a short, strong stick (or similar object) on the half knot and tie a full knot.
4. Twist the stick until bleeding is stopped.
5. Secure the stick in place.
6. Attach a note to the victim giving the location of the tourniquet and the time it was applied.
7. Once the serious decision to apply the tourniquet has been made, the tourniquet should not be loosened except on the advice of a physician.
8. Treat for shock and get medical attention for the victim immediately (pp. 203-204).

Shock

A depressed state of the vital bodily functions resulting from injury or a traumatic event is called shock. Shock has a number of causes; the most common are due to:

- loss of body fluids (due to heavy perspiration, vomiting, burns, etc.)
- severe bleeding
- infection
- heart attack or stroke
- poisons
- limited breathing
- inability to handle stress

Due to the seriousness of shock if proper attention is not given, it is important to be able to recognize these symptoms:

- skin color is pale or bluish and feels quite cool. For dark-skinned victims, the pale flesh under the fingernails, inside the mouth or under the eyelids provides the tell-tale signs

- breathing is usually faster than normal unless the chest has been damaged (breathing will most likely be shallow due to the pain)
- victim shows little strength or vitality (lifeless)
- pulse rate may be weak and rapid (generally over 100 beats per minute) and may also be irregular in its pattern
- severe vomiting
- large dilated pupils
- blood pressure may be low and the skin appears blotched or spotted

First Aid for Shock

The best first aid for victims with shock is to attempt to keep the vital functions of the body at normal. Circulation of the blood, adequate oxygen through breathing, and a normal body temperature are critical to recovery. In order to stabilize the bodily functions and return them to normal, first aid occurs in three forms:

1. lay the victim down and calm her
2. keep the victim warm by covering
3. obtain medical assistance as quickly as possible

Care must be taken to insure that the victim doesn't get up and move around. If neck or back injuries are suspected, the victim should not be moved. If transportation is a necessity, it should not be done until the body is prepared properly using a method described in the section to follow on spinal injuries.

As a final suggestion for victims without head or facial injury, the feet may be raised up to approximately 12 inches. However, if breathing becomes labored or additional pain occurs, the feet should be returned to their normal position.

There is often a natural tendency for the first aid giver to offer liquids to the victim in shock. These general rules apply to offering fluids:

1. give water or a baking soda solution (1 teaspoon of salt and one-half teaspoon baking soda per quart of water) only if the medical assistance is delayed for more than one hour
2. offer a glass half full of water or water solution every 15 minutes
3. offer one-fourth of a glass to children ages 1-12 years, and half that amount for those one year old or less
4. stop all liquids if vomiting or sickness occurs
5. resume normal fluid intake after 2 to 4 hours if the victim can keep from vomiting

Spinal Injuries

One of the hazards of working with severely retarded individuals is often their inability to tell you what is wrong when an accident occurs. If proper precautions are not followed immediately, you may run the risk of causing further injury or death.

If the instructor suspects that a student has sustained an injury to the spinal column such as fracturing or dislocating a vertebra, extreme care must be taken during movement to avoid any twisting or bending.

The most immediate caution is—don't move the victim unless you have to. Signal for medical help and keep the victim immobile, comfortable, and warm. If the individual absolutely must be moved from the swimming pool, gym, or training area, make sure these rules are followed:

1. Find others, preferably three or four people, to help
2. Brief those helping in the techniques of lifting (practice several lifts on a noninjured person before moving the victim)

The fundamental procedure to follow for individuals with spinal injuries is to first offer first aid to stop any bleeding, restore breathing using artificial respiration, and splint any broken limbs. Second, place a rigid board (door, ironing board, plank) next to the victim. With minimal lifting and no twisting of the victim, the board is slid under the back. Third, as an additional precaution to protect the victim from sliding or rolling, straps, wraps, or materials should be secured around the body. As a last precaution, if a support board or device is not available, people can be placed on each side of the victim and another at the victim's head. Lifting must occur simultaneously with firm support given to keep the head and neck level with the victim's back.

SUDDEN ILLNESSES

Excessive activity with the loss of body fluids, faulty body perspiration mechanisms, and sickness may result in conditions known as heat stroke, heat cramps, and heat exhaustion.

Heat Stroke

This condition results from a problem with the sweating mechanism and a reaction to high temperatures. Difficulty usually occurs when an individual is active on an unusually hot day. If large amounts of water and/or salt are lost due to perspiration, the body becomes overheated, and an immediate life-threatening situation exists.

The basic heat stroke signs to watch for are:

- extreme temperature (often reaches higher than 105 degrees Farenheit)
- skin color is red, hot to touch, and very dry
- a fast and strong pulse
- unconscious victim

First aid must be administered immediately in order to restore the body temperature to its normal level. If the body temperature reaches the 105 degree Farenheit level, the following first aid procedures are appropriate:

1. remove the victim's clothing and begin sponging the body with cool water or rubbing alcohol. Victim can also be placed in a tub of cool water. As temperature drops, dry victim off
2. place victim near a fan or air-conditioning unit and monitor temperature (Note: cover victim with light towel or sheet to maintain modesty during the cooling process.)

Heat Cramps

During heavy activity, an individual may experience a cramp or muscular pain due to an imbalance within the salt/fluid levels. In most cases, cramps occur in the legs or abdomen first and may later spread to other parts of the body if first aid is not forthcoming. First aid should include:

- massaging or rubbing the affected muscles to relieve the contraction
- offer the victim small amounts of a salt-water solution (1 teaspoon per glass). Give approximately a half of a glass every 15 minutes for a one-hour period.

Heat Exhaustion

If an individual is actively participating in games, exercises, or sports and becomes extremely tired, weak, and suddenly collapses, the problem may be due to heat exhaustion. This situation occurs when large amounts of sweat are lost and are not replaced by a proportional amount of fluid.

When this condition occurs, more than one of the following symptoms will generally prevail:

- weak, tired feeling
- sweating profusely

- possible fainting, vomiting, and upset stomach
- headache and cramps
- clammy skin, which has lost its normal color

First aid should include:

- offer the victim small amounts of a salt-water solution (1 teaspoon per glass) Give approximately one-half glass every 15 minutes for a one-hour period
- place the victim on the back and elevate the feet 8 to 12 inches
- loosen tight-fitting clothing
- place the victim near a fan or air-conditioner and/or apply cool wet cloths
- if vomiting occurs, do not give fluids and seek immediate medical treatment
- allow victim to rest and remain in a cool area until strength and salt/fluid level returns to normal

Severely retarded individuals are subject to numerous illness conditions. Because fitness and conditioning levels are often low, problems can be expected when increased physical demands and high environmental temperatures occur simultaneously.

Epilepsy

In closing, one condition must be touched upon briefly as its prevalence is much higher in the mentally retarded population when compared to the nonhandicapped. This chronic disease is know as epilepsy.

In its most severe form (grand mal seizures) the victim may be forewarned by a unique feeling or sensation (aura) and be able to lie down before the convulsions begin. Jerky, uncontrolled contractures will continue resulting in the loss of consciousness and often bladder control.

When a grand mal seizure occurs, first aid should be administered as follows:

1. place the victim on his back
2. remove all objects (furniture, rocks, people) from the immediate area
3. protect the victim's head from any fall or banging action
4. loosen any tight clothing from around the victim's neck
5. keep the airway open by tilting the head back if there is breathing difficulty (do not place sticks or objects between teeth to pry the mouth open)
6. if breathing stops, give artificial respiration
7. after the convulsion stops allow victim to rest and assist with any clean-up
8. remove other children or spectators and explain what has occurred

AQUATIC INSTRUCTION

Once participants are dressed for swimming, movement to the pool area should follow a preplanned and systematic procedure. Adherence to a few simple rules can prevent many accidents and increase valuable instructional time. The following are several worthwhile considerations:

- assemble students in pairs, lines, or small groups when moving to the pool area
- avoid wet spots and remove all benches or obstacles
- make no stops along the way to the pool
- once in the pool area, seat all students on specified mats or bleachers

Frequently aides and volunteers are used during locker room activities, travel to the pool area, and aquatic instruction. In their willingness to help, they frequently carry the slower participants far more than is necessary. In the case of ambulatory students, walking or crawling must be encouraged whenever possible. When wet floor surfaces make movement unsafe, common pathways should be covered with vinyl or rubber mats. If wheelchairs are used with nonambulatory participants, travel problems should not occur; however, extra care must be taken when transferring them to the water. In some cases the task can be simplified using a full body carrier or cage attached to the ceiling. Others may enter from a wheelchair if a ramp leading into the water is available, or in other situations hand carrying may be the only alternative.

Hand Carrying

Due to pool construction limitations, hand carrying is a common technique used to transfer nonambulatory students to the water. For the small individual, the one-person carry can be accomplished by slipping one hand behind the back and the other under the knees. Next, the student is raised from the wheelchair using a straightening action of the carrier's legs, thus preventing any excessive back strain. Once in carrying position, the instructor walks to the pool's edge and places the student in a sitting position with her feet in the water. If necessary, someone may need to steady the student until the carrier can enter the water.

A student can also be passed directly from pool side to someone in the water. If this is appropriate, the instructor simply carries the student to the water's edge, assumes a half-kneeling position, and passes the student to the instructor in the water. In making this transfer, the instructor in the water places his hand above the carrier's, allowing the carrier to merely slide his hands away as the student grasps the instructor in the water.

A nearly identical technique is the two-person carry. In this transfer, both people initiate the pickup from opposing sides by slipping one hand around the student's back and the other under the knees. A good safety precaution is to grasp the arm or wrist to guard against slipping. Once the student is lifted from the chair, she is placed in a sitting position at pool side with her feet dangling in the water. If the student is ready to enter the water, one instructor should stand behind her and lift under the shoulders, thus easing her into the water to the awaiting arms of the second instructor.

Instructional Procedures

The complication of numerous physiological and behavioral characteristics can make aquatic instruction for the severely retarded a trying experience for both teacher and student. Students commonly exhibit one or a combination of the following categories:

- severe physical involvement (athetoid, spastic, missing limbs, etc.)
- lethargic or apathetic behavior
- excessive fear of the water

A goal of instruction must be to attempt to meet the individual needs of each student. Therefore, handling procedures will often vary depending on the disability and overt behaviors. Following are several general suggestions for handling individuals displaying spasticity, lethargy, and fear:

1. *Spasticity*—generally circulation is restricted and the body temperature drops, therefore water temperature should be in the low 90s.
   a. Body movement in the water such as rocking the student side-to-side or spinning slowly tends to increase body temperature and lower muscular tension.
   b. Spastic individuals carried or handled improperly tend to become more rigid, requiring that they be carried in a semiflexed position at the waist, with the shoulders rounded forward and the knees apart.

2. *Lethargy*
   a. Listless and apathetic individuals can receive increased stimulation through assisted movements. Instructors should assist the individual in making turning, twisting, reaching, splashing, and kicking motions.
   b. Spinning or rocking an individual while wearing a life vest or while seated on an inner tube also supplies increased stimulation.

3. *Fear*
   a. Patience, routine, repetition, and coaxing are needed to help individuals overcome their fear.
   b. Gradual introduction to the water through play at pool side is the first step.
   c. Students who become frightened in the water should be held away from the instructor's shoulders and neck.
   d. Finger and toe nails should be trimmed before students receive instruction. Frightened students may claw or scratch unknowingly.

Instructional Phases

A successful aquatic therapy program does not mean that each participant must learn to swim. For some individuals with serious physical impairments, swimming may be beyond their capability. However, much can still be accomplished to benefit the student's total development.

Instructional formats in aquatics programs vary, yet nearly all include the four basic phases of: (1) adjusting to water, (2) buoyancy, (3) propulsion and stroking, and (4) deep water activities. Aquatics checklist Table 13-1 identifies the common subskills within the four phases.

Phase Number 1—Adjusting to Water

Possibly the most trying aspect of aquatic instruction presents itself in the water accommodation phase. In order to make the student feel safe and secure in and about the water, it is often necessary to use a number of coaxing tactics. First, in a one-to-one situation the teacher may sit at pool side with the student and watch the others in the water. Gradually the student is coaxed into coming closer until seated on the pool's edge or steps. At this point a bucket and several corks, dry sponges, or wash cloths are introduced. As the student begins to play with these, the bucket is filled with water and the student is again encouraged to continue playing. In the next step the instructor enters the water and plays with the student from that point. Gradually the student is led into the water always maintaining direct physical contact with the teacher.

On paper the transition from the pool side bleachers to entering the water appears to require little time; yet in reality, it may take weeks of constant repetition and coaxing. The instructor must keep in mind that it may take weeks to reduce the fear of the water; however, once a sense of security is established, future tasks can be accomplished much faster.

Table 13-1 Aquatic Therapy Checklist

Phase 1—Adjusting to Water
  A. Entering and Exiting Water
    ___ 1. Requires instructor's assistance
    ___ 2. Descends steps (assisted)
    ___ 3. Descends steps (unassisted)
    ___ 4. Descends ladder (assisted)
    ___ 5. Descends ladder unassisted, but instructor watches for safety
    ___ 6. Descends ladder without aid
    ___ 7. Leaves water using steps (assisted)
    ___ 8. Leaves water using steps (unassisted)
    ___ 9. Ascends ladder (assisted)
    ___10. Ascends ladder (unassisted)

  B. Sitting Locomotor Movements
    ___ 1. Sits in waist deep water
    ___ 2. Walks ten steps holding teacher's hand
    ___ 3. Stands alone
    ___ 4. Walks across pool pushing kickboard
    ___ 5. Walks across pool width in water chest height
    ___ 6. Walks across pool splashing with hands
    ___ 7. Walks across pool—arms simulating crawl stroke
    ___ 8. Runs across pool (assisted or unassisted)
    ___ 9. Hops across pool

  C. Facial Accommodation
    ___ 1. Allows instructor to wet face with sponge
    ___ 2. Wets own face with sponge
    ___ 3. Touches chin to water
    ___ 4. Touches ears to water (assisted and unassisted)
    ___ 5. Touches forehead to water
    ___ 6. Blows bubbles through plastic tube
    ___ 7. Blows Ping Pong balls ten feet
    ___ 8. Cups water in hands
    ___ 9. Blows water from cupped hands
    ___10. Splashes self with water in hand
    ___11. Puts mouth in water
    ___12. Puts face in water
    ___13. Blows bubbles in water (5 consecutive times)
    ___14. Bobs under water (3 consecutive times)
    ___15. Touches bottom or toes with hands
    ___16. Opens eyes under water
    ___17. Retrieves objects from bottom of pool (shallow)
    ___18. Seesaw bobbing with a partner
    ___19. Bobbing down and coming up under a hat
    ___20. Bobbing into inner tubes

Table 13-1 continued

Phase 2—Body Buoyancy
__ 1. Assumes horizontal position (with assistance)
__ 2. Floats on back with arm cuffs, barbell floats
__ 3. Floating block and instructor's support
__ 4. Floats on front (same as #3)
__ 5. Jellyfish float with artificial support-recovery
__ 6. Floats on back with arm cuffs and floating blocks
__ 7. Floats on front (same as #6)
__ 8. Floats on back with floating block
__ 9. Floats on front with floating block
__10. Front float no support 5 seconds
__11. Jellyfish float no support 5 seconds
__12. Back float no support 5 seconds
__13. Turns over front to back (artificial support)
__14. Turns over back to front (artificial support)
__15. Turns over front to back (no support)
__16. Turns over back to front (no support)

Phase 3—Propulsion and Coordinated Stroking-Leg Action
__ 1. Flutter kick on front (with support)
__ 2. Flutter kick on back (with support)
__ 3. Flutter kick on front (no support)
__ 4. Flutter kick on back (no support)

     Propulsion and Coordinated Stroking-Arm Action
__ 5. Alternate arms (with support)
__ 6. Walking across pool with alternate arm action
__ 7. Finning on back with support
__ 8. Paddling on front with support

     Combined Movements
__ 9. Prone glide and flutter kick (with support)
__10. Prone glide and flutter kick (no support)
__11. Back glide and flutter kick (with support)
__12. Back glide and flutter kick (no support)
__13. On front—paddle and flutter kick
__14. On back—fin and flutter kick
__15. Front crawl 5 yards (with support)
__16. Front crawl 5 yards (no support)
__17. Front crawl 10 yards (with support)
__18. Front crawl 10 yards (no support)

Phase 4—Deep Water Training
__ 1. Front crawl 20 yards including deep water (with support)
__ 2. Front crawl 20 yards including deep water (no support)
__ 3. Touch bottom in deep water with feet
__ 4. Touch bottom in deep water with hand
__ 5. Retrieves small objects from bottom in deep water from surface dive
__ 6. Sitting jump from pool side into deep water (with assistance)
__ 7. Sitting jump from pool side into deep water (without assistance)

Table 13-1 continued

___ 8. Standing jump from pool side into deep water (with assistance)
___ 9. Standing jump from pool side into deep water (without assistance)
___10. Jumps from 1 meter diving board (artificial support)
___11. Jumps from 1 meter diving board (without support)
___12. Jump in—level off to front crawl (with artificial support)
___13. Jump in—level off—front crawl
___14. Sitting dive from pool side
___15. Kneeling dive from pool side
___16. Standing dive from pool side
___17. Standing dive from 1-meter board

Phase Number 2—Body Buoyancy

Body buoyancy or the quality of floating differs among individuals. A person with large quantities of fat cells (adipose tissue) will be able to float much easier than someone whose weight is primarily muscle and bone. As a general rule women are more buoyant than men, just as Caucasians are more buoyant than blacks.

The key to floating vertically lies in maintaining one's center of buoyancy (CB) at a point where it is vertical to one's center of gravity (CG). For an obese person, the center of buoyancy is usually located in the lower portion of the hip region. In contrast, the CB for a thin person may be in the chest area. Due to the fact that one's CB and CG must align vertically in order to balance (floating), it is impossible for a thin person to maintain a horizontal position in the water without moving the arms and legs. As the reader can see in Figure 13-2 buoyancy or the floating position depends solely upon the individual's body mass.

Figure 13-2 Effects of Buoyancy on Floating Explain Why There Are Many Correct Ways

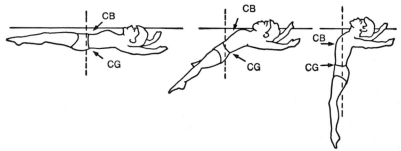

A Above average buoyancy.   B Average buoyancy.   C Below average buoyancy.

Source: From *Adapted physical education and recreation: A multidisciplinary approach,* by C. Sherrill, p. 277, ©1976. Reprinted by permission of Wm.C. Brown Co., Dubuque, Iowa.

For nearly all swimmers, once initial fears are overcome, floating becomes an enjoyable and relaxing activity. Its accomplishment also serves as a natural step to teaching the elementary strokes of swimming. In teaching the skill of floating, many assistive devices such as arm cuffs, vests, floating blocks, and barbell floats can be used. During the beginning stages of instruction, it may be necessary to use one type or another in addition to the instructor's support. As skill improves, support can be gradually reduced, finally reaching a point where it is no longer necessary. For some participants, especially those with cardiac problems, floating should be done on the back, and not so that the breath must be held. In these cases the face float, bobbing activities, front crawl, and glide must be omitted.

Phase Number 3—Propulsion and Coordinated Stroking

Teaching the severely retarded techniques of propelling themselves requires very little technical knowledge and large amounts of patience and repetitive activities. Arm and leg strokes should be taught using land as well as water drills. In both settings it is usually necessary to manipulate the student's limbs through the desired patterns, at the same time telling the performer in one- or two-word statements what he is doing. Next the student should be told repeatedly to kick, splash, etc. while slowly fading physical prompts.

Stroke instruction can begin with the glide while incorporating leg action using the flutter kick. If the flutter kick appears unteachable, the trudgen frog or dolphin kicks may be effective substitutes. Arm action includes splashing, finning (pushing the palms of the hands against the water in a direction opposite to the way the student wants to go), sculling, paddling, and the front crawl strokes. Combined strokes, synchronized breathing, and distance swimming are included as phase three instructional skills; however, their attainment is not essential before entering phase four.

Phase Number 4—Deep Water Training

Extreme care should be taken in this phase to insure safety at all times. Even the most proficient swimmers should never be left unsupervised when working on deep water skills of jumping and diving, treading water, and distance swimming.

ACTIVITIES FOR INSTRUCTION

There are endless activities that can be used when instructing the retarded in aquatic therapy. Those suggested in Table 13-2 are intended to provide a creative springboard for the instructor's imagination. Activities have been provided in each of the four instructional phases and correspond to the subskill areas identified in the Aquatic Therapy Checklist (Table 13-1).

Table 13-2 Instructional Activity Suggestions for Aquatic Therapy

Phase 1—Adjusting to Water
  Entering and Exiting Water
  1. Sit in bleachers or near pool side and watch others play in the water
  2. Coax student to the edge of the pool—use primary and secondary reinforcers
  3. Introduce a bucket and sponges to the student and let him play with them—gradually introduce water by filling the bucket
  4. Play with student while both student and instructor sit with feet dangling in the pool
  5. Have students sponge the edge of the pool, steps, and ladder
  6. Fill buckets with water by squeezing out the sponges
  7. Students attempt to catch and hold on to a rope with a towel attached to the end. The instructor controls the rope.
  8. Over and under towel relay
  9. Simon Says

  Sitting and Locomotor Movements
  1. Splash water in open topped floating objects to sink them
  2. Throw objects into floating inner tubes
  3. Pull floating toys across water
  4. Standing in water, submerge small inner tubes
  5. Walk across the pool holding on to inner tubes
  6. With instructor and student inside a Hoola-Hoop walk across pool
  7. March in shallow water to music
  8. Carry the flag—students carry cloth or flag to other side of pool without letting it touch the water
  9. Knee press relay—student holds ball between the knees and carries it across the pool, hopping, walking, or running
  10. Use inner tubes as walkers for students unable to walk independently
  11. Follow the leader—standing in the water, have participants imitate actions such as splashing, kicking, floating, and bobbing. Students must do as the instructor does.
  12. Ring toss—floating an inner tube, have the student bob, duck down, and come up inside. Also have the student try to throw the inner tube around the neck of the kneeling instructor.

  Facial Accommodations
  1. Students wash face and various named body parts with a washcloth or sponge
  2. Throw and catch large sponges
  3. Play keep away with washclothes or sponges
  4. Blow bubbles with plastic tubing
  5. Students select different colored and shaped sponges from the water
  6. Students stand or walk on sponges
  7. Blow toys, Ping-Pong balls, and balloons across the water

Table 13-2 continued

8. Jumping up for rags or flags suspended by clothes pins on a line stretched across the pool
9. Retrieve toys from the bottom of the pool
10. Parachute games using a plastic sheet or round table cloth
11. Tug-of-war between two students or teacher and students using a towel

Phase 2—Body Buoyancy
   1. Place the student on a piece of heavy plastic or canvas. Using several adults, float the child as if he were on a magic carpet
   2. Hold student's hands and pull him through the water in a horizontal position
   3. Pull student through the water using a towel or kickboard
   4. Using a Hoola-Hoop, student assumes a prone position in order to pass through it
   5. Students hold onto the edge of the pool or gutter and let feet rise to a horizontal position (this is called bracketing)
   6. Use arm cuff, floating block, etc., to practice floating

Phase 3—Propulsion and Coordinated Stroking
   Leg Action
   1. Land drills:
      a. Lying on back, assimilate the leg action of riding a bicycle
      b. Student lies on his back with lower legs resting on air mattress or air pillow. Teacher assists student in kicking action against the cushion.
      c. Using a bench the student lies prone with legs extending over the edge. Practice in flutter kicking may be assisted by instructor.
   2. Holding on to the pool's edge or gutter, students assume a horizontal position and are assisted in kicking action
   3. Practice flutter kicking while holding on to kickboards or while suspended by floatation device
   4. Student sits in inner tube, propels himself across pool using flutter kicks
   5. Students take a position for the flutter kick (holding gutter, sitting at pool side, sitting on steps, etc.). Call out 1, 2, 3, 4—anyone kicking after you call 4 is out.
   6. Shooting baskets with nerf, beach ball, or light playground ball.

   Arm Action
   1. Land drills:
      a. Students imitate teacher's actions of climbing a ladder as teacher says "reach up, pull down, reach up, pull down," set, crawl, stroke to rhythm
      b. While lying on their back or stomach, students perform angels-in-the-snow arm action to assimilate sculling. Initially the teacher assists the participant by moving the arms through the pattern.
      c. Arm action can be practiced lying on a bench.
      Note: Individuals with cerebral palsy should practice arm strokes in the water due to the relaxing effect of the warm water on the muscles. If a limb is paralyzed, a small float can be attached to offer support.

Table 13-2 continued

2. A wide belt or sling is placed under the swimmer's stomach and held by two instructors, one on each side. Initially, nearly all of the swimmer's weight is supported by the belt as he makes a crawling action with the arms.
3. The floating block, barbells, and arm cuffs can be used as support while the swimmer practices the paddle or crawl stroke
4. Walk across pool making arm strokes

Combined Movements
1. Using floatation equipment, the student pushes off the side or a step with the legs and assumes the glide position. The push off may be practiced using this land drill: student lies on his back with hands above head in glide position and the knees bent toward chest. At the command of push, the instructor assists the student in extending the legs in an explosive manner. For safety, an air mattress should be placed under the feet, as many students will bang their heels after each push.
2. Hoola-Hoop crawl—have students swim through hoops held on edge
3. Relay races using the floating block for support
4. Novelty crawl—swimmers hold a pie plate (aluminum) in each hand and swim across pool
5. Clothing relay—each team of swimmers must put on a clothing article (hat, shirt, etc.) before walking or swimming across the finish line

Phase 4—Deep Water Training
    At this level, target jumping, diving for objects, relays, and water basketball are only a few of the many activities available. For an elaborate list of suggestions consult the works of Reynolds, 1973; Seamons, 1966; Neishloss, 1973; Fender, 1973; and Lawrence and Hackett, 1973. In addition, the United Cerebral Palsy Association, YMCA, YWCA, and the American and Canadian Red Cross are excellent resources.

The Total Program

It is important for the severely retarded to feel secure and comfortable in the water and to enjoy the freedom of movement that it can bring.

The aquatic program should be an integral part of the special student's entire educational plan. It provides an environment not only conducive to play, but to the teaching of skills related to self-help, perceptual development, motor, social behavior, and leisure time. As a member of the multidisciplinary team, the aquatic therapist, adapted physical education specialist, therapeutic recreator, or special teacher can evaluate, reinforce, and reemphasize the developmental skills taught in all curricular areas. This concept holds true for even the curricular area of speech development, as holding one's breath under water, blowing bubbles through a plastic straw, blowing Ping-Pong balls, and exhaling under water are all important prespeech activities.

SUMMARY

The swimming or therapy pool provides a unique environment for educational training for the severely retarded. Individuals responsible for administering and/or instructing aquatic programs must not only determine what instructional approach(es) will be used, but the administrative and program components as well. Pool construction, safety practices, barriers, health and first aid considerations must all be examined before aquatic programs begin. Instructional staff should possess knowledge of handling procedures, first aid skills, an understanding of program goals, and know how to determine individual student objectives. Coupling this information with the fundamentals of instructional procedures and their phases, appropriate learning activities can be carried out which offer an enjoyable and challenging atmosphere.

REFERENCES

American Red Cross. *Swimming for the handicapped–instructor's manual* (rev. ed.). Washington D.C.: American Red Cross, 1975.

———— *Lifesaving: Rescue and water safety.* Garden City, New York: Doubleday, 1977.

Aquatic therapy for the severely and profoundly retarded child. Berks County, Pennsylvania: Unpublished manuscript, 1976.

Fait, H. *Special physical education: Adapted, corrective, developmental.* Philadelphia: W.B. Saunders, 1978.

Fender L. *Aquatic/swimming orientation manual.* Bethany, Oklahoma: Children's Convalescent Hospital, January 1973.

Karpovich, P.V., & Sinning, W.E. *Physiology of muscular activity.* Philadelphia: W.B. Saunders, 1971.

Lawrence, C.C., & Hackett, L.C. *Waterlearning: A new adventure.* Palo Alto, California: Peek, 1973.

Neishloss, L. *Swimming for the handicapped child and adult.* Chicago: National Easter Seal Society for Crippled Children and Adults, October 1973.

Reynolds, G.D. (Ed.). *A swimming program for the handicapped.* New York: Association Press, 1973.

Seamons, G. *Swimming for the blind.* Provo: Brigham Young University, 1966.

Sherrill, C. *Adapted physical education and recreation: A multidisciplinary approach.* Dubuque, Iowa: Wm. C. Brown, 1976.

United Cerebral Palsy Associations, Inc. *Swimming for the cerebral palsied.* New York: United Cerebral Palsy Associations, Inc.

S-G

Grand Mal Epilepsy: Diagnosis and Management (30 min.)
National Epilepsy League
6 North Michigan
Chicago, IL 60602

Presents an overview of epilepsy with actual seizures.

S/P-G

Moments of Joy (24 min.)

Wombat Productions
77 Tarrytown Rd.
White Plains, NY 10607

The complete modification of Ohio's state mental institutions are shown. Living conditions, program alterations and training techniques are revealed.

P-G

Teaching the Mentally Retarded—A Positive Approach (25 min.)

Du Art Film Laboratory
245 W. 55th St.
New York, NY 10019

A four-month training program involving four profoundly retarded children shows that even the lowest functioning retardates can learn the basic skills of toilet training, dressing, eating, and manners.

S-L

Janet Is a Little Girl (28 min.)

University of California
Extension Media Center
Berkeley, California 94720

Down's syndrome severely retarded children are shown in language skills programs at Sonoma State Hospital. Teaching techniques are demonstrated in the classroom with ten nonverbal five-year-olds.

S-L

Where to Begin with Nonverbal Children (17 min.)

National Audiovisual Center
General Services Admin.
Attn. Order Section
Washington, D.C. 20409

Explains a process for assessing language levels in nonverbal children.

S-MS

Watch Us Move (21 min.)

University of California
Extension Media Center
2223 Fulton St.
Berkeley, CA 94720

This film describes the need and potential benefits of "sensory integration" as a curricular component in a preschool age program for the retarded.

P-MS

Development of Perceptual Motor Skills in a Profoundly Retarded Child (6 min.)

University of Kansas
Audiovisual Center
Film Rental Service
746 Massachusetts St.
Lawrence, Kansas 66044

A child diagnosed as profoundly retarded is placed on a program designed to improve the perceptual motor skills involved with using the hands. Operant conditioning and systematic training with medical supervision are shown through a series of training lessons.

S-MS

I Can (Four 12 min. films)

Hubbard Co.
Box 104
Northbrook, Illinois 60062

Fundamental locomotor skills and object control are taught through the "I Can" program. The films focus on planning and organization, systematic evaluation and instruction, and re-evaluation and recordkeeping within the motor skills area.

S/P-MS

Patterns (17 min.)

Title III Physical Education Research Grant
Austin State School
P.O. Box 1269
Austin, TX 78767

The central theme of this film is the need for physical education programs for the severely and profoundly retarded. Teaching activities and the need for them are presented by physical education staff members.

S/P-MS

P.E. Lever to Learning (20 min.)
Stuart Finley Inc.
3428 Mansfield Rd.
Falls Church, Virginia 22041

This rather dated film continues to have merit in that it demonstrates the implementation of inexpensive equipment such as logs, used tires, boards, and ladders in a physical education program.

S-MS

Somebody's Waiting (24 min.)

University of California
Extension Media Center
2223 Fulton St.
Berkeley, CA 94720

The film demonstrates the effects of appropriate handling upon severely mentally retarded, physically handicapped, and emotionally disturbed. The focus is upon environmental stimulation and appropriate therapeutic techniques.

S/P-T

Genetic Defects: The Broken Code (87 min.)

Indiana University
Audio Visual Center
Bloomington, IN 47401

The recessive, dominant, and sex-linked gene patterns of inheritance are discussed. Interviews with affected individuals and a discussion of moral, legal, and ethical implications are included.

S/P-T

Piaget's Developmental Theory: The Growth of Intelligence in the Preschool Years (30 min.)

Sterling Educational Films
241 E. 34th Street
New York, NY 10016

The thinking behaviors of children 3-6 years of age are demonstrated as they perform a variety of tasks. This film offers a summary of Piaget's theory with young children.

S/P-T

Task Analysis: An Introduction to a Technology of Instruction (18 min.)

Film Productions of Indianapolis
128 E. 36th Street
Indianapolis, IN 46205

Mark Gold, originator of the Try Another Way Approach, demonstrates the methodology of breaking tasks into small teachable units.

S/P-T

Content and Process: Two Components of Task Analysis (12 min.)

Film Productions of Indianapolis
128 E. 36th Street
Indianapolis, IN 46205

Two individuals are taught to assemble electronic circuit boards using different steps to accomplish the same outcome.

S/P-T

Formats for Single Pieces of Learning: Subcategories of Process Task Analysis (13 min.)

Film Productions of Indianapolis
128 E. 36th Street
Indianapolis, IN 46205

The process component of Dr. Gold's task analysis system is presented. Instructional formats such as match to sample, paired associate learning, oddity, recognition, and successive and simultaneous presentation are covered.

S/P-WS

Like Everybody Else (32 min.)

Stanfield House
900 Euclid Street
Santa Monica, CA 90403

A description of the sheltered workshop is provided, in addition to an in-depth look at the retarded adults' living style and interaction within the community.

S/P-WS

Try Another Way (27 min.)

Film Productions of Indianapolis
128 E. 36th Street
Indianapolis, IN 46205

This film introduces the training techniques used by Mark Gold to teach complex assembly tasks to the mentally retarded. All training takes place at the Children's Research Center, University of Illinois.

One source that may prove extremely helpful in selecting the latest in educational training films is the *National Catalog of Films in Special Education*. This publication may be acquired by contacting:

Ohio State University Press
Publication Sales Division
2070 Neil Avenue
Columbus, Ohio 43210

COMMERCIAL AND NONCOMMERCIAL EQUIPMENT

There is an abundance of commercial special education products on the market purporting to possess educational and/or therapeutic value. In an attempt to reduce the confusion involved with selecting appropriate equipment and manufacturers, a list is provided below. This roster is an attempt to identify the many commonly used pieces of equipment found in educational training centers for the severely retarded. It has been divided into five instructional areas with the name and address of at least one distributor or manufacturer where the product can be purchased.

Adapted Physical Education/Recreation/Fundamental Motor Skills —Equipment and Materials

Equipment:	Distributor:
Prone Board Balance Barrel Balance Board Stimulation Board	Motor Development Equipment Co. P.O. Box 4054 Downey, CA 90241
Leg Abduction Chair Corner Chair Parallel Bars	J.A. Preston Co. 71 Fifth Ave. New York, NY 10003

Special Chairs
Guidance Chairs
   (Battery Powered)
	Mulholland Growth
	   Guidance Equipment
	Los Angeles, CA 93003

	Ortho-Kinetics, Inc. 1225 Pearl St. Waukesha, Wisconsin 53186
Exercise Bike Game Equipment (Basketball, Baseball, Floor Hockey, etc.) Floor Seat Balance Beam Shatterproof Mirrors Weights Folding Mats Plastic Hoops Foot Placement Ladder	Flaghouse Inc. 18 W. 18th St. New York, NY 10011

A styrofoam block with a belt positioned through its center can offer floatation support for beginning swimmers. The belt is attached about the student's waist allowing him to float on the stomach or back.

Barbells/Floatation

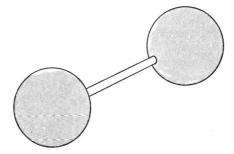

Source: Rudolph.

Styrofoam barbells can be constructed to offer support in the water. They may be positioned under the armpits, supplying support in a front float position. Barbells can also be used for kicking practice by holding them in the hands with the arms extended.

PRINTED MATERIALS

This section presents a sampling of textbooks and printed materials that may be of interest to the student or professional working with the severely retarded. These are sources with excellent resource value. The descriptions after some of these entries are supplied by the publisher(s).

As was the case with films, a coding system is used to assist the reader in selecting books in areas of interest.

BM—behavior modification
G—general
L—language
MS—motor skills
OT—occupational therapy
PT—physical therapy
R—recreation
S—social skills
T—theory

BM

Holland, J.G., & Skinner, B.F. *The analysis of behavior: A program for self-instruction.* New York: McGraw-Hill, 1961.

Contents—Reflex Behavior. Operant Conditioning: Elementary Concepts. Operant Conditioning: Precise Contingencies. Shaping. Intermittent Reinforcement. Stimulus Control. Deprivation. Emotion I. Avoidance and Escape Behavior. Emotion II. Punishment. Scientific Analysis and the Interpretation of Complex Cases. Self-control.

G

Baldwin, V.L., Fredericks, H.D., & Brodsky, G. *Isn't it time he outgrew this? or A training program for parents of retarded children.* Springfield: Charles C. Thomas, 1976.

Basic principles of behavior modification including cues, behaviors, and reinforcements are explained in layman's terms and are applied to all areas of concern for parents of retarded children. Parents are taught how to use learning principles in the areas of self-help skills and language. Behavior modification techniques are described for the handling of behavior problems. Each area is described in sufficient detail to allow the parents to set up home training programs.

Haring, N., & Brown, L. (Ed.). *Teaching the severely handicapped* (2 Vol.). New York: Grune & Stratton, 1976.

These volumes are the first of a yearly series presented by the American Association for the Education of the Severely/Profoundly Handicapped. The purpose is to provide instructional materials—guidelines, procedures, curricula—for direct classroom use.

Gibson, D., and Brown, R.I. (Eds.). *Managing the severely retarded: A sampler.* Springfield: Charles C. Thomas, 1976.

This volume brings together a representative sample of recent information and arranges it in sequence from rudimentary self-help skill training to contact skill development. Early chapters are concerned with feeding, dressing, toileting behaviors, abuse abatement and sensorimotor upgrading. Contact skill training is organized around encouraging communication skills, enhancing play skills, developing social and affective capacity, and reducing stereotypy. New gains in overall group management are explored and emphasis is placed on the need to monitor and evaluate outcomes.

DeVore, S.M. *Individualized learning program for the profoundly retarded.* Springfield: Charles C. Thomas, 1977.

This book, written to aid both professional instructors and parents of profoundly and severely retarded children, combines a series of lesson plans with an easy method of collecting data and recording the progress attained by the child. Special education students, paraprofessionals, and volunteers in care centers for the retarded will also benefit from these new and useful techniques. Comprising the major portion of the text, the lesson plans are divided into six sections that individually cover programs for teaching self-care, socialization, communication, cognitive function, gross motor skills, and fine motor skills. The accompanying progress reports each contain a list, in developmental order, of the various goals to be attained. Special procedures needed to accomplish a given goal are included along with advice to the instructor or parent on observing, measuring, and recording pertinent information.

Blatt, B., Biklen, D., & Bogdan, R. (Eds.). *An alternative textbook in special education; people, schools, and other institutions.* Denver: Love, 1977.

This book suggests that special education may be connected more with ideological than pedagogical issues, and that instruction for the handicapped has been individualized but expectations have not. The volume covers the problems associated with traditional concepts and also the promises of alternative concepts and settings, offering challenging questions and suggestions. It includes discussion of research orientations, approaches to mental retardation, normalization, legal views, advocacy, and psychological aspects of special education.

Dempsey, T. (Ed.). *Community services for retarded children.* Baltimore: University Park Press, 1975.

This is a primary sourcebook for professionals serving families with retarded children, for policy makers who design service systems, and for students and teachers in mental retardation. It is the first major work on this subject that evaluates community services for retarded children in terms of a consumer-provider relationship—a refreshingly pragmatic new approach to this complex but critically important problem.

Community Services for Retarded Children is an unquestionably significant, original contribution to the goal of improved services for the mentally retarded that offers much-needed insight for everyone working in this field.

Begab, M., & Richardson, S. *The mentally retarded and society.* Baltimore: University Park Press, 1975.

The information, scientific studies and reviews, evaluations, surveys, and perspectives presented in this work form one of the most important and far-ranging volumes available on the contemporary sociological aspects of mental retardation.

The Mentally Retarded and Society provides an expertly organized synthesis and review of an unusually wide range of key topics in mental retardation, including the controversial and often divergent views of authorities in the field. It also identifies limitations or gaps in current theory and research to serve as definitive guidelines for all scientists, practitioners, policy makers, and other professionals working toward practical, attainable goals for the mentally retarded and their families.

Anderson, R., & Greer, J. *Educating the severely and profoundly retarded.* Baltimore: University Park Press, 1976.

This volume compiles from the current literature fifty of the most innovative and successful studies on educating severely and profoundly retarded children and meets the changing needs of professional and nonprofessional people who work with these children in school settings. It presents a thorough, well-organized, and challenging review of a subject that is of growing concern as a result of "right to education" decisions in the courts. It contains ten major sections, each presenting several selected articles.

Adams, J.L. *An education curriculum for the moderately, severely, and profoundly mentally handicapped pupil.* Springfield: Charles C. Thomas, 1975

The purpose of this book is to set in a sequential format the curriculum content necessary to provide groups of trainable and subtrainable children in an educational program with appropriate learning experiences in the areas of self-help skills, cognitive skills, physical-motoric skills, communication skills, and socialization skills. The philosophy of normalization and the principles of behavior modification are recommended to meet the individualized needs, both present and future, more efficiently.

Donlon, E., & Burton, L. *The severely and profoundly handicapped.* New York: Grune & Stratton, 1976.

The first part of the book is devoted to a procedure for providing descriptions of those behaviors that are of most concern, and to outlining some of the behaviors that occur in many severely and profoundly handicapped children. Also presented is a system for structured observation which has been effective in describing the child's development and in providing a basis for prescriptive programming.

The second section provides a sampling of techniques which have been useful in the authors' work with these children. Acceptance or rejection of specific ideas and development of new ones depend greatly on the reader's creativity and ability to apply them practically and appropriately to the individual child's needs at that time. The last section of the book deals with total life planning and other considerations.

Snell, M. (Ed.). *Systematic instruction of the moderately and severely handicapped*. Columbus, Ohio: Charles E. Merrill, 1978.

Kelley, M.J. (Ed.). *Yes they can! A primer for educating the severely and profoundly retarded*. Watertown, Wisconsin: Bethesda Lutheran Home, 1978.

The skills of following simple commands, eating, preworkshop tasks, dressing, closures, grooming and play are described in a task analysis format. The introductory sections of the text identify the how, why, and when to teach the practical and functional skills required for daily living.

Johnson, V.M., & Werner, R.A. *A step by step learning guide for older retarded children*. Syracuse, New York: Syracuse University Press, 1977.

A description of a skill-centered approach to learning is presented for severely retarded teenagers. Specific skills are broken down into small components for a wide range of areas including: self-care, fine motor, gross motor, language, and perception.

Behavioral Characteristics Progression. Austin, Texas: Texas Department of Mental Health and Mental Retardation, 1977.

This observation manual offers a sequential listing of general living and academic skills. Many of the statements are appropriate to the lower functioning retardate.

L

Kent, L. *Language acquisition program for the retarded or multiply impaired*. Champaign, Illinois: Research Press, 1974.

Language Acquisition Program is designed to teach a language system which may be predominantly oral, manual, or some combination of both. The Preverbal Section covers the acquisition of prerequisite attending behaviors and motor imitation. The Verbal Sections outline the procedures for the acquisition of selected receptive and expressive language skills, which are sequenced according to difficulty.

A manual signing system is included for use with students who are unable to produce or perfect understandable words.

Extremely practical, this program is designed for use with no further preparation or source material.

Christopher, D. *Manual communication*. Baltimore: University Park Press, 1976.

Manual Communication contains forty-eight lessons that clearly illustrate, with step-by-step written instructions, more than 800 signs and letters. These are presented in a sophisticated professional format intended for specialists and career-minded students, and include encoding and decoding practice exercises with each lesson.

The book first introduces the American Manual Alphabet and basic number concepts, then develops the basic vocabulary of traditional (American Sign Language) signs that are the building blocks needed to communicate in sign language. The lessons form self-contained teaching units covering twenty signs each (suitable for normal class sessions) covering both function and content words so students quickly learn to formulate and communicate in sentences. Signs for morphemic elements are also presented early in the text to encourage students to master the skill of communicating in the Simultaneous Method.

The final four lessons of the book apply manual communication to hearing, speech, and language evaluation in clinical practice. These cover children's case histories, hearing aid evaluation, and related topics.

Vanderheiden, G. and Grilley, K. *Nonvocal communication techniques and aids for the severely physically handicapped.* Baltimore: University Park Press, 1976.

Based upon edited transcriptions of the National Workshop Series conducted by the Trace Center, University of Wisconsin-Madison, this volume reviews and describes currently available nonvocal communication aids and techniques. Designed for clinicians and teachers, it forms a much-needed introductory text and sourcebook summarizing information on nonvocal communication aids and techniques that have been developed and applied around the world.

The first section of the book reviews the problem of communication in the severely handicapped, discusses the development of alternate communication systems, and introduces nonvocal communication techniques and aids including scanning, encoding, and direct selection. The second section deals with the tools with detailed training sections on each technique. Section three reviews results as seen in four actual programs while the fourth and final section covers what is needed now in terms of the present state of the art and future requirements for progress in nonvocal communication.

Rieke, J, Lynch, L; & Soltman, S. *Teaching strategies for language development.* New York: Grune & Stratton, 1977.

The primary aim of this book is to foster the use of team approaches to communication, and to build into communication and language programs the developmental basis for approaching children's problems. It is written to enable teachers and language disorders specialists to individualize language programs that can be used in classroom settings with generalization to the home and other environments.

Body Control

Log Roll	Dynamic Balances
Shoulder Roll	Inverted Balances
Forward Roll	Bounce on Trampoline
Backward Roll	Drops on Trampoline
Static 2-point Balances	Airborne on Trampoline
Static 1-point Balances	

3. Health/Fitness

Basic physical fitness is the focus of this instructional area. Activities are designed to improve muscular strength, stamina, endurance, and posture. Following is a listing of activity areas:

Fitness and Growth

Abdominal Strength and Endurance	Trunk and Leg Flexibility
Arm/Shoulder/Chest Strength and Endurance	Relaxation
	Weight Maintenance
Stamina and Heart/Lung Strength and Endurance	Charts
	Weight Training

Posture

Standing	Pulling
Sitting	Pushing
Walking	Holding, Carrying
Ascending, Descending Stairs	Lifting Objects
	Lowering Objects

4. Aquatics

The development of fundamental water skills is covered in this instructional component. Instructional activities are available at all ability levels within the following areas:

Basic Skills

Adjustment to Water	Front Flutter Kick
Breath Control	Back Flutter Kick
Front Buoyancy	Wedge Kick
Back Buoyancy	

Swimming and Entry Skills

Front Crawl	Tread Water
Back Crawl	Survival Float
Finning	Jump into Water
Elementary Backstroke	Front Dive

The "I Can" program is a comprehensive instructional approach to adapted physical education complete with teacher guides, performance record sheets, and training films. It may be purchased through Hubbard Co., P.O. Box 104, Northbrook, Illinois 60062, in individual components or in a complete program for approximately $400.00.

PROJECT A.C.T.I.V.E.

The project A.C.T.I.V.E. program (All Children Totally Involved Exercising) began as a funded grant through the New Jersey State Department of Education under provisions of the Elementary and Secondary Education Act of 1965, Title III. Under the direction of Dr. Thomas M. Vodola, project A.C.T.I.V.E. has given the handicapped an opportunity to participate in a comprehensive physical education program.

The A.C.T.I.V.E. program was validated by the standards and guidelines of the United States Office of Education in 1974. This approval is offered only to those programs that prove successful, cost-effective, and exportable. As a result, the program has received continued funding for the dual purposes of training of interested educators and for the reproduction of materials for national consumption and replication.

The project staff identify the following features of their program:

- a comprehensive, individualized-personalized program designed to cope with children who evidence Low Motor Ability, Low Physical Vitality, Postural Abnormalities, Nutritional Deficiencies, Learning Disabilities, Breathing Problems, Motor Disabilities or Limitations, and Communication Disorders
- diagnostic-prescriptive teacher practicum experiences working with the handicapped
- student learning experiences to "totally" involve the handicapped child in the learning process
- criterion-referenced norms for determining teacher achievement of specific competencies
- formative and summative strategies for assessing individual student achievement
- compliance with P.L. 94-142/T & E Legislation

The following materials were developed by the project staff and are also available for a nominal fee:

Teacher Training Manual
Low Motor Ability Manual

Low Physical Vitality Manual
Nutritional Deficiencies Manual
Postural Abnormalities Manual
Motor Disabilities or Limitations Manual
Communication Disorders Manual
Breathing Problems Manual
Motor Ability Duplicating Masters
Forms: Test, Administrative Requests Duplicating Masters
Motor Ability Resource Tasks and Activities
Physical Fitness Resource Tasks and Activities
Motor Ability Filmstrip
Teacher Training Filmstrip
To Help Your Child
ACTIVE's Inservice Program
Technical Brief
Film: A Child Involved
Film: The Hidden Handicap
ACTIVE Administrative Guidelines Manual
Teacher Resource Manual
Research Monograph
Norms Manual (Norms are not available for the Severe and Profound)
Prescriptive Reinforcement Duplication Masters

The A.C.T.I.V.E. program incorporates the diagnostic-prescriptive instructional approach; therefore, assessment instruments have been developed to identify strengths and weaknesses. Several instruments are available that measure levels of motor achievement for: (1) severely or profoundly retarded, (2) trainable mentally retarded, and (3) educable mentally retarded or normal.

Motor fitness instruments are also available. Level I is used with low fitness students (severe, profound, and low trainable), and Level II accommodates students possessing a higher degree of fitness.

Although the project staff is available to train educators to implement the A.C.T.I.V.E. program, an interested party can gain valuable information through reading the training manuals. Further information may be obtained from:

> Dr. Thomas M. Vodola, Project Director
> Director, Research and Evaluation
> Township of Ocean School District
> Dow Avenue
> Oakhurst, New Jersey 07755
> (201) 531-6600 Extension 365

Index

A

Academic instruction, 254
Action words, 236
Activity center programs, 249-251
  academics, 254
  communication skills, 255
  community skills, 254
  household skills, 253
  occupational training, 261-266
  prevocational training, 255-259
  priority skill areas, 255
  public school setting, 260-261
  recreation, 254-255
  social skills, 252-253
  self-help skills, 251-252
  work, 251
Adapted physical education
  assessment, 296
  commercial instructional programs,
    389-393
  defined, 293
  equipment and material sources,
    372-374
  film resources, 368-369
  function, 293-294, 321-323
  need for, 294
  perceptual motor skills, 305-309
  program organization, 309-311
  sensorimotor skills, 296, 301-305
  Special Olympics, 321-323

  staff, 294-295
  teaching methods, 310, 312-313
  See also Play; Therapeutic recreation;
    Total body activity
Adapted physical educators, 314
Adaptive behavior
  assessment, 25-27
  criterion-referenced testing, 37-41
  defined, 23-25
  mental retardation and, 10, 11
  norm-referenced testing, 27-37
  task analytical approach, 37-39
Adaptive Behavior Scale, 29, 32-36
Adaptive Behavior Scale Public School
  Version, 29, 36
Aggression, 186
Alpern-Boll Developmental Profile, 29
American Association on Mental
  Deficiency (AAMD)
  adaptive behavior scales, 29, 32-36
  mental retardation definition, 10, 11
Anxiety, 185-186
Appearance, 175-176
Aquatic therapy, 334, 358
  activities, 355-358
  adjusting to water, 351
  artificial respiration, 340-342
  buoyancy, 354-355
  checklist, 351-354
  content format, 350-355
  deep water training, 355

equipment sources, 378-379
facilities, 336-337
film resources, 362
first aid, 338-348
health considerations, 337-338
objectives, 335
pool entry procedures, 349-350
propulsion, 355
safety practices, 338
teaching methods, 334-335
Artificial respiration, 340-342
Arts and crafts, 211, 366
Asphyxiation, 340
Assessment
criterion-referenced testing, 37-41
defined, 25
entry skill level, 46
film resources, 362, 368
gross motor skills, 90-91
language skills, 24, 32, 106-108, 115
methods, 26-27
mobility training, 220, 221, 224, 225
norm-referenced testing, 27-37
physical education, 296
play areas, 194-197
play performance, 200-209
postural reflexes, 87-89
progress, 54, 76-78
recreation performance, 315
righting and equilibrium reactions,
   82-84
social skills, 163
task analytical approach, 37-41, 54
toileting patterns, 137
Ataxia, 90
Athetosis, 82, 90, 94-95
Attempted grasp, 99-100
Attention
focusing, 72-76
reinforcement with, 63
seeking, 247, 252
Auditory discrimination, 308
Auditory expression, 109
Auditory reception, 108-109
Automatic recording, 49-50
Aversion methods

application of, 71
chemical intervention, 70
counterconditioning, 67
desensitization, 67
electric shock, 70
ignoring, 66-67
Level I, 66-67, 71
Level II, 67-69, 71
Level III, 69-71
overcorrection, 68-69
positive practice, 69
punishers, 69-70
reinforcer removal, 68
restraint, 70-71
satiation, 67
time out, 68, 70
Awareness, 303-304

B

Backward chaining, 59-60, 152, 226
Bagging buttons, 273, 274
Balance, 81-86, 308
Ball playing, 101, 102
Balthazar Scales of Adaptive Behavior,
   29
Basic Movement Performance Profile,
   296-300
Bathing, 168-169
Bead stringing, 101, 210
Bed wetting, 141
Behavioral objectives, 50-51
Behavior modification, 61-62
appropriate behavior reinforcement,
   61-65
film resources, 362-363
inappropriate behavior, 65-71
principles of, 62
printed resources, 380
Behavior recording, 26
Behaviors, 62
Belt buckling, 160
Birth control, 181
Biting reflex, 146
Bladder control, 136
Bleeding, 342-344

Resources for Individuals Working with the Severely Retarded

This appendix contains three major areas: (1) film resources, (2) commercial and noncommercial equipment, and (3) printed materials. The information should serve as an instructional resource in the preparation of teachers and paraprofessionals. Additionally, it can be used by program administrators and supervisors to evaluate equipment needs, analyze program components, and meet additional professional training needs.

ANNOTATED FILM RESOURCES

A number of films have been produced that focus on the mentally retarded. The majority of those included in the list to follow were produced in the 1970s and tend to reflect a more contemporary attitude.

In order to assist the reader in the selection of appropriate films, each production is coded according to its general level of application. Subject matter relative to the severely mentally retarded is prefaced by the code letter "S." Material dealing with the profoundly mentally retarded is prefaced by the letter "P."

Following the general application code letters are additional letters which identify the specific area(s) of emphasis for each film. The film key is as follows:

General Application Code Letters
S—severely mentally retarded
P—profoundly mentally retarded

Areas of Emphasis
A—aquatics
AS—assessment
BM—behavior modification

G—general viewing
L—language
MS—motor skills
ST—sensory training
T—theory
WS—work skills

The films are listed by areas of emphasis and in sequence beginning with A (aquatics) and ending with WS (work skills).

S/P-A

Splash (20 min.)
Documentary Films
3217 Trout Gulch Rd.
Aptos, California 95003

Aquatics are introduced to youngsters with multiple handicaps. Fundamental motor skills, dressing and self-help skills are discussed as they relate to the swimming environment.

S-AS

Operant Audiometry with Severely Retarded Children (15 min.)
University of Kansas
Audio Visual Center
Film Rental Service
746 Massachusetts St.
Lawrence, Kansas 66044

Positive reinforcement techniques are used in testing the hearing acuity of a severely handicapped 13-year-old. The training sessions illustrate how a person is conditioned to wear the headset and how he is taught to respond to the auditory cues.

S-BM

A Token System for Behavior Modification (8 min.)
University of Kansas
Audiovisual Center
Film Rental Service
746 Massachusetts St.
Lawrence, Kansas 66044

This film demonstrates how behavior modification and the use of a token economy can be applied to training the severely and moderately retarded. The primary focus is on self-help occupational skills needed for community living.

S-BM

Reinforcement Therapy (45 min.)
Consolidated Film Industries
959 Seward St.
Hollywood, California 90028

The treatment of autistic, retarded children and chronic schizophrenic adults using behavior modification techniques is illustrated in this film. Although this is a 1966 production, the principles and techniques are excellent.

S-BM

Token Economy: Behaviorism Applied (21 min.)
Martin and Cricks, LTD
c/o Weston Woods Studios
Weston, CT 06880

The use of tokens in a reinforcement therapy program is demonstrated with retarded and delinquent adolescents. Scheduling, extinction, punishment, and types of reinforcers are discussed by Dr. B.F. Skinner.

S/P-G

All My Buttons (28 min.)
H & H Enterprises, Inc.
Box 3342
Lawrence, Kansas 66044

The contemporary problems and issues of introducing developmentally disabled into the mainstream (normalization) are presented. The film creates a springboard for discussion and offers several solutions to these problems.

S-G

And Crown Thy Good (35 minutes)
Orchard School
8600 Grosse Point Rd.
Skokie, Illinois 60076

The accomplishments of one community in their efforts to provide for the severely retarded are provided in this film.

S-G

Cast No Shadow (27 min.)
Professional Arts, Inc.
P.O. Box 8484
Universal City, CA 91608

A comprehensive program of recreational activities for physically handicapped, severely mentally retarded, multi-handicapped and emotionally disturbed individuals of all ages are shown. This program takes place at the Recreation Center for the Handicapped, Inc., San Francisco, California.

S-G

Control of the Naturalistic Social Behavior of Severely Retarded Boys (18 min.)
Penn State University
Psych Cinema Register
AV Services
6 Willard Bldg.
University Park, Pennsylvania 16802

Institutional behaviors such as establishing territoriality, dominance hierarchy, and cooperation within a group are illustrated. Controlling techniques and varying amounts of supervision are exposed.

S/P-G

Graduation (17 min.)
Stanfield House
900 Euclid St.
Santa Monica, CA 90403

This film illustrates what happens to a retarded adolescent when he does not attend an activity center or sheltered workshop upon leaving the public school.

P-G

Growth and Development of a Multiply Handicapped Infant (10 min.)
New York University Film Library
26 Washington Place
New York, NY 10003

The first three and a half years of life of a profoundly retarded blind child are followed. Clinical examination and the child's general home life at twenty-two months is shown in addition to the family's decision for institutional placement.

S-G

The Music Child (45 min.)
Benchmark Films
145 Scarborough Rd.
Briarcliff Manor, N.Y. 10510

The use of improvised music as an intervention strategy for developing communication skills in children with various handicapping conditions.

S-G

Moving True (19 min.)
Music Therapy Center
251 W. 51st Street
New York, New York 10019

A dance session is presented which provides instruction in music therapy.

S-G

Reach Inside: Learning Through Music (30 min.)
Bradley Wright Films
Number 1 Oak Hill Drive
San Anselmo, CA 94960

Activities that draw out natural musical tendencies are presented. Creative exploration and individual responses to music are examined.

S-G

Problems in Transporting the Handicapped (27 min.)
VISUCOM
P.O. Box 3536
Stanford, CA 94305

Presents problems bus drivers face daily in transporting special education students. Problem-solving strategies are offered for seizures, disruptive behavior, injuries, etc.

S-G

As We Are (29 min.)
Phoenix Films
470 Park Ave. South
New York, NY 10016

Art activities for the retarded are presented using the Tempus Art Center as a model.

S-G

Free (18 min.)
Hawaii Association for Retarded Children
245 North Kukui St.
Honolulu, HI 96815

Arts and crafts activities, music and rhythm games, puppetry, play, perceptual-motor and fitness activities are presented.

S-G

Individualized Education Programs (25 min.)
Instructional Media
128 East Pittsburg St.
Greensburg, PA 15601

The I.E.P. process is discussed along with the interaction and involvement between parent and teacher.

Equipment:	Distributor:
Trampoline Adjustable Chin-up Bar Floor Ladder High Stepper Gym Scooter	Jayfro P.O. Box 400 Waterford, Conn. 06385
Play Scapes Net Climbers Swings Hollow Building Blocks Sand Tables Crawl Tunnel Wood Rocker "Rolling Head" Cue Sticks Billiard tables Table tennis tops Hand grip bowling balls Bowling ramps	North American Recreation Convertibles, Inc. P.O. Box 758 33 Knowton St. Bridgeport, Conn. 06601

Outdoor Equipment (slides,
   swings, net climbers, play
   scapes)
Gym Forms
Saf-T-Trike (Chain-
   driven tricycle)
	Markham Distributors Co.
	507 Fifth Avenue
	New York, NY 10017
	   and
	J.A. Preston Co.
	71 Fifth Avenue
	New York, NY 10003

Airflow Mats
Builder Logs
Creative Foam Shapes
Foam Balls
Creative Shapes
Floor Systems
Folding Mats
	Skill Development
	   Equipment Co.
	Box 6300
	1340 North Jefferson
	Anaheim, CA 92807
	   and
	United Canvas and Sling Inc.
	248 River St.
	Hackensack, NJ 07601

Musical Instruments (Rhythm) Records (Hap Palmer, Ella Jenkins, Lou Stallman, etc.) Rhythmic Activities	Beckley-Cardy (General Office) 1900 N. Narragansett Chicago, Ill. 60639

Riding Toys (wagons, trikes,
   wheelbarrows, wooden trucks,
   etc.)
	Constructive Playthings
	1040 E. 85th Street
	Kansas City, MO 64131

Equipment:	Distributor:
Training Staircase Climbing Stools Climb and Slide with Handrails	Achievement Products Inc. P.O. Box 547 Mineola, NY 11501
Porta-Pools	Universal Bleacher Co. P.O. Box 638 Champaign, Illinois 61820
Floatation Equipment	Stacks Aquatic Co. 35126 Cannon Rd. Chargin Falls, Ohio 44022
Rhythm Balls Audi-Ball	AMF Voit 3801 South Harbor Blvd. Santa Ana, CA 92704
Aquatic Kickboards	Pull-Buoy, Inc. 2511 Leach Auburn Heights, MI 48057
Schwimmflugel Inflatable Cuffs	Belleair International 1016 Ponce de Leon Blvd. Miami, Florida 33134
Speedo Aqualift Swimsuit	Blue Grass Industries Carlisle, Kentucky 40311
Playground Equipment (Swedish gym sets)	Delmar F. Harris Co. Box 278 Concordia, Kansas 66901

Fine Motor/Occupational Skills—Equipment and Materials

Equipment:	Distributor:
Sequencing Beads Perma Clay (nonhardening clay) Water Play Trough Wire Frame Sequence Boards Multi-Link Cubes Jumbo Size Plastic Nuts & Bolts	Childcraft Education Corp. 20 Kilmer Rd. Edison, NJ 08817

Equipment:	Distributor:
Easy Grip and Double-handled Scissors Lacing Boards Rolling Threader Shapes Sorting Box Shapes Templates Pegs & Peg Boards Colored Inch Cubes Attribute & Parquetry Blocks Sorting Cards/Sorting Box	Developmental Learning Materials 7440 Natchez Ave. Niles, IL 60648 and Teaching Resources Co. 100 Boylston St. Boston, MA 02116
Dexterity Centers (lacing, knots, zippers, snaps, buckles, etc.)	United Canvas and Sling Inc. 248 River Street Hackensack, NJ 07601
Tactile Discrimination (varied texture cylinders) Latches and Locks Shape Concept Templates	Childcraft Education Corp. 20 Kilmer Rd. Edison, NY 08817
Stacking Shape Puzzles Shape Boards	Exceptional Play Inc. P.O. Box 1015 Lawrence, Kansas 66044

Personality and Play—Equipment and Materials

Equipment:	Distributor:
Stuffed Toys	Exceptional Play, Inc. P.O. Box 1015 Lawrence, Kansas 66044
Infant Musical Ball Stack Rings Infant Creep and Crawl	

Social/Self-Help—Equipment and Materials

Equipment:	Distributor:
The Gripper: used to secure the hand around an object which is being held (i.e., spoon, stick, toothbrush, etc.) Three-way table mirror	Childcraft Education Corp. 20 Kilmer Rd. Edison, NJ 08817

Equipment:	Distributor:
Adaptive Eating Utensils (plastic and nonplastic coated)	Childcraft Education Corp. 20 Kilmer Rd. Edison, NJ 08817 and Achievement Products P.O. Box 547 Mineola, NY 11501
Tongue Thrust Therapy Program	Learning Concepts 2501 N. Lamar Austin, TX 78705
Toilet Aids (seats, trainers, etc.) Protective Helmets Modified Furniture (table, desks, etc.) Snap Rings Walking Aids (full body suspension walkers, crutches, canes, kiddie walkers, etc.)	Achievement Products Inc. P.O. Box 547 Mineola, NY 11501
Walking Aids also available from	J.A. Preston Co. 71 Fifth Ave. New York, NY 10003

Language—Materials and Equipment

Equipment:	Distributor:
Zygo Communicator: This electronic visual communicator features 16 display areas each with a signal light and form with an audible alarm. The visual board can be controlled via touch, breathing, biting, etc.	Everest and Jennings Inc. 1803 Pontius Ave. Los Angeles, CA 90025

Equipment:	Distributor:
Bliss Symbol Scanner Alphabet-Message Scanner	Prentke Romich Co. R.D. 2 Box 191 Shreve, Ohio 44676
Sign Products: Exit, Stop, First Aid, Men, Women, etc. are available in standard sizes.	Flaghouse Inc. 18 W. 18th St. New York, NY 10011
Hand Puppets Geometric Figures (hand size)	Childcraft Education Corp. 20 Kilmer Rd. Edison, NJ 08817
Phonic Mirror Handivoice Communicator	HC Electronics, Inc. 250 Camino Alto Mill Valley, CA 94941

Miscellaneous Noncommercial Equipment and Materials

Throwing Apparatus

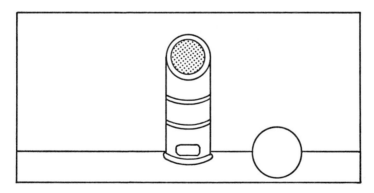

Source: L. Rudolph, *Physical Skills for the Severely and Profoundly Handicapped,* © 1977, reprinted by permission.

The "Bally Ho" throwing device can be produced inexpensively by connecting two laundry detergent barrels, which are then covered with contact paper. As the ball is thrown into the upper opening, it automatically returns at the bottom (Rudolph, 1977).

Aquatic Equipment: Water Wings

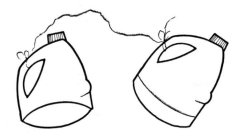

Source: Rudolph.

Two empty bleach bottles are connected by a strap and used to support the head, neck, and shoulders when the student is in the supine floating position.

Arm Cuffs—for Floatation Aid

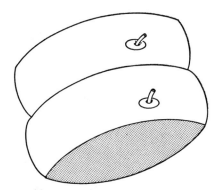

Source: Rudolph.

To assist the student to maintain buoyancy, cuffs can be worn on the upper arm. Cuffs can be adjusted to fit varying sizes by simply regulating the air pressure.

Floating Block

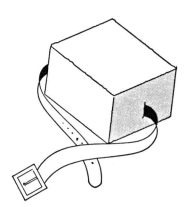

Source: Rudolph.

Emphasis is placed upon communicative interaction as a basis for language development with suggestions for the classroom teacher.

MS

Fiorentino, M.R. *Normal and abnormal development: The influence of primitive reflexes on motor development.* Springfield: Charles C. Thomas, 1978.

Provides both physicians and therapists with a graphic representation of normal reflex development and persistent primitive reflexes, a useful guide to the evaluation of newer techniques in therapy. Invaluable in the early diagnosis of the cerebral palsied child under one year of age. Development of the normal child in contrast to the abnormal development of the cerebral palsied child is discussed. Certain reflexes, including the Moro, asymmetrical tonic neck, and positive supporting, are considered and their effect on the child with cerebral palsy emphasized.

Morrison, D., Pothier, P.C., & Hon, K. *Sensory-motor dysfunction and therapy in infancy and early childhood.* Springfield: Charles C. Thomas, 1978.

The theory of and research into sensory-motor therapy are investigated in the first section of this book. Topics covered in this area include the role of sensory-motor dysfunction in infancy and early childhood, intervention, and Piagetian concepts of sensory-motor intelligence and dysfunction. The second group of chapters focuses on assessment and therapy, with excellent reviews of normal sensory development, motor development and dysfunction, and habilitation and remediation of infants and young children. The final portion of the text explores the relationship between sensory-motor and emotional development. Sensory-motor therapy with a young emotionally disturbed child, interventions for early occurring emotional disturbances, and movement therapy are the primary subjects for discussion in this section. Helpful appendixes are provided on assessment of primitive reflex remnants, righting, and equilibrium reactions; defining and assessing the abilities of a child; and resources for equipment.

A manual for cerebral palsy equipment. Chicago, Illinois: The National Society for Crippled Children and Adults.

Hofmann, R. *How to build special furniture and equipment for handicapped children.* Springfield, Illinois: Charles C. Thomas, 1970.

Before buying ready-made furniture for the handicapped child, consider the fact that it is often prohibitive in price and must frequently be modified to meet the needs of each particular child. By applying a few principles one can build the equipment at a fraction of the cost and with more satisfactory results.

This manual will serve as a guide for persons who might have a need to build special equipment for a handicapped child. The equipment and furniture shown are functional, attractive and simple to construct without the use of expensive woodworking tools and materials. The directions for building each piece of equipment are simple and easy to understand. All pieces can be made with scrap wood in a limited space with very few tools and still will be sturdy enough to withstand much hard use.

Macey, P. *Mobilizing multiply handicapped children: A manual for the design and construction of modified wheelchairs.* Lawrence, Kansas: Division of Continuing Education, University of Kansas, 1974.

Robinault, I. *Functional aids for the multiply handicapped.* Hagerstown, Maryland: Harper and Row, 1973.

AIM Adventures in movement for the handicapped. Dayton, Ohio: AIM for the Handicapped, Inc., 1974.

McCormack, J.E. *Manual of alternative procedures: Motor development.* Medford, Mass: Massachusetts Center for Program Development and Evaluation, no date.

Wehman, P. *Helping the mentally retarded acquire play skills.* Springfield, Illinois: Charles C. Thomas, 1977.
The problem, theory, and techniques for teaching leisure-time skills are presented in a sequential manner. The theoretical construct of operant learning is applied to training the mentally retarded to play and to use their leisure time appropriately.

Anderson, F.B. *Fay's first fifty: Activities for the young and the severely handicapped.* Augusta, Georgia: Strother's Printing Inc., 1976.
This is one of a series of five books that present gross and fine motor training activities for children experiencing a variety of handicapping conditions.

Information system for adaptive, assistive, and recreational equipment (I.S.A.A.R.E.), Texas Area Learning Resource Center, 1912 Speedway, Room 348, Austin, Texas, 78712.
The I.S.A.A.R.E. provides an information resource base which identifies and describes specific equipment that can be used with the physically handicapped. This service can be extremely valuable to individuals working with the severely and profoundly retarded.

Cratty, B.J. *Developmental games for physically handicapped children.* Palo Alto, California: Peek, 1969.

This publication contains numerous games and activities for children experiencing a variety of movement problems. Alterations have been made in rules and physical requirements, yet the general objectives of providing social and physical stimulation are emphasized.

R

Kay, J.G. *Crafts for the very disabled and handicapped.* Springfield: Charles C. Thomas, 1977.

This is a book of crafts designed for use by both professionals and volunteers involved with very disabled persons. The projects are geared toward a wide range of clients, from the physically able but very senile to the extremely disabled but mentally alert. All the crafts are limited to a low level of difficulty and are rated on a sliding scale. They are inexpensive, utilize materials which are both safe and readily available, and can be completed in one session. They are suitable for use at home with individuals, at the bedside, or in crafts groups. This book is especially unique for its inclusion of explicit instructions and numerous detailed patterns and diagrams. These will make the work of the crafts director infinitely easier and more effective.

Slivey, M.A. and Geelan, K.E. *Manual of alternative procedures: Recreational activities.* Medford, Massachusetts: Massachusetts Center Program Development and Evaluation, no date.

A practical guide for teaching the mentally retarded to swim. Washington, D.C.: AAHPER, 1969.

Wehman, P. *Helping the mentally retarded acquire play skills.* Springfield: Charles C. Thomas, 1977.

Although the phenomenon of play is considered spontaneous and natural, as it may well be with normal children, this frequently is not the case with the mentally retarded. Some degree of intervention or environmental arrangement must occur initially for play to take place. This book describes how behavioral training methods may be applied to the play problems of the mentally retarded. Specific instructional direction and an empirical rationale for program guidelines are provided, considering the needs of all ages and functioning levels of the mentally retarded. This text is directed toward special educators, recreation and occupational therapists, social workers, pediatric nurses, and university students involved in therapeutic recreation and special education.

Alpha chi omega toy book: Self-help toys to make for handicapped children. Indianapolis, Indiana: Alpha Chi Omega National Headquarters, 1975.

Reynolds, G. *A swimming program for the handicapped.* New York: Association Press, 1973.

Sherrill, C. (Ed.). *Creative arts for the severely handicapped.* Fort Worth: Perko, 1977.

S

A resource guide in sex education for the mentally retarded. Hempstead, New York: SIECUS, 1971.

An overview of curriculum concepts and content with sample lessons and a detailed list of written and audio-visual materials, coded by difficulty level and topic covered.

Gallender, D. *Eating handicaps: Illustrated technique for feeding disorders.* Springfield: Charles C. Thomas, 1978.

This well-illustrated text emphasizes the structures involved with the intake and initial processing of food. Among the topics discussed are the appropriate corrective movements for the tongue (tongue thrusts), chewing, swallowing, bite and gag reflexes, lip closure, and jaw stability. The book is divided into two parts. Part I deals with the anatomy and physiology of the bone, muscle, gland, and nerve structures as each relates to the eating process. Part II concerns itself with feeding disorders and techniques that may be applied when working with those having specific disorders. Contained in the second part is a visual framework using sequential pictures, diagrams, and illustrations.

OT

Copeland, M., Ford, L., & Solon, N. *Occupational therapy for mentally retarded children.* Baltimore: University Park Press, 1976.

This combination teaching textbook and professional reference provides a thorough introduction to mental retardation for occupational therapy aides and certified assistants specializing in mental retardation. It develops an understanding of mental retardation and its causes, the effects of mental retardation on growth and development, and the role of the occupational therapist in treatment. It focuses on the skills and knowledge needed by aides and assistants who provide supportive and management services to registered occupational therapists.

Chapter by chapter, the book covers occupational therapy and mental retardation, characteristics of the retarded, management of the retarded child, transportation and transfers, adapted equipment, activities of daily living, crafts, and progress reporting. The information is presented in order of rank so that competency is demonstrated at one level before aides are asked to assume responsibility at the next higher level.

T

Foxx, R., & Azrin, N. *Toilet training the retarded.* Champaign, Illinois: Research Press, 1973.

This text describes a toilet training procedure that has proven extremely successful with over 1000 institutionalized students in approximately 50 institutions.

Ellis, N.R. *Handbook of mental deficiency: Psychological theory and research.* New York: McGraw-Hill, 1963.

A definitive presentation of all the significant theoretical approaches to the study of mental deficiency. Its purpose is to assess the status of behavioral research and theory in the field. The material is divided into two parts: Part I is devoted to the exposition and evaluation of theories of defectives' behavior. Part II summarizes the literature pertaining to the area of mental deficiency and evaluates the available data, pointing out the relevant aspects as well as the shortcomings.

COMMERCIAL PROGRAMS IN ADAPTED PHYSICAL EDUCATION

Several total programs and their instructional materials are commercially available in the area of adapted physical education. These programs have a general emphasis toward higher functioning retardates and all other handicapping conditions, but can accommodate the severe and profoundly retarded as well.

The following two programs began as funded projects through the Office of Education, United States Department of Health, Education, and Welfare, Bureau of Education for the Handicapped.

I Can

The "I Can" physical education curriculum package was developed and field tested by the field service unit of Michigan State University under the direction of Dr. Janet A. Wessel. "I Can" is a comprehensive instructional system for physical education that structures lessons at the child's level of performance. The program identifies the individual's abilities and assists the student in building from this point at his own pace. The "I Can" model incorporates six fundamental steps which include:

1. setting physical education goals for the school system
2. designing a yearly physical education program complete with performance objectives

3. instruction and the determination of present performance levels
4. individual activity prescriptions based upon assessed performance levels
5. ongoing assessment and prescription of activities
6. records of performances and report writing

The program materials which were field tested with 5 to 14 year-old, trainable and severely mentally retarded children contain four primary areas: (1) fundamental skills, (2) body management, (3) health/fitness, and (4) aquatics.

1. Fundamental Skills

Locomotor skills, rhythm and object control are covered in this instructional area. The following teaching components are contained:

Locomotor Skills and Rhythm

Run	Slide
Leap	Skip
Horizontal Jump	Move to Even Beat
Vertical Jump	Move to Uneven Beat
Hop	Accent
Gallop	Communication

Object Control

Underhand Roll	Underhand Strike
Underhand Throw	Overhand Strike
Overhand Throw	Forehand Strike
Kick	Backhand Strike
Continuous Bounce	Sidearm Strike
Catch	

2. Body Management

This instructional area is designed to provide motor and cognitive growth through environmental interaction and sensory motor training. Many of the activities are closely associated with the subject areas of art, numbers, music, language, and self-help skills. The following areas are covered:

Body Awareness

Body Parts	Directions in Space
Body Actions	Personal Space
Body Planes	General Space
Shapes and Sizes	

Bliss Symbol System, 125
Blocks, 101
Blowing, 127
Body image, 118-121, 308
Body positions, 308
Bowel control, 136-137
Bristol Social Adjustment Guides, 29
Brushing teeth, 167
Buckling, 160
Buoyancy, 354
Button bagging, 273, 274
Button cutting, 273, 275
Buttoning, 153, 155, 159

C

Cain-Levine Social Competency Scale,
    29, 36-37
Care of belongings, 176-178
Certification, 5-6
Chaining formats, 59-60, 152, 226
Channel drawing, 245
Checklists
    aquatic therapy, 351-354
    developmental, 46
    motor skills, 91
    play area, 194-197
    progress, 77
    recreational skill areas, 316-320
Chemical intervention, 70
Chewing, 127, 144
Circuit training, 309-310
Clay, 210
Clothing care, 176-178
Coats
    putting on, 158-159
    removing, 154
Cognitive development, 14-15, 25
Color
    discrimination, 242-243
    matching, 241-242
Columbus Community Center, 218
Combing hair, 170
Communication boards, 126
Communication levels, 117-118
    See also Language skills

Community skills. *See* Mobility training
Component skills, 53
Conditioning. *See* Behavior
    modification
Consent. *See* Permission
Continuous training, 310
Contract procurement managers, 281
Cooking, 253
Cooperative work, 248
Copying, 101-102
Correction, 68-69, 246
Counseling, 223
Counterconditioning, 67
Cramps, 347
Crawling, 94-95, 312
Crayons, 210
Creeping, 95
Criterion-referenced tests
    development of, 39-41
    language skills, 108
    task analytical approach, 37-39
Cruising, 96
Cuing, 73-75, 128, 235
Curriculum content, 18-19
Curriculum materials. *See* Resource
    materials
Cutting
    food, 149-150
    scissor use, 211-212

D

Deafness, 16
Demonstration, 74
Denton State School, 125
Desensitization, 67
Differential reinforcement, 67
Dimensions, 72
Directions, 74
Directors, 280-281
Documentation. *See* Assessment;
    Checklists; Recording
Down's Syndrome, 337
Dresses
    putting on, 157
    removing, 154

Dressing
    assessment, 31
    clothing care, 176-178
    physical appearance, 175
    putting on clothes, 155-161
    removing clothes, 153-155
    teaching methods, 152-153
Dressing frames, 153
Drill press operation, 273, 275
Drinking
    cup use, 59-60, 145-146
    swallowing, 142-143
Drugs, 70
Duration recording, 48

E

Eating
    assessment, 31
    chewing, 144
    cutting, 149-150
    drinking, 59-60, 145-146
    finger feeding, 145
    fork use, 147
    group behavior, 151-152
    holding food in mouth, 143-144
    knife use, 149-150
    napkin use, 148-149
    Orff-Schulwerk activities, 329
    passing food, 152
    pouring liquids, 150
    serving food, 150-151
    spoon use, 146-147
    swallowing, 142-143
    word identification, 122-123
Edible reinforcers, 62
Educational programs
    content, 18-19
    public school programs, 17, 255-261,
        287-290
    service needs, 17-18
Education of All Handicapped
    Children's Act of 1975 (P.L.
    94-142), 13, 76-77
Electrical equipment, 249
Electric shocks, 70

Elicited language tests, 107
Emergency warnings, 249
Emotional development, 15
Employees. See Staff
Enuresis, 141
Epilepsy, 348, 367
Equilibrium 81-86, 308
Equipment sources, 372-379
Evaluation. See Assessment
Event recording, 47
Exhaustion, 347-348
Expectancy of failure, 187
Explanation-demonstration approach,
    334
Extinguishing techniques, 66-67
Eye coordination, 99-102, 244-245, 309

F

Face
    appearance, 176
    washing, 167-168
Fading, 65-66, 71, 73, 75
Failure expectancy, 187
Fairview Behavior Battery for the
    Mentally Retarded, 29
Fear, 67, 351
Feedback, 61, 226
Feminine hygiene, 171-173
Film resources, 361-371
Fine motor skills, 98
    copying, 101-102
    equipment and material sources,
        374-375
    eye-foot coordination, 102
    eye-hand coordination, 100-101,
        244-245
    grasping, 99-100
    hand dexterity, 101, 243-244
    hands to midline, 99
    reaching, 100
    release, 100
    sorting, 102
    visual fixation, 99
    visual tracking, 99
    See also Perceptual motor skills

Finger dexterity, 101, 243-244
Finger feeding, 145
Finger painting, 211
Fist aid
  bleeding, 342-344
  breathing problems, 340-342
  epilepsy, 348
  general, 338-340
  heat-related illness, 346-348
  shock, 344-345
  spinal injuries, 346
Fixation, 99
Floating, 354-355
Focusing attention
  cuing, 73-74
  dimensions, 72
  fading, 73
  feedback, 61
  modeling, 74
  oral directions, 74
  prompting, 75-76
  redundancy, 72-73
Folding
  business paper, 262-263
  cardboard sheets, 261-262
  jewelry box liners, 273
  occupational training, 261-263
  play activities, 212
Foot-eye coordination, 102, 309
Fork use, 147
Form
  discrimination, 240-241
  perception, 239-240
Forward chaining, 59
Frustration, 186
Functional levels, 46, 53

G

Gagging reflex, 143
Gait, 97
Games
  language skills, 127
  motor skills, 95, 97-98, 101, 102
  Orff-Schulwerk, 323-329
  play, 191

reinforcement with, 64
Gardner Behavior Chart, 29
Gestures, 74, 75, 118, 125
G.O.A.L., 108
Gold, Marc, 13
Grasping, 100
Gripper, 146
Grooming. *See* Hygiene; Personal
  appearance
Gross motor skills
  assessment, 90-91
  crawling, 94-95
  creeping, 95
  cruising, 96
  head control, 92
  hitching, 94
  jumping, 98
  rolling, 93
  running, 97-98
  sitting, 94
  standing, 95-96
  walking, 96-97
Grouping, 210

H

Hair care, 169-170
Hand assembly, 273
Hand carrying, 349-350
Hand dexterity, 101, 243-244
Hand-eye coordination, 100-101,
  244-245, 309
Handicrafts, 211, 366
Handling procedures
  carrying, 349-350
  film resources, 369
  positioning, 82
Hand press operation, 273, 274
Hands to midline, 99
Hand tools, 248
Hand washing, 166-167
Hanging clothes, 176-177
Haptic discrimination, 102
Head control, 91, 92
Head-eye coordination, 309
Hearing, 16, 117

Heat stroke, 346-347
Hemophilia, 337
Hitching, 94
Hospital Adjustment Scale, 29
Household skills, 121, 253
Houston Test of Language
    Development, 107
Huay, Valentin, 269
Hydrocephalis, 337
Hygiene
    activity center programs, 251-252
    bathing and showering, 168-169
    face washing, 167-168
    feminine, 171-173
    hair combing, 170
    hair washing, 169-170
    hand washing, 166-167
    nose care, 168
    shaving, 170-171
    teeth brushing, 167
    word identification, 123-125
Hypotonia, 90

I

I Can program, 368-369, 389-392
Idiosyncratic reinforcers, 63
Ignoring, 66, 140, 142
Illinois Program, 108
Illinois Test of Psycholinguistic Ability,
    107
Imitation, 128, 308, 325
Inappropriate activities, 252
Inappropriate behavior, 252-253
Incontinence, 136, 137, 141
    See also Toilet training
Independent functioning, 23, 24, 36-37,
    247-248
Initiative, 247
Inner language, 108
Instructional objectives, 50-51
Intelligence
    mentally retarded, 10, 11, 14-15
    play and, 193
    travel skills and, 216-217, 219
    visual discrimination and, 238-239

Intermittent schedules, 65
Interval recording, 48-49
Interval schedules, 65
Interval training, 310
Interviewing, 31, 36-37, 64
Isolated time out, 70
Isolation rooms, 70

J

Jackets
    putting on, 158-159
    removing, 154
Jaw exercises, 127
Jobs. See Activity center programs;
    Occupational training; Sheltered
    workshops; Staff
Judgments, 26
Jumping, 98

K

Kennedy, Joseph P., Jr., Foundation,
    321, 322
Kiwanis Club of Portland, Oregon, 316
Knife use, 149-150

L

Lacing shoes, 160-161
Laminator operation, 273, 276
Language Acquisition Program for the
    Retarded or Multiply Impaired, 108,
    112-115
Language comprehension tests, 107
Language Intervention Program, 107,
    112-117
Language skills, 105-106, 129
    assessment, 24, 32, 106-108, 115
    basic skills, 108-109
    communication boards, 126
    communication levels, 117-118
    equipment and material sources,
        376-377
    expressive, 127-129
    film resources, 365, 367-368

instructional programs, 110-117
occupational training, 235-237, 255
Orff-Schulwerk activities, 328-329
play activities, 193
printed resources, 383-385
program development principles,
    117-125
signing, 115, 118, 125-126
skill sequencing, 109-110
speech, 108-109, 127-129
total body activity approach, 118-122
word identification, 118-125, 174,
    235-237
Laus Orientation and Mobility Program
    for Sighted Mentally Retarded
    Individuals, 218-226
Leg extension, 95
Leisure skills. *See* Therapeutic
    recreation
Lethargy, 350
Lets-Play-to-Grow, 322
Lift/carry/put down, 236-237
Limited time out, 68
Lincoln-Oseretsky Motor Development
    Scale, 91
Lips
    control, 143
    exercises, 127, 328-329
Locomotion, 31, 305

M

Manipulation, 304
Manners, 174
Matching, 210, 241-242
Match-to-sample formats, 59
Materials. *See* Resource materials
Meal preparation, 253
Mean length utterance (MLU), 106-107
Memory, 308
Menstruation, 171-173
Mental health, 15, 192
Mental retardation
    defined, 10-11
    See also Severely mentally retarded

Mobility training
    candidate selection, 219-221
    instructional process, 223-226
    occupational training programs, 254
    parental cooperation, 220, 222-223
    programs, 215-218
Modeling, 74, 223, 325
Monitoring. *See* Assessment; Recording
Motivation, 243
Motor action sequencing, 308
Motor skills, 81
    assessment, 24
    equilibrium reactions, 81-86
    film resources, 368-369
    physical education and, 310, 312-313
    postural reflexes, 87-90
    printed resources, 385-387
    righting reactions, 81-86
    See also Fine motor skills; Gross
        motor skills; Perceptual motor
        skills
Mouth exercises, 328-329
Mouth to mouth respiration, 340-342
Mouth to nose respiration, 341-342
Movement, 304, 308
Movement exploration approach,
    334-335
Murdock C & Y program, 78
Muscle tone, 16
Music, 212, 323-329, 365, 366

N

Name games, 323-324
Napkin use, 148-149
Narrative data, 26, 47
National Association for Retarded
    Children, 270
Nesting objects, 101
Newman-Doby Measure of Social
    Competence, 29
Nonisolated time out, 68
Nonverbal communication, 117-118
Normalizing tone, 87
Norm-referenced tests
    Adaptive Behavior Scale, 32-36

Adaptive Behavior Scale Public
   School Version, 36
Cain-Levine Social Competency
   Scale, 36-37
inventory approach, 28-30
level of functioning, 28
shortcomings, 27
social maturity, 28-30
types, 27-30
Vineland Social Maturity Scale,
   30-32
Northside Industrial Workshop, 284-287
Northwest Syntax Screening Test, 107
Nose care, 168
Nut and bolt assembly, 264-265

O

Observation, 26, 47-50, 64, 70
Occupational training, 229-230
assessment, 32
basic skills, 230-235
equipment and material sources,
   374-375
film resources, 363, 371
language skills, 235-237
perceptual motor skills, 238-245
prevocational training, 255-259
printed resources, 388
social skills, 237-238
supervision, 237-238, 247
work adjustment skills, 245-249
See also Activity center programs;
   Sheltered workshops
Oddity formats, 59
On-task behavior, 237-238
Operant conditioning model, 62
Oral directions, 74
Orff, Carl, 323
Orff-Schulwerk, 323
food activities, 329
modeling and imitation, 325
musical instrument activities,
   324-325
name games, 323-324
sensorimotor skills, 326-328

voice activities, 328-329
Overcorrection, 68-69
Overprotection, 220-223

P

Passing food, 152
Pasting, 211
Patterning, 194, 310, 312-313
Peabody Picture Vocabulary Test, 107
Pegboards, 210
Peg playing, 101
Pennsylvania Training Model;
   Individual Assessment Guide, 46
Perceptual motor skills, 238-239
color discrimination, 242-243
color matching, 241-242
finger dexterity, 243-244
form discrimination, 240-241
form perception, 239-240
physical education, 305-309
speed and accuracy, 243-245
visual discrimination, 238-239
Performance tests, 49, 107-108
Perkins Institute for the Blind, 270
Permission
aquatic therapy, 337
aversion methods, 66, 67, 69
sex education, 180
mobility training, 220
Perseverance, 248, 251
Personal appearance, 175-176
Personal belongings, 176-178
Personality
anxiety, 185-186
characteristics, 15, 183-185
defined, 184-185
expectancy of failure, 187
frustration and aggression, 186
psychological needs, 188-190
reaction tendencies, 186
self-concept, 187-190
Personnel. *See* Staff
Physical appearance, 175-176
Physical education. *See* Adapted
   physical education

Physical prompts, 75
Physical therapists, 82
Pittsburgh Public School System, 218-226
Play
  area design, 193-194
  characteristics of, 191
  defined, 190
  equipment, 197, 375
  goals for, 191-193
  handicrafts, 211-212
  music activities, 212
  need for, 190-191
  performance assessment, 200-209
  socialization, 194
  stations, 197-199
  structured, 194, 197-200
  success, 197
  table activities, 209-210
Portland State University, 316
Positive practice, 69
Positive reinforcers, 63
Posture, 16, 81, 87-90, 176, 304-305, 308
Pouring liquids, 150
Precise teaching technology, 45
  decreasing inappropriate behavior, 66-71
  entry level assessment, 46
  focusing attention, 72-76
  objective writing, 50-51
  progress assessment, 76-78
  reinforcement procedures, 61-66
  skill sequencing, 51-52
  targeting behavior, 46-50
  task analysis, 52-57
  task analysis structure, 54, 57-61
Pre-operational period, 14, 15
Preschool Educational Attainment Record, 29
President's Panel on Mental Retardation, 229
Pressure points, 343
Preverbal communication, 118
Prevocational centers
  instructional program, 261-266

skill areas and subabilities, 255-259
Printed materials, 379-389
Printmaking, 211
Production managers, 281
Production monitoring, 238
Programmed Conditioning for Language Curriculum, 107, 108, 111-115
Progress Assessment Chart of Social Development, 29
Project A.C.T.I.V.E., 392-393
Prompting, 73-74
Proprioceptive neuromuscular facilitation (PNF), 90
Psycho-educational assessment, 27-37
Pull and push, 236
Pullover shirts
  putting on, 157
  removing, 154
Punctuality, 245-246
Punishers, 69-70, 71
Pushing, 236
Puzzles, 210

R

Rainier School, 194, 310, 312-313
Rating scales, 26
Ratio schedules, 65
Reaching, 100
Reactional tendencies, 186
Recording
  automatic, 49-50
  duration, 48
  event, 47
  interval, 48-49
  narrative, 47
  products of behavior, 48
  test method, 49
  time sampling, 49
Recreation. *See* Therapeutic recreation
Recreation intern program, 322
Recreation specialists, 314-315
Redundancy, 72-73
Reinforcers
  activities, 64
  behavior modification and, 62

differential, 67
dispensing of, 64-66
film resources, 362-363
idiosyncratic, 63
inappropriate, 252-253
positive, 63
rate scheduling, 65-66
removal of, 68
selection of, 64
token system, 64
Release, 100
Repetitive behavior, 15
Representational play, 190-191
Resource materials
commercial instructional programs,
389-393
equipment and material sources,
372-379
films, 361-371
printed resources, 379-389
Responsibility, 23, 24, 246-247
Restraints, 70-71
Rewards. See Reinforcers
Righting reactions, 81-86
Role modeling, 223
Role playing, 174
Rolling, 93
Running, 97-98

S

Safety
aquatic therapy, 338
workshop, 248-249
Salaries, 3-5
Satiation, 67
Self-concept, 187-190
Self-direction, 32
Self-help skills
activity center programs, 251-252
basic skill areas, 133-136
dressing, 152-161
eating, 142-152
equipment and material sources,
375-376
toileting, 136-142

Self-mutilation, 15
Sensorimotor skills, 14, 15
awareness, 303-304
physical education, 296, 301-305
play, 190
postural reflexes, 87, 90
recreational activities, 326-328
Sensory defects, 16
Serving food, 150-151
Severely mentally retarded
cognitive characteristics, 14-15
educational provision, 17-19
emotional characteristics, 15
functional level, 12-14
health, 16
personality characteristics, 15
physical defects, 16
Sewing, 212
Sex education
biological aspects, 179, 180
health aspects, 179, 181
menstruation, 171-173
need for, 178-179
social aspects, 179, 180-181
Shape perception, 239, 240
Shaving, 170-171
Sheltered workshops
film resources, 371
history, 269-270
industrial, 282-287
job skill training, 276-277
layout of, 277-278
program planning, 271-276
public school setting, 287-290
staff, 279-282
subtask skills, 272-276
types, 270-271
work categories, 270
Shining shoes, 177-178
Shock, 344-345
Shoes
lacing, 160-161
putting on, 157-158
removing, 154-155
shining, 177-178
tying, 161

Showering, 168-169
Shriver, Eunice Kennedy, 321
Shriver, Sargent, 321
Shuffling, 97
Signing, 115, 118, 125-126
Sitting, 94
Size perception, 239-240, 241
Skill sequencing, 51-52
  language skills, 109-111
Social amenities, 174
Social behavior, 24, 25, 32, 192, 194,
  364
Social Competence Rating, 29
Social maturity, 24, 28-32
Social Quotient (SQ), 31
Social skills
  activity center programs, 252-253
  basic skill areas, 163-165
  care of belongings, 176-178
  equipment and material sources,
    375-376
  grooming and hygiene, 166-173
  manners, 174
  on-task behavior, 237-238
  physical appearance, 175-176
  printed resources, 388
  sex education, 178-181
  timing of training, 173-174
  See also Self-help skills
Socks
  putting on, 156
  removing, 153
Sorting
  colors, 241-242
  fine motor skills, 102, 241-242
  occupational training, 241-242, 261,
    263-264
  parquetry blocks, 261, 263-264
  play skills, 210
Spasticity, 82, 87, 94, 350
Spatial relations, 308
Special Olympics, 321-323
Special physical education. *See* Adapted
  physical education
Speech. *See* Language skills
Spinal injuries, 346

Spoon use, 146-147
Staff
  competency areas, 2-3
  job seeking, 9
  personal characteristics, 2
  physical education programs,
    294-295
  qualifications, 5
  recreational programs, 314-315, 322
  salary range, 3-5
  sheltered workshops, 279-283
  teacher certification, 5-6
Standing, 95-96
Stand/sit, 237
Stanford-Binet, 11, 107
Stop/start, 237
Stringing beads, 210
Success, 197
Sucking, 127
Swallowing, 142-143
Sweaters
  putting on, 158-159
  removing, 154
Swimming. *See* Aquatic therapy
Symbolic play, 190-191
Systematic Language Instruction, 108

T

Taping, 265-266
Target behavior, 46-47
Task analysis
  assessment, 37-41, 78
  content format, 58-59
  decision-making process, 57-58
  feedback, 61
  film resources, 370-371
  general format, 52-54
  method selection, 58
  process phase, 59-61
  structure, 54-57
Teachers, 5-9
Teaching methods. *See* Precise teaching
  technology
Tearing paper, 212
Teeth brushing, 167

Territoriality, 186
Testing. *See* Assessment
Texture, 240, 241
Therapeutic recreation, 313-314
  activity center programs, 254-255
  assessment, 315
  equipment and material resources,
    372-374
  film resources, 364
  goals, 316
  objectives, 315
  Orff-Schulwerk, 323-329
  printed resources, 387-388
  skill areas, 316-320
  Special Olympics, 321-323
  staff, 314-315
  See also Adapted physical education;
    Play
Thorndike model, 62
Time out, 68, 70
Time sampling, 49
Toilet training
  accidents, 140, 142
  entry level assessment, 137-138
  nighttime, 141-142
  procedures, 138-140
  readiness, 136-137
  self-initiation, 140
Token systems, 64, 68, 363
Tongue
  exercises, 127, 328-329
  thrust reflex, 143
Total body activity (TBA), 112-114,
  118-122
Tourniquets, 344
Tracking, 99, 244-245
Travel skills. *See* Mobility training
Trousers
  placing on hanger, 176-177
  putting on, 156-157
  removing, 153-154
Try-another-way approach. *See* Task
  analysis
T-shirts
  putting on, 157
  removing, 154

Turning, 237
Tying shoe laces, 161

U

Unbuttoning, 155
Underwear
  putting on, 156
  removing, 153-154
Undressing, 153-155
Uniform Performance Assessment
  System (UPAS), 46
Utah Test of Language Development,
  107

V

Verbal cues, 74
Very Special Olympics, 322
Vineland Social Maturity Scale, 29-32
Visual acuity, 16
Visual cues, 128
Visual discrimination, 102, 238-239
Visual fixation, 99
Visual tracking, 99, 244-245
Vives, Juan Luis, 269
Voluntary movement, 81

W

Walking, 96-97, 176
Washing
  bathing and showering, 168-169
  face, 167-168
  hair, 169-170
  hands, 58-59, 166-167
Weaving, 212
Wechsler Intelligence Scale for
  Children, 11, 107
Word identification
  action words, 236
  body parts, 118-121
  classroom, 121
  eating, 122
  grooming, 123-125
  household, 121

occupational training, 236
social amenities, 174
Work adjustment skills
activity center programs, 251
correction, 246
independence, 247-248
initiative, 247
perseverance, 248, 251
punctuality, 245-246

responsibility, 246-247
safety, 248-249
Work evaluators, 281-282
Work foremen, 282
Workshops. *See* Sheltered workshops

Z

Zipping, 155, 159

About the Authors

DR. ALLEN A. MORI is an associate professor of special education at the University of Nevada, Las Vegas. His previous experience includes teaching both secondary and elementary educable mentally handicapped students. Dr. Mori also worked for two years at a state institution for the mentally retarded. As a recreation counselor, camp counselor, summer camp director, and classroom teacher, he has had varied experiences with all age levels of severely retarded individuals. He received his B.A. degree in government from Franklin and Marshall College, his M.Ed. in special education from Bloomsburg State College, and his Ph.D. in special education from the University of Pittsburgh. Dr. Mori has published extensively in his areas of interest including another textbook on intervention with handicapped infants coauthored with Jane E. Olive and published by Aspen Systems Corporation.

DR. LOWELL F. MASTERS is director of rehabilitative services for Southern Nevada Mental Retardation Services. Prior to this position he was an assistant professor of adapted physical education at the University of Arkansas, an assistant professor of special education at the University of Nevada, Las Vegas, a classroom teacher of the learning disabled, and a teacher of the moderately and severely retarded at the Samuel Kirk Training Center in Illinois. Dr. Masters received his B.S. degree in physical education from Eastern Oregon State College, his M.S. degree in adapted physical education from Indiana State University, and his Ed.D. in special education from the University of Northern Colorado. Dr. Masters has published in professional journals in his area of interest.